1001876091

SO-EBW-456

City Centre
HN
51
.A78
1994/95

LEARNING RESOURCE
CENTRE
GRANT MacEWAN
COMMUNITY COLLEGE

SOCIAL PROBLEMS
94/95

Twenty-Second Edition

Editor

Harold A. Widdison
Northern Arizona University

Harold A. Widdison, professor of sociology at Northern
Arizona University in Flagstaff, holds degrees in Sociology
and Business Administration from Brigham Young University
and Case-Western Reserve University. Employed as an
education specialist with the U.S. Atomic Energy
Commission, he was awarded a Sustained Superior
Performance Award. As a medical sociologist, Dr. Widdison
is actively involved in his community with the local medical
center's neonatal committee, a founding member of
Compassionate Friends, a member of the board of directors
of the Hozhoni Foundation for the mentally handicapped,
and a consultant on death, dying, and bereavement.

Annual Editions
A Library of Information from the Public Press

DATE DUE		
DEC 2 6 1994	RECEIVED APR 1 9 1996	
	RECEIVED JAN 2 5 1996	
MAY 0 8 1996		
FEB 2 8 1997		
NOV 2 2 1999		
DEC 1 0 2005		

The Dushkin Publishing Group, Inc.
Sluice Dock, Guilford, Connecticut 06437

The Annual Editions Series

Annual Editions is a series of over 60 volumes designed to provide the reader with convenient, low-cost access to a wide range of current, carefully selected articles from some of the most important magazines, newspapers, and journals published today. Annual Editions are updated on an annual basis through a continuous monitoring of over 300 periodical sources. All Annual Editions have a number of features designed to make them particularly useful, including topic guides, annotated tables of contents, unit overviews, and indexes. For the teacher using Annual Editions in the classroom, an Instructor's Resource Guide with test questions is available for each volume.

VOLUMES AVAILABLE

Africa
Aging
American Foreign Policy
American Government
American History, Pre-Civil War
American History, Post-Civil War
Anthropology
Biology
Business Ethics
Canadian Politics
Child Growth and Development
China
Comparative Politics
Computers in Education
Computers in Business
Computers in Society
Criminal Justice
Drugs, Society, and Behavior
Dying, Death, and Bereavement
Early Childhood Education
Economics
Educating Exceptional Children
Education
Educational Psychology
Environment
Geography
Global Issues
Health
Human Development
Human Resources
Human Sexuality
India and South Asia
International Business
Japan and the Pacific Rim

Latin America
Life Management
Macroeconomics
Management
Marketing
Marriage and Family
Mass Media
Microeconomics
Middle East and the Islamic World
Money and Banking
Multicultural Education
Nutrition
Personal Growth and Behavior
Physical Anthropology
Psychology
Public Administration
Race and Ethnic Relations
Russia, Eurasia, and Central/Eastern Europe
Social Problems
Sociology
State and Local Government
Third World
Urban Society
Violence and Terrorism
Western Civilization, Pre-Reformation
Western Civilization, Post-Reformation
Western Europe
World History, Pre-Modern
World History, Modern
World Politics

Library of Congress Cataloging in Publication Data
Main entry under title: Annual Editions: Social problems. 1994/95.
     1. United States—Social conditions—1960.—Periodicals. I. Widdison, Harold A., comp.
II. Title: Social problems.
309′.1′73′092′05   73–78577   ISBN 1–56134–288–2
HN51.A78

© 1994 by The Dushkin Publishing Group, Inc., Guilford, CT 06437

Copyright law prohibits the reproduction, storage, or transmission in any form by any means of any portion of this publication without the express written permission of The Dushkin Publishing Group, Inc., and of the copyright holder (if different) of the part of the publication to be reproduced. The Guidelines for Classroom Copying endorsed by Congress explicitly state that unauthorized copying may not be used to create, to replace, or to substitute for anthologies, compilations, or collective works.

Annual Editions® is a Registered Trademark of The Dushkin Publishing Group, Inc.

Twenty-Second Edition

Printed in the United States of America

Printed on Recycled Paper

Editors/ Advisory Board

Members of the Advisory Board are instrumental in the final selection of articles for each edition of Annual Editions. Their review of articles for content, level, currentness, and appropriateness provides critical direction to the editor and staff. We think you'll find their careful consideration well reflected in this volume.

EDITOR

Harold A. Widdison
Northern Arizona University

ADVISORY BOARD

Thomas Arcaro
Elon College

Sylven Beck
George Washington University

Mamie Bridgeforth
Essex County College

T. Jesse Dent, Jr.
Johnson C. Smith University

Roger G. Dunham
University of Miami

Kurt Finsterbusch
University of Maryland
College Park

Lorraine Greaves
Fanshawe College of
Applied Arts and Sciences

Ray Helgemoe
University of New Hampshire

Brian Jones
Villanova University

Bruce D. LeBlanc
Blackhawk College

John Lynxwiler
University of Central Florida

Kathryn Mueller
Baylor University

Robert Newby
Central Michigan University

Marie Richmond-Abbott
Eastern Michigan University

Dean G. Rojek
University of Georgia

Larry Rosenberg
Millersville University

Leslie Samuelson
University of Saskatchewan

Donald F. Smith
George Mason University

Joseph L. Victor
Mercy College

STAFF

Ian A. Nielsen, Publisher
Brenda S. Filley, Production Manager
Roberta Monaco, Editor
Addie Raucci, Administrative Editor
Cheryl Greenleaf, Permissions Editor
Diane Barker, Editorial Assistant
Lisa Holmes-Doebrick, Administrative Coordinator
Charles Vitelli, Designer
Shawn Callahan, Graphics
Steve Shumaker, Graphics
Lara M. Johnson, Graphics
Libra A. Cusack, Typesetting Supervisor
Juliana Arbo, Typesetter

LEARNING RESOURCE
CENTRE
GRANT MacEWAN
COMMUNITY COLLEGE

To the Reader

In publishing ANNUAL EDITIONS we recognize the enormous role played by the magazines, newspapers, and journals of the *public press* in providing current, first-rate educational information in a broad spectrum of interest areas. Within the articles, the best scientists, practitioners, researchers, and commentators draw issues into new perspective as accepted theories and viewpoints are called into account by new events, recent discoveries change old facts, and fresh debate breaks out over important controversies.

Many of the articles resulting from this enormous editorial effort are appropriate for students, researchers, and professionals seeking accurate, current material to help bridge the gap between principles and theories and the real world. These articles, however, become more useful for study when those of lasting value are carefully *collected, organized, indexed,* and *reproduced* in a *low-cost format,* which provides easy and permanent access when the material is needed. That is the role played by *Annual Editions.* Under the direction of each volume's *Editor,* who is an expert in the subject area, and with the guidance of an *Advisory Board,* we seek each year to provide in each *ANNUAL EDITION* a current, well-balanced, carefully selected collection of the best of the public press for your study and enjoyment. We think you'll find this volume useful, and we hope you'll take a moment to let us know what you think.

Welcome to *Annual Editions: Social Problems 94/95.* Since the last edition, significant changes in the political structure of our society have occurred, necessitating major revisions in this edition. The election of President Bill Clinton and the Democratic control of both houses of Congress introduced a new political agenda. Some have hailed this new agenda as the end of political gridlock, the start of meaningful political reforms, and a chance to overhaul governmental bureaucracy.

President Clinton lost no time in attempting to implement his campaign promises. He tried to drop the ban on gays in the military, to pass an economic stimulus package, to "reinvent" government, to pass NAFTA (North American Free Trade Agreement), and to pass a universal health care package. Each of these programs was designed to address a significant societal problem, and each has met with mixed results. This edition of *Annual Editions: Social Problems* has been revised to reflect the implications of these attempts to make significant changes in governmental programs and individual behaviors.

In addition, a number of readers have suggested that the text needed a section on crime, delinquency, and violence. We have created such a unit by pulling articles from other units and introducing new ones. The problem we faced in this edition was deciding which of many high-quality articles should be included. Many of the possible choices not only were well-written, timely, and stimulating, but also contained unique information. To make room for the new materials, some very good articles that had become dated had to be eliminated.

This edition begins with an introduction and overview of social problems, and it includes eight units. Unit 1 clusters articles concerning the basic unit of society, the family, including the changes it is experiencing and the implications of these changes for society. The second unit is new. It includes articles examining the increase in crime rates, delinquency, and violence in our society and what, if anything, can be done to control them. Unit 3 looks at problems facing society because of the increasing proportion of older people. Unit 4 looks at the issues surrounding health care policies and practices and how they are affecting individuals, groups, and society in general. Unit 5 examines issues, trends, and public policies impacting on poverty and inequality. Unit 6 looks at the implications of existing immigration policies and the utility or dysfunctions of cultural pluralism. Unit 7 examines the growing problems associated with teen sex, homosexuality, and drug abuse. The final unit examines global issues that transcend national geographic boundaries.

To assist the reader in identifying specific topics or issues covered in the various articles, we have created a *topic guide.* This guide lists various topics in alphabetical order and the articles in which they are discussed. If you are doing research on a specific topic, be sure to check this guide first.

A number of the articles' authors express concern about the troubled state of our cities, of families, the economy, of America's deteriorating position as a world power, and the conditions of Earth's environment. While this book is about social problems, not all authors feel there is no hope. Some do see hope for the family, for solutions to the spread of violence, and for the future.

If you have suggestions for articles or topics to be included in future editions of this series, please write and share them. You are also invited to use the form provided on the last page of this book for rating the articles.

Harold A. Widdison
Editor

Contents

Introduction

This introduction summarizes the three major theoretical approaches to studying social problems: symbolic interactionism, functionalism, and conflict.

Unit 1

Parenting and Family Issues

Six selections examine how the socially stabilizing force of the family has been assaulted by the dynamics of economic pressure, unemployment, and homelessness.

The concepts in bold italics are developed in the article. For further expansion please refer to the Topic Guide and the Index.

Unit 2

Crime, Delinquency, and Violence

Six articles discuss the extent and significance of crime and delinquency in today's society.

The concepts in bold italics are developed in the article. For further expansion please refer to the Topic Guide and the Index.

Unit 3

Aging: Problems New and Old

Four articles discuss some of the realities of growing old in America. Topics include elderly health, the economy, and cultural segregation.

Unit 4

Health and Health Care Issues

Four articles discuss the problems inflicted on society by the health care system. Topics include the cost of health insurance, industrial migration due to extensive domestic regulation, and the AIDS pandemic.

The concepts in bold italics are developed in the article. For further expansion please refer to the Topic Guide and the Index.

Unit 5

Poverty and Inequality

Six selections examine how inequality affects society and the institutions of education, women's rights, the economy, and welfare.

Unit 6

Cultural Pluralism: Race and Ethnic Relations

Four selections discuss various aspects of cultural pluralism: that it has been minimized, that diverse differences promote unity, and that diversity is the sign of social maturity.

The concepts in bold italics are developed in the article. For further expansion please refer to the Topic Guide and the Index.

Unit 7

Drug and Sexual Issues

Five selections examine the dynamics of social control of the private lives of a society's citizens.

Unit 8

Global Issues

Six articles discuss common human social problems faced by people worldwide. Topics include the environment, inflation, and cultural misunderstanding.

The concepts in bold italics are developed in the article. For further expansion please refer to the Topic Guide and the Index.

The concepts in bold italics are developed in the article. For further expansion please refer to the Topic Guide and the Index.

Topic Guide

This topic guide suggests how the selections in this book relate to topics of traditional concern to students and professionals involved with the study of social problems. It is useful for locating articles that relate to each other for reading and research. The guide is arranged alphabetically according to topic. Articles may, of course, treat topics that do not appear in the topic guide. In turn, entries in the topic guide do not necessarily constitute a comprehensive listing of all the contents of each selection.

TOPIC AREA	TREATED IN:	TOPIC AREA	TREATED IN:
Abortion	32. Born or Bred? 34. Truth and Consequences: Teen Sex	**Divorce**	3. American Family, 1992
African Americans	4. Endangered Family 28. American Melting Plot 31. Is White Racism the Problem?	**Drugs**	6. Everyday Life in Two High-Risk Neighborhoods 8. Whole Child Approach to Crime 13. Los Angeles Riots 35. CIA Connection 36. Society of Suspects
Aging/Elderly	14. Old Money 15. New Face of Aging 16. Unplanned Parenthood 17. Story of a Nursing Home Refugee	**Economy**	4. Endangered Family 12. When Cities Run Riot 21. Confronting the AIDS Pandemic 22. Front Lines of Welfare Reform 27. When Problems Outrun Policy 30. Japan's Influence on American Life 41. Outer Limits to America's Turn Inward
AIDS	21. Confronting the AIDS Pandemic 33. Shape Up or Ship Out 34. Truth and Consequences: Teen Sex		
Asians	28. American Melting Plot 30. Japan's Influence on American Life	**Education**	5. Bringing Up Father 13. Los Angeles Riots 28. American Melting Plot 29. America: Still a Melting Pot?
Business/Industry	14. Old Money 19. Risky Business 20. Deadly Migration 38. Rape of the Oceans	**Energy**	42. Decade of Discontinuity
		Environment	20. Deadly Migration 37. Enough Is Enough 38. Rape of the Oceans 39. Benefits of Global Warming 42. Decade of Discontinuity
Children	2. America's Family Time Famine 3. American Family, 1992 5. Bringing Up Father 6. Everyday Life in Two High-Risk Neighborhoods 8. Whole Child Approach to Crime 9. Danger in the Safety Zone 10. Ganging Up Against Violence 11. Honey, I Warped the Kids 16. Unplanned Parenthood	**Family**	2. America's Family Time Famine 3. American Family, 1992 4. Endangered Family 5. Bringing Up Father 6. Everyday Life in Two High-Risk Neighborhoods 8. Whole Child Approach to Crime 16. Unplanned Parenthood 22. Front Line of Welfare Reform 23. Going Private 26. New Faces of Poverty
Civil Liberties	36. Society of Suspects		
Conservation	20. Deadly Migration 37. Enough Is Enough 38. Rape of the Oceans		
Crime and Delinquency	3. American Family, 1992 5. Bringing Up Father 6. Everyday Life in Two High-Risk Neighborhoods 8. Whole Child Approach to Crime 9. Danger in the Safety Zone 10. Ganging Up Against Violence 12. When Cities Run Riot 13. Los Angeles Riots 25. No Exit 35. CIA Connection 36. Society of Suspects	**Fathering**	4. Endangered Family 5. Bringing Up Father
		Foreign Policy	21. Confronting the AIDS Pandemic 29. America: Still a Melting Pot? 35. CIA Connection 37. Enough Is Enough 38. Rape of the Oceans 39. Benefits of Global Warming 40. Islam's Violent Improvisers 41. Outer Limits to America's Turn Inward

TOPIC AREA	TREATED IN:	TOPIC AREA	TREATED IN:
Future	15. New Faces of Aging 28. American Melting Plot 42. Decade of Discontinuity	**Population**	21. Confronting the AIDS Pandemic 37. Enough Is Enough
Gangs	10. Ganging Up Against Violence	**Poverty**	3. American Family, 1992 6. Everyday Life in Two High-Risk
Grandparents	16. Unplanned Parenthood		Neighborhoods 7. American Nightmare:
Greenhouse	39. Benefits of Global Warming		Homelessness 12. When Cities Run Riot
Health	14. Old Money 17. Story of a Nursing Home Refugee 18. Wasted Health Care Dollars 19. Risky Business 20. Deadly Migration 21. Confronting the AIDS Pandemic 23. Going Private 34. Truth and Consequences: Teen Sex		13. Los Angeles Riots 22. Front Lines of Welfare Reform 24. Manufacturing Poverty 25. No Exit 26. New Faces of Poverty 27. When Problems Outrun Policy 31. Is White Racism the Problem? 37. Enough Is Enough
		Race and Ethnic Issues	12. When Cities Run Riot 28. American Melting Plot 29. America: Still a Melting Pot? 30. Japan's Influence on American Life 31. Is White Racism the Problem?
Homeless	7. American Nightmare: Homelessness		
Homosexuality	32. Born or Bred? 33. Shape Up or Ship Out	**Religion**	40. Islam's Violent Improvisers
Housing	7. American Nightmare: Homelessness 26. New Faces of Poverty	**Riots**	12. When Cities Run Riot 13. Los Angeles Riots
Immigration	29. America: Still a Melting Pot? 30. Japan's Influence on American Life	**Sex**	34. Truth and Consequences: Teen Sex
Infrastructure	27. When Problems Outrun Policy	**Single Parents**	3. American Family, 1992 4. Endangered Family 5. Bringing Up Father 25. No Exit 27. When Problems Outrun Policy
Marriage	4. Endangered Family 5. Bringing Up Father		
Medicine	18. Wasted Health Care Dollars 19. Risky Business 23. Going Private	**Violence**	9. Danger in the Safety Zone 10. Ganging Up Against Violence 11. Honey, I Warped the Kids 12. When Cities Run Riot 13. Los Angeles Riots 40. Islam's Violent Improvisers
Middle East	40. Islam's Violent Improvisers		
Migration	20. Deadly Migration		
Military	33. Shape Up or Ship Out	**Welfare**	22. Front Lines of Welfare Reform 23. Going Private 26. New Faces of Poverty 34. Truth and Consequences: Teen Sex
Multicultural/ Cultural Pluralism	28. American Melting Plot 29. America: Still a Melting Pot?		
NAFTA (North American Free Trade Agreement)	24. Manufacturing Poverty	**Work/Dual Careers**	2. America's Family Time Famine
		World Leadership	41. Outer Limits to America's Turn Inward
Pollution	20. Deadly Migration 24. Manufacturing Poverty 39. Benefits of Global Warming 42. Decade of Discontinuity		

Introduction

Before initiating any analysis of social problems, it is always useful to agree on what it is we are talking about. Something that to one group seems to represent a serious social problem might be seen by others as a symptom of a much larger problem, or even as no problem at all.

In this section, the authors try to help the reader explore the complexities of social problems. While some individuals take a very simplistic black-and-white approach in defining social problems and, in turn, what must be done to eliminate them, sociologists realize how complex and intertwined social problems are in all aspects of social life. But even sociologists do not agree as to the best approach to take in the study of social issues. Here, the authors introduce the reader to sociology's three dominant theoretical positions and give examples of how those espousing each theory would look at specific issues. The three theories—symbolic interactionism, functionalism, and conflict—represent three radically different approaches to the study of social problems and their implications for individuals and societies. The perceived etiology of social problems and their possible resolutions reflect the specific orientations of those studying them. As you peruse the subsequent articles, try to determine which of the three theoretical positions the various authors seem to be utilizing.

The authors conclude their article by suggesting several approaches that students may wish to consider in defining conditions as "social" problems and how they can/should be analyzed.

The editor felt it desirable to introduce this book of readings with a discussion of this type in order to help readers understand the social and sociological aspects of problems and issues plaguing modern society. The 42 articles included in this edition range from what it is like to live in a drug-infested slum to the pending destruction of the world's environment. The reader should ask why the issue covered in each article is a social problem. Is it a case of rights in conflict, a case of conflicting values, or a consequence of conflicting harms? To find out, the reader might first skim over each article to get a general idea of where the author is coming from, i.e., his or her theoretical position. Then reread the article to see just what the author indicates as the cause of the problem and, by implication, what can or should be done to resolve or eliminate it.

SOCIAL PROBLEMS:
Definitions, Theories, and Analysis

Harold A. Widdison
and H. Richard Delaney

Northern Arizona University

INTRODUCTION AND OVERVIEW

When asked, "What are the major social problems facing humanity today," college students' responses tend to mirror those highlighted by the mass media such as AIDS, poverty, child abuse, war, famine, racism, sexism, crime, riots, state of the economy, environment, abortion, euthanasia, homosexuality, and affirmative action. These are all valid subjects for study in a social problems class but some give rise to very great differences of opinion and even controversy. Dr. Jack Kevorkian in Michigan and his killing machine is one example that comes to mind. To some he evokes images of Nazi Germany with its policy of murdering the infirm and helpless. On the other hand, others see Dr. Kevorkian as a solution to the slow and agonizing death of individuals with terminal illnesses. Dr. Kevorkian is not symbolic of a potentially devastating social issue to them, but the solution to an escalating social problem.

The same controversy exists at the other end of life, specifically, what obligations do pregnant women have to themselves as opposed to the unborn? Some individuals see abortion as a solution to the problems of over population, child abuse, disruption of careers, dangers to the physical and emotional health of women, as well as the prevention of the birth of damaged fetuses, and they regard it as a right to self-determination. Others look at abortion as attacking the sanctity of life, abrogating the rights of a whole category of people, and violating every sense of moral and ethical responsibility.

Affirmative action is another issue that can be viewed as both the problem and the solution to a problem. As a solution, affirmative action attempts to reverse the effects of hundreds of years of discrimination. Doors that have been closed to specific categories of people for many generations are, it is hoped, forced open. Individuals, regardless of race, ethnicity, and gender, have access to professional schools, good jobs, and the assurance that they will be promoted. On the other hand, affirmative action forces employers, recruiting officers, and housing officials to give certain categories of individuals a preferred status. While affirmative action is promoted by some as a necessary policy to compensate for centuries of exclusion and discrimination, others claim that it is still discrimination disguised under a new label but with different groups being discriminated against. If race, sex, age, ethnicity, or any characteristic other than merit is used as the primary criterion for selection or promotion, then discrimination is occurring. Discrimination hurts both sides. William Wilson, a black social scientist, argues that it is very damaging to the self-esteem of black individuals to know that the primary reason they were hired was to fill quotas.

Both sides to the debate of whether these issues themselves reflect a social problem or are solutions to larger societal problems have valid facts and use societal level values to support their claims. Robin William, Jr. (1970) identified a list of 15 dominant value orientations that represent the concept of the good life to many Americans;

1. Achievement and success as major personal goals.
2. Activity and work favored above leisure and laziness.
3. Moral orientation, that is, absolute judgments of good/bad, right/wrong.
4. Humanitarian motives as shown in charity and crisis aid.
5. Efficiency and practicality; a preference for the quickest and shortest way to achieve a goal at the least cost.
6. Process and progress; a belief that technology can solve all problems and the future will be better than the past.
7. Material comfort as the American Dream.
8. Equality as an abstract ideal.
9. Freedom as a person's right against the state.
10. External conformity; the idea of going along, joining, and not rocking the boat.
11. Science and rationality as the means of mastering the environment and securing more material comforts.
12. Nationalism; a belief that American values and institutions represent the best on Earth.
13. Democracy based on personal equality and freedom.
14. Individualism, emphasizing personal rights and responsibilities.

15. Racism and group superiority themes that periodically lead to prejudice and discrimination against those who are racially, religiously, and culturally different from the white northern Europeans who first settled the continent.

This list combines some political, economic, and personal traits that actually contradict one another. This coexistence of opposing values helps explain why individuals hold conflicting views of the same behavior and why some issues generate such intense feelings.

It is the intent of this article and the readings included in this book to help students see the complex nature of a social problem and the impact that various values, beliefs, and actions have on them.

In the next segment, the authors will look at specific examples of values in conflict and the problems created by this conflict. Subsequently the authors will look at the three major theoretical positions that sociologists use to study social problems. The article will conclude with an examination of various strategies and techniques used to identify, understand, and resolve various types of social problems and their implications for those involved.

As noted above, contemporary American society is typified by values that both complement and contradict each other. For example, the United States capitalistic free enterprise system stresses rugged individualism, self-actualization, individual rights, and self-expression. This economic philosophy meshes well with Christian theology, particularly that of many Protestant denominations. This fact was the basis of Max Weber's (1964) *The Protestant Ethic and The Spirit of Capitalism.* He showed that the concept of grace (salvation is a gift—not something you can earn), predestination (the fact that some people have this gift while others do not), and a desire to know if the individual has grace, gave rise to a new idea of what constituted success. Whereas, with the communitarian emphasis of Catholicism where material success was seen as leading to selfishness and spiritual condemnation, Protestantism viewed material success as a sign of grace. In addition, it was each individual's efforts that resulted in both their economic success and their spiritual salvation. This religious philosophy also implied that the poor are poor because they lack the proper motivation, values, and beliefs (what is also known as the culture of poverty), and they are reaping the results of their own inadequacies. Attempts to reduce poverty have frequently included taking children from "impoverished" cultural environments and placing them in "enriched" environments to minimize the potentially negative effects parents and a bad environment could have on their children. These enrichment programs attempt to produce attitudes and behaviors that assure success in the world but, in the process, cut children off from their parents. Children are forced to abandon the culture of their parents, if they are to "succeed." Examples of this practice include the nurseries of the Kibbutz in Israel and the Head Start programs

in America. This practice is seen by some social scientists as a type of "cultural genocide." Entire cultures have been targeted (sometimes explicitly, though often not intentionally) for extinction in this way.

This fact upsets a number of social scientists. They feel it is desirable to establish a pluralistic society where ethnic, racial, and cultural diversity exist and flourish. To them, attempts to "Americanize" everyone are a sign of racism, sexism, bigotry, and prejudice. Others point to the lack of strong ethnic or racial identities as the unifying strength of the American system. When immigrants came to America, they put ethnic differences behind them, they learned English and democratic values, and they were assimilated into American life. In nations where immigrants have maintained their ethnic identities and held to unique cultural beliefs, their first loyalty is to their ethnic group. Examples of the destructive impact of strong ethnic loyalties can be seen in the conflict and fragmentation now occurring in the former Soviet Union, Czechoslovakia, and Yugoslavia.

THEORETICAL PERSPECTIVES: SYMBOLIC INTERACTION, FUNCTIONALISM, AND SOCIAL CONFLICT

In their attempts to understand social phenomena, researchers look for recurring patterns, relationships between observable acts, and unifying themes. The particular way in which researchers look at the world reflects not only their personal views and experiences, but their professional perspective as well. Sociologists focus on interactions between individuals, between individuals and groups, between groups, and between groups and the larger society in which they are located. They try to identify those things that facilitate or hinder interaction and the consequences of each. But not all sociologists agree as to the most effective/appropriate approach to take and tend to divide into three major theoretical camps. These are symbolic interactionism, functionalism, and social conflict. These three approaches are not mutually exclusive, but they do represent radically different perspectives of the nature of social reality and how it should be studied.

Symbolic Interaction

This theoretical perspective argues that no social condition, however unbearable it may seem to some, is inherently or objectively a social problem until a significant number of politically powerful people agree that it is contrary to the common good.

Scientists, social philosophers, religious leaders, and medical people may "know" that a specific action or condition has or will eventually have a devastating effect on society or a specific group in society, but, until they can convince those who are in a position to control and perhaps correct the condition, it is not considered a social problem. Therefore, it is not the social condition, but how the condition is defined and by whom, that determines if it is or will become a social problem. The social process whereby a specific condition moves from the level of an individual concern to a societal level issue can be long and arduous or very short. An example of the latter occurred in the mid-1960s when some physicians noticed a significant increase in infants born with severe physical deformities. Medical researchers looking into the cause of the deformities made a connection between them and the drug thalidomide. Pregnant women suffering from severe nausea and health threatening dehydration were prescribed this drug that dramatically eliminated the nausea and appeared to have no bad side effects. But the babies were born with terrible deformities. Once the medical researchers discovered the connection, they presented their findings to their colleagues. When the data were reviewed and found to be scientifically valid, the drug was banned immediately. Thus a small group's assessment of an issue as a serious problem quickly was legitimized by those in power as a societal level social problem and measures were taken to eliminate it.

Most situations are not this clear cut. In the mid-1960s various individuals began to question the real reason(s) why the United States was involved in the war in Southeast Asia. They discovered data indicating that the war was not about protecting the democratic rights of the Vietnamese. Those in power either ignored or rejected their claims as politically motivated and as militarily naive. Reports from the Vietcong about purported U.S. military atrocities were collected and used as supportive evidence. These claims were summarily dismissed as communistic propaganda. Convinced of the validity and importance of their cause, the protesters regrouped and collected still more data including data collected by the French government. This new information was difficult for the U.S. government to ignore as the French were our allies and former administrators of the area. Nevertheless, these new claims were also rejected as being somewhat self-serving since the Vietcong had defeated the French in Indochina and the French government could justify their failure if the United States also failed.

Over the years the amount of data continued to accumulate augmented by new information collected from disenchanted veterans. This growing pool of evidence began to bother legislators who demanded an accounting from U.S. government and the Department of Defense, but none was forthcoming. Increasing numbers of students joined the antiwar movement, but their protests were seen as unpatriotic and self-serving, i.e., an attempt to avoid military service. The increasing numbers of protesters began to cause some legislators to look closely at the claims of the antiwar protesters. As the magnitude of the war and the numbers of individuals sent to Vietnam grew, the number of people affected by the war grew as well. Returning veterans' reports of the state of the war, questionable military practices (such as the wholesale destruction of entire villages), complaints of incompetent leadership in the military, and corrupt Viet Nam politicians, supported the antiwar movement's earlier claims and convinced additional senators and representatives to support the stop the war movement, even though those in power still refused to acknowledge the legitimacy of the movement.

Unable to work within the system and convinced of the legitimacy of their cause, increasing numbers of people began to resort to unconventional and illegal actions such as burning their draft cards, refusing to register for the draft, seeking refuge in other countries, attacking ROTC buildings on college campuses, and even bombing military research facilities. These actions were initially interpreted by government officials as criminal activities of self-serving individuals or activities inspired by those sympathetic with the communistic cause. The government engaged in increasingly repressive efforts to contain the movement. But increasing disaffection with the war fueled by the rapidly growing numbers of casualties, coupled with the discontent within the ranks of the military, eventually forced those in power to acquiesce and accept the claims that the war was the problem and not the solution to a problem. Reaching this point took nearly fifteen years.

For the symbolic interactionist, the fact that socially harmful conditions are thought to exist is not the criterion for what constitutes a social problem. Rather, the real issue is to understand what goes into the assessment of a specific condition as being a social problem. To the symbolic interactionist, the appropriate questions are, (a) How is it that some conditions become defined as a social problem while others do not? (b) Who, in any society, can legitimate the designation of a condition as a social problem? (c) What solutions evolve and how do they evolve for specific social problems? (d) What factors exist in any specific society that inhibit or facilitate resolution of social problems?

In summary, symbolic interactionists stress that social problems do not exist independently of how people define their world. Social problems are socially constructed as people debate whether or not some social condition is a social problem and decide what to do about it. The focus is on the *meanings* the problem has for those who are affected by it and not on the *impact* it is having on them.

Functionalism

A second major theory sociologists use to study social problems is functionalism. Functionalists argue that society is a social system consisting of various integrated parts. Each of these parts fulfills a specific role that contributes to the overall functioning of society. In well-integrated systems, each part contributes to the stability of the whole. Functionalists examine each part in an attempt to determine the role it plays in the operation of the system as a whole. When any part fails, this creates a problem for the whole. These failures (dysfunctions) upset the equilibrium of the system and become social problems. To functionalists, anything that impedes the system's ability to achieve its goals is, by definition, a social problem. Unlike the symbolic interactionists, the functionalists argue that a social problem is not contingent on someone's assessment that it is a problem. Serious social problems may exist without anyone being aware of the detrimental effects they are having on various members of society or on society itself. Functionalists examine the stated objectives, values, and goals of a group, observe the behaviors of the members of the group, and analyze how their behaviors impact on the abilities of the group to achieve their goals.

Many times the stated objectives (what sociologists call the manifest functions) produce results that were not desired or intended (what sociologists call latent functions) and, in fact, are working against the group's abilities to accomplish its goals. Sociologists attempt to make the members of the group aware of the consequences of specific behaviors. For example, in an attempt to help single mothers of infants to provide for their children adequately, the American government created a program (Aid to Families with Dependent Children [AFDC]) to provide single mothers with enough money to feed, clothe, and house their children so that the children would not suffer. This program was motivated by the Judeo/Christian philosophy that society is obligated to care for those who cannot care for themselves. In this regard the program was a success. But it also had a dark side in that it discouraged the establishment of stable households with a father present since families consisting of both mothers and fathers did not qualify for aid. If a woman got married or was known to be living with a man, she lost her eligibility and her benefits. As a result, males were pushed to the periphery of the family. Many lower class unskilled males could not earn as much as a single mother under AFDC. This did not mean that men were not around, only that they could not become permanent fixtures in these families. As a result, a program designed to help families ended up altering the structures of families and in the process created a whole new social problem.

Functionalists also argue that if a behavior or social institution persists, it must be meeting some need within the society. Merely defining a behavior as a problem does not assure its demise. To eliminate any behavior, researchers/society must first find out what functions it is serving, remove or make the behavior dysfunctional, and then the behavior will disappear. As poverty, crime, and inequality exist and persist in all societies, the task of the social scientist is to discover how and why. In this regard, most individuals would argue that poverty is not desirable and should, if possible, be eliminated. Yet, as discussed by Herbert J. Gans in his article, "The Uses of Poverty: The Poor Pay All," poverty benefits a significant portion of society. The incentive to eradicate poverty is neutralized by specific benefits to the nonpoor. Five of the thirteen functions Gans identified are:

1. Poverty insures that society's "dirty work" will be done. Poverty functions to provide a low-wage labor pool that is willing or rather, unable to be unwilling, to perform dirty work at low cost.
2. Because the poor are required to work at low wages, they subsidize a variety of economic activities that benefit the affluent.
3. Poverty creates jobs for a number of occupations and professions that serve or "service" the poor, or protect the rest of society from them, such as social workers, police, and prison staff.
4. The poor buy goods others do not want thus prolonging the economic usefulness of such goods, i.e., day old bread, fruit, and vegetables that would otherwise have to be thrown out, secondhand clothes, and deteriorating automobiles and buildings.
5. The poor, being powerless, can be made to absorb the costs of change and growth in American society. Urban renewal and expressways, for example, have typically been located in poor neighborhoods.

Though not explicitly stated by Gans, the poor cannot afford the ever spiraling costs of health care and become those upon which the fledgling physician can practice his or her profession. As part of the learning process, mistakes are common and the poor are thus likely to have a lower level of medical expertise. Many medical, dental, and nursing schools are located within the inner city. In exchange for free or greatly reduced fees, poor people become guinea pigs to help student nurses, doctors, and dentists become experienced enough to practice on the more affluent.

The functionalists examine conditions, behaviors, and institutions in an attempt to try to understand the functions being met by these specific phenomena. To eliminate any of these problems they have to become dysfunctional. But because many of the functional alternatives to each problem would be dysfunctional for the affluent and powerful members of society, there is an incentive for the behavior to persist.

In summary, functionalists emphasize the interrelationship of the various parts of a system and believe that changes in one part will have significant implications for other parts. Any particular social problem is only a part of a larger whole. Which means that in order to understand a social problem, one must place it in a broader context. A social problem is a consequence of the way a social system is put together.

Conflict Theory

Those social scientists adhering to the conflict perspective view life and all social interaction as a struggle for power and privilege. They see every person and every group as being in competition for scarce and valued resources. They believe that even though people occasionally may have to cooperate with each other or even form alliances, they are still essentially in conflict. As soon as the alliance is no longer beneficial, conflict will often ensue. Unlike the functionalists who see the elements of a society as harmoniously working together and contributing to the whole, conflict theorists view all the parts as being in competition with each other. They see the guiding principle of social life as disequilibrium and change, not equilibrium and harmony. But, like the functionalists, they argue that social problems can and do exist independently of people's assessments of them. They argue that whether people are aware of it or not, they are enmeshed in a basic struggle for power and survival. Each group in society is attempting to achieve gains for itself that must necessarily be at the expense of other groups. It is this consistent conflict over limited resources that threatens societal peace and order.

Whereas the functionalists try to understand how different positions of power came into existence (Davis & Moore 1945), the conflict theorists show how those in power attempt to stay in power (Mills 1956). The conflict theorists see social problems as the natural and inevitable consequences of groups in society struggling to survive and gain control over those things that can affect their ability to survive. Those groups who are successful then attempt to use whatever means they must to control their environment and consolidate their position, thus increasing their chances of surviving. According to conflict theorists, those in power exploit their position and create poverty, discrimination, oppression, and crime in the process. The impact of these conditions on the exploited produces other pathological conditions such as alienation, alcoholism, drug abuse, mental illness, stress, health problems, and suicide. On occasions, such as that which occurred in Los Angeles in the summer of 1991 when policemen were found innocent of excessive force in the beating of a man named Rodney King, the feelings of helplessness and hopelessness can erupt as rage against the system in the form of violence and riots or as in Eastern Europe, as rebellion and revolution against repressive communistic governments.

The conflict theorists argue that drug abuse, mental illness, various criminal behaviors, and suicide are symptoms of a much larger societal malaise. To understand and eliminate these problems, society needs to understand the basic conflicts that are producing them. The real problems stem from the implications of being exploited. Being manipulated by the powerful and denied a sense of control tends, (a) to produce a loss of control over one's life (powerlessness), (b) to lead to an inability to place one's productive efforts into some meaningful context (meaninglessness), (c) to not being involved in the process of change but only to experience the impact resulting from the changes (normlessness), and (d) to cause one to find oneself isolated from one's colleagues on the job (self-isolation). Conflictists see all of these problems as the product of a capitalistic system that alienates the worker

from himself and his or her fellow workers (Seeman 1959).

To protect their positions of power, privilege, prestige, and possessions, those in power use their wealth and influence to control organizations.

For example, they manipulate the system to get key individuals into positions where they can influence legislation and decisions that are designed to protect their power and possessions. They might serve on or appoint others to school boards to assure that the skills and values needed by the economy are taught. They also assure that the laws are enforced internally (the police) or externally (the military) to protect their holdings. The war in the Persian Gulf is seen by many conflict theorists as being over oil rather than to free Kuwait.

When the exploited attempt to do something about their condition by organizing, protesting, and rebelling, they threaten those in power. For example, they may go on a strike that might disrupt the entire nation. Under the pretext that it is for the best good of society, the government may step in and stop the strike. Examples are the air-controller's strike of 1987 and the railroad strike in 1991. In retaliation the workers may engage in work slow down, stoppage, and even sabotage. They may stage protests and public demonstrations and cast protest votes at the ballot boxes. If these do not work, rebellions and revolutions may result. Those in power can respond very repressively as was the case in Tiananmen Square in China in 1989, threaten military force as the Soviet Union did with the Baltic countries in 1990, or back down completely as when the Berlin wall came down. Thus reactions to exploitation may produce change but inevitably lead to other social problems. In Eastern Europe and the former Soviet Union, democracy has resulted in massive unemployment, spiraling inflation, hunger, crime, and homelessness.

Sometimes those in power make concessions to maintain power. The conflict theorists look for concessions and how they placate the poor while still protecting the privileged and powerful. The rich are viewed as sharing power only if forced to do so and only to the extent absolutely necessary.

Robert Michels (1949), a French social philosopher, looked at the inevitable process whereby the members of any group voluntarily give up their rights, prerogatives, and power to a select few who then dominate the group. It may not be the conscious decision of those who end up in positions of power to dominate the group but, in time, conscious decisions may be made to do whatever is necessary to stay in control of the group. The power, privilege, and wealth they acquire as part of the position alters their self-images. To give up the position would necessitate a complete revision of who they are, what they can do, and who they associate with. Their "self" has become fused/confused with the position they occupy and in an attempt to protect their "self," they resist efforts to remove them from the role/position. Threats to them are seen as threats to the organization and are vigorously resisted. According to Michels, no matter how democratic an organization starts out to be it will always become dominated and controlled by a few. The process whereby this occurs he called "The Iron Law of Oligarchy." For example, hospitals that were created to save lives, cure the sick, and provide for the chronically ill, now use the threat of closure to justify/force rate increases. The hospital gets its rate increase, the cost of health goes up and the number of individuals able to afford health care declines resulting in increased health problems in the community. Though not explicitly stated, the survival of the organization (and its administrators) is more important than the health of the community.

In summary, the conflict theoretical model stresses the fact that key resources such as power and privilege are limited and distributed unequally among the members/ groups in a society. Conflict is therefore a natural and inevitable result of various groups pursuing their interests and values. To study the basis of social problems, researchers must look at the distribution of power and privilege because these two factors are always at the center of conflicting interests and values. Moreover, whenever social change occurs, social problems inevitably follow.

Conflict and Functionalism: A Synthesis

While the conflict theorist's and functionalist's explanations of what constitutes the roots of social problems appear to be completely contradictory, Dahrendorf (1959) sees them as complementary. "Functionalism explains how highly talented people are motivated to spend twenty-five years of study to become surgeons; conflict theory explains how surgeons utilize their monopoly on their vital skills to obtain rewards that greatly exceed that necessary to ensure an adequate supply of talent." (See also Ossowski 1963; van de Berghe 1963; Williams 1966; Horowitz 1962; and Lenski 1966 for other attempts at a synthesis between these two theoretical models.)

SOCIAL PROBLEMS: DEFINITION AND ANALYSIS

Value Conflicts

It is convenient to characterize a social problem as a conflict of values, a conflict of values and duties, a conflict of rights (Hook, 1974), or a social condition that leads to or is thought to lead to harmful consequences. Harm may be defined as (a) the loss to a group, community, or society of something to which it is thought to be entitled, (b) an offense perceived to be an affront to our moral sensibilities, or (c) an impoverishment of the collective good or welfare. It is also convenient to define values as individual or collective desires that become attached to social

objects. Private property, for example, is a valued social object for some while others disavow or reject its desirability and, because of the public disagreement over its value, is also an example of a conflict of values. A conflict of values is also found in the current controversy surrounding abortion. Where pro-life supporters tend to see life itself as the ultimate value, supporters of pro-choice may, as some have, invoke the Fourteenth Amendment's right to privacy clause as the compelling value.

Values vs. Duties Conflicts

A second format that students should be aware of in the analysis of social problems is the conflict between values and obligations or duties. This approach calls our attention to those situations in which a person, group, or community must pursue or realize a certain duty even though we may be convinced that doing so will not achieve the greater good. For example, educators, policemen, bureaucrats, and environmentalists may occupy organizational or social roles in which they are required to formulate policies and follow rules which, according to their understanding, will not contribute to the greater good of students, citizens, or the likelihood of a clean environment. On the other hand, there are situations in which, we, as a person, group, or community, do things that would seem not to be right in our pursuit of what we consider to be the higher value. Here students of social problems are faced with the familiar problem of using questionable, illogical, or immoral means to achieve what is perhaps generally recognized as a value of a higher order. Police officers, for example, are sometimes accused of employing questionable, immoral, or deceptive means (stings, scams, undercover operations) to achieve what are thought to be socially helpful ends and values such as removing a drug pusher from the streets. Familiar questions for this particular format are: Do the ends justify the means? Should ends be chosen according to the means available for their realization? What are the social processes by which means themselves become ends? These are questions to which students of social problems and social policy analysis should give attention since immoral, illegal, or deceptive means can themselves lead to harmful social consequences.

Max Weber anticipated and was quite skeptical of those modern bureaucratic processes whereby means are transformed into organizational ends and members of the bureaucracy became self-serving and lose sight of their original and earlier mission. The Central Intelligence Agency's (CIA) efforts to maintain U.S. interests in Third World countries led to tolerance of various nations' involvements in illicit drugs. Thus the CIA actually contributed to the drug problem the police struggle to control. A second example is that of the American Association of Retired Persons (AARP). To help the elderly obtain affordable health care, life insurance, drugs, and so forth, the AARP established various organizations to provide or contract for services. But now the AARP seems to be more concerned about its corporate holdings than it is about the welfare of its elderly members.

Rights in Conflict

Finally, students of social problems should become aware of rights vs. right moral conflicts. With this particular format, one's attention is directed to the conflict of moral duties and obligations, the conflict of rights and, not least, the serious moral issue of divided loyalties. In divorce proceedings, spouses must try to balance their personal life and career against the obligations and duties to the other spouse and children. We may want to meet our full obligations to both our family and our occupation, but often this is not possible because of finite time and means.

There is a complex interaction between the rights an individual has and the consequences of exercising specific rights. For example, if an individual elects to exercise his or her right to consume alcoholic beverages, this act then nullifies many subsequent rights because of the potential harm that can occur. The right to drive, to engage in athletic events, or to work, is jeopardized by the debilitating effects of alcohol. Every citizen has rights assured him or her by membership in society. At the same time, rights can only be exercised to the degree to which they do not trample on the rights of other members of the group. If a woman elects to have a baby, she abrogates her right to consume alcohol, smoke, consume caffeine, or take many drugs. The consequences of these drugs on the developing fetus are potentially devastating because the rights of the child to a healthy body and mind are threatened. Fetal Alcohol Effect/Syndrome is the number one cause of preventable mental retardation in the United States, and it could be completely eliminated if pregnant women never took an alcoholic drink. Caring for individuals with Fetal Alcohol Effect/Syndrome is taking increasingly greater resources that could well be directed toward other pressing issues.

Rights cannot be responsibly exercised without individuals weighing their potential consequences. Thus a hierarchy of rights, consequences, and harm exists and the personal benefits resulting from any act must be weighed against the personal and social harm that could follow. The decision to use tobacco should be weighed against the possible consequences of a wide variety of harms such as personal health problems and the stress it places on society's resources to care for tobacco-related diseases. Tobacco-related diseases often have catastrophic consequences for their users that cannot be paid for by the individual, so the burden of payment is placed on society. Millions of dollars, many hospital beds and health care personnel must be diverted away from other patients to care for these individuals with self-inflicted tobacco-related diseases. In addition to the costs in money, personnel, and medical resources, the diseases these individ-

uals get takes a tremendous emotional toll on those closest to them. To focus only on one's rights without consideration of the consequences associated with those rights often deprives other individuals from exercising their rights.

Our Constitution guarantees individual rights without clearly specifying what the rights really entail. Logically one cannot have rights without others having corresponding obligations. Specifically, what obligations does each right assure and what limitations do these obligations and/or rights require? Rights for the collectivity are protected by limitations placed on each individual, but limits on collective rights are also mandated by laws assuring that individual rights are not infringed on. Therefore, we have rights as a whole that often differ from those we have as individual members of that whole. For example, the right to free speech may impinge in a number of ways on a specific community. To the members of a small Catholic community, having active proselyting non-Catholic missionaries preaching on street corners and knocking on doors could be viewed as a social problem. Attempts to control their actions, such as the enactment and enforcement of "Green River" ordinances (laws against active solicitation), could eliminate the community's problem but could trample on the individual's constitutional rights of religious expression. To protect individual rights, the community may have to put up with individuals pushing their personal theological ideas in public places. For the Catholic community, aggressive non-Catholic missionaries are not only a nuisance but a social problem that should be banned. To the actively proselyting churches, restrictions on their actions are violations of their civil rights and hence a serious social problem.

Currently, another conflict of interests/rights is dividing many communities and that is smoking. Smokers argue that their rights are being seriously threatened by aggressive legislation restricting smoking. They argue that society should not and cannot legislate morality. Smokers point out how attempts to legislate alcohol consumption during the Prohibition Era of the 1920s and 1930s was an abject failure and, in fact, created more problems than it eliminated. They believe that exactly the same process is being attempted today and will prove to be just as unsuccessful. Those who smoke then go on to say that smoking is protected by the Constitution's freedom of expression and that no one has the right to force others to adhere to their personal health policies which are an individual choice. They assert that if the "radicals" get away with smoking restrictions, they can and will move on to other health-related behaviors such as overeating. Therefore, by protecting the constitutional rights of smokers, society is only protecting the constitutional rights of everyone.

On the other hand, nonsmokers argue that their rights are being violated by smokers. They point to an increasing body of research data that shows that secondhand smoke leads to numerous health problems such as emphysema, heart problems, and throat or lung cancer. They not only have a right not to have to breathe smoke-contaminated air, but society has an obligation to protect the health and well-being of its members from the known dangers of breathing smoke.

These are only a couple of examples of areas where rights come into conflict. Others include environmental issues, endangered species, forest management, enforcement of specific laws, homosexuality, mental illness, national health insurance, taxes, balance of trade, food labeling and packaging, genetic engineering, rape, sexual deviation, political corruption, riots, public protests, zero population growth, the state of the economy, and on and on.

It is notable that the degree to which any of these issues achieves widespread concern varies over time. Specific problems are given much fanfare by politicians and special interest groups for a time, and the media tries to convince us that specific activities or behaviors have the greatest urgency and demand a total national commitment for a solution. However, after being in the limelight for a while, the importance of the problem seems to fade and new problems move into prominence. If you look back over previous editions of this book, you can see this trend. It would be useful to speculate why, in American society, some problems remain a national concern while others come and go.

The Consequences of Harm
To this point it has been argued that social problems can be defined and analyzed as (a) conflicts between values, (b) conflicts between values and duties, and (c) conflicts between rights. Consistent with the aims of this article, social problems can be further characterized and interpreted as social conditions that lead, or are generally thought to lead, to harmful consequences for the person, group, community, or society.

Harm, and here we follow Hyman Gross's (1979) conceptualization of the term, can be classified as (a) a loss, usually permanent, that deprives the person or group of a valued object or condition it is entitled to have, (b) offenses to sensibility, that is, harm that contributes to unpleasant experiences in the form of repugnance, embarrassment, disgust, alarm, or fear, and (c) impairment of the collective welfare, that is, violations of those values possessed by the group or society.

Harm can also be rank ordered as to its potential for good. Physicians, to help their patients, often have to harm them. The question they must ask is, "Will this specific procedure, drug, or operation produce more good than the pain and suffering it causes?" For instance, will the additional time it affords the cancer patient be worth all the suffering associated with chemotherapy? In Somalia, health care personnel are forced to make much harder decisions. They are surrounded by starvation, sickness, and death. If they treat one person, another cannot be treated and will die. They find themselves forced to allocate their time and resources not according to who needs it the most, but according to who has the greatest chance of survival.

Judges must also balance the harm they are about to inflict on those they must sentence against the public good and the extent to which the sentence might help the individual reform. Justice must be served in that people must pay for their crimes, yet most judges also realize that prison time often does more harm than good. In times of recession, employers also must weigh harm when they are forced to cut back their work force. Where should the cuts occur? Who will be affected? Should they keep employees of long standing and cut those most recently hired (many of which are minorities hired through affirmative action programs), or should they keep those with the most productive records, or those with the greatest need for employment? No matter what they do, harm will result to some. The harm produced by the need to reduce their work force must be balanced by the potential good of the company's surviving and sustaining employment for the rest of the employees.

The notion of harm also figures into the public and social dialogue between those who are pro-choice and those who are pro-life. Most pro-lifers are inclined to see the greatest harm of abortion to be the loss of life while most pro-choicers argue that the compelling personal and social harm is the taking away of a value (the right to privacy) they are entitled to. A further harmful consequence of abortion for most pro-lifers is that the value of life will be cheapened, the moral fabric of society will be weakened and the taking of life could be extended to the elderly and disabled, for example. Most of those who are pro-choice, on the other hand, are inclined to argue that the necessary consequence of their position is keeping government out of their private lives and bedrooms. In a similar way this "conflict of values" format can be used to analyze, clarify, and enlarge our understanding of the competing values, harms, and consequences of other social problems. We can, and should, search for the competing values underlying such social problems as, for example, income redistribution, homelessness, divorce, education, and the environment.

Loss, then, as a societal harm consists in a rejection or violation of what a person or group feels they are entitled to have. American citizens, for example, tend to view life, freedom, equality, property, and physical security as ultimate values. Loss is a rejection or violation of these values that is thought to constitute a serious social problem since such a loss diminishes our sense of personhood. Murder, violence, AIDS, homelessness, environmental degradation, the failure to provide adequate health care, and abortion can be conveniently classified as social problems within this class of harms.

Offenses to our sensibilities constitute a class of harm which, when they are serious enough, become a problem affecting moral issues and the common good of the members of a society. Issues surrounding pornography, prostitution, and the so-called victimless crimes are examples of this class of harm. Moreover, some would argue that environmental degradation, the increasing gap thought to exist between the very rich and the very poor in our society, and the problem of the homeless should be classified within this class of harm.

A third class of harms, namely impairments to the collective welfare, is explained, in part, by Gross (1979: 120) as follows:

Social life, particularly in the complex forms of civilized societies, creates many dependencies among members of a community. The welfare of each member depends upon the exercise of restraint and precaution by others in the pursuit of their legitimate activities, as well as upon cooperation toward certain common objectives. These matters of collective welfare involve many kinds of interests that may be said to be possessed by the community.

In a pluralistic society such as ours, matters of collective welfare are sometimes problematic in that there can be considerable conflict of values and rights between various segments of our society. There is likely to remain, however, a great deal of agreement that those social problems whose harmful consequences would involve impairments to the collective welfare would include poverty, poor education, mistreatment of the young and elderly, excessive disparities in income distribution, discrimination against ethnic and other minorities, drug abuse, health and medical care, the state of the economy, and problems of the environment.

BIBLIOGRAPHY

Dahrendorf, R., *Class and Class Conflict in Industrial Society*, Stanford, California: Stanford University Press, 1959.

Davis, Kingsley & Wilbert E. Moore, "Some Principles of Stratification," *American Sociological Review*, Vol. X, 1945:242–249.

Gans, Herbert J., "The Uses of Poverty: The Poor Pay All," *Social Policy*, New York: Social Policy Corporation, 1971.

Gross, Hyman, *A Theory of Criminal Justice*, New York: Oxford University Press, 1979.

Hook, Sidney, *Pragmatism and the Tragic Sense of Life*, New York: Basic Books, 1974.

Horowitz, M.A., "Consensus, Conflict, and Cooperation," *Social Forces*, Vol. 41, 1962:177–88.

Lenski, G., *Power and Privilege*, New York: McGraw-Hill, 1966.

Michels, Robert, *Political Parties: A Sociological Study of the Oligarchical Tendencies of Modern Democracy*, New York: Free Press, 1949.

Mills, C. Wright, *The Power Elite*, New York: Oxford University Press, 1956.

Ossowski, S., *Class Structure in the Social Consciousness*, translated by Sheila Patterson. New York: The Free Press, 1963.

Seeman, Melvin, "On The Meaning Of Alienation," *American Sociological Review*, Vol. 24, 1959:783–791.

van den Berghe, P., "Dialectic and Functionalism: Toward a Theoretical Synthesis," *American Sociological Review*, Vol. 28, 1963:695–705.

Weber, Max, *The Protestant Ethic and the Spirit of Capitalism*, translated by Talcott Parsons. New York: Scribner, 1964.

William, Robin, Jr., *American Society: A Sociological Interpretation*, 3rd Edition, New York: Alfred A. Knopf, 1970.

Williams, Robin, "Some Further Comments on Chronic Controversies," *American Journal of Sociology*, Vol. 71, 1966:717–721.

Wilson, William, *The Declining Significance of Race*, Chicago: University of Chicago Press, 1978.

CHALLENGE TO THE READER

As you read the articles that follow, try to determine which of the three major theoretical positions each of the authors seems to be using. Whatever approach the writer uses in his or her discussion suggests what he or she thinks is the primary cause of the social problem/issue under consideration.

Also ask yourself as you read each article, (1) What values are at stake or in conflict? (2) What rights are at issue or in conflict? (3) What is the nature of the harm in each case, and who is being hurt? (4) What solutions do the authors see or imply could resolve each social problem?

Parenting and Family Issues

- **The Family (Articles 2–6)**

- **Homelessness (Article 7)**

Throughout history, the family has been seen as the most effective and primary transmitter (for good or ill) of values, beliefs, and behaviors. Since the 1960s, the family has been under assault. Some individuals argue that it is not so much an assault as it is a restructuring of an old and antiquated social institution. Single parents, couples with no children, single individuals, people living together, homosexual couples—almost any combination of people living under a common roof is being classified by some as a family.

Questions raised by the articles in this section include: (a) Just what is a family? (b) What impact is the "new" family structure having on its members, especially the children? (c) What impact are other social institutions having on the family? (d) How does what is happening in the family impact on other institutions? (e) What can and should be done to strengthen the family?

"America's Family Time Famine" covers some of the implications of dual careers, disrupted families, and one-child families. As the value placed on careers increases, the time available for spending with children decreases. The trend against parenting seems to be nationwide, and with this trend, the implications for children and parents who wish to be effective are not promising.

"The American Family, 1992" examines what happens to children raised in single-parent homes. This article raises questions about our basic values and the impact that divorce and careerism are having on children.

"Endangered Family" looks at the unique problems facing black families. This article is not an indictment of blacks, but an attempt to understand why a black child has only one chance in five of growing up with two parents. The economy is a significant culprit. While opportunities for work declined for black men, many opportunities for employment opened for black women, making it possible for them to survive without men. At the same time, governmental programs were created that inadvertently pushed black men out of the family. Increasingly, black leaders are realizing that if the black family is to be saved, it is up to the black community.

"Bringing Up Father" focuses on the subtle and not so subtle messages given males that they are superfluous. Society, employment, schools, health care providers, and even their own wives tend to push them to the fringes of the family. A sociologist discovered, "Fathers, except in rare circumstances, have not yet become equal partners in parenthood." As a result, record numbers do not stick around at a time when they are needed more than ever.

"Everyday Life in Two High-Risk Neighborhoods" provides two short research field reports from inner-city neighborhoods. Philippe Bourgois lived with a family in a tenement in East Harlem. He used classical participant observation methods, spending hundreds of nights on the streets and in crack houses. Linda Burton focuses on the impact of illicit drug trafficking on families. The paired articles picture how social problems, in this case drugs and poverty, touch inner-city children.

"American Nightmare: Homelessness" argues that national economic policies, not lack of drive or incentive, are the primary cause of homelessness. The solution to homelessness lies not in changing the attitudes and values of the homeless but in providing jobs and low-income housing.

Looking Ahead: Challenge Questions

What personal experiences have you had with problems in your family?

Is it possible to have a successful career and be an effective parent? If not, which would you choose and why?

Is the current high divorce rate good or bad for society?

How do the problems facing children of single parents differ from those of children with two parents?

In what ways are the lives of American children, particularly minority children, in peril?

Why are men, especially black men, not as involved in parenting as are women?

What are the primary causes for homelessness? To what extent is homelessness an individual or a societal problem?

What is it like to try and raise children in the inner city?

What is it like to be forced to survive on welfare?

In what key ways would the approaches of symbolic interactionists, functionalists, and conflict theorists differ in the study of family issues?

What conflicts in rights, values, and duties seem to underlie each issue?

America's Family Time Famine

William R. Mattox, Jr.

William R. Mattox, Jr. is a policy analyst who focuses on work and family issues for the Family Research Council. This article is adapted from a piece published in the Winter, 1991 edition of the Heritage Foundation's Policy Review.

Many parents in America today are out of time. Out of gas. Running on empty. "On the fast track of two-career families in the go-go society of modern life, the most rationed commodity in the home is time," observes syndicated columnist Suzanne Fields. And the children of today's overextended parents are starving — starving from a lack of parental time, attention and affection.

Parents today spend 40 percent less time with their children than did parents in 1965, according to data collected from personal time diaries by sociologist John Robinson of the University of Maryland. In 1965, parents spent approximately 30 hours a week with their kids. By 1985, parent-child interaction had dropped to just 17 hours a week.

These changes are presenting significant challenges to American family life. Parents today employ a variety of time-management strategies to meet their work and family responsibilities. In roughly one-third of all two-income families today (one-half of those with preschoolers) spouses work complementary

Mom and Dad on their way to work

 By William R. Mattox, Jr., from *Children Today*, November/December 1990, pp. 9-11, 31. Reprinted by permission.

Here Sis and I are doing homework

shifts to maximize the amount of time children are cared for by at least one parent. The most common "tag-team" arrangement is one in which the father works a standard 9-to-5 job and the mother works part-time in the evenings or on weekends.

Other two-income households work concurrent shifts. Families in which the youngest child is of school age often choose this strategy to minimize the amount of time parents are unavailable to children during non-school hours. Same-shift arrangements are also common among families in which both parents have a high attachment to their careers and in those in which limited employment opportunities leave few alternatives.

Whether couples adopt a tag-team arrangement or a same-shift strategy, two-income households spend considerably less time with their children than do breadwinner-homemaker households. (Although there are certainly some traditional families that suffer from father absence due to the time-demanding nature of the sole breadwinner's work.)

This discrepancy is most pronounced in maternal time with children. In fact, research by University of Virginia sociologists Steven Nock and Paul William Kingston shows that employed mothers of preschool children on average spend less than half as much time with their children as full-time mothers at home. Moreover, Nock and Kingston show that employed mothers do not compensate for this shortage in quantity of time by devoting a higher proportion of the time they do spend with children to "high quality" child-centered activities such as playing with dolls, going to the park, or reading.

Time pressures can be especially daunting for single parents—and especially harmful to their children. Children in single-parent homes usually receive less parental attention and supervision than other children. Not only is one parent absent from the home (and research by sociologist Frank Furstenberg shows that three-fourths of all children of divorce have contact with their fathers less than two days a month), but the other parent is overloaded with money-making and household tasks. Indeed, Robinson's

data show that, on average, single mothers spend 33 percent less time each week than married mothers in primary child-care activities such as dressing, feeding, chauffeuring, talking, playing, or helping with homework.

Moreover, children in single-parent families often have very irregular schedules. One study found that preschool children of single mothers sleep two fewer hours a night on average than their counterparts in two-parent homes, in part because harried mothers find it difficult to maintain a consistent bedtime routine.

Sibling Revelry

Kids aren't just missing out on time with their parents. Thanks to the "birth dearth," they are also missing out on interaction with siblings.

In 1975, 62 percent of all women aged 40-44 had given birth to three or more children over the course of their lifetimes. In 1988, only 38 percent had done so. The percentage of those giving birth to just one child rose from 9 to 15 percent during this same time period.

Some regard the decline in family size

as a positive development because it means children today receive more individualized attention from their parents than did children a generation ago.

Even if this were true—and sociologist Harriet Presser reports "not only are Americans having fewer children than ever before, they are spending less time with the children they have"—it can hardly be argued that a one-child family generally has as rich a family experience as a larger family. Even if an only child receives more individualized parental attention, he still misses out on the intimate joys of having brothers and sisters—playing wiffle ball in the backyard, exchanging gifts at Christmas time, double-teaming Dad in a wrestling match on the family room floor, attending a sibling's ballet recital, and (later in life) reminiscing about old times at family reunions.

Today's fast-paced family life is also eroding the development of other aspects of what sociologist David Popenoe of Rutgers University says "is arguably the ideal child-rearing environment":

a relatively large family that does a lot of things together, has many routines and traditions, and provides a great deal of quality contact time between adults and children; regular contact with relatives, active neighboring in a supportive neighborhood, and contact with the world of work; little concern on the part of children that their parents will break up; and the coming together of all these ingredients in the development of a rich family subculture that has lasting meaning and strongly promulgates such family values as cooperation and sharing.

Eating dinner together is one time-honored family tradition some believe is on its way out. "The family meal is dead," columnist Jonathan Yardley has written. "Except on the rarest occasions—Christmas, Thanksgiving, certain religious holidays—when we reach down to the innermost depths of the tribal memory and summon up turkeys and pies, roasts and casseroles, we have given up on what was once a central element in American domestic life."

Research on the prevalence of regular family mealtimes is mixed. Some reports claim as many as 75 percent of all families regularly dine together, while others suggest less than 35 percent do so. Whatever the case, polls taken by the Roper organization show that the proportion of families that dine together regularly declined 10 percent between 1976 and 1986. This helps explain why heat-and-eat microwavable dinners for children to prepare alone are "the hottest new category in food products," according to a food industry spokesperson.

Whatever the virtues of microwavable meals and other convenience foods, there is reason to be concerned about children routinely feeding themselves. As Suzanne Fields observes, "The child who grazes, standing in front of a microwave eating his fried chicken, biscuits, or refried beans, won't starve, but he may suffer from an emotional hunger that would be better satisfied if only Mom and Dad were there to yell at him for every pea he slips onto the knife."

So Many Bills, So Little Time

So how did American families run out of time? Growing economic pressures have a lot to do with the American family time crisis.

One of the supreme ironies of recent economic developments is that while America has experienced steady growth in its gross national product, the economic pressures on families with children have risen significantly. How can it be that at the same time we hear so much about the longest peacetime economic expansion in our nation's history, we also hear talk that economic pressures have grown so much that many families today must have two incomes?

Wage stagnation is one big reason. During the 1970s and '80s, constant dollar earnings of American husbands grew at less than 1 percent per year compared to a real growth rate of 3 percent per year in the 1950s and '60s. Moreover, for some occupational and demographic groups—particularly non-supervisory workers and males under age 25—real wages have actually fallen since 1973.

While wages have stagnated, taxes have risen dramatically. In 1950, a median-income family of four paid 2 percent of its annual gross earnings to the federal government in income and payroll taxes. Today, it pays 24 percent. In addition, state and local taxes, on average, take another 8 percent from the family's gross income.

Moreover, the erosion in the value of the personal exemption (the tax code's chief mechanism for adjusting tax liability to reflect differences in family size) has shifted more of the federal income tax burden onto the backs of families with dependents. Had the exemption kept pace with inflation since 1950, it would now be worth close to $7,000. Instead, it stands at $2,050.

On top of this, families are finding their take-home pay does not go as far as it once did. As economist Sylvia Ann Hewlett puts it, families today are "like hamsters on a wheel," running hard just to keep up.

Over the past 25 years, increases in the cost of several major family expenses—housing, health care, transportation, and higher education—have significantly outpaced the general inflation rate. For example, Joseph Minarik of the Congressional Joint Economic Committee has calculated that the typical 30-year-old man could get a mortgage on a median-priced home in 1973 with 21 percent of his income. By 1987, a median-priced home mortgage would take 40 percent of a typical 30-year-old's gross income.

The cost of housing, which is typically a family's single greatest expense, is tied directly to crime rates and school districts. As crime rates have risen and school performance has declined, an under-supply of housing in good school districts with low crime rates has driven the price of housing in such neighborhoods way up. Thus, parents who value safety, education, and time with children must either live in areas with poorer schools and higher crime or divert time from children to market their labor in order to purchase a home in a safe neighborhood with good schools. That is a quintessential Hobson's choice.

Perrier and Teddy Bears

Growing economic pressures aren't the only reason families have less time together. A number of cultural factors have also played a major role.

"Unbridled careerism" is partly responsible for the decline in family time, says Karl Zinsmeister of the American Enterprise Institute. "For years, one of the most cogent criticisms of American sex roles and economic arrangements has been the argument that many fathers get so wrapped up in earning and doing at the workplace that they become dehumanized, losing interest in the intimate joys of family life and failing to participate fairly in domestic responsibilities," he writes. "Now it appears workaholism and family dereliction have become equal opportunity diseases, striking mothers as much as fathers."

The devaluation of motherhood stands behind such trends. As Zinsmeister notes, "Today, women are more likely to be admired and appreciated for launching a catchy new ad campaign for toothpaste than they are for nurturing and shaping an original personality." Ironically, this has a detrimental impact on fatherhood as well. So long as child-rearing is viewed as a low calling for women, it is unlikely that it will take on increased significance for men.

Apart from unbridled careerism, some of the reduction in family time has been driven by a rampant materialism that places a higher premium on obtaining or retaining a "Perrier and Rolex life-style" than on investing time in a larger kin group.

"Increasingly, Americans are pursuing a selfish individualism that is inconsistent with strong families and strong communities," writes University of North Carolina sociologist Peter Uhlenberg. "This movement is fueled by the media, most especially television (both in its programming and advertising), which suggests that personal happiness is the highest good and that it can be achieved by pursuing pleasure and material goods."

Indeed, it has become all too common for parents to buy material goods for their children in an attempt to compensate for their frequent absence from the home. Harvard University child psychiatrist Robert Coles calls this the "teddy bear syndrome":

Some of the frenzied need of children to have possessions isn't only a function of the ads they see on TV. It's a function of their hunger for what they aren't getting—their parents' time. The biggest change I have seen in 30 years of interviewing families is that children are no longer being cared for by their parents the way they once were. Parents are too busy spending their most precious capital—their time and their energy—struggling to keep up with MasterCard payments. They're depleted. They work long hours to barely keep up, and when they get home at the end of the day they're tired. And their kids are left with a Nintendo or a pair of Nikes or some other piece of crap. Big deal.

Swimming Upstream

Of course, not all parents are trying to "buy off" their children with Teenage Mutant Ninja Turtles gear or overpriced sneakers. Many are struggling to raise responsible children and to transmit family values such as sharing, responsibility, commitment, and self-control. But these families are finding themselves swimming upstream against an increasingly unfriendly culture that instead promotes casual sex, instant gratification and selfish individualism.

Whereas once institutions outside the family, such as schools, churches, the mass media, and businesses, formerly reinforced the inculcation of traditional values, today they are often indifferent or downright hostile to family values and the rights of parents to pass on such values to their children. Many parents sense that they are being undercut by larger institutional forces. And they recognize that children who lack the self-esteem that comes from parental attention and affection are especially vulnerable to negative peer and cultural influences.

"Doing Things Together"

Some opinion leaders in government, academia, and the mass media view initiatives designed to increase family time—especially those that recognize the legitimacy and strengths of the breadwinner-homemaker family model—as an attempt to "turn back the clock"

rather than "facing the realities" of modern family life. These leaders overlook the fact that concerns about family time are not limited to those who believe the traditional family model is ideal.

A 1989 Cornell University study found that two-thirds of all mothers employed full-time would like to work fewer hours so that they could devote more time to their families. And when respondents to a 1989 survey commissioned by the Mass Mutual Insurance Company were asked to identify "extremely effective" ways to strengthen the family, nearly twice as many opted for "spending more time together" than listed "full-time parent raising kids."

Moreover, most Americans do not sneer at the past the way elitists do. As Whitehead observes:

In the official debate (on family issues), the remembered past is almost always considered a suspect, even unhealthy, guide for the present or future.... But for the parents I met, the remembered past is not a dusty artifact of the good old days; it is an important and vital social resource. Parents take instruction from their own family's past, rummaging through it for usable truths and adopting—or modifying or occasionally rejecting—its values.... In the official language, the family isn't getting weaker, it's just "changing." Most parents I met believe otherwise.

Americans believe "parents having less time to spend with their families" is the most important reason for the family's decline in our society, according to a recent survey. And most parents would like to see the work-family pendulum swing back in the direction of home.

To be sure, most children would not object to spending more unhurried time with their parents. Indeed, when 1,500 schoolchildren were asked, "What do you think makes a happy family?" social scientists Nick Stinnett and John DeFrain report that children "did not list money, cars, fine homes, or televisions." Instead the answer most frequently offered was "doing things together."

THE AMERICAN FAMILY, 1992

Everyone knows how vastly it has been transformed, but we are just learning how profoundly disturbing the implications are for kids—and for American society.

Myron Magnet

I KNOW BY THE WORRY in their eyes that my children are not kidding when they ask, every couple of months or so, "Are you and Mommy getting a divorce?" And this in a close-knit family committed to solidarity. Yet so pervasive is family collapse and turmoil that virtually no American child, seeing the distress of friends whose parents are splitting apart, can escape the thought that the family structure anchoring his childhood may not prove secure.

In this as in many other ways, the revolution in families that we see all around us— the result of an epidemic of divorce, remarriage, redivorce, illegitimacy, and new strains within intact families—has precipitated a revolution in the inner lives of our children. And a torrent of recent research makes plain that this revolution within the minds and hearts of the next generation has deeply troubling implications for the American social order. It affects companies through their workers, and some employers are wisely responding.

We're so accustomed to talking about the divorce revolution and the explosion of single parent families that we've become numbed to how vast these changes really are. The most basic unit of our social organization has undergone transformations so sweeping that changes of similar magnitude in economic or industry data over the same period—or in the average temperature of the earth over 20 centuries—would make us gape in amazement.

Consider the numbers afresh for a moment. During the Fifties—culturally and socially as far away as Shangri-La—the divorce rate fell 11% to an infinitesimal 9.2 per thousand married women each year. But then in the Sixties, as the first rockets

REPORTER ASSOCIATES *Kate Ballen, Catherine Guthrie*

headed for outer space, the divorce rate soared straight up with them. At its height in 1979 it stood at 22.7, 147% higher than 1960's rate. At the last measurement in 1988 it had subsided to 20.7 per thousand—hopeful, but still more than double the 1950 number.

Over half of all first marriages now end in divorce. And proving Dr. Johnson's adage that remarriage is the triumph of hope over experience, a similar proportion of subsequent marriages dissolve in redivorce.

The problem is that the majority of people who get divorced—57%—have children under 18. Over a million kids a year have to weather the breakup of their parents' marriage. An epidemic rise of out-of-wedlock births—from under 4% of children born in 1950 to a startling 27% in 1989—has further swollen the number of children in single-parent families. Two of every three black children are born out of wedlock today, and one of every five white children.

As a result of their parents' inability to preserve their marriages or to marry at all, almost a quarter of American children live in single-parent, usually female-headed, households. More than half can expect to live in such households, typically for an extended period, before they turn 18. Says David Blankenhorn, president of the Institute for American Values, a New York family-issues research outfit: "The experience of fatherlessness is approaching a rough parity with the experience of having a father as an expectation of childhood."

Contrary to the longstanding received opinion that children recover quickly from divorce and flourish in families of almost any shape, these changes have harrowed and damaged kids. Though of course many single-parent families work very well, lovingly nurturing children fully capable of

happiness and success—and though everyone knows intact families that exemplify Franz Kafka's dictum that the middle-class family is the closest thing to hell on earth— in general, children from single-parent families have more trouble growing up and bear more scars than children from two-parent families. Says Princeton sociologist Sara McLanahan, who studies children of divorce as they enter adulthood: "Almost anything you can imagine not wanting to happen to your children is a consequence of divorce." That goes for out-of-wedlock birth too, as recent research amply, and depressingly, bears out.

Experts back in the Sixties confidently predicted that child poverty would fall markedly between 1960 and 1988, assuming trends continued. Instead, the child poverty rate rose from around 15%, to 20.3%, with almost all the increase coming in the 1980s. Analyzing every variable, Penn State researchers recently concluded that the explosion of single-parent families is crucial to so dramatic and unexpected a rise. Had family breakdown not deprived many families of a male breadwinner, the child poverty rate would have declined to 13.8% in 1988. Changes in the composition of families, researchers calculate, account for one-third of the increase in child poverty among whites during the Eighties and two-thirds of it among blacks, who constitute 44% of America's poor children.

Kids in single-parent families have less than one-third the median per capita income of kids from two-parent families, and half of them fall below the poverty line in any given year, compared with 10% of their counterparts in intact families. Around 75% of single-parent children will sink into a spell of poverty before they reach 18, vs. 20% of kids from two-parent families. After

From *Fortune,* August 10, 1992, pp. 42-47. © 1992 by The Time Inc. Magazine Company. All rights reserved. Reprinted by permission.

divorce, a Census Bureau study discovered, kids are twice as likely to be in poverty as before. As for out-of-wedlock children, a large proportion are underclass kids, their poverty and illegitimacy part of a tangle of social pathology that mars their life chances.

Growing up in a single-parent family puts its mark not just on a child's external economic circumstances but on his or her innermost psyche as well. A vast National Center for Health Statistics study found that children from single-parent homes were 100% to 200% more likely than children from two-parent families to have emotional and behavioral problems and about 50% more likely to have learning disabilities. In the nation's hospitals, over 80% of adolescents admitted for psychiatric reasons come from single-parent families.

A RECENT long-term study found that elementary school children from divorced families, especially boys, on average scored lower on reading and math tests, were absent more often, were more anxious, hostile, and withdrawn, and were less popular with their peers than their classmates from intact families. Single-parent children are twice as likely to drop out of high school as two-parent children. In later life, adults who grew up in divorced homes are more likely than others to tell investigators that they are unhappy, in poor health, and dissatisfied with their lives. Men from divorced families are 35% more likely—and women fully 60% more likely—than their intact family counterparts to get divorced or separated. Ominously, the most reliable predictor of crime is neither poverty nor race but growing up fatherless.

No scale can measure the deepest wounds of divorce for children, and impressive recent research suggests they are wounds that never heal. Psychologist Judith Wallerstein, who for 15 years has intimately followed 130 children of divorce, was shocked by the extent of the harm she found, not just right after the divorce but years later, Wallerstein, co-author of *Second Chances: Men, Women, & Children a Decade after Divorce,* had at first assumed that an unhappy marriage must be unhappy for children too: While they would feel pain at the divorce, they would also feel relief and would be just fine as time passed and their parents grew happier. Not at all.

She was taken aback by the intensity of the pain and fear that engulfed these kids when their parents split up. "The first reaction is one of pure terror," Wallerstein says. Though most were middle-class children of executives and professionals, they worried who was going to feed and care for them. Preschool children feared that now that one parent had abandoned the other, both would abandon the child, leaving him unprotected in a scary world.

After the divorce, many of the boys started having learning and behavior trouble in school, even though most were bright; in adolescence and young adulthood a significant number began to drift. The girls in Wallerstein's study did much better, as they do in other surveys—even better than girls from intact families, according to one study, leading some researchers to believe that divorce leaves girls unscathed. But the girls' success, Wallerstein found, tended to be fragile. Says she: "These girls were on super behavior, consciously trying to be good little girls—at a high inner cost." Many of them couldn't keep it up. "In adolescence and in young adulthood," Wallerstein says, "girls from divorced families have a very difficult time, and there's a steep decline."

By young adulthood, years after the divorce, boys and girls were having equal difficulty forming intimate, loving relationships. Fearful of being alone, fearful that men would abandon and betray them rather than form the lasting relationship they desperately wanted, many of the girls, as if militantly trying to disprove their fears, flung themselves into affair after affair. They married early, often unsuitably, divorcing at a very high rate. Why? Says Wallerstein: "To exercise a good choice takes a sense of who you are and the inner sturdiness to stand there on the threshold of adulthood and say, 'Now let me take a little bit of time.' A lot of these girls are too anxious for that."

The boys, by contrast, typically held themselves back from relations with girls as they grew up. Says Wallerstein: "They were really very lonely and scared to take a chance. As one of them said, 'I'm afraid that when she gets to know me, she won't love me.'"

Surprisingly, children with stepparents don't do any better than children in single-parent families, even though remarriage greatly improves the children's economic situation. According to the National Center for Health Statistics, they are at least as likely as children from single-parent families to have learning disabilities and emotional and behavioral problems. Remarkably often, girls in such families wind up locked in conflict with their mothers. As these consequences make plain, solidifying a new marriage while keeping the children from feeling excluded or discarded isn't easy. Plainly, too, as sociologist McLanahan says, for children "remarriage is not the solution."

But—it's reasonable to ask—aren't the bad consequences of divorce really caused not by the divorce itself but by the family disharmony that precipitated the split? Here too investigators have come up with clear answers, differing in degree but not in overall conclusion. A British study concludes that around half the learning difficulties that boys from divorced families have—but almost none for girls—are explained by preexisting family problems. But that is the biggest effect any researcher has found. The most recent study finds that preexisting problems account for none of the difficulties that beset children of divorce.

What caused the enormous changes in the American family? Some attribute them to economic forces. Real wages stagnated and in some cases even declined in the Eighties, making two-earner families and longer work hours an economic necessity and thus burdening marriage and parenthood with unprecedented strains that a government lacking a family policy does nothing to alleviate, according to this view. Says Congresswoman Patricia Schroeder (D-Colorado): "People get into a marriage, they have children—all of a sudden everything becomes such a tough, stressful thing that they say, 'Wait a minute, this is not what I bought into,' and one or the other runs."

But since family breakup began in the Sixties, while wages were rising strongly, and since the Eighties' 15% or so decline in the real wages of low-skill young workers, while extremely significant, is not cataclysmic, economic change would seem to explain, if anything, only a modest fraction of earth-shattering family change.

Nor is there some vast evolutionary force that over the course of history regularly shapes and reshapes family life. Quite the contrary. Says historian Christopher Lasch: "The structure of the family has been very stable over a long period of time, and it's only over the last generation that we've had this enormous change."

INSTEAD, if ever proof were needed of the overwhelming power of ideas to shape society, the changes in the family provide it eloquently. American culture shifted radically in the 1960s, and three key cultural changes worked powerfully to restructure family life. First, the Sixties' quest for personal liberation and gratification, the decade's rebelliousness against authority and convention, took the glamour away from the family life personified by upright, uptight Mom and Dad, with their stultifying rules and routine. Says George Washington University sociologist Amitai Etzioni: "The Sixties attacked all authority and institutions, including families and fathers." The spirit of the age also devalued commitments to others made for better, for worse, for richer, for poorer—diametrically opposed to the new, radically individualist ethic of, "If it feels good, do it," as a Sixties slogan put it.

Second, once the sexual revolution licensed promiscuity, the domestication of sex within marriage could seem less of a fulfillment and more of a restriction. The whole culture's glorification of the joy of sex without reference to marriage allowed married people to feel an unprecedented self-justification in the pursuit of sexual adventure, even if it broke up their marriages.

Third, the most vocal contingent of the women's movement devalued what feminist Betty Friedan called the "comfortable concentration camp" of traditional family life. This attitude encouraged some women to see family life's inevitable constraints as an oppression from which they needed liberation. Moreover, it encouraged women to value themselves for their career achievements but not for motherhood.

These new beliefs about what happiness was, coupled with the belief that children's happiness was a function of their parents' happiness or unhappiness, set the stage for three decades of family disintegration. Says Vanderbilt University political scientist Jean Elshtain: "Kids have been the unwitting volunteers for all sorts of experiments in uncharted territory. If the standard is how well the kids are doing, the changes are not for the better."

Unexpectedly, these attitudes had disproportionate consequences for those at the bottom of society, undermining their family life in a particularly destructive way. For these attitudes not only helped shape America's pernicious welfare system but also helped encourage many of the poor to embrace that system. After all, only a culture both sexually permissive and cavalier about the traditional family could create a welfare system that makes no distinction between legitimate and out-of-wedlock children, and that virtually on demand gives an income with more buying power than a minimum wage job to unwed teenage girls who have a baby before even finishing high school. And only in a culture that both vibrates with the celebration of sexual thrills and also has removed the stigma from having out-of-wedlock children will significant numbers of women permit themselves to get enmeshed in that system.

Enabled by these conditions, welfare has become a malign mechanism for perpetuating the dysfunctional families that make up America's underclass. Such families have all the economic and psychological disadvantages that go with fatherlessness. In addition, they are typically headed by unschooled mothers unprepared to support children economically or guide their moral and cognitive development with the almost heroic competence needed to make single-parent families work well. Consequently, such families often end up hopelessly imprisoned in poverty and failure.

The cultural changes of the last generation transformed intact families too, notably by sending battalions of moms into the work force. This is a giant gain for America's economy, but it can be a loss for America's children if mothers are not at home to bond with their babies in the crucial early months, or if no one is around to look after schoolchildren when they come home in the afternoon. As a recent

The prime determinant of drinking or drug use is how many hours the child is left alone during the week.

study of junior high school kids has shown, the prime determinant of drinking or drug use is how long the child is left alone during the week, and whether a child does his homework correlates strongly with whether an adult is home to supervise.

This predicament hits FORTUNE readers directly, since many of us have, or are, or are married to employees facing it. Says Cornell University family expert Urie Bronfenbrenner: "After those at the bottom of society, the second most threatened group are those at the top, those who are supposed to be the leaders of the world—the college graduates who are having children at the start of their careers."

Men with executive or professional careers notoriously don't have enough time for family. And women in high-powered professions similarly put in more than 40-hour workweeks, travel, take office work and worries home with them, and don't dare slacken the pace or take time out for their children for fear of getting left by the wayside in the race for advancement. And so children are left with "quality time," which means little time, from parents, and with what Amitai Etzioni calls "quality phone calls: 'Honey, I won't be home. I love you.' " Though not neglect in intent, this can turn out to be neglect in effect.

The worry is, what does this do to the children? It of course means that children can feel unvalued and insecure. Says Harvard law professor Mary Ann Glendon: "It's easy to dress up as duty things that you don't really have to do. 'Why didn't you come to my school play? Oh, you had a client? Do we really need that much money?' "

It means that the parents are not around to participate in the thousands of daily interactions that make up a child's intellectual, moral, and emotional education, and so, unless the child is a latchkey kid, babysitters are left to do it, as well or ill as they are able and willing. Socializing children, restraining their impulses, awakening their faculties, encouraging their talents, forming their values—all take time.

And parents who don't give it run the risk that their kids won't achieve all they can achieve, even that they'll go wrong. What's more, says Mary Ann Glendon, "middle- and upper-income people who don't spend a lot of time with their kids are not teaching how members of a community live together and respect each other's rights. When parents put personal goals ahead of family goals, how will kids learn the opposite?"

Families are the institution in which character is formed, and what kinds of characters are being forged, what kinds of citizens are being molded to carry on our society, when our principal socializing institution has had so much parental time withdrawn from it and so many Americans bear such scars from what has happened in their families? The answer is dismayingly clear for dysfunctional underclass families, whose children so often turn out flagrantly antisocial, with such high rates of delinquency and criminality.

But several studies have also found disquieting character distortions in children from well-educated, middle-class divorced families. Many are withdrawn and lonely; many others, while gregarious and popular, choose their friends for the status they confer, manipulate them, and can't keep them for long. It is worrisome, too, to wonder about the ultimate consequences of fatherhood's decline. Says Glendon: "Will a man who hasn't had a father know how to be a father?" And it is disturbing that the family life of so many otherwise privileged children is so thin and unnourishing a medium for the cultivation of sturdy souls.

There are two classes of solution to America's family problem. One class contains specific solutions to each aspect of the problem; the other addresses our family situation in its entirety. First, the specifics:

■ **Reform the nation's child-support laws.** These should be federalized, the levels of support greatly increased, and contempt-of-court procedures should be streamlined to strengthen enforcement. Says Glendon: "Suppose they were to tell you in school, 'This is how much you'll make at your job, and this is what you'll make if you have two children and get a divorce.' " Let everyone know before conceiving a child that he or she can't escape at least the economic responsibility for that child.

That will enforce the notion that parenthood is not something to be entered into lightly. It goes for unmarried parents too. Michigan has found it's not hard to establish the paternity of out-of-wedlock children and to make the fathers pay support.

■ **Reform the welfare system** to strengthen families and not encourage the proliferation of dysfunctional ones. It's said that America has no family policy, and that's why 40% of America's poor are children.

The reality is that the nation has a vast, powerful family policy: welfare. That policy helps explain why millions of those poor children are underclass children whose mothers have been enabled to have them because welfare will provide an income to support both mother and child—in poverty, if you don't count such noncash benefits as food stamps and Medicaid. If underclass children turned out to be mainly productive citizens—if they didn't have such epidemic rates of crime, school dropout, drug use, unwed teenage pregnancy, and poverty—welfare might be considered a boon. But it isn't.

In the current ferment of reformist spirit, policymakers should try to make welfare what it was established in the Depression to be: a safety net for children who have lost their fathers through death or, more rarely, divorce, not a subsidy to unmarried mothers. At the least, policymakers should remember that children, not mothers, should be the primary focus of a welfare program. A first step might be to stop setting up unwed teenaged mothers in their own apartments but instead to require them to live in group residences, where they can be taught the skills of mothering and children can be enrolled in Head Start–type programs.

■ **Government should adopt family-strengthening policies.** The inflation-eroded value of the dependent *exemption* on income tax returns should be restored (to around $6,000 per child), or the same effect should be achieved in other ways, such as the $1,000-per-child refundable tax *credit* in the Downey/Hyde bill described in the previous article. Says Harvard's Glendon: "It's legitimate for the law to accord special preference to child-rearing households, for all of us have a stake in the socialization of each new generation."

■ **Industry should adopt enlightened child care policies.** Businesses have a big stake in retaining the talented young women they have hired and in keeping their productivity high: Helping them be good mothers as well as good employees is a key ingredient in doing that. IBM believes its enlightened child care policies—including unpaid leave of up to three years—save money by cutting employee turnover. The company also lets employees work part-time while caring for young children. Aetna allows employees caring for young children to work part of the week at home or arrange their working hours at the office with great flexibility.

If families can afford it, it's much better for mothers to take at least a year off to tend very young children than to put them in all-day institutional day care. Says Yale psychologist Edward Zigler: "The most important family value is: When a woman has a baby, let her stay home to bond properly with the child. That determines his future." Unfortunately not everyone has this option, and for them, as well as for parents of older children, Patagonia, a clothing company in Ventura, California, has devised as good a day care system as there is. Its day care center is at headquarters, so parents are right next door and can drop in during the day. Patagonia trains child care workers and subsidizes their wages, keeping the quality of staff high and turnover low. The company sends buses to pick up older children from school and bring them to the center for afternoon activities, and it runs a day camp for such kids in summer.

But beyond these particular solutions is the more general cultural problem: how to make children and families, if not as glamorous as in the Ozzie and Harriet era, at least not as devalued as they have been in the Donald and Ivana decade. Fortunately, the wilder excesses of all the liberations of the past 30 years have begun to pall for most Americans. Says Institute for American Values researcher Barbara Whitehead: "The experimentalist generation is beginning to understand the costs of that period of experimentation."

NOW WE NEED to reflect on what we've learned: that children are important, that they don't grow up well unless we bring them up, that they need two parents, that our needs can't shoulder theirs aside, that commitments and responsibilities to others have to take precedence over personal gratification, that nothing is more gratifying than to see children flourish. What is our life for, if not for that?

ENDANGERED FAMILY

*For many African-Americans, marriage and childbearing do not go together.
After decades of denial and blame, a new candor is emerging as
blacks struggle to save their families.*

Late on a sultry summer morning, Dianne Caballero settles onto her porch in the New York suburb of Roosevelt, bemused by the scene playing out across the street. Behind electric clippers, a muscular black man is trimming hedges with the intensity of a barber sculpting a fade; nearby, his wife empties groceries from the car. In most quarters, they might elicit barely a nod. But in this largely black, working-class community, the couple is one of the few intact families on the block. All too common are the five young women who suddenly turn into view, every one of them pushing a baby stroller, not one of them married. Resigned, Caballero says with a sigh, "Where are the men?"

A black child has only one chance in five of growing up with two parents

---

It's a lament she knows too well. Like her mother before her and her daughter after, Caballero, who is black, had a child out of wedlock at 16. Twenty-three years later, even she is astounded at the gulf between motherhood and marriage. When her mother got pregnant in the '50s, she says, she was considered unique. When Caballero had a baby in 1970, no one ostracized her, though it still wasn't something "nice" girls did. But by the time her daughter had a baby seven years ago, it was regarded as "normal." Now, Caballero says regretfully, it's commonplace. "And there doesn't

This article was reported by Farai Chideya, Michele Ingrassia, Vern E. Smith and Pat Wingert. It was written by Michele Ingrassia.

seem to be anything happening to reverse it."

That prospect troubles black leaders and parents alike, those like Caballero, who worries that her granddaughter is destined to be the fourth generation in her family to raise a child without a man. The odds are perilously high:

- For blacks, the institution of marriage has been devastated in the last generation: 2 out of 3 first births to black women under 35 are now out of wedlock. In 1960, the number was 2 out of 5. And it's not likely to improve any time soon. A black child born today has only a 1-in-5 chance of growing up with two parents until the age of 16, according to University of Wisconsin demographer Larry L. Bumpass. The impact, of course, is not only on black families but on all of society. Fatherless homes boost crime rates, lower educational attainment and add dramatically to the welfare rolls.

- Many black leaders rush to portray out-of-wedlock births as solely a problem of an entrenched underclass. It's not. It cuts across economic lines. Among the poor, a staggering 65 percent of never-married black women have children, double the number for whites. But even among the well-to-do, the differences are striking: 22 percent of never-married black women with incomes above $75,000 have children, almost 10 times as many as whites.

Nearly 30 years ago, Daniel Patrick Moynihan, then an assistant secretary of labor, caused a firestorm by declaring that fatherless homes were "the fundamental source of the weakness of the Negro Community." At the time, one quarter of black families were headed by women. Today the situation has only grown worse. A majority of black families with children—62 percent—are now headed by one parent. The result is what

Johns Hopkins University sociologist Andrew Cherlin calls "an almost complete separation of marriage and childbearing among African-Americans."

It was not always so. Before 1950, black and white marriage patterns looked remarkably similar. And while black marriage rates have precipitously dipped since then, the desire to marry remains potent: a NEWSWEEK Poll of single African-American adults showed that 88 percent said that they wanted to get married. But the dream of marriage has been hammered in the last 25 years. The economic dislocations that began in the '70s, when the nation shifted from an industrial to a service base, were particularly devastating to black men, who had migrated north in vast numbers to manufacturing jobs. The civil-rights movement may have ended legal segregation, but it hasn't erased discrimination in the work force and in everyday life. "When men lose their ability to earn bread, their sense of self declines dramatically. They lose rapport with their children," says University of Oklahoma historian Robert Griswold, author of "Fatherhood in America."

Some whites overlooked jobs and discrimination as factors in the breakdown of the black family. Back in the '60s, at the peak of the battle over civil rights, Moynihan infuriated blacks by describing a pattern of "pathology." Understandably, blacks were not willing to tolerate a public discussion that implied they were different—less deserving—than whites. The debate quickly turned bitter and polarized between black and white, liberal and conservative. Emboldened by a cultural sea change during the Reagan-Bush era, conservatives scolded, "It's all your fault." Dismissively, this camp insisted that what blacks need are mainstream American values—read: *white* values. Go to school, get a job, get married, they exhorted, and the family

From *Newsweek*, August 30, 1993, pp. 17-27. © 1993 by Newsweek, Inc. All rights reserved. Reprinted by permission.

Steep Rise in Out-of-Wedlock Births

Since the sexual revolution, the rate has shot up for both races. But the numbers are much higher for black women than white women.

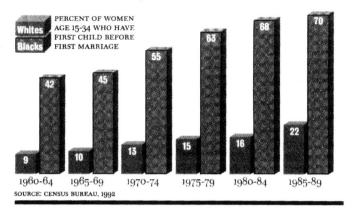

PERCENT OF WOMEN AGE 15-34 WHO HAVE FIRST CHILD BEFORE FIRST MARRIAGE

Whites / Blacks

1960-64	1965-69	1970-74	1975-79	1980-84	1985-89
9 / 42	10 / 45	13 / 55	15 / 63	16 / 68	22 / 70

SOURCE: CENSUS BUREAU, 1992

NEWSWEEK POLL

WHAT BLACK ADULTS THINK

How important are the following reasons young, unmarried black people today are having children?

(Percent saying very important)

53% They don't understand sex or birth control

48% They won't use birth control or have abortions for personal or religious reasons

38% They want something all their own

37% They want to prove they are adults

35% They are following the examples of older people they know

THE NEWSWEEK POLL, AUGUST 12-15, 1993

will be just fine. Not so, liberals fired back. As neoliberal University of Chicago sociologist William Julius Wilson argued in "The Declining Significance of Race," the breakdown of the African-American family resulted from rising unemployment, not falling values. Liberals have regarded the conservative posture as "blaming the victim," a phrase that, not coincidentally, white psychologist William Ryan coined in a 1965 assessment of Moynihan's study. To this camp, any family structure is good, as long as it's nurturing. "Marriage is important in the black community, just not the most important thing," says Andrew Billingsley, the University of Maryland sociologist who wrote the pioneering "Black Families in White America." "It is not an imperative for black people who can afford it."

Who's right? Both sides are too busy pointing fingers to find out. "We're never going to get to where we need to be if we first have to settle whose fault it is," says writer Nicholas Lemann, whose 1991 book, "The Promised Land," chronicles the great migration of blacks from the rural south to the industrialized North. But if there is any optimism, it is that now, after more than two decades on the defensive and with a Democratic president in the White House for the first time in 12 years, the African-American community is beginning to talk a little more openly about its problems. "Because of all the debate about morality, social programs, individual responsibility, it became very difficult to have an honest discussion," says Angela Glover Blackwell, who heads the Children's Defense Fund's Black Community Crusade for Children. "I'd like to think we've

entered an era where we're willing to accept that there is a dual responsibility" between government and ordinary citizens.

Without question, government must do more to help. But increasingly, African-Americans are unwilling to wait for White America to step in. "During integration," says Virginia Walden, who owns a day-care center in Washington, D.C., "we kept saying that the white people did us wrong, and that they owed us. Well, white people did us wrong, but I tell my children, "Don't nobody owe you anything. You've got to work for what you get'." In response, many African-American men and women have thrown themselves into a range of grassroots efforts from volunteer work in their communities to adopting children—stopgap efforts, perhaps, but to many, also cathartic and energizing. In many neighborhoods, the black church has led the awakening. Ministers began chastising themselves for sidestepping some basic moral issues. "We don't use 'family values' as an ax," says Wallace Smith, pastor of Shiloh Baptist Church in Washington. "But if someone is shacked up, we encourage them to get married." Smith is remarkably blunt about his own belief in the importance of a stable marriage. "Dan Quayle," he says, "was right."

At their kitchen tables and in their church basements every day, black families talk to each other, as they always have, about their fears. And part of what worries them is the growing tension between black men and black women, who are quick to blame each other for the massive retreat from marriage. "Black men say black women are 'Sapphires,'

trying to dominate," explains Harvard psychologist Alvin Poussaint, referring to the wife of Kingfish in "Amos 'n' Andy," who epitomized the bitchy, bossy black woman. But Boston anchorwoman Liz Walker believes that many black men mistake self-reliance for highhandedness. "I don't think black women have thrown black men out," says Walker, who sparked a controversy when she became pregnant out of wedlock six years ago, long before TV's Murphy Brown knew what a home pregnancy test was. "I think black women have been abandoned."

More commonly, though, black women feel the fallout of the economic and psychological battering the African-American male has taken in the last generation. Of course black women want love and commitment. But not with a man whose chief qualification for marriage is that he's, well, a man. The remarkable success of Terry McMillan's 1991 novel, "Waiting to Exhale," underscores that passion. The book's main characters are four strong-minded black women who can't seem to find men who measure up. They clearly struck a nerve. "When Terry McMillan wrote that book, the reason it was so popular was because it was us," says Walker, 42. Giddy one night from too much birthday champagne and pepperoni pizza, McMillan's quartet—Robin, Gloria, Bernadine and Savannah—get to the essential question: what's happened to all the men, they ask. Where are they hiding?

NEWSWEEK

POLL

WHAT BLACK
ADULTS THINK

Which one
can do
most to
improve the
situation
for black
families to-
day?

41%	**Black families themselves**
25%	**Churches**
14%	**Community organizations**
14%	**Government**

FOR THIS SPECIAL
NEWSWEEK POLL, PRINCE-
TON SURVEY RESEARCH AS-
SOCIATES INTERVIEWED A
NATIONAL SAMPLE OF 600
BLACK ADULTS BY TELE-
PHONE AUGUST 12-15. THE
MARGIN OF ERROR IS +/- 5
PERCENTAGE POINTS. "DON'T
KNOW" AND OTHER RE-
SPONSES NOT SHOWN. THE
NEWSWEEK POLL © 1993 BY
NEWSWEEK, INC.

They're ugly.
Stupid.
In prison.
Unemployed.
Crackheads.
Short.
Liars.
Unreliable.
Irresponsible.
Too possessive . . .
Childish.
Too goddam old and set in their ways.

The litany drives the women to tears. But does marriage really matter? Or is a family headed by a single mother just as good as the nuclear unit? The evidence come down solidly on the side of marriage. By every measure—economic, social, educational—the statistics conclude that two parents living together are better than one. Children of single mothers are significantly more likely to live in poverty than children living with both parents. In 1990, Census figures show, 65 percent of children of black single mothers were poor, compared with only 18 percent of children of black married couples. Educationally, children in one-parent homes are at greater risk across the board—for learning problems, for being left back, for dropping out. Psychiatrist James P. Comer, who teaches at Yale University's Child Study Center, says that the exploding population of African-American children from single-parent homes represents "the education crisis that is going to kill us. The crisis that we're concerned about—that American kids don't achieve as well as European kids and some Asian kids—won't kill us because [American students are] scoring high enough to compete. The one that will kill us is the large number of

bright kids who fall out of the mainstream because their families are not functioning."

Statistics tell only part of the story. Equally important are the intangibles of belonging to an intact family. "Growing up in a married family is where you learn the value of the commitments you make to each other, rather than seeing broken promises," says Roderick Harrison, chief of the Census Bureau's race division. "It deals with the very question of what kind of personal commitments people can take seriously."

Boys in particular need male role models. Without a father, who will help them define what it means to be a man? Fathers do things for their children that mothers often don't. Though there are obviously exceptions, fathers typically encourage independence and a sense of adventure, while mothers are more nurturing and protective. It is men who teach boys how to be fathers. "A woman can only nourish the black male child to a certain point," says Bob Crowder, an Atlanta lawyer and father of four, who helped organize an informal support group for African-American fathers. "And then it takes a man to raise a boy into a man. I mean a real man." Mothers often win the job by default, and struggle to meet the challenge. But sometimes, even a well-intentioned single mother can be smothering, especially if her son is the only man in her life. Down the road a few years, she hears erstwhile daughters-in-law lament how she "ruined" him for every other woman. Like the street-smart New Yorker she is, Bisi Ruckett, who is Dianne Caballero's daughter, says flat out that she can't "rule" her boyfriend. And just as quickly, she concedes she can't compete with his mom. "If he tells her he needs a zillion dollars, she'll get it," says Ruckett, 23.

Without a father for a role model, many boys learn about relationships from their peers on the street. In the inner city in particular, that often means gangs; and the message they're selling is that women are whores and handmaidens, not equals. Having a father does not, of course, guarantee that the lessons a young male learns will be wholesome. But research shows that, with no father, no minister, no boss to help define responsibility, there's nothing to prevent a boy from treating relationships perversely. University of Pennsylvania professor Elijah Anderson, who authored a 1990 study on street life, says that,

among the poor, boys view courting as a "game" in which the object is to perfect a rap that seduces girls. The goal: to add up one's sexual conquests, since that's the measure of "respect."

Often, for a girl, Anderson says, life revolves around the "dream," a variation of the TV soaps in which a man will whisk her away to a life of middle-class bliss—even though everywhere she looks there are only single mothers abandoned by their boyfriends. Not surprisingly, the two sexes often collide. The girl dreams because she must. "It has to do with one's conception of oneself: 'I will prevail'," Anderson says. But the boy tramples that dream because he must—his game is central to his vision of respect. "One of the reasons why, when a woman

---

Wallace Smith, pastor of Washington's Shiloh Church, puts it bluntly: 'Dan Quayle was right.'

---

agrees to have a baby, these men think it's such a victory is that you have to get her to go against all the stuff that says he won't stick around."

For teenage mothers not mature enough to cope, single parenthood is not the route to the dream, but entrapment. They have too many frustrations: the job, the lack of a job, the absence of a man, the feeling of being dependent on others for help, the urge to go out and dance instead of pacing with a crying child. Taken to its extreme, says Poussaint, the results can be abuse or neglect. "They'll see a child as a piece of property or compete with the child—calling them dumb or stupid, damaging their growth and education to maintain superiority," he says. The middle class is not exempt from such pain. Even with all the cushions money could buy—doctors and backup doctors, nannies and backup nannies—Liz Walker says that trying to raise her son, Nicholas, alone was draining. "Certainly, the best situation is to have as many people in charge of a family as possible," says Walker, who is now married to Harry Graham, a 41-year-old corporate-tax lawyer; together, they're raising her son and his two children from a previous marriage. "I can see that now," she adds. "Physically, you *need* it."

Not Just an Underclass Problem

In every economic group, black women are two to six times more likely to have a child before marriage than white women.

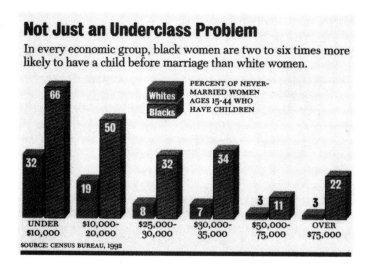

PERCENT OF NEVER-MARRIED WOMEN AGES 15-44 WHO HAVE CHILDREN

Whites / Blacks

UNDER $10,000	$10,000-20,000	$25,000-30,000	$30,000-35,000	$50,000-75,000	OVER $75,000
32 / 66	19 / 50	8 / 32	7 / 34	3 / 11	3 / 22

SOURCE: CENSUS BUREAU, 1992

More and more, black men aren't there to build marriages or to stick around through the hard years of parenting. The question we're too afraid to confront is why. The biggest culprit is an economy that has locked them out of the mainstream through a pattern of bias and a history of glass ceilings. "The economic state of the African-American community is worse in 1993 than it was in 1963," says NAACP head Benjamin Chavis Jr. He could be speaking, just as easily, about the black family, since the two fell in tandem.

A man can't commit to a family without economic security, but for many African-American men, there is none. The seeds of modern economic instability date back to the 1940s, when the first of 6½ million blacks began migrating from the rural South to the urban North as farm mechanization replaced the need for their backs and hands. At first, black men built a solid economic niche by getting factory jobs. But just as the great migration ended in the '70s, the once limitless industrial base began to cave in. And as steel mills and factories swept offshore, the "last hired, first fired" seniority rules disproportionately pushed black men out. During that time, says Billingsley, unemployment for blacks became twice as high as it was for whites, "and it has rarely dropped below that [ratio] since." Unarguably, economic restructuring hit whites as well as blacks, but the new service sector favored those with education—and there were many more educated white men than blacks in the '70s as vast numbers of baby boomers streamed out of the nation's colleges looking for jobs.

Ironically, just as the job market collapsed for black men, it opened for black women, who went to college while black men went to war. Armed with the college degrees that black males didn't have and pushed by the burgeoning women's movement, growing numbers of black women found spots in corporate America. As with white women in the '80s, that bought them greater independence. But the jobs of black women came at the expense of black men. Throughout the workplace, says Yale's Comer, "there was a trade-off. The one black woman was a two-fer: you got a black and a woman." Since then, the gap between white women's income and black women's has disappeared—black women's salaries are the same as whites'.

But the chasm between black and white men has barely moved. In 1969, black men earned 61 cents for every dollar white men earned; by 1989, the number had increased to only 69 cents. And that's for black men who were working; more and more, they found themselves without jobs. During the same time, the number of black men with less than a high-school education who found jobs dropped from two thirds to barely half. And it's likely to worsen: in the last 25 years, the proportion of black men in college has steadily eroded. "America has less use for black men today than it did during slavery," says Eugene Rivers, who helps run computer-training programs as pastor of Boston's Azusa Christian Community.

Though he is scarcely 11, Luqman Kolade dreams of becoming an electrical engineer. But he already wears the grievous pain of a man who feels left out. Luqman is a small, studious, Roman Catholic schooler from Washington,

D.C., who will enter the sixth grade this fall, a superb student who won the archdiocese science fair with a homemade electric meter. Unlike most boys in the Male Youth Project he attended at Shiloh Baptist Church, his parents are married. His mother works for the Department of Public Works; describing what his father does doesn't come easy. "My father used to be a [construction] engineer. He left his job because they weren't treating him right; they would give white men better jobs who did less work. Now he drives an ice-cream truck."

Black men were hurt, too, by the illegal economy. As the legitimate marketplace case them aside, the drug trade took off, enlisting anyone lured by the promise of fast money. Ironically, says Comer, "you had to make a supreme and extra effort to get into the legal system and no effort to get into the illegal system." For many on the fringes, there was no contest. "It overwhelmed the constructive forces in the black mainstream," he says. Disproportionately, too, black men are in prison or dead. While African-Americans represent only 12 percent of the population, they composed 44 percent of the inmates in state prisons and local jails in 1991; and, in 1990, homicide was the leading cause of death for young black men.

The economy explains only one part of what happened. The sexual revolution in the '70s was the second great shift that changed the black family. Although the social tide that erased taboos against unwed motherhood affected all women, whites and blacks took different paths. White women delayed both marriage and childbearing, confident that, down the road, there would be a pool of marriageable men. Not so for black women, who delayed marriage but not children because they were less certain there would be men for them. In what they called a "striking shift," Census officials reported earlier this year that less than 75 percent of black women are likely to ever marry, compared with 90 percent of whites.

More dramatic is the childbearing picture. Between 1960 and 1989, the proportion of young white women giving birth out of wedlock rose from 9 to 22 percent, markedly faster than it did for blacks. The slower rate of increase for blacks was small comfort. Their rate—42 percent—was already so high by 1960 that if it had kept pace with the white race, ti would have topped 100 percent by now. As things stand, it's 70 percent.

Rejecting Marriage

Before 1950, young black women were actually more likely to get married than white women.

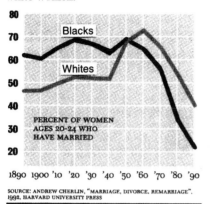

PERCENT OF WOMEN AGES 20-24 WHO HAVE MARRIED

SOURCE: ANDREW CHERLIN, "MARRIAGE, DIVORCE, REMARRIAGE". 1992, HARVARD UNIVERSITY PRESS

Traditionally, the extended family has served as a safety net. But the terrible irony of history is that it has also hurt the black family. While intended as a cushion, the network, in effect, enabled more single women to have children. And that helps explain why not only poor black women, but middle- and upper-class blacks as well, have had children out of wedlock at higher rates than white women. Historically, white women have had only themselves to rely on for child rearing, and so marriage became more of an imperative. For blacks, the network of extended kin is a tradition rooted in African customs that emphasize community over marriage. Although historians say that most black children grew up in two-parent households during slavery, as well as in the 19th and early 20th centuries, high rates of poverty, widowhood and urban migration reinforced the need for interdependence that continues today. The oft-repeated African proverb "It takes a whole village to raise a child" echoes back to that.

Now the extended family is breaking down. Yet the black family's expectations for it haven't diminished. Both sides feel the strains. With the soaring number of teenage mothers, grandparents today are getting younger and more likely to be working themselves. A 32-year-old grandmother isn't necessarily eager, or able, to raise a grandchild, especially when that child becomes a teenager and the problems multiply. And, after generations of no fathers, there are no grandfathers, either. What's more, the tradition of a real neighborhood is disappearing. "It used to be that everyone looked out for everyone else," said community activist Claudette Burroughs-White of Greensboro, N.C. "Now I think people are kind of estranged. They don't get involved. It's safer not to." Many families left in the inner city—the ones most in need of support—are increasingly isolated from relatives able to flee to the suburbs. "Not every poor black mother is in a strong kinship network," says Cherlin. "Many are living alone, hiding behind double-locked doors in housing projects."

What's the solution? Nearly 30 years after Lyndon Johnson launched the War on Poverty, experts on the black family return again and again to the same ideas—better education, more jobs, discouraging teen pregnancy, more mentoring programs. But now the question is, who should deliver—government or blacks themselves? Ever since the government started abandoning social programs in the '70s and early '80s, black families have been left on their own to find a way out. Those who would argue against funneling in more government dollars say we tried that, but "nothing works." Lemann, who believes that most of the positive social changes in Black America were sparked by government

intervention, dismisses the conceit that spending on social welfare failed. The War on Poverty, he says "threw out some untested ideas, some of which worked"— like Head Start, the Job Corps and Foster Grandparents—"and some of which didn't." Beyond the all-or-nothing extremes, there is room for solutions. Moynihan believes the nation has been in a collective "denial phase" about the black family for the last 25 years. But he says he's encouraged. "We're beginning to get a useful debate on this."

Will self-help do it? Though few African-American leaders expect what they call "White America" to come to the rescue, they're equally skeptical that the thousands of programs filling church rec rooms and town-hall meeting rooms can, on their own, turn things around. "People who are trying to salvage a lot of the children are burnt out, they think it's like spitting into the ocean," says Poussaint, who doesn't dispute the pessimism. "The problems are overwhelming. It's like treating lung cancer and knowing that people are still smoking."

There aren't many places left to look for answers. When black leaders peak with one voice, it is about the deep crisis of faith and purpose that came with integration: the very promise that African-Americans would be brought into the American mainstream has left many by the wayside. What's the penalty for doing nothing? "We could revert to a caste society," says Moynihan. Others are just as bleak. There are sparks of hope, says Comer, but he warns: "It's getting late, very late." The problems of the black family have been apparent for decades. And so has our collective understanding that we must take them on. What we need to find now is a voice to start the dialogue.

BRINGING UP FATHER

The message dads get is that they are not up to the job. And a record number don't stick around—even as fathers are needed more than ever.

NANCY R. GIBBS

"I don't have a dad," says Megan, 6, a tiny blond child with a pixie nose who gazes up at a visitor and talks of her hunger. "Well, I do have a dad, but I don't know his name. I only know his first name, Bill."

Just what is it that fathers do?

"Love you. They kiss you and hug you when you need them. I had my mom's boyfriend for a while, but they broke up." Now Megan lives with just her mother and older brother in Culver City, California.

What would you like to do with your dad?

"I'd want him to talk to me." She's hurting now. "I wish I had somebody to talk to. It's not fair. If two people made you, then you should still be with those two people." And she's sad. "I'm not so special," she says, looking down at the floor. "I don't have two people."

She imagines what it would be like for him to come home from work at night.

"It would be just like that commercial where the kids say, 'Daddy, are you all right?'" She smiles, dreaming. "The kids show the daddy that they care for him. They put a thermometer in his mouth. They think he's sick because he came home early. They are sitting on the couch watching TV, and it's like, wow, we can play with Dad!"

Megan thinks her father is in the Navy now. "One day when I get older, I'm gonna go back to Alabama and try to find him."

More children will go to sleep tonight in a fatherless home than ever in the nation's history. Talk to the experts in crime, drug abuse, depression, school failure, and they can point to some study somewhere blaming those problems on the disappearance of fathers from the American family. But talk to the fathers who do stay with their families, and the story grows more complicated. What they are hearing, from their bosses, from institutions, from the culture around them, even from their own wives, very often comes down to a devastating message: We don't really trust men to be parents, and we don't really need them to be. And so every day, everywhere, their children are growing up without them.

Corporate America, for a start, may praise family life but does virtually nothing to ease it. Managers still take male workers aside and warn them not to take a paternity leave if they want to be taken seriously. On TV and in movies and magazine ads, the image of fathers over the past generation evolved from the stern, sturdy father who knew best to a helpless Homer Simpson, or some ham-handed galoot confounded by the prospect of changing a diaper. Teachers call parent conferences but only talk to the mothers. When father arrives at the doctor's office with little Betsy, the pediatrician offers instructions to pass along to his wife, the caregiver presumptive. The Census Bureau can document the 70 million mothers age 15 or older in the U.S. but has scant idea how many fathers there are. "There's no interest in fathers at all," says sociologist Vaughn Call, who directs the National Survey of Families and Households at the University of Wisconsin. "It's a nonexistent category. It's the ignored half of the family."

Mothers themselves can be unwitting accomplices. Even women whose own progress in public life depends on sharing the workload in private life act as "gatekeepers" in the home, to use Harvard pediatrician T. Berry Brazelton's description. Dig deeply into household dynamics, and the tensions emerge. Women say they need and want their husbands to be more active parents but fear that they aren't always reliable. Men say they might like to be more involved, but their wives will not make room for them, and jealously guard their domestic power.

Most troubling of all to some social scientists is the message men get that being a good father means learning how to mother. Among child-rearing experts, the debate rages over whether men and women parent differently, whether there is some unique contribution that each makes to the emotional health of their children. "Society sends men two messages," says psychologist Jerrold Lee Shapiro, father of two and the author of *A Measure of the Man,* his third book on fatherhood. "The first is, We want you to be involved, but you'll be an inadequate mother. The second is, You're invited into the birthing room and into the nurturing process—but we don't want all of you. We only want your support. We're not really ready as a culture to accept men's fears, their anger or their sadness. This is the stuff that makes men crazy. We want men to be the protectors and providers, but we are scared they won't be if they become soft."

So now America finds its stereotypes crushed in the collision between private needs and public pressures. While some commend the nurturing nature of the idealized New Father, others cringe at the idea of genderless parenting and defend the importance of men being more than pale imitations of mothers. "If you become Mr. Mom," says Shapiro, "the family has a mother and an assistant mother. That isn't what good fathers are doing today." And fathers themselves wrestle with memories of their own fathers, vowing to do it differently, and struggling to figure out how.

THE DISAPPEARING DAD

Well into the 18th century, child-rearing manuals in America were generally addressed to fathers, not mothers. But as industrialization began to separate home and work, fathers could not be in both places at once. Family life of the 19th century was defined by what historians call the feminization of the domestic sphere and the marginalization of the father as a parent. By the 1830s, child-rearing manuals, increasingly addressed to mothers, deplored the father's absence from the home. In 1900 one worried observer could describe "the suburban husband and father" as "almost entirely a Sunday institution."

What alarms modern social scientists is that in the latter part of this century the father has been sidelined in a new, more disturbing way. Today he's often just plain absent. Rising divorce rates and out-of-wedlock births mean that more than 40% of all children born between 1970 and 1984 are likely to spend much of their childhood living in single-parent homes. In 1990, 25% were living with only their mothers, compared with 5% in 1960. Says David Blankenhorn, the founder of the Institute for American Values in New York City: "This trend of fatherlessness is the most socially consequential family trend of our generation."

Credit Dan Quayle for enduring the ridicule that opened the mainstream debate over whether fathers matter in families. In the year since his famous Murphy Brown speech, social scientists have produced mounting evidence that, at the very least, he had a point. Apart from the personal politics of parenting, there are larger social costs to reckon in a society that dismisses fathers as luxuries.

Studies of young criminals have found that more than 70% of all juveniles in state reform institutions come from fatherless homes. Children from broken families are nearly twice as likely as those in two-parent families to drop out of high school. After assessing the studies, economist Sylvia Hewlett suggested that "school failure may well have as much to do with disintegration of families as with the quality of schools."

Then there is the emotional price that children pay. In her 15 years tracking the lives of children of divorced families, Judith Wallerstein found that five years af-

ter the split, more than a third experienced moderate or severe depression. After 10 years a significant number of the young men and women appeared to be troubled, drifting and underachieving. At 15 years many of the thirtyish adults were struggling to create strong love relationships of their own. Daughters of divorce, she found, "often experience great difficulty establishing a realistic view of men in general, developing realistic expectations and exercising good judgment in their choice of partners."

For boys, the crucial issue is role modeling. There are psychologists who suggest that boys without fathers risk growing up with low self-esteem, becoming overly dependent on women and emotionally rigid. "Kids without fathers are forced to find their own ways of doing things," observes Melissa Manning, a social worker at the Boys and Girls Club of Venice, Cali-

It Takes Two

WOMEN'S VOICES ARE MORE SOOTHING. THEY CAN READ THE SIGNALS A CHILD SENDS BEFORE HE OR SHE CAN TALK. BUT AS TIME PASSES, THE STRENGTHS THAT FATHERS MAY BRING TO CHILD REARING BECOME MORE IMPORTANT.

fornia. "So they come up with their own ideas, from friends and from the gangs. Nobody is showing them what to do except to be drunk, deal drugs or go to jail." Then there are the subtler lessons that dads impart. Attorney Charles Firestone, for instance, recently decided it was time to teach his 11-year-old son how to play poker. "Maybe it will help if he knows when to hold 'em, when to fold 'em," he says.

THE ANTI-FATHER MESSAGE

Given the evidence that men are so vital to a healthy home, the anti-father messages that creep into the culture and its institutions are all the more troubling. Some scholars suggest that fatherhood is by its very biological nature more fragile than motherhood, and needs to be encouraged by the society around it. And yet for all the focus on the New Father (the kind who skips the corporate awards dinner to attend the school play), the messages men receive about how

they should act as parents are at best mixed and often explicitly hostile.

Employers that have been slow to accommodate the needs of mothers in their midst are often even more unforgiving of fathers. It is a powerful taboo that prevents men from acknowledging their commitment to their children at work. A 1989 survey of medium and large private employers found that only 1% of employees had access to paid paternity leave and just 18% could take unpaid leave. Even in companies like Eastman Kodak, only 7% of men, vs. 93% of women, have taken advantage of the six-year-old family-leave plan.

Those who do soon discover the cost. "My boss made me pay a price for it emotionally," says a prominent Washington executive who took leaves for both his children. "He was very generous with the time, but he never let me forget it. Every six seconds he reminded me what a great guy he was and that I owed him really, really big. You don't get a lot of points at the office for wanting to have a healthy family life." Men, like women, are increasingly troubled by the struggle to balance home and work; in 1989, asked if they experienced stress while doing so, 72% of men answered yes, compared with 12% a decade earlier, according to James Levine of the Fatherhood Project at the Families and Work Institute of New York City.

Many men will freely admit that they sometimes lie to employers about their commitments. "I announced that I was going to a meeting," shrugged a Washington journalist as he left the office in midafternoon one day recently. "I just neglected to mention that the 'meeting' was to watch my daughter play tennis." Now it is the fathers who are beginning to ask themselves whether their careers will stall and their incomes stagnate, whether the glass ceiling will press down on them once they make public their commitment as parents, whether today's productivity pressures will force them to work even harder with that much less time to be with their kids. In the higher reaches of management, there are not only few women, there are also few men in dual-income families who take an active part in raising their children. "Those who get to the top today," says Charles Rodgers, owner of a 10-year-old family-research organization in Brookline, Massachusetts, called Work/Family Directions, "are almost always men from what used to be the traditional family, men with wives who don't work outside the home."

Many men insist that they long to veer off onto a "daddy track." In a 1990 poll by the Los Angeles *Times*, 39% of the fathers said they would quit their jobs to have more time with their kids, while another survey found that 74% of men said they would rather have a daddy-track job than a fast-track job. But in real life, when they are not talking to pollsters, some fathers recognize the power of their atavistic impulses to earn bread and compete, both of which often leave them ambivalent about their obligations as fathers.

George Ingram, 48, lives on Capitol Hill with his sons Mason, 15, and Andrew, 10. He is the first to admit that single fatherhood has not helped his career as a political economist. "We're torn between working hard to become Secretary of State and nurturing our kids," he says. "You make the choice to nurture your kids, and people think it's great. But does it put a crimp on your career? Yes, very definitely. When I finish this process, I will have spent 15 years on a professional plateau." Ingram finds that his colleagues accept his dual commitments, his leaving every night before 6, or by 5 if he has a soccer practice to coach. In fact they are more accepting of his choices than those of his female colleagues. "I get more psychic support than women do," he says. "And I feel great about spending more time with my kids than my father did."

MATERNAL GATEKEEPERS

The more surprising obstacle men say, arises in their own homes. Every household may be different, every division of labor unique, but sociologists do find certain patterns emerging when they interview groups of men and women about how they view one another's parenting roles. Men talk about their wife's unrealistic expectations, her perfectionism, the insistence on dressing, feeding, soothing the children in a certain way. "Fathers, except in rare circumstances, have not yet become equal partners in parenthood," says Frank Furstenberg, professor of sociology at the University of Pennsylvania. "The restructuring of the father role requires support and encouragement from wives. Presumably, it is not abnormal for wives to be reluctant to give up maternal prerogatives."

Many men describe in frustration their wife's attitude that her way of doing things is the only way. "Dad is putting the baby to bed," says Levine. "He's holding his seven-month-old on his shoulders and walking around in circles. Mom comes in and says, 'She likes it better when you just lay her down on her stomach and rub her back.' Dad gets mad that Mom is undermining his way of doing things, which he thinks works perfectly well."

In most cases, it is still the mother who carries her child's life around in her head, keeping the mental daybook on who needs a lift to piano practice and who needs to get the poetry folder in on time. After examining much of the research on men's housework and child care, Sylvia Hewlett concluded that married men's average time in household tasks had increased only 6% in 20 years, even as women have flooded the workplace. Psychologists Rosalind Barnett and Grace Baruch found that fathers were often willing to perform the jobs they were assigned but were not responsible for remembering, planning or scheduling them.

Women often respond that until men prove themselves dependable as parents, they can't expect to be trusted. A haphazard approach to family responsibilities does nothing to relieve the burdens women carry. "Men haven't been socialized to think about family appointments and how the household runs for kids," notes Marie Wilson of the Ms. Foundation for Women, who constantly hears of the hunger women feel for their husbands to participate more fully at home. "They don't really get in there and pay attention. Mothers often aren't sure they can trust them—not just to do it as they do it, but to do it at a level that you can get away with without feeling guilty."

Some women admit that their own feelings are mixed when it comes to relinquishing power within the family. "I can probably be overbearing at times as far as wanting to have it my way," says the 35-year-old wife of a St. Louis, Missouri, physician. "But I would be willing to relax my standards if he would be more involved. It would be a good trade-off." Here again the attitude is changing with each generation. Women under 35, researchers find, seem more willing than older women, whose own fathers were probably less engaged, to trust men as parents. Also, as younger women become more successful professionally, they are less fearful of relinquishing power at home because their identity and satisfaction come from many sources.

THE NEW FATHER

The redefinition of fatherhood has been going on in virtually every arena of American life for well over 20 years. As women worked to broaden their choices at home and work, the implicit invitation was for men to do likewise. As Levine has observed, Dr. Spock had carefully revised his advice on fathers by 1974. The earlier version suggested that fathers change the occasional diaper and cautioned mothers about "trying to force the participation of fathers who get gooseflesh at the very idea of helping to take care of a baby." The new version of *Baby and Child Care*, by contrast, offered a prescription for the New Fatherhood: "The father—any father—should be sharing with the mother the day-to-day care of their child from birth onward ... This is the natural way for the father to start the relationship, just as it is for the mother."

By the '80s, bookstores were growing fat with titles aimed at men: *How to Father,* *Expectant Father, Pregnant Fathers, The Birth of a Father, Fathers Almanac* and *Father Power.* There were books about child-and-father relations, like *How to Father a Successful Daughter,* and then specific texts for part-time fathers, single fathers, stepfathers and homosexual fathers. Bill Cosby's *Fatherhood* was one of the best-selling books in publishing history, and *Good Morning, Merry Sunshine,* by Chicago *Tribune* columnist Bob Greene, a journal about his first year of fatherhood, was on the New York *Times* best-seller list for almost a year. Parents can now pick up *Parents' Sports,* a new magazine dedicated to reaching the dad market with stories on the joys of soccer practice.

Institutions were changing too. In his book *Fatherhood in America,* published this month, Robert L. Griswold has traced the history of a fast-changing role that today not only allows men in the birthing room (90% of fathers are in attendance at their child's birth) but also

Mixed Emotions

"WE'RE NOT READY TO ACCEPT MEN'S FEARS . . . OR THEIR SADNESS. WE WANT MEN TO BE THE PROTECTORS . . . BUT WE ARE SCARED THEY WON'T BE IF THEY BECOME SOFT."

offers them postpartum courses in which new fathers learn how to change, feed, hold and generally take care of their infant. Some fathers may even get in on the pregnancy part by wearing the "empathy belly," a bulge the size and weight of a third-trimester fetus. Suddenly available to men hoping to solidify the father-child bond are "Saturday with Daddy Outings," special songfests, field trips and potlucks with dads. Even men behind bars could get help: one program allows an inmate father to read children's stories onto cassette tapes that are then sent, along with the book and Polaroid picture of Dad, to his child.

"It's become cool to be a dad," says Wyatt Andrews, a correspondent for CBS News who has three children: Rachel, 8, Averil, 7, and Conrad, 5. "Even at dinner parties, disciplinary techniques are discussed. Fathers with teenagers give advice about strategies to fathers with younger kids. My father was career Navy. I don't think he ever spent two seconds thinking about strategies of child rearing. If he said anything, it was 'They listen to me.' "

BRING BACK DAD

These perceptual and behavioral shifts have achieved enough momentum to trigger a backlash of their own. Critics of the New Fatherhood are concerned that something precious is being lost in the revolution in parenting—some uniquely male contribution that is essential for raising healthy kids. In a clinical argument that sends off political steam, these researchers argue that fathers should be more than substitute mothers, that men parent differently than women and in ways that matter enormously. They say a mother's love is unconditional, a father's love is more qualified, more tied to performance; mothers are worried about the infant's survival, fathers about future success. "In other words, a father produces not just children but socially viable children," says Blankenhorn. "Fathers, more than mothers, are haunted by the fear that their children will turn out to be bums, largely because a father understands that his child's character is, in some sense, a measure of his character as well."

When it comes to discipline, according to this school of thought, it is the combination of mother and father that yields justice tempered by mercy. "Mothers discipline children on a moment-by-moment basis," says Shapiro. "They have this emotional umbilical cord that lets them read the child. Fathers discipline by rules. Kids learn from their moms how to be aware of their emotional side. From dad, they learn how to live in society."

As parents, some psychologists argue, men and women are suited for different roles at different times. The image of the New Fatherhood is Jack Nicholson surrounded by babies on the cover of *Vanity Fair,* the businessman changing a diaper on the newly installed changing tables in an airport men's room. But to focus only on infant care misses the larger point. "Parenting of young infants is not a natural activity for males," says David Popenoe, an associate dean of social studies at Rutgers University who specializes in the family. He and others argue that women's voices are more soothing; they are better able to read the signals a child sends before he or she can talk. But as time passes, the strengths that fathers may bring to child rearing become more important.

"At a time when fatherhood is collapsing in our society," warns Blankenhorn, "when more children than ever in history are being voluntarily abandoned by their fathers, the only thing we can think of talking about is infant care? It's an anemic, adult-centered way of looking at the problem." Why not let mothers do more of the heavy lifting in the early years and let fathers do more of the heavy lifting after infancy when their special skills have more relevance? As children get older, notes William Maddox, director of research and policy at the Washington-based Family Research Council, fathers become crucial in their physical and psychological development. "Go to a park and watch father and mother next to a child on a jungle gym," he said. "The father encourages the kid to challenge himself by climbing to the top; the mother tells him to be careful. What's most important is to have the balance of encouragement along with a warning."

This notion that men and women are genetically, or even culturally, predisposed to different parenting roles strikes other researchers as misguided. They are quick to reject the idea that there is some link between X or Y chromosomes and, say, conditional or unconditional love. "To take something that is only a statistical tendency," says historian E. Anthony Rotundo, "and turn it into a cultural imperative—fathers must do it this way and mothers must do it that way—only creates problems for the vast number of people who don't fit those tendencies, without benefiting the children at all." While researchers have found that children whose fathers are involved in their early rearing tend to have higher IQs, perform better in school and even have a better sense of humor, psychologists are quick to say this is not necessarily a gender issue. "It has to do with the fact that there are two people passionately in love with a child," says Harvard's Brazelton.

The very fact that psychologists are arguing about the nature of fatherhood, that filmmakers are making movies based entirely on fatherlove, that bookstores see a growth market in father guides speaks not only to children's well-being but to men's as well. As much as families need fathers, men need their children in ways they are finally allowed to acknowledge, to learn from them all the secrets that children, with their untidy minds and unflagging hearts, have mastered and that grownups, having grown up, long to retrieve.

—*Reported by Ann Blackman/Washington, Priscilla Painton/New York and James Willwerth/Los Angeles*

EVERYDAY LIFE IN TWO HIGH-RISK NEIGHBORHOODS

Growing Up

PHILIPPE BOURGOIS

Philippe Bourgois is an assistant professor of anthropology at San Francisco State University and a visiting scholar at the Russell Sage Foundation in New York. He is writing a book entitled, In Search of Respect: Selling Crack in Spanish Harlem, *published by Little, Brown & Co.*

I live with my family in a tenement in East Harlem opposite a large complex of public housing projects where I have been engaged since 1985 in ethnographic research. I am using the classical anthropological methodology of participant-observation fieldwork, focusing on a network of youths and adults who participate intensively in the underground economy—primarily street-level, retail crack distribution. This means I have spent hundreds of nights on the streets and in crack houses observing and tape recording dealers and addicts. I visit their families, attend their parties and intimate reunions—from Thanksgiving dinners to New Year's Eve celebrations—in order to collect life history interviews and to befriend their children, spouses, lovers, siblings, mothers, grandmothers, and—when possible—fathers and stepfathers. This allows me to situate the street dealing scene in its larger family and community context.

East Harlem, also referred to as *"El Barrio,"* or Spanish Harlem, is a 200-square-block neighborhood in New York City's upper East Side. Although the population is between 40 and 45 percent African-American, it is considered by both its residents and outsiders to be New York's quintessential Puerto Rican community. Most of the individuals I interact with are second- or third-generation New York-born Puerto Ricans.

According to 1980 census data, 29 percent of the population in East Harlem was at 75 percent of the poverty level, 48 percent at 125 percent, and 68 percent at 200 percent. In other words, if one were to adjust for New York City's exorbitant cost of living, well over half of the population would fall into the ranks of the "working poor." One in three families in East Harlem is dependent on public assistance, and approximately half of all households are headed by women. The schools in the neighborhood have one of the highest drop-out rates in the country.

The neighborhood is visibly poor. Abandoned buildings, vacant lots, and streets strewn with rubbish are the rule here rather than the exception. My block is not atypical: I can get heroin, crack, powder cocaine, hypodermic needles, methadone, Valium, PCP, and mescaline within a two-block radius of my apartment.

Despite this active street scene and the visible social and economic crisis it reflects, the majority of the adult population of East Harlem abhors drugs. Most heads of households work nine-to-five-plus-overtime at entry-level jobs and shun illegal activity. Nonetheless, this majority, mainstream, working-class and working-poor sector is in retreat. Many residents,

From *The American Enterprise*, Vol. 2, No. 3, May/June 1991, pp. 28-37. © 1991 by The American Enterprise Institute for Public Policy Research. Distributed by The New York Times Special Features.

especially the elderly, live in terror, venturing outside only during daylight hours.

The street-level drug dealers I study are resented and shunned by the majority of the community. Unfortunately, however, they control the streets. Worse yet, they are offering on a daily basis an all-too-persuasive, violent, and self-destructive alternative to the youths growing up in the neighborhood.

Most of the hard-core inner-city "unemployables" have, in fact, worked at legitimate pursuits at some time or other in their lives. All of the crack dealers and addicts whom I have interviewed have worked at one or more legal jobs in their early youth. In fact, most entered the labor market at an earlier age than the typical teenager. Before their twelfth birthday, many were bagging groceries at the supermarket for tips, stocking beers (off the books) in local *bodegas*," or shining shoes. In fact, many dropped out of school in order to make money to obtain the childhood "necessities"—candy, sneakers, basketballs, baseball cards—that most preteens throughout the rest of America are able to buy with their allowances. What happens to these "eager-beaver" 12-year-olds that transforms them into the adult felons who terrorize their neighbors?

Income-Generating Opportunities: School Versus Drugs

The drug economy, especially retail crack sales, is currently out-competing the legal, entry-level economy for the "hearts and minds" of inner-city youth. Tragically, crack/cocaine is the only growing, dynamic, equal-opportunity-employer industry in East Harlem today. According to police records, millions of dollars worth of drug sales are going on within a stone's throw of the youths living in my building. Why should we be surprised when they drop out of school to "get some of mine's"? And why should we wonder why they refuse low-prestige jobs in the service sector in favor of building up crack/cocaine enterprises where their identities, rooted in street culture, become an asset rather than a liability?

The youths on my block are not disorganized or apathetic. On the contrary, they are overly organized and energetic. Their mobilization, however, is destroying them and their community. The most determined, lucky, and ruthless of the children on my block are running thousand-dollar-a-day drug sales networks and are not yet 18. They keep regular hours and supervise half a dozen employees who work on consignment or on an hourly wage.

The most successful drive their Mercedes, Jaguars, and Porsches up to the fire hydrant

WHAT OPPORTUNITIES FOR THE YOUNG?

on the block to be washed and waxed by local crack addicts while they stand triumphantly ten yards away and watch the neighborhood kids ogle their "ride" (car). To be this successful, they have to cultivate an aggressive and violent presentation of self or else they will lose credibility and be forced out of business, perhaps even killed. They believe with a vengeance in the traditional American dream: rags to riches through private entrepreneurship.

At the same time, contrary to what we hear in the media, the vast majority of the street sellers are not, in fact, making much money—on an average night, they might get $6 or $8 an hour. Of course, that is already twice minimum wage. But what is more important is that they are able to earn these "good wages" without having to demean themselves in jobs they believe compromise their sense of personal dignity. They do not want to adapt to the rules of a hostile outside world that is uncomfortable with their form of dress, their language, and their culture in general. In the crack economy, there is also a real possibility for dramatic advancement that is not easily replicated in the entry-level service sector, which is where the jobs available to them are located once they drop out of high school.

During the course of their lives, most of the street sellers cycle in and out of legal, just-above-minimum-wage jobs. Even the most hard-core sellers frequently talk about "going legit." In fact, one young man left the crack business when he was given a temporary job over the holidays with the Postal Service. Another street dealer recently took a union job as a porter for Woolworths; another now works as a bus driver for the New York City Transit Authority; yet another joined the Army. This shows that despite the strength of the underground economy, the situation is not hopeless. There is still an arena within which the mainstream economy can compete for their allegiance.

The Crack House: Youth Center and Day-Care Facility

In this neighborhood after 8:30 p.m. on a hot summer night, the only air-conditioned place open to teenagers is the crack house. Most teens do not yet use drugs or even drink beer, but they hang out in the crack house hallways to escape the heat and to watch the excitement: the money changing hands, the power plays of rising entrepreneurs, the well-dressed people coming and going, the emaciated addicts flitting by in various stages of cocaine psychosis. There is no mainstream institution competing with the crack house for their attention after dark.

One hot June evening, I walked into a crack house and saw three baby carriages parked near the video machines at the entrance. The mothers were teenagers vying to be noticed by the manager of the night shift. These girls were typical of those who are there every night: they are not only looking for someone to supplement their AFDC checks, they are also seeking excitement and searching for an identity that does not compromise their status as young mothers. They turn their backs on their babies to dance or to talk in private outside. When out of sight from their infants, they remain "confident" that should their babies wake up or start crying, one of the dozen or so crack-house habitués will attend to them.

The situation for the babies of the young mothers who resist the seduction of crack and who get jobs in the mainstream economy is often not that much better. The mothers' wages (even if combined with the fathers' income) will not pay the market rate for licensed day care in New York City. (As a point of reference, I pay $900 a month for first-class care at a full-time day-care facility!) If a relative is not able to care for the babies while the parent works, then they are left with a neighbor in an often inadequate, bootleg "family day-care setting." In one such "day-care" arrangement that a colleague of mine happened upon, the "caregiver" had just locked a two-year-old in a broom closet because the baby was "crying too much." We cannot expect working-class children to grow up unscarred in those kinds of situations. The irony is that these are precisely the families that are trying to "do the right thing": they work hard at legal jobs and refuse public subsidy.

The Breakdown of the Public and Private Sectors

The telephone company took six weeks to install my phone; the garbage trucks don't make their rounds at least once a month; about as often, the letter carrier fails to appear; and careless oil truck operators frequently spill heating oil all over the sidewalk when they fill the underground storage tanks of the tenement buildings. Neither Express Mail nor Federal

> **THE TELEPHONE COMPANY TOOK SIX WEEKS TO INSTALL MY PHONE; THE GARBAGE TRUCKS DON'T MAKE THEIR ROUNDS ... THE LETTER CARRIER FAILS TO APPEAR. IN SHORT, NOTHING WORKS ADEQUATELY.**

Express deliver on time in my neighborhood. In short, nothing works adequately—regardless of whether it is publicly or privately owned. Market mechanisms should normally be able to come into play to encourage providers of services, but the infiltration of organized crime into the local economy is an obvious obstacle to this process in East Harlem. Even 12-year-olds know that the Mafia controls the private contracting companies, the garbage collection services, and a critical proportion of the private-sector labor unions.

The miles and miles of abandoned buildings are powerful testimony to a profound infrastructure crisis. For the second summer in a row, the public swimming pool two blocks away that was the one healthy, popular, city-run activity center for youths in the neighborhood has been closed down while a corrupt construction company "renovates" it at a snail's pace. For the third year in a row, the basketball courts hedged in between the public housing towers are marred by deep potholes; only every other hoop on the courts is still in place, and the lighting systems for nighttime play never operate. Broken beer bottles, human feces, crack vials, and an occasional hypodermic needle litter the jungle gym where I take my two-year-old son to play on weekends.

It is unrealistic to expect most of the eight-and ten-year-olds playing tag in the ruins of the abandoned buildings or the preteenagers sifting through mounds of garbage piled on the sidewalks to develop healthy notions of public good and personal responsibility. The "common sense" emerging among this newest generation is that "The System" hates them. A disproportionate number of adults and teenagers believe virulent conspiracy theories about "The Plan"—that is, the evil intentions of the wealthy white-power-structure elite toward poor African-Americans and Puerto Ricans living in Manhattan. A fringe group has even postered the bricked-up abandoned buildings along several blocks with a picture of a black family struggling into the distance, carrying their possessions on their backs. The word "Genocide!" is written above the picture in red ink. This kind of rage and frustration will filter down in one form or another to the bulk of the children in the neighborhood, including those living in stable working households.

Perhaps the most ironic failing of the public sector is that the biggest crack-house landlord is the City of New York. Crack is most frequently sold out of abandoned building storefronts or in housing project stairways. Most people in the neighborhood assume that the police are paid off to ignore this activity, but in fact they do not need to be. The police are overwhelmed by the magnitude of crime; their morale is low; they cannot relate culturally to the community; and inadequate budgets are poorly managed.

Our tax dollars are not spent as effectively in the inner city as they are in the suburbs. How else can one explain the chipped paint and dirty floors of the local post offices, or the complaint scrawled on the blackboard in my neighborhood's police precinct last January: "No more arrests until we get some heat in here!"

The schools offer the most blatant testimony of an irrational public-sector breakdown. Why is the beautiful but abandoned turn-of-the-century school building around the corner from me being renovated with tax incentives into commercial lofts? Two blocks away, my neighborhood's primary school is so overcrowded that special-education classes are being held in "renovated" broom closets. (On a more positive note, the extraordinary energy and commitment of New York's new chancellor of schools, Joseph Fernandez, is a hopeful sign. He is cleaning up school board corruption, ousting incompetent managers, and attempting to fire dysfunctional principals. More important, if his management technique is more than media hype, then he could be a public-sector model for the revitalization of crucial services without politically unrealistic infusions of new funds.)

It is not a question of providing a "special opportunity" or an "easy street" for the youths on my block. Instead, the necessity is to guarantee them what the rest of the nation takes for granted: streets where they do not have to witness gunfights; hot and cold running water in their homes; heat at recreation centers; public safety officers who do not curse at them when they stand on the corner; child care that is not abusive; schools where they do not have to peer through the keyhole of the bathroom before entering for fear of being raped; principals and teachers who do not smoke crack; regular garbage pickups and mail deliveries; abandoned buildings that are either renovated

or ripped down rather than left standing for years; a local economy and job structure that is not perversely distorted by narco-dollars; and supervisors in the entry-level economy who do not subject them to cultural ridicule because of their inner-city ethnic identity. In short, let us begin by offering them a level playing field.

Conclusion

Scholars studying urban America are debating whether or not the structural transformations of the 1970s and 1980s have created a qualitatively as well as quantitatively new dynamic of poverty different from the one faced by new immigrants at the turn of the century or prior to World War II. As our cities have shifted from manufacturing to service economies, high school graduates can no longer find stable, unionized jobs that provide health and retirement benefits and pay a family wage. The debate over the social implications of these long-term structural transformations in our nation's economy is not academic; it has important policy ramifications. The inner-city crisis is "Made in the U.S.A."; it is not caused by new immigrants or by residual cultural influences. Right now, we are not even reaching out to the boys and girls who want to play by the rules.

Because I come from a discipline that systematically analyzes cultural processes, I have reached the conclusion that the experience of second-generation urban poverty in America today is qualitatively different from what it was in the recent past. Political and socioeconomic forces have coalesced, rendering street culture more persuasive and "economically logical" than it was in past generations. Concretely, this means that a much higher percentage then ever before of our best and brightest inner-city youths are pursuing careers with rugged determination that lead to violence and drug addiction. Worse yet, current public-sector policies and private-sector practices are merely compounding this crisis rather than addressing it.

> I HAVE REACHED THE CONCLUSION THAT THE EXPERIENCE OF SECOND-GENERATION URBAN POVERTY IN AMERICA TODAY IS QUALITATIVELY DIFFERENT FROM WHAT IT WAS IN THE RECENT PAST.

Caring For Children

LINDA M. BURTON

Linda M. Burton is associate professor of human development at the Pennsylvania State University. Her primary area of research focuses on the effects of teen pregnancy on multigeneration family systems.

The continuing debate about the underclass has intensified the interest of scholars and policymakers in the child-care strategies of poor families who live in high-risk neighborhoods. Much of the research explores how census tract data on the rates of crime, male joblessness, welfare dependency, and nonmarital fertility are related to a narrowly defined range of child-care arrangements these families use. While the research offers important information on the suggested link between the characteristics of the neighborhood and how families are faring, it provides little insight into neighborhood and family child-care *processes*—that is, how day-to-day activities in high-risk communities influence child-care arrangements in families.

Because of its impact on families, illicit drug trafficking is one ongoing activity in high-risk neighborhoods that has received considerable attention. High-volume drug activity in neighborhoods affects the lives of families, particularly children, in several ways. It provides local opportunities for recruiting children, adolescents, and their parents as drug dealers and users. It also increases the type and frequency of dangers that families are exposed to in the neighborhood. Exposure to these temptations and dangers prompts families to develop arrangements for taking care of their children that are appropriate to the situation.

The range of strategies used by these families is influenced by other factors as well as the dangers related to the local drug trade: the number of available and responsible child-care providers among local kin (such as grandparents) and friendship networks, parental work schedules, and parental drug use.

Using preliminary data from a community-based ethnographic study, this article describes several child-care strategies used by families consisting of two or more generations living in a neighborhood where there is considerable illicit drug activity. The types of strategies outlined are linked specifically to the daily timing of drug sales in the neighborhood, the work schedules of parents and grandparents, and parental illicit drug use.

The data here are from a larger ongoing study of the effects of teenage childbearing on persistent and working-poor black multigeneration families. The data on drug-trafficking schedules and child-care strategies were obtained fortuitously—it was not my intention at the outset of the larger study to focus on these issues. After only one month of field research, however, it became apparent that understanding the connection between drug-trafficking schedules and child-care strategies was essential to being able to understand the day-to-day routines of young families that live in one particularly high-risk neighborhood.

The data were collected during the first year of the study. The study is being conducted in a poor, predominantly black neighborhood encompassing eight city blocks in a moderate-sized northeastern city. The drug trafficking and other related dangers in this neighborhood are extreme. The neighborhood is the only one of its kind in the city. The vast majority of poor black families in this city do not live in such environments.

To date, 127 males and females, 5 to 78 years old, have been interviewed in this neighborhood. In addition to these interviews, I have used a variety of qualitative field research techniques to collect data, including direct observation of neighborhood activities at various times of the day (8:00 a.m., 3:00 p.m., and 2:00 a.m.), focus group discussions with neighborhood residents, and informal observation of community and family events.

Neighborhood Drug-Trafficking Schedules

In industry, there is shift work; similarly, in this particular neighborhood there are daily shift-like patterns in the sale of illicit drugs and related environmental dangers. Three distinct drug activity shifts operate in this neighborhood: a morning shift (7:00 a.m.–4:00 p.m.), an afternoon/evening shift (4:00 p.m.–10:00 p.m.), and a night shift (10:00 p.m.–6:00 a.m.).

The morning shift is best described as having a low level of drug activity and the dangers such as crime that accompany it. Participants in the study indicate that this is the time of day when most drug dealers and users sleep. Consequently, neighborhood residents who are not involved in the local drug trade (which is the majority of families) use the safe morning hours to do their grocery shopping and banking, visit with friends in the neighborhood, attend church activities, deliver and pick up children from school, and take toddlers and preschool children out for walks. Community residents describe this as the "family time of day."

At approximately 4:00 p.m., the neighborhood "climate" changes. Around this time, the small-time drug dealers open for business on neighborhood corners. Older residents, parents not involved in the local drug economy, and their children retreat inside their homes. Young children and adolescents who have no adult supervision hang out on the street. The local automobile traffic increases dramatically as people who live outside the neighborhood stop on their way home from work to purchase drugs. Uniformed police officers are nowhere to be found. As night falls, the stench of urine and vomit emanates from the local bars, alleys, and church steps. Community residents call this the "p.m. shift"—it is the time that dealers have "stolen" from families to promote the drug economy.

At 10:00 p.m., the neighborhood undergoes yet another transformation. Hard-core drug dealers make their appearance on the street. Young-adult, heavily addicted drug users lie around, seemingly dead, in alleys and doorways of churches and local businesses. The presence of undercover police officers is easily discernible. The stench of urine and vomit becomes more intense. Community residents agree that this is the most dangerous time of day in their neighborhood. They call it "the night shift."

Drug Shifts and Child-Care Strategies

In each of the drug-trade shifts described above, I observed a number of distinctly different child-care strategies that families in the neighborhood use. The arrangements involve a range of providers (parents, grandparents, teenage siblings, and elderly and young-adult males who are friends of the family) and child-monitoring activities. Participants in the study describe these strategies as responses to the dangers in the area associated with local drug activity, the work schedules of parents, and drug use among some of the neighborhood children's parents.

During the morning shift, employed and unemployed parents, grandmothers, retired "surrogate grandfathers," and a few young unemployed males take care of infants, toddlers, and school-age children of drug-addicted parents. A number of these caregivers offer insightful explanations about why they are child-care providers and why they monitor the children the way they do. A fairly common situation was described by Mary, a 68-year-old great-grandmother who is currently caring for her drug-addicted 36-year-old daughter's eight children. The children range from 1 to 20 years of age. Four of the children have mental and physical handicaps possibly related to their mother's drug use. Mary told me quite candidly why she was the child-care provider: "I ain't no different than any of the other grandmommas in my neighborhood that has a dopehead for a kid. We all have to take care of our children's mistakes. If we don't, ain't nobody else gonna do it. Who cares how it affects us? I'm real sick. I got heart trouble and diabetes. I'm tired myself. But there ain't nobody else to do it."

Mary explained how she takes care of her grandchildren: "In the morning, I get up early, get the babies ready, and hits the streets. At 7:00 in the morning, I let the kids go out to play—them that don't have school. Then about 10:00 o'clock, I pack up the babies, and we go to the store and the doctor. I'm always home by 2:00 in the afternoon so we can all go inside. That's when shit starts to change around here. Them no-good women and men dope dealers takes over the streets. I done lost one child to dope. I ain't letting her babies get lost too."

Sam, a 65-year-old retired factory worker who currently takes care of his three nieces, had this comment: "We gets ready really early in the morning. I comb the girls' hair. I dress and feed them. Then I take them to school. Then I go and hang out with my buddies until it's time to pick my babies up. We hurry up and walk home because I want to be in the house by three o'clock. I don't want them to see the trash on the street. I don't want them to turn out like the low-life drugheads their momma and daddy are."

Shirley, a 27-year-old mother of three, also engages in close monitoring of her children but she speaks more defiantly than Mary and Sam about allowing the neighborhood drug trade to dictate the structure of her life and that of her children: "Sometimes I get so mad. It's not right to have to keep your kids inside after school. Sometimes I take my kids outside anyway . . . but I'm right there with them the whole time. I dare anyone to mess with them."

When Mary, Sam, Shirley, and others like them go inside with their children, and the parents and grandparents who work the swing shift in local factories leave for work, a second type of child-care strategy becomes apparent in the neighborhood for families without providers like Mary, Sam, and Shirley. It involves child-care provided by neighborhood teens or older siblings.

Ordinarily, this kind of child-care would be considered a safe, natural alternative for families. Unfortunately, however, in a high-volume drug-trafficking neighborhood, this strategy is often very risky. A few of the teens and older siblings who are responsible for the care of younger children "hang out" on the street from 4:00 p.m. to 9:00 p.m.—the time of day when children on the streets are exposed to heightened dangers related to the drug economy, including increased automobile traffic and street fighting. It is quite common to see young children and adolescent child-care providers being solicited by small-time dealers to buy or sell drugs. When I asked Walter—a 14-year-old who was babysitting for his three younger siblings on a street corner—what impact the neighborhood drug activity had on his child-care responsibilities, he said: "I got to be out here where it's happening. I'm out here learning them the streets. Just 'cuz I got to watch my sisters and brother don't mean I got to stay inside with them."

Walter, his friends, and their siblings are usually in the house by 10:00 p.m.—just in time for their parents' arrival home from work. For families in which there are working parents, the child-care responsibilities of teens and older siblings are usually turned back to par-

> "I'M ALWAYS HOME BY 2:00 IN THE AFTERNOON SO WE CAN ALL GO INSIDE. . . . THEM NO-GOOD WOMEN AND MEN DOPE DEALERS TAKES OVER THE STREETS. I DONE LOST ONE CHILD TO DOPE. I AIN'T LETTING HER BABIES GET LOST TOO."
> —Mary, Age 68

ents when they return from work. These parents are deeply concerned about the dangers their children are exposed to while they are at work. Walter's mother, for example, stated: "I know he is out there [on the streets] when I'm at work. I don't have any other way right now to have someone watch my children . . . . I hope and pray that I taught Walter the right things, though. He knows too that when I'm home he better be straight. The Lord only knows, I have to believe that what I taught him, the good I taught him, will bring him through and make him a good man."

Steven, a 37-year-old single parent of three teenage boys expressed his concern for his children and talked about the arrangements he makes for their care: "Yes, I worry about them. There is so much here to get into, too . . . . But I call my boys every hour and come home on my break. They know they better be here when I come."

For a small number of families in which parents' are unemployed and both parents and grandparents have serious drug addictions, there is no available adult supervision for children and a third child-care strategy prevails. This is a strategy of the "night shift" and, fortunately, is not a frequent pattern in the neighborhood I studied. Children as young as five take care of their younger siblings during the late night to early morning hours while their parents or grandparents buy and get high on "serious drugs" (crack, cocaine, heroin, ice). Tameka, a seven-year-old who takes care of her five-year-old brother, two-year-old twin sisters, and two-month-old brother, described her child-care responsibilities to me: "My momma and my grandmomma have to go out every night so they can feel better. They take something that makes them sleep and feel better sometimes. Sometimes they get sick. I know they take drugs. I'm not stupid. Since they ain't got it together, I got to take care of the little ones. I feed them all. Change diapers. Put them to bed. I know how to do all of it. In the morning, I get my brother dressed for school. I stay home all the time to take care of my real little sisters and brother because everybody is sleep. I haven't been to school for a long time."

I visited with only three children like Tameka in the neighborhood but was told by community residents and school officials that other children in the community live in similar circumstances. Children like Tameka are extreme cases and are clearly the most at risk. They receive very little, and rarely continuous, care themselves, they are subjected to myriad household and neighborhood dangers, and they miss, on average, 80–100 days of school per year.

Implications of Preliminary Findings

How many children are there like Tameka in the nation? How do we identify them, and how do we help them and the other children in these neighborhoods? Although the data presented here are preliminary and focus on child-care arrangements used by families who live in one small, high-risk neighborhood, they nonetheless call attention to three issues that policymakers, social service providers, and community leaders should consider in developing child-care programs for communities like these. First, the relationship between child-care strategies and neighborhood drug-trafficking shifts indicates that children whose parents work swing shifts or are addicted to drugs are at greater risk of exposure to dangers in the neighborhood during the late afternoon, night, and early morning hours when they have no responsible adult supervision. Clearly, programs designed to fill the gaps in responsible child care should be implemented in these high-risk neighborhoods.

Second, we observed that in order to protect children in high-risk neighborhoods, responsible caregivers feel that they have to literally lock children indoors to keep them safe. We need to know what the implications of this child-monitoring strategy are for children's healthy development. Can safe programs be instituted in these neighborhoods to allow children to have positive experiences outside after 3:00 p.m.?

Third, this research highlights the efforts of several important child-care providers—grandmothers, retiree surrogate grandfathers, and young unemployed black males. Although these people perform valuable services for children and families, it is important to note that, particularly in the case of grandmothers, the care they provide is not without personal cost. Many of the older-generation caregivers experience social, psychological, and physical problems in caring for the young children. If these caregivers are to continue providing this valuable service for children, it is clear that they, too, must have support from local community groups and social-services agencies to meet their own needs as well as the children's.

We do not know how prevalent this type of neighborhood and the child-care strategies employed within it are in other inner-city communities throughout the nation. Further research is needed. But certainly, social scientists, policymakers, and community leaders need to look more closely at how activities in high-risk neighborhoods affect the lives of families and children who are trying to survive and thrive.

American Nightmare: Homelessness

In the worst housing crisis since the Depression, many families face the spectre of homelessness. Restoring the homeownership dream means shifting national spending priorities and taking housing out of the speculative market.

Peter Dreier and Richard Appelbaum

Peter Dreier is Director of Housing at the Boston Redevelopment Authority. Richard Appelbaum is Chairman of the Department of Sociology at the University of California at Santa Barbara.

During the 1980s, a new ingredient was added to the landscape of America's cities—millions of people sleeping in alleyways and subways, in cars and on park benches.

The spectacle of homeless Americans living literally in the shadow of luxury condos and yuppie boutiques symbolized the paradox of the decade: It was a period of both outrageous greed and outrageous suffering. The media gave us "lifestyles of the rich and famous," but they also offered cover stories about homeless families. And while the 1980s were often characterized as the "me decade"—an orgy of selfishness and self-interest—more Americans were involved in social issues, as volunteers and activists, than at any time in recent memory.

These contrasts are even more striking in light of the billions of dollars invested in speculative commercial real estate during the 1980s, which has led, according to a recent Salomon Brothers report, to an unprecedented high office vacancy rate. Rampant real estate speculation also contributed to the savings-and-loan debacle. The S&L bailout, perhaps the biggest rip-off in American history, may cost taxpayers over $500 billion, a regressive burden that will divert funds from much-needed economic and social recovery programs. Meanwhile, housing starts—particularly construction of low-rent apartments—have reached a postwar low while, according to a new U.S Conference of Mayors survey, demand for emergency shelter continues to grow.

What will the 1990s bring?

Everyone from President Bush to the late advocate for the homeless Mitch Snyder has agreed that homelessness is a national tragedy and an embarrassment to America in the court of world opinion. Most Americans acknowledge that something must be done, that no great and affluent nation should tolerate such fundamental misery. And public opinion polls show that a vast majority of Americans now put solving the problem of the homeless near the top of the national agenda. According to these polls, Americans are even willing to pay higher taxes, if the funds go to assist the homeless.

It is clear to most Americans that "a thousand points of light" cannot stem the rising tide of homelessness. Public policy was responsible for creating this epidemic, and changes in public policy will be required to resolve

From *Challenge* Magazine, Vol. 34, No. 2, March/April 1991, pp. 46-52. Reprinted by permission of M. E. Sharpe, Inc., Armonk, New York 10504.

this mounting problem. But as long as politicians, housing activists, and academic experts disagree on how many people are homeless, who they are, and why America suddenly found itself with so many people living on the streets, it will be difficult to forge a consensus on what to do. In this article, we seek to answer these questions.

Middle class crisis

No other major industrial nation has such widespread homelessness. Even Canada, a country quite similar to ours in most political and economic features, has neither the slums to match the physical and social deterioration of our inner cities, nor the level of homeless people sleeping in shelters, streets, and subways. This suggests that there is something unique about the way the United States deals with its most needy citizens; but it also suggests that a solution is within reach. Indeed, there is no reason why the United States cannot solve its homeless problem by the end of the twentieth century, if we can mobilize the political will to do so.

The growing epidemic of homelessness is only the tip of the iceberg. The United States faces its worst housing crisis since the Great Depression. The underlying problem is a widening gap between what Americans can afford to pay and what it costs to build and maintain housing. This has always been a problem for the poor; now it is a growing problem for the middle class.

The "American Dream" of homeownership is fading fast for a large segment of the middle class. Thanks to postwar federal housing programs, the rate of homeownership rose steadily for three decades, from 43.4 percent in the late 1940s to 65.6 percent in 1980. Since then, however, it has steadily declined, reaching 64.0 percent in 1989. The problem is particularly troubling for young families. For example, among twenty-five to thirty-four- year- olds, the homeownership rate dropped from 52.3 percent in 1980 to 45.2 percent in 1989. The median price of a new single-family home climbed from $69,300 in 1982 to about $120,000 today. While in 1973 it took roughly one-quarter of the median income of a young family with children to carry a new mortgage on average-priced housing, today it takes over half of a young family's income. In some regions of the country, housing prices have started to drop, but because of wage and employment trends as well as interest rates, this has not made a significant dent in overall housing affordability.

High rents make it impossible for most young families to save money for a downpayment. As a result, about the only people who can afford to purchase a home are those who already own one. Even among those who manage to buy a home, a growing number are in danger of losing their homes to foreclosure by banks.

Rents have reached a two-decade peak, according to a recent Harvard University study. This is especially a problem for the poor, who are now competing with the middle class for scarce apartments. Some 85 percent of low-income renters (5.8 million households) are paying at least 30 percent of their income for housing. Two-thirds of the poor are paying at least half of their income just for housing. The typical young single mother pays over 70 percent of her meager income just to keep a roof over her children's heads.

Perhaps the most important statistic is this: Only one-quarter of poor households receive any kind of housing subsidy—the lowest level of any industrial nation in the world. The swelling waiting lists for even the most deteriorated subsidized housing projects are telling evidence of the desperation of the poor in the private housing market.

Is it any wonder that the ranks of the homeless are growing?

Fundamental economic shifts

The initial stereotype of the homeless person was an alcoholic or mentally ill middle-aged man or "bag lady"—many of them victims of deinstitutionalization resulting from the Community Mental Health Act of 1963. But when more low-rent housing was available, including many rooming houses that have since been lost to gentrification, even people on the margins of society could afford a roof over their heads.

The homelessness crisis is not, as some suggest, primarily a problem of personal pathology. It is, rather, a symptom of some fundamental shifts in the nation's economy.

The most important involves the deindustrialization and gentrification of our urban areas. The past fifteen years have been characterized by a tremendous flight of previously high-wage industries to low-wage countries. Since the early 1970s, the electronics revolution has hastened the development of a global economy. Foot-loose firms have moved their manufacturing operations to more favorable locations—with low wages, lax environmental laws, tax breaks, and other subsidies—whether these be in suburbs, rural areas, or Third World countries.

As a result of this geographic realignment, it is unlikely that American industry will soon again enjoy the once-privileged postwar position that enabled our standard of living to rise steadily for almost three decades. Many American cities have still not recovered from the loss of blue-collar industry and jobs. As factories closed down, tax bases declined, waterfronts were left vacant, and downtown department stores went out of business, some cities began to resemble ghost towns.

During the past decade, many observers have hailed the "services revolution" as the savior of cities. It is true that many cities have now shifted from what University of North Carolina sociologist John Kasarda calls "centers of production and distribution of goods to centers of administration, finance and information exchange." Cities sought to revitalize their downtown areas with new office buildings, medical and educational complexes, hotels, urban shopping malls, convention centers, and even sports complexes. But such efforts, even when successful, do not stem the growing tide of poverty only blocks away from the glittering glass and steel. In the shadow of its downtown skyscrapers, Los Angeles resembles a Third World city, its streets teeming with economically precarious low-wage workers and homeless men, women, and children.

Why? Because the services economy is predominantly a low-wage economy, and most of its jobs offer no career ladder or upward mobility. According to Bennett Harrison and Barry Bluestone, in *The Great U-Turn* (see For Further Reading), the majority of jobs created since the 1970s have offered poverty-level wages. Working full-time is no longer a guarantee of escaping poverty. Even relatively low levels of unemployment in some cities mask the deepening poverty and desperation.

As Robert Reich has noted, the American economy has two escalators—a small one moving upward and a much larger one moving downward. More than 33 million Americans—one out of seven—now live below the poverty line. The figure for children is even more alarming: one of every four (and one-half of all black children) live in poverty. Today's poor people are poorer and likely to remain poor for longer periods of time. During the 1980s, both the minimum wage and Aid For Dependent Children (AFDC) benefit levels fell far behind the rate of inflation.

Not surprisingly, more and more of America's homeless are families with children and people with jobs. A survey released in December 1990 by the U.S. Conference of Mayors found that almost one-quarter of the homeless work, but have wages too low to afford permanent housing. Apart from those who live on the streets or in shelters, there are millions more who live doubled-up or tripled-up in overcrowded apartments, and millions of others who pay more than they can reasonably afford for substandard housing. As a result of this situation, millions of low-income Americans are only one rent increase, one hospital stay, one layoff away from becoming homeless.

Things are getting worse for the middle class as well. In recent years, the average middle class American has seen family income stagnate. In 1960, the typical thirty-year old head of household could expect family income to increase by 50 percent during the next decade. Today, he or she can expect family income (real buying power) to decline. According to a recent Children's Defense Fund report, young families (headed by someone under thirty) have seen their incomes erode by one-quarter over the past fifteen years; among Hispanics, the decline has been one-third; among Blacks, one half.

For a small, but very visible, segment of the population, however, these new economic forces have led to the up-escalator. The services economy has created a stratum of highly-educated, well-paid management and professional workers. They, along with top-level executives and owners of wealth, did well during the decade of corporate takeovers and leveraged buyouts. The share of national income now going to the wealthiest 20 percent is the highest since World War II. Meanwhile, the share going to the poorest 40 percent is the lowest in that period. By dramatically lowering tax rates of the affluent and big business, the Reagan Administration exacerbated these trends and redistributed income from the working class to the wealthy. President Bush's proposal to cut capital gains taxes would continue this trend.

All this pertains directly to housing. While America was witnessing a growing disparity of incomes, the affluent began viewing a house less as a home than as an investment, as valuable for its tax benefits as for its Victorian details. Young baby boom generation professionals moved into urban neighborhoods, especially those close to the downtown core, where they found work in the growing service sector. Housing that had been abandoned or devalued decades earlier became more attractive to so-called "yuppies." As the affluent and the poor began to compete for scarce inner-city housing, prices skyrocketed. Low-rent apartments were converted to high-priced condominiums. Rooming houses, the last refuge of the poor, were torn down or turned into upscale apartments. Businesses catering to the poor and working class families were replaced by high-priced shops and restaurants.

The housing market failed to expand significantly overall number of apartments, because it simply isn't profitable to build housing for the poor. The situation was made worse when the Reagan Administration removed the two props that once served to entice some private investors into providing low-rent housing—subsidies which bring housing costs and poor peoples' incomes into line, and tax shelters which indirectly produce the same result.

The role of government

The dramatic escalation of housing prices during the 1980s—and the ongoing affordability gap—stems from three basic factors. First, nearly everyone involved in housing is trying to maximize profits—including land development, materials manufacture, construction, rentals, and capital gains. For example, the average price of a residential lot has increased 813 percent in the past twenty years, from $5,200 in 1969 to $42,300 in 1989; more than half of that increase occurred in the last five years alone. Second, the cost of credit (the money borrowed to build and buy housing) adds a large and permanent cost to every housing unit. For homeowners, roughly two out of every three housing dollars goes to pay off the mortgage. For renters (who pay these costs indirectly), the proportion is often higher. Third, because housing is viewed as an investment by developers, landlords, and most homeowners, home prices and rents are often much higher than what it actually costs to build and operate housing. Both homeowners and landlords expect to sell their buildings for much more than they paid for them—a psychological and economic factor known as speculation. Government policies can exacerbate or curb these market-driven forces.

One way for the federal government to help close the gap between incomes and housing expenses is through a variety of consumer and developer subsidies. The magnitude of federal housing resources was never adequate, but the Reagan Administration made the situation even worse. Housing shouldered the largest burden of the Reagan budget axe. Since 1981, federal housing assistance has been slashed from about $33 billion to less than $8 billion a year. The number of new federally subsidized apartments built each year dwindled from over 200,000 in the 1970s to less than 15,000 last year. To put this in perspective, in 1981 the federal government was spending seven dollars for defense for every one dollar is spent on housing. By 1989, it spent over forty dollars on defense for every housing dollar.

The increase in homelessness parallels these federal housing cuts. And although President Bush and Housing and Urban Development (HUD) Secretary Jack Kemp have promised to deal with the nation's homelessness scandal, the Bush Administration actually proposed further housing cutbacks in its 1991 budget proposal, but was rebuffed by Congress. Bush's 1992 budget proposed further housing cuts.

The single housing subsidy that did *not* fall to the Reagan (and now Bush) budget axe is the one that goes to the very rich. The federal tax code allows homeowners to deduct all property tax and mortgage interest from their income taxes. This cost the federal government $34 billion in 1990 alone—more than four times the HUD budget for low-income housing. Over three-quarters of the foregone tax revenue goes to the 15.1 percent of taxpayers who earn over $50,000 annually; one-third of this subsidy goes to the 3.1 percent of taxpayers with incomes over $100,000. Over half of all homeowners do not claim deductions at all. Tenants, of course, don't even qualify. In other words, our nation's housing subsidies disproportionately benefit homeowners with high incomes, often with two homes. The *Washington Post* recently revealed, for example, that Sen. John D. (Jay) Rockefeller of West Virginia receives a tax subsidy worth about $223,000 a year just on his $15.3-million Washington mansion.

Another housing role for federal and state governments is to regulate lenders in order to guarantee a supply of credit for builders and homeowners. The government can control interest rates, require banks to meet community credit needs, and protect savings-and-loans to guarantee credit for the average homeowner. The Reagan Administration, however, dismantled most of the federal policies designed to regulate lenders. Reagan's policies resulted in a frenzy of speculative lending, mismanagement, and corruption by the nation's savings-and-loan industry during the past decade. President Bush has proposed a bailout of failing savings-and-loans which will fall primarily on low- and middle-income taxpayers, and which now looks as if it will swell to over $500 billion. And Bush's new plan to restructure the nation's banks does nothing to promote lending for homeownership or to encourage community development.

Finally, state and local governments can regulate land use, through zoning laws, to promote affordable housing development. Instead, most localities, particularly suburbs, use these regulations (''snob zoning'') to keep out the poor. They can establish codes regulating the safety and health of new and existing buildings, but few state or local governments allocate adequate resources to enforce these laws, particularly in poor neighborhoods. They can also protect consumers by regulating rents, evictions, and condominium conversions. However, only a few local politicians are willing to buck the powerful real estate industry.

The politics of housing

In the past, the major political force for housing programs was the real estate industry—developers, mortgage bankers, landlords, and brokers. They, of course, wanted Congress to enact policies to help build more housing for the middle class or to provide subsidies to make it lucrative to house the poor. Developers, realtors, and mortgage bankers have been the most generous contributors to congressional and presidential candidates, and their national associations have strong political action committees, deep pockets, and effective local networks. In turn, many members of Congress have ties to developers and have lobbied HUD or bank regulators on their behalf.

But even the housing industry's clout couldn't offset the Reagan Administration's determination to slash federal housing funds, which suffered the biggest cuts of any domestic program. Recently, some conservative politicians and editorial writers have cynically used the corruption scandal at HUD as an excuse to dismantle federal housing programs even further. House Minority Whip Newt Gingrich (R-Ga.), *The Wall Street Journal*, and *The New Republic* have called for folding up HUD's tent and replacing it with a voucher program, an approach long-advocated by HUD Secretary Jack Kemp. But rent vouchers, on their own, won't solve the problem. About one million low-income households already receive such vouchers, which are intended to help them pay rent for apartments in the private market. But in cities with low rental vacancy rates, handing out vouchers is like providing food stamps when the grocery shelves are empty. About half the low-income tenants who now receive vouchers return them unused because apartments are so scarce. Clearly, we must increase the overall *supply* of low-income housing.

The Bush Administration has never acknowledged that more affordable housing is the only workable solution to homelessness. His proposed budget significantly *reduced* funding for new housing, while providing only minimal increases for emergency shelters and vouchers. In October, Congress enacted legislation that called for a slight increase in new housing funds. In January, however, Bush unveiled a 1992 budget proposal that called for *reduced* funding for new housing, while providing only minimal increases for emergency shelters and vouchers.

Ironically, one hopeful sign is that Jack Kemp's political ambitions have made him the most vocal and visible HUD Secretary in memory. In sharp contrast to his predecessor, Samuel Pierce, Kemp has been a high-profile Cabinet member, although his clout within the Bush Administration does not appear to parallel his public visibility. He visits shelters, meets with advocates and builders, and testifies before Congress. Although his approach to urban housing problems (vouchers, selling off public housing, creating "enterprise zones" in inner cities) and his budget proposals are woefully inadequate, his enthusiasm and visibility have helped keep the hous-

ing issue in the media. History suggests that social movements and social reform are best sown in the soil of "rising expectations." Kemp's rhetoric is clearly setting the stage for a revolt against broken promises.

Grassroots organizing for housing

If there was one silver lining during the 1980's housing crisis, it was the emergence of locally based efforts to address community housing needs. A combination of community organizations, municipal governments, unions, and business groups developed a wide range of innovative local programs and strategies to cope with the impact of federal housing cutbacks, and the changes in local housing markets. These forces have gained momentum in the 1980s—in part, as a result of the growing visibility of homelessness.

The fledgling grassroots housing movement is composed of tenant groups, homeless advocacy organizations, shelters and soup kitchens, church-based institutions, community-based nonprofit developers, neighborhood associations, senior citizen groups, women's organizations, and civil rights groups.

These groups have spent much of the past decade working, primarily on the local level, to plug some of the gaps left by the federal government's withdrawal from housing programs. They fix up abandoned buildings and construct new homes for the poor. They apply pressure on local governments to protect tenants against unfair evictions. They lobby for stricter enforcement of health and safety codes, and for municipal funds to be placed in banks with good records of investment in low-income neighborhoods ("linked deposits"). They persuade banks to open up branches in minority neighborhoods and increase available mortgage loans for low-income consumers. They publish reports to dramatize the plight of the homeless, to highlight the widening gap between incomes and housing prices, and to expose the continuing practice of bank redlining. They pressure and work with city and state housing agencies to expand available funds for affordable housing and to target more assistance to community-based groups.

But these have been primarily defensive efforts—brushfire battles to keep things from getting worse. Only the federal government has the resources needed to address housing issues and the problem of homelessness in a significant way. Despite the good work of groups like the National Low-Income Housing Coalition, the Association of Community Organizations for Reform Now (ACORN), and the National Coalition for the Homeless, and despite periodic bursts of mobilization like the Housing Now march (which brought 200,000 Americans to

Washington in October 1989), the housing movement has been relatively weak at the national level.

For the housing issue to move to the top of Congress' agenda, advocates must broaden the constituency and organize more effectively. The housing movement must mobilize people to influence Congressmembers through meetings and public accountability sessions, and letter-writing campaigns. It must do a better job of shaping the public debate, particularly getting the attention of the mainstream media to discuss alternative policies and local success stories.

Equally important, the housing movement must address the growing housing concerns of the middle class as well as the poor. As homeownership declines, and as more young adults are forced to live with their parents, the potential for a broad-based agenda grows. As Cushing Dolbeare, founder of the National Low-Income Housing Coalition, has pointed out, "political demographics" work against an exclusively low-income focus.

"The majority of Congress represent areas where low-income problems are not a major issue," observed Dolbeare. "[A]sking Members of Congress to vote for low-income housing is often asking them to vote against their own political interests." Last year, the National Housing Institute, a think tank based in Orange, New Jersey, issued a Congressional scorecard based on twenty key votes on housing issues. More than one-third of Congresspeople received an "F" for voting against affordable housing at least half the time.

The housing agenda has always made the most headway when the concerns of the poor and the middle class were joined. In the Progressive era, that meant improving health standards for tenements for immigrant workers in the teeming slums, as well as building apartment houses for the middle class. In the Depression and the postwar years, it meant building subsidized housing for the working class and shoring up homeownership for the middle class.

But the political vehicles to fashion this coalition need to be rebuilt if the issue is to move from the margins to the mainstream of the nation's agenda.

The plight of the homeless confronts millions of middle class Americans on a daily basis. Most, of course, pass them by as they walk through the downtown sections of our cities, occasionally handing them spare change out of compassion or guilt. But a growing number of middle class Americans meet the homeless in different settings, especially as volunteers in soup kitchens and shelters. They parallel the settlement house reformers who pushed for improved tenement conditions at the turn of the century and for public housing during the Depression.

While some of the more militant advocates for the homeless criticize the "shelter industry" as a new form of institutional oppression, most shelter staff and volunteers would like nothing more than to eliminate the need for shelters. Their concerns and political skills have yet to be effectively mobilized.

Some mayors and governors have felt the local political heat to address the homelessness problem. They have become vocal allies of anti-poverty and housing advocates for a stronger federal role.

The labor movement—once a formidable advocate for federal housing policy—has barely recognized that a renewed federal housing agenda would provide jobs, as well as homes, for its members and for those it seeks to recruit. A large-scale housing production and rehabilitation program should be a major part of our anti-recessionary effort for job and economic recovery. Unions are becoming increasingly involved in the housing issue, but it is still not near the top of the unions' agenda. In Boston, for example, the Hotel Workers Union recently negotiated a contract requiring the hotels to contribute five cents an hour to a trust fund which the union will use to provide housing subsidies for members. The local union waged a successful campaign to amend the Taft-Hartley Act to allow unions to bargain for housing benefits. A number of unions, including the Bricklayers, have become successful nonprofit housing developers in a few cities. And the AFL-CIO was a sponsor of the "Housing Now" march.

Some sectors of the business community are also beginning to recognize the importance of the housing problem for their own bottom lines. Like health care and child care, high housing costs are increasingly becoming a barrier to business profits. In recent years, a growing segment of the business community has become sympathetic to some version of government-sponsored universal health care and universal child care. As high housing prices make it increasingly difficult for employers to attract workers (creating a labor shortage in many parts of the country), key business leaders are potential advocates for a federal housing program to subsidize housing costs for low-wage workers. But the U.S. Chamber of Commerce, trade associations, and other business groups have not yet signed on to the housing agenda.

The progressive housing agenda

In light of the HUD scandal, the public is correctly skeptical of programs that offer big profits to politically connected developers and consultants in the name of housing the poor. However, the solution is not to scrap federal housing programs, but to build on the cost-effective successes that have recently emerged in communities across the country.

The key to a successful housing policy is to increasingly remove housing from the speculative market and transform it into limited equity, resident-controlled housing, funded through direct capital grants rather than long-term debt. That is how a significant segment of the housing industry in Canada, Sweden, and other social democratic countries is organized. In the United States, the non-profit (or "social") sector is relatively small but it has grown significantly during the past decade.

Congressman Ron Dellums of California already has sponsored legislation tailored to this goal. The National Comprehensive Housing Act, drafted by an Institute for Policy Studies task force, calls for an annual expenditure of $50 billion. The federal government would make direct capital grants to nonprofit groups to build and rehabilitate affordable housing, as well as to purchase existing, privately owned housing for transfer to nonprofit organizations. These homes would remain in the "social" sector, never again to be burdened with debt. Occupants would pay only the operating costs, which would dramatically lower what poor and working class families are currently paying for housing. The Dellums bill is clearly a visionary program—a standard for judging progress on long-term housing goals—but not yet a winnable bill in the current political climate.

In fact, the major housing bill passed in Congress in October and signed by President Bush in November, if fully funded, is a mix of good and bad news. After a decade of housing cutbacks, Congress would finally increase the federal commitment to housing. After months of political wrangling, the House and Senate agreed on legislation to add only $3 billion to the current housing budget. The bill, a compromise of versions sponsored by Senator Alan Cranston (D-Cal.) and Rep. Henry Gonzalez (D-Tex.), would provide some funding to assist first-time homebuyers, to preserve the existing inventory of public and subsidized housing, to expand housing vouchers for the poor, and to expand the capacity of non-profit builders. But it would not even restore the commitment of federal government to the pre-Reagan level of housing assistance, much less move us forward. The bill incorporates a progressive initiative, the Community Housing Partnership Act, sponsored by Rep. Joseph Kennedy (D-Mass.) at the urging of Boston Mayor Ray Flynn. It targets federal funds specifically to the non-profit "social" housing sector.

This year, housing advocates hope to make the Mickey Leland Housing Assistance Act the centerpiece of their efforts. Named after the late Texas Congress-

man, the bill would add $125 billion in new housing funds over a five-year period.

In broad terms, there are five key areas in national housing policy that need attention:

• Expanding the supply of low- and moderate-income housing, particularly through the vehicle of non-profit housing builders. We need to build at least five million new units (500,000 a year) this decade.

• Preserving the existing inventory of public housing (1.3 million units) and subsidized private housing (two million units), which are at risk because of expiring subsidies and long-term neglect—and giving residents a greater role in management.

• Providing adequate income subsidies to the seven-to-eight million low-income families who currently receive no housing assistance and cannot afford market rents.

• Providing working class and lower-middle class young families opportunities for homeownership, in part by putting a cap on the homeownership tax subsidy for the affluent while expanding it for the rest.

• Strengthening the government's regulation of banks and other financial institutions, particularly in terms of allocating credit for homebuyers, eliminating discrimination in lending, making the wealthy pay for the S&L bail-out, and putting consumer representatives on the Federal Reserve Bank.

In light of the war in the Persian Gulf, there is no guarantee that we will see a "peace dividend" to invest in housing, child care, health care, education, rebuilding the infrastructure, and other much-needed domestic programs. Without it, however, the nation cannot address its other gulf crises—the widening gulf between the wealthy and the rest of America, as well as the growing gulf in competitiveness between the United States and the rest of the world. There is no question that we must shift national spending priorities to solve our formidable domestic crises, including the lack of adequate housing for our population. This is the most urgent political issue we face today. And whether the nation's leaders seize this historic moment to act effectively in our best domestic national interests, is a question of political will, not resources.

For Further Reading

Richard Appelbaum and John Gilderbloom, *Rethinking Rental Housing,* Temple University Press, Philadelphia, 1988.

Martha Burt and Barbara Cohen, *America's Homeless: Numbers, Characteristics, and Programs That Serve Them,* Urban Institute Press, Washington, D.C., 1989.

Peter Dreier and J. David Hulchanski, "Affordable Housing: Lessons from Canada," *The American Prospect,* Summer 1990.

Peter Dreier, David Schwartz, and Ann Greiner, "What Every Business Can Do About Housing," *Harvard Business Review,* September-October 1988.

Bennett Harrison and Barry Bluestone, *The Great U-Turn: Corporate Restructuring and the Polarizing of America,* Basic Books, New York, 1988.

Clifford M. Johnson, Andrew M. Sum, and James D. Weill, *Vanishing Dreams: The Growing Economic Plight of America's Young Families,* Children's Defense Fund and Center for Labor Market Studies, Northeastern University, Washington, D.C., 1988.

Paul A. Leonard, Cushing Dolbeare, and Edward B. Lazere, *A Place to Call Home: The Crisis in Housing the Poor,* Center on Budget and Policy Priorities and Low-Income Housing Information Service, Washington, D.C., 1989.

Sandra J. Newman, *Subsidizing Shelter: The Relationship Between Welfare and Housing Assistance,* Urban Institute Press, Washington, D.C., 1988.

Crime, Delinquency, and Violence

The probability that every American will at sometime in his or her life be subjected to a criminal act and that act will involve some degree of violence is becoming greater. With the ever-increasing crime rate, especially in major cities, confidence in law enforcement is declining, and citizens feel forced to arm themselves and turn their homes into minifortresses. What must be done to make our streets safe to walk, our highways safe to drive, and our homes safe from unwanted intrusions?

In "The Whole Child Approach to Crime," U.S. attorney general Janet Reno argues that the solution to crime starts with the family. The juvenile justice system cannot correct societal damage that produces violent children. It is her belief that a solution to youth violence necessitates a coordinated effort of all federal, state, and local agencies that touch the lives of children. The best institution for caring for children, for nurturing them, for giving them a strong and healthy environment is the family, and all governmental agencies should refocus their efforts to strengthen the family, not replace its functions.

"Danger in the Safety Zone," examines the impact that random violence is having on the sense of safety and security of individual Americans. Former havens of safety and security are no longer safe or secure. No one and no place is immune from violent acts. From the quiet solitude of a local library to a busy hospital emergency room, people are being beaten, shot, and killed. Amitai Etzioni, a major sociologist, observed, "There is a new level of fright, one that is both overdone and realistic at the same time."

"Ganging Up Against Violence" looks at the social factors resulting in the explosion of violent street gangs. Major cities such as Chicago, Los Angeles, and New York City are no longer the only domains of street gangs. They have graduated into the heartland of America. What can be done to control these violent, alienated young men? Beefed-up police departments, specialized training of officers, and new legislation and social action programs have met with limited success and mixed results.

"Honey, I Warped the Kids" explores the interrelationship between violence on television and violence in society. The author argues that a massive amount of research data clearly documents a direct cause-and-effect relationship between violence on television and subsequent violence in society. While eliminating all violence on televi-sion will not eliminate all violence in society, it would make a significant impact. However, any attempt to limit violent television programing would run into issues of free speech, artistic expression and license, and censorship.

"When Cities Run Riot" is an interesting study by a French sociologist. He has studied cities in Western societies and discovered that riots are associated with a significant increase in the societies' levels of social inequality. This inequality, coupled with declines in economic opportunities for minorities, a growing sense of racial injustice, and a loss of faith in the system, makes for a very volatile situation.

The Los Angeles riots forced many politicians, law enforcement personnel, and academic researchers to try and understand what happened and why. The authors of "The Los Angeles Riots: Causes and Cures" believes that there is no simple explanation. Many major cities are experiencing severe declines in revenues that cannot keep up with increasing demands for new or expanded services. These cities will increasingly be unable to meet the needs of a growing proportion of their residents, resulting in a general sense of frustration and loss of faith in the system. The question that the author finds intriguing is why such riots do not erupt more often.

Looking Ahead: Challenge Questions

What effect does being a victim of crime have on the individual?

How can fear of becoming a victim actually make you a victim?

In what major ways is delinquency the product of other social problems?

Do most delinquents grow up to become adult criminals?

Why is violence on the increase in the United States?

What social institutions seem to be the most effective in curbing violence?

What seem to be the major underlying causes of urban riots?

Why have some cities experienced riots while others of comparable size have not?

How would a functionalist's and a conflict theorist's approaches to the problem of crime, delinquency, and violence differ?

Unit 2

The Whole Child Approach to Crime

The juvenile justice system cannot labor by itself to reverse societal damage done to children, our new U.S. attorney general told the Coalition for Juvenile Justice in April. The following excerpts from her address tell what needs to be done to help prevent youth violence.

Janet Reno

Janet Reno is Attorney General of the United States.

When I first took office as prosecutor in Dade County Fla., I wanted to do everything I could to beef up our juvenile division; make it one of the best possible. I started focusing on 14-, 16- and 17-year-olds but quickly learned that we would never have enough money to change all the delinquent children unless we started much earlier.

Then we looked at dropout programs in the middle schools and that was too late. We tried early intervention programs in the elementary schools and that was too late.

During the crack epidemic advent in Dade County in 1985, doctors took me to the neonatal unit at Jackson Memorial Hospital, but they pointed out to me that it was too late even for small babies.

I began to hear about child welfare and see juvenile justice people and the child welfare people. But too often they don't seem to talk to each other and if they do, they don't talk in a coordinated way.

What we have at stake is not just one component, not just an adult prosecutor or people who focus on juvenile justice or people who focus on child welfare or people who focus on pediatric issues. What we have at stake is children and families throughout America.

I became convinced that unless we as a nation focused on children, all my efforts as prosecutor would be for naught. Everything I saw as a prosecutor—crime and drugs, delinquency and dropouts, youth gangs, teen pregnancy, teen suicide and the great increase in the number of homeless children—was the symptom of a deeper problem in society. For the last 30 or 40 years America has forgotten and neglected its children.

Everything I saw as a prosecutor—crime and drugs, delinquency and dropouts, youth gangs, teen pregnancy, teen suicide and the great increase in the number of homeless children—was the symptom of a deeper problem in society. For the last 30 or 40 years America has forgotten and neglected its children.

I would like to challenge us all—myself and the Department of Justice included—to start to work with others, with the Department of Education, the Department of Health and Human Services and all the federal, state and local agencies that touch children.

We've got to forge a bond between Washington and local government. It can't be Washington saying we know best. It's got to be us asking the people in communities what the problems are and what the best solutions are. The best solutions are out in the communities and the neighborhoods of America.

There are bold, innovative programs being tried at every level, and we've got to come together to take the limited resources of government and provide a national agenda for children.

The first step is to focus on the parents. We've got to support parents, understanding that the best institution for caring for children, for nurturing them, for giving them a strong and healthy environment is the family.

A single mother can do a beautiful job if she's given some support, a helping hand, a little push to get her off to a fresh start and to self-sufficiency. But she can't do it if she struggles to get a minimum wage job and finds herself worse off than if she hadn't gone to work in the first place.

Let's make sure that every child in America has appropriate and preventive health care. There is something terribly wrong with a nation that is interested in dollars and cents but hasn't made sure that all of its children are inoculated.

We've got to make sure that education is available to all our children in a manner that reflects the diversity of America, that appreciates our cultural difference.

We have got to make sure that education is relevant to our children. They want to learn.

But as we focus on education, let us understand why so many of our children aren't going to school. Let's not wait

Reprinted with permission from *Spectrum*, Vol. 66, No. 3, Summer 1993, pp. 31-36. © 1993 by The Council of State Governments.

until they are delinquent at 13, when at eight years old they were out of school 15 days in three months and nobody checked on them.

Nothing frustrates me more than to see the police taking a child to school, the school calls home, nobody comes to get the child and the child is sent home on the bus.

Let's forge an alliance among the social service agencies, the police and schools in every neighborhood of America to make sure that when that mother does not come, the child is taken home by community-friendly police officers and social workers to try to force an action to prevent the problem in the future, rather than waiting until that child at 13 holds somebody up with a gun and gets into real trouble.

Let's save him early but let's do it without labeling. More people tell me that if they transfer a kid from one school to another, he gets rid of the label and starts over again. We shouldn't have to transfer him from one school to another.

We've got to realize that kids develop at different rates, that they've got to be given a chance, that they can make a difference, that they want to be somebody and that if we peel that label off and never put it on we can make such a difference.

Let's understand that children want to socialize with their peers, but they like having adults around, too. If they're drifting around the housing development in the afternoon while their mother is working, or drifting around the middle-class neighborhood while both parents are working and nobody is really focusing on them, we don't know what they're going to get into.

Let's look at the after-school time and the night-time hours. If we make an investment, not just recreation and sports but a variety of programs, after school and in the evening, we can make such a difference. Those programs don't cost that much and they save us millions of dollars in terms of crime prevented.

Let's teach children relevant skills. Has it ever puzzled you to watch somebody graduate from high school without a skill that can enable them to earn a living wage? They go on to college and get a degree in English literature. They can tell you what Blake means in *The Tiger*, but can they get a job? No. They might be able to get a job as a paralegal if they take a special course at the junior college.

Let us suggest to all American high schools that students be required not only to have a certain number of years of algebra or geometry or foreign language, but that they've got to graduate with a skill that can enable them to earn a living wage.

When a person graduates from college with a degree in English literature, he can at least be the radiologist or the X-ray technician at the local hospital dealing with the latest new machines.

Let's give them an opportunity to contribute to their community. I don't think I have ever met a youngster who didn't want to be somebody, who didn't want to contribute, who didn't want to make a difference. Let's let each one of them know that in big and small ways they can make a difference.

Let's give them an opportunity to belong, not to a youth gang that tears the fabric of society around them, but to constructive groups that can build the fabric of society around a neighborhood.

Let's give them an opportunity to feel competent. If a youngster doesn't know how to play a sport but is marvelous on the computer, if he brings to school a polished piece of carving, if he writes a poem or puts two lines together, figure out the way to make him feel competent.

Let's give our youth an opportunity to be involved, to contribute through public service programs such as the Civilian Conservation Corps that helped give youth an opportunity during the depression, or the Peace Corps.

When you raise children, you set guidelines, you punish them when they violate the guidelines, but you also, if you're a good parent, give them love and support and encouragement along the way.

Let's understand that we can do something about violence up front. One of the extraordinary lessons that the 1980s taught us is that drug abuse education, prevention and treatment worked far better than jail.

Let's look at violence in the same way. Let's not wait until a 14-year-old puts a gun to a tourist's head. Let's understand the patterns when that child is in elementary school through conflict resolution programs, which are springing up in elementary schools and middle schools throughout this nation.

Let's understand that violence is one of the greatest public health problems in America today. It is not going to be solved just by adult jails or by juvenile detention facilities or by youth in prisons.

It is going to be solved by working together up front to provide a nurturing environment where a child can learn that we don't solve problems by conflict that leads to violence.

Let's start challenging TV. My mother would never let us have a television because she thought it would contribute to mind rot. I think if she were raising children now, she would also say it contributes to violence.

We put labels on our cigarettes because they cause cancer. I didn't think the Federal Communications Commission should prevent us from putting labels or taking steps to ensure TV programs for children don't promote violence.

A large number of kids who come into the juvenile justice system as delinquents maybe will be there a second time. But after the second time they won't be back, no matter what we do.

Let's try to identify them, get them off on the right foot with the limited resources we have and wish them well. But let us understand that there are children in America today who are coming into the juvenile justice system with the fabric of society literally ripped away because we have forgotten children for the last 30 years. We not only have to wish them well and say let's work on this young man, we have to reknit the fabric of society around them. And we can't do it by diverting them into a program when there are obvious gaps.

We cannot take a 13-year-old child of a crack addict who has helped raise his five siblings and been bounced from his grandmother to his uncle, put him in a diversion program and think he will succeed.

Let's get rid of the categories and labels, such as "delinquent" and "abused." Let's understand that there are children crying out for help, and we have to work together in a comprehensive effort to help these children have a chance.

2. CRIME, DELINQUENCY, AND VIOLENCE

Youth violence is the greatest single crime problem in America today. Many people suggest it's drugs, but too many of us have seen a kid walk into a courtroom or detention center, not on drugs but totally cynical and mean. If you get to know that child, there is strength and warmth and love. He's just been deprived for too long.

Let us understand that children are thumbing their nose at police officers. We've got to work together with the police to develop reasonable, fair, humane sanctions for our children that send a message. We've got to see that those fair and humane sanctions are carried out when appropriate.

Most of all, we've got to give our children a chance to live in a nurturing, thriving environment and I analogize it to this: When you raise children, you set guidelines, you punish them when they violate the guidelines, but you also, if you're a good parent, give them love and support and encouragement along the way.

Somehow or another we have to devise that environment, particularly in the case of children who don't have the nurturing support around them. We've got to give them the opportunity to grow, but we have got to spell out boundaries and sanctions that can have an impact.

Most of all, we have got to send a message that we will not, we cannot and we won't lose a generation.

We've got to be bold. We've got to give juvenile court judges more authority than they've had. Their hands have been tied because of excesses over the years.

We've got to look at what we are doing with children in America. There is a tendency to think a child's violent, so put him in the detention center and throw the key away; he's committed two violent crimes, so send him to the adult system. I have done that when there was no other way because the juvenile justice system was bankrupt, but we cannot forget that child in detention, we cannot forget that child in the jail.

Let's look at juvenile detention and correctional facilities. Let's look at the overcrowding, the lack of health care and the lack of substance-abuse treatment. Otherwise, we are never going to change those children's lives and some of the situations of confinement we have them in.

Let's understand what we're doing in terms of confining kids. If we confine them and then dump them back into the community with nothing more, it's not going to make any difference. If we send them off to that wonderful school upstate where they learn how to take care of cows and then bring them back to Liberty City without aftercare and a coherent pattern of treatment, that's going to be a big waste of everybody's dollars.

Let's try to develop programs within our community that understand that in most cases, if a child is properly supervised, he will not have to be detained.

There will be rare exceptions. There is always going to be that terrible person who is the exception, but we can do so much if we understand that he is coming back to the community in pretty short order, anyway, and that we can make a difference by providing a coherent pattern.

Let's understand that we've got to forge new ideas. A year ago, we developed a team in a neighborhood plagued by a terrible youth gang, by drugs and crime. A team made up of a highly respected police officer, a social worker, a public health nurse and a community organizer began working in a housing development.

The police officer and social worker would go to court, tell the judge that a kid, with supervision by the police officer and community, could stay out of detention and asked if they could place him in this special program and monitor him.

Crime was so significantly reduced by August 1992 that the police wanted to replicate this program in other jurisdictions with similar problems.

We can do so much if we form youth teams, new ideas, new concepts.

The single most important message we have to send is that somehow or other in America we are going to have to place children first again.

DANGER IN THE SAFETY ZONE

As violence spreads into small towns, many Americans barricade themselves

JILL SMOLOWE

"PAGING DR. STRONG. PAGing Dr. Strong." When that seemingly routine message squawked over the public address system last Monday evening at the Corona Regional Medical Center, nearly all employees froze. Just weeks earlier, the 148-bed hospital in Southern California had established new security precautions. Staff members now knew the potentially deadly meaning of those six words: someone with a gun was in the building.

The terrifying drama that unfolded over the next 10 minutes has become all too familiar not only in America's hospitals but in virtually all public places once regarded as safe havens. At 6:20 p.m., Sophia White, 31, entered the facility and calmly made her way to the third-floor nursery where six infants lay. Drawing a .38-cal. revolver, White wildly fired six shots at nurse Elizabeth Staten, striking her in the abdomen and hand. The wounded Staten fled down a stairwell to the first-floor emergency room, with White in pursuit. "She caught up with Liz at the chart desk and pistol-whipped her. Then she shot her," says veteran nurse Joan Black, 62, who was in the triage area at the time. "She said [to Liz], 'You've destroyed my life. You've taken my husband and my kids. Prepare to die. Open your mouth.'"

As White took aim yet again, Black crossed the room and wrapped her right arm around White. "I figured if she could feel my body, maybe she wouldn't kill me," Black recalls. Tightening the hug, Black placed her left hand over the gun and began a soothing patter. "You're in pain. I understand, and we can work it out." After five, maybe 10 minutes, White told Black she would give her the gun. Only after police handcuffed White did Black break down in sobs. "I don't know why the hell I did what I did," Black says. "It was just instinct." Instinct, that is, born of experience. "I've taken handguns out of the purses of little old ladies, and I've had people take a swing at me," she says. While this incident had no tragic ending—Staten survived the assault and is in stable condition—Black is wary of what may happen the next time. "You can't deny rapid access to an emergency room," she notes. "But nurses are terrified."

So, it appears, are most Americans. Bingeing on a diet of local news stories that graphically depict crime invading once safe ports—schools, restaurants, courtrooms, homes, libraries—Americans are rapidly coming to regard the summer of '93 as a season in hell. Indeed, a spate of events in the past two weeks seemed to argue that no one and no place was immune, not a respected schoolteacher living in a small town in Texas, not even the father of a megastar athlete driving a car down the highway.

The epidemic of shooting sprees in malls, McDonald's restaurants and movie theaters has fostered the perception that almost no place is safe anymore. Fear has led to a boom in the security industry and the transformation of homes and public places into fortresses. "People are worried more. They're worried sick," says Amitai Etzioni, a sociologist at George Washington University. "There is a new level of fright, one that is both overdone and realistic at the same time."

Newly released FBI statistics show two different trends in crime rates: occurrences of violence in cities and towns with populations under 1 million are nudging upward, while such incidents are declining in the densest urban enclaves. In a TIME/CNN poll conducted last week, 30% of those surveyed think suburban crime is at least as serious as urban crime—double the number who said that was true five years ago.

The broadening of targets to include suburban and rural preserves—and the savageness of the crimes that fill the news—has left far more Americans feeling vulnerable. "The fear is getting worse because there is no pattern to the crime," says James Marquart, a criminal-justice professor at Sam Houston State University. "It is random, spontaneous and episodic." These days, everyone has a story to tell. Says Pam Lychner, 34, who six weeks ago founded a Houston-based citizens' action group called Justice for All: "People used to know one crime victim. Now they know five—or they are one themselves." According to the National Victim Center, victim-advocacy groups have multiplied nearly eightfold since 1985.

The past two weeks, in fact, provided a frightening new list of victims who found themselves suddenly vulnerable in places they thought they would be safe—a burger joint, a mall, the courtroom, a car. Here is a brief catalog of unexpected mortality:

A CAUSE CELEBRE No one knew who "John Doe" was when they fished him from South Carolina's Gum Swamp Creek

From *Time*, August 23, 1993, pp. 29-33. © 1993 by The Time Inc. Magazine Company. All rights reserved. Reprinted by permission.

A RHYTHM TO THE MADNESS

Is there a link between crime and population growth? And how does social change aggravate the current crime surge? James Q. Wilson, professor of management and public policy at UCLA *and author of* Thinking About Crime *and* The Moral Sense, *gave his views last week in an interview with* TIME *assistant editor Susanne Washburn. Excerpts:*

Any historian knows that crime waves, in fact, are cyclical. Earlier ones occurred in the 1830s, the late 1860s and the 1920s. The question is, What causes the cycles, and what affects their timing? Crime was abnormally low in the 1940s and 1950s and began to rise around 1963 and peaked in the late 1970s. The increase in crime from 1963 to 1980 was enormous—and it occurred in a period of general prosperity. Part of the explanation is that the population got younger, because of the baby boom—and younger men are more likely to commit crime than older ones.

Then in the early 1980s, almost all forms of crime began to decline for a while. The baby boom got old, so the baby boomers were no longer in the crime-prone years. We saw this in declining public-school enrollments. Now, however, if you look at what's happening in elementary schools, enrollments are going up because the children of baby boomers are starting to move through the cycle. My guess—and the guess of many other criminologists—is that by the end of this decade we will see an increase in the general crime rate regardless of what the government does.

Obviously, we want to do everything possible to moderate its severity. And public policy ought to be directed toward that end. The public expects it. I think politicians will face up to it. But we simply have to realize we are in an era when our ability to moderate the severity of crimes is substantially reduced from what it once was. We are much more reliant on public policy, which is a crude and not very effective

instrument. And we are much less dependent on informal social controls, which, when they work, are the most powerful controls.

The most significant thing in the last half-century has been the dramatic expansion in personal freedom and personal mobility, individual rights, the reorienting of culture around individuals. We obviously value that. But like all human gains, it has been purchased at a price. Most people faced with greater freedom from family, law, village, clan, have used it for good purposes—artistic expression, economic entrepreneurship, self-expression—but a small fraction of people have used it for bad purposes. So just as we have had an artistic and economic explosion, we have had a crime explosion. I think the two are indissolubly entwined. When that prosperity puts cars, drugs and guns into the hands of even relatively poor 18-year-olds, young people can do a great deal more damage today than they could in the 1940s or 1950s.

on Aug. 3. He had a bullet wound in his chest and no identification. Only two days later, after a car was found about 60 miles away, did clues and apprehensions start coming together. Last Friday, Chicago Bulls fans and friends went numb when they learned that John Doe was James Jordan, 57, the father of megastar Michael Jordan.

The senior Jordan disappeared after attending the North Carolina funeral of a friend on July 22. At the time, his family thought little of it: the elder Jordan often took off for days at a time without warning. Alarms began to sound on Aug. 5 when sheriffs in Cumberland County, North Carolina, found his car on a wooded back road. The red 1993 Lexus had been stripped of its tires, stereo system and vanity license plates. Though the windows were smashed, there was no evidence of foul play: no blood, no bullet holes, no ransom note. Then Cumberland County authorities learned of the John Doe corpse in a neighboring state.

Dental records confirmed the Jordan family's dread. Last week the FBI opened a kidnapping investigation, and a 16-year-old boy was arrested by sheriffs' deputies in connection with the stripped car. But as yet, the murder remains a mystery. What was the motive? Is there a link to the gambling allegations that have dogged the su-

perstar? James Jordan was an infectiously affectionate man, known as Pops not only to his famous son but to friends as well. The most chilling possibility is that his death was just the result of another carjacking—and that this could have been anyone's dad.

MC DONALD'S MASSACRE Kirk Hauptmann, 18, had just bitten into his cheeseburger last Tuesday in the no-smoking section of the McDonald's in Kenosha, Wisconsin, when he noticed Dion Terres, 25. "I looked up and said, 'Oh, he's got a gun,' but I thought it wasn't real," says Hauptmann. Moments later, Terres yelled, "Everybody out of here!" and began shooting a .44-cal. Magnum pistol. As 10 panicked patrons dove for the exit door, Terres unloaded four shots. Two middle-aged customers were killed, and Hauptmann was shot in the right forearm. Terres turned the fourth bullet on himself, splattering his brain on the walls and ceiling.

Later police found a 40-minute tape in Terres' apartment. The rambling message pointed to several possible motives. Terres spoke of being under psychiatric care a few years ago and admitted to fantasizing about killing people for more than a year. The tape made reference to several notorious mass murderers, including Jeffrey Dahmer and Ted Bundy. It also referred to a 1984 bloodbath at a McDonald's in San

Ysidro, California—and police speculated that Terres' rampage might have been a copycat massacre. On tape, Terres stated, "Society screwed me, and now it's payback time." He may have been referring to the company that he claimed fired him in March, or to the 16-year-old girlfriend who dumped him in July.

As police continue to gather details about the disturbed and reclusive young man, those who survived Terres' perverse revenge are trying to resume their lives. Hauptmann returned to the same McDonald's the next day. "I had to go back," says the college sophomore. "My stomach was in knots, but it's still a public place."

MURDER IN THE MALL Paula Clouse, 43, and her 15-year-old son were among the dozen patrons who turned up last Tuesday at the Metro North Mall in Kansas City, Missouri, for the 5:20 p.m. showing of *Robin Hood: Men in Tights*. About 25 minutes after the theater darkened, the teenager allegedly took out a handgun and pumped four bullets into his mother's head. The boy then left the theater and strolled into the mall, followed by stunned onlookers. An arrest swiftly followed, but police have yet to come up with a motive.

"Apparently the parents were going through a divorce, and it was a very bitter divorce," says Captain Vince McInerney. "There were arguments over custody. The

A CONVICT'S VIEW: "PEOPLE DON'T WANT SOLUTIONS"

Wilbert Rideau, 51, has been imprisoned since 1962 at the Louisiana State Penitentiary at Angola, serving a life sentence for murder. During that time, Rideau has gained renown as a journalist, author and advocate of prison reform. In a conversation with TIME *Houston bureau chief Richard Woodbury, Rideau gave a scathing critique of the prison system:*

Q. *What do you think of Clinton's crime package?*

A. Public fear is out of control, so he has to put more police on the streets. Boot camps can help, but often they're just another feel-good device for punishing criminals. I'd like to see more efforts aimed at really improving people. Crime is a social problem, and education is the only real deterrent. Look at all of us in prison: we were all truants and dropouts, a failure of the education system. Look at your truancy problem, and you're looking at your future prisoners. Put the money there.

Q. *How have the increases in violent crime over the years contributed to a tougher mood in the country?*

A. It's a self-fulfilling hypothesis. If you scare people enough and make them believe the world is crumbling around them, at some point they'll start reacting. The news media have helped set the tone of rabid crime, and the politicians just pick up the theme and go with the flow.

Q. *What has been the fallout on prisons of this get-tough mood? Is their basic role changing?*

A. Since the 1970s, they have increasingly become just giant warehouses where you pack convicts to suffer. Look around me in this place. It's a graveyard, a human wasteland of old men—most of them just sitting around waiting to die. Of the 5,200 inmates here, 3,800 are lifers or serving sentences so long they will never get out. America has embraced vengeance as its criminal-justice philosophy. People don't want solutions to crime, they only want to feel good. That is what politicians are doing, they're making people feel secure. They offer them a platter of vindictiveness.

Q. *You don't feel that the tougher sentences are in any way a restraining influence on the criminal mind?*

A. Not at all. The length of a prison sentence has nothing to do with deterring crime. That theory is a crock. I mean, I've lived with criminals for 31 years. I know these guys, and myself. That's not the way it works. When the average guy commits a crime, he's either at the point where he doesn't care what happens to him, or more likely he feels he is going to get away with it. Punishment never factors into the equation. He just goes ahead because he feels he won't get caught.

Q. *Then what will stop violent crime?*

A. Only one thing: the certainty of apprehension. If a criminal fears that he's going to get caught, he will think twice before he robs or steals. And it won't matter whether the sentence is one year or 100 years.

Q. *What would have deterred you?*

A. I've thought a lot about that. I know that if I hadn't been able to walk into a pawnshop and buy a handgun as easily as I did, I wouldn't have robbed that bank. That applies to just about everybody in this prison who ever held up anybody. Nobody robs a place with a knife or a can of Mace. I was 19, an eighth-grade dropout. If I'd known that things weren't as helpless as I thought they were, that would have stopped me. I wouldn't have felt so frustrated.

Q. *How would you go about paying for education programs you propose, given the cash-starved nature of most government budgets?*

A. By shortening sentences. Sure, that's a hot button, but the public must come to realize that it can't enjoy its full measure of vengeance and expect at the same time to reduce bulging inmate populations. The citizenry must determine the minimum amount of punishment that it is willing to settle for, and then channel the millions it has saved into schools and preventive programs.

Q. *Given the level of public outrage, how would you deal with those who do commit serious crimes?*

A. You don't go handing out 99-year, no-parole sentences all over the place. That's ridiculous. States can't afford to keep locking people away for eternity. It takes $1 million to house a lifer. Look at these convicts around me. They're old men at 50, like me, or even 40. The fire's been burned out of them years ago. Most of them you'll never have to worry about again.

Q. *Isn't the notion of shorter sentences an incendiary idea in today's political climate?*

A. Probably. But the public has been sold a bill of goods on prisons, just like it's been given a distorted, negative picture of recidivism and parole. Most of the guys in this prison will never return to Angola, I can tell you that from being here. And parole can and does work, and I would expand it. I'd much rather pay for parole officers to supervise nondangerous people than build $100,000 cells.

---

boy was living with his dad, and a younger sister lived with the mom and the mother's parents." The gun reportedly belonged to the boy's father; police have not determined whether the murder was premeditated or the father was involved. "Disputes used to be settled with a shouting match or a punch in the nose," sighs McInerney.

AN ASSAULT IN SMALL TOWN, U.S.A. Tomball, Texas (pop. 6,370), is the safe sort of town where many residents leave their front doors unlocked at night. The quiet middle-class community may rethink such nocturnal habits after the strangling death last Tuesday of 82-year-old Mildred Stallones, a retired schoolteacher. A respected member of the community who was known for her generosity to children, Stallones was found in her old frame house. Police are still trying to determine if rape was involved. Beyond a forced entry into the house, police have little to offer: no motive, no suspects, no signs of theft.

Until now Tomball has suffered only the occasional property crime. "This is a wake-up call for anyone in Tomball who may have got complacent about living here," says police chief Paul Michna. "Nowhere is safe." Since Stallones was found, some of the town's elderly citizens have asked to move in with their children. Stallones' former daughter-in-law, Kerri Harrington, has barely slept since learning of the murder. "Before, I felt safe," she says. "Now I know this horrible crime could happen anywhere to anyone."

COURTROOM CARNAGE Federal judges have been so jittery about courthouse crime that since the early '80s, most federal courts have been outfitted with airport-style X-ray machines, designed to detect concealed weapons. Even so, the bloodletting continues. On Aug. 6, a man scheduled to be sentenced for drug dealing stormed the federal courthouse in Topeka, Kansas, firing two guns and lobbing pipe bombs. Before Jack McKnight, 37, killed himself by detonating explosives strapped to his body, he killed a security guard and wounded five people. "There's now a tacit assumption that people can vent their frustrations almost anywhere," says Dr. Allwyn Levine, a New Jersey psychiatrist. "We've become a much more lawless society."

While experts agree that the summer's rash of too-close-to-home crimes has deepened Americans' anxiety, they disagree on the triggers that have touched off the violence. Some believe the crime waves are cyclical (*see box*). Many fault Hollywood, which rushes sordid re-creations to TV and cinema screens before the corpses are even cold. "We have created a culture that increasingly accepts and glamourizes violence," says Dewey Cornell, a clinical psychologist at the University of Virginia. "I don't care what the network executives say. It does desensitize you." Others point accusingly at the media. "Every crackpot out there knows that if he can take an automatic weapon into a fast-food restaurant, the more people he can shoot, the more attention he's going to get," says Houston homicide sergeant Billy Belk. "So it encourages these weirdos."

Many experts dig deeper—but the roots they pull up are a messy tangle of societal ills. "We have a whole generation of kids suffering from neglect," says sociologist Stephen Klineberg of Houston's Rice University. "There is no one at home when they return from school, and this neglect in socialization results in increased violence." Others cite neglect's twin evil, child abuse, or that distant relative, school truancy. Liberals decry poverty; conservatives fault the decline of family values.

As the experts argue, many Americans are taking safety matters into their own hands. "When people are besieged with new reports of crime every day, the perception grows that, by golly, maybe the cops are ineffective," says crime expert Marquart. "It reinforces the perception of the criminal-justice system not working,

and the next thing you know, people are mobilizing to protect themselves."

IN THE PAST FIVE YEARS SECURITY PRE-cautions have increased at hospitals, schools, shopping malls, offices, courthouses and even libraries. And for good reason. Within the past year, librarians have been attacked and killed behind their desk in Sacramento, California, and Buckeye, Arizona. Incidents of violence against health-care workers have increased 400% since 1982, says Ira A. Lipman, chairman of the National Council on Crime and Delinquency and head of Guardsmark, Inc., the nation's fifth largest security company. "Companies are very concerned because one incident in a shopping mall can destroy business."

Across the U.S., companies that offer security devices report booming sales in both low-tech paraphernalia (Mace, burglar bars, door alarms) and high-tech apparatus (video doorbells, motion-detection devices). Meanwhile, existing forms of high technology are being pressed into the services of security. Cellular phones are popular not only with businessmen but also with people who fear being stranded because of auto trouble or attacked while on the road. As their cost goes down, many are buying them for emergency use only.

Last year an estimated 16% of all U.S. homes installed electronic systems. Video surveillance is becoming more popular. Says Steve Gribbon of the Alert Centre Protective Services, a Colorado-based security company with 200,000 customers in 48 states: "Five or six years ago, only estates in the $700,000-to-$1 million range used them. We're now seeing them in $200,000 homes." Says Anthony Potter, a private security consultant in Atlanta: "In the past, people thought home-security systems were too expensive—that it was only for people with diamond collections." But, he adds, "they are seeing that it is not that expensive. It cuts their homeowner's insurance." Many are also thinking of gun ownership. Says Potter: "I know a lot of people who five years ago would not have thought about asking me about guns. Now they're asking me what kind they should buy."

"Many people who are most fearful of crime have the least reason to be fearful," says James Q. Wilson, a social scientist at

UCLA. "If you map the fear of crime and map the actual crime range, you note that they don't overlap." But, he says, "that doesn't mean people are irrational. It simply means that everyone is aware that we live in a far more dangerous society and, in fact, the self-protective measures they take do tend to protect them. They are acting correctly, rationally."

From coast to coast, people are sealing off their homes and neighborhoods with iron gates, razor-ribbon wire and iron spikes. The home of Billy Davis in Pico Rivera, southeast of Los Angeles, offers a glimpse of the paranoia that is fast turning homes into fortresses. His two-story frame house is outfitted with motion-sensitive floodlights, video monitors, infrared alarms and a spiked fence topped with razor wire. A metal cage surrounds the patio. Bars adorn every window. A Doberman pinscher guards the yard. And a security guard patrols the driveway. "The wrong people are behind bars," says Anne Seymour of the National Victim Center. "People are putting themselves behind bars because we as a nation have failed to put the right people behind bars."

While such precautions make some people feel safer, others worry about the "Balkanization" of America. "All of this leads to a breakdown of any sense of community," says Camilo José Vergara, who has been photographing the gradual fortressing of urban areas over the past 20 years. "Each family tries to make a living within its own fort and is unconcerned about what goes on outside." Moreover, homegrown solutions often breed new problems. When neighborhoods barricade themselves in, they often cut the access of police, ambulance drivers and fire fighters. When public institutions, like courts and libraries, erect barriers, the concept of access in a democratic society is threatened.

In the end, gates, gadgetry and gizmos may not be enough. "I don't think you can build gates high enough to eradicate the fear," says Los Angeles city councilwoman Rita Walters. "You've got to eliminate the source of the fear." Until then, the public arena can suddenly become a coliseum of blood sport. No place is sacred. All sanctuaries are suspect. —*Reported by Julie Johnson/ Washington, Elaine Lafferty/Los Angeles, Ken Myers/Cleveland, Lisa Towle/Raleigh and Richard Woodbury/Houston*

Ganging Up Against Violence

Criminal street-gangs have spread across the country, creating fear and challenging policymakers to prevent or suppress their activities.

Donna Hunzeker

Donna Hunzeker is NCSL's criminal justice expert.

While fires smoldered in riot-torn sections of Los Angeles last year, observers blamed police incompetence, pervasive poverty and resonating racism. Also blamed were juvenile gangs, whose members reportedly were responsible for much of the violence and who have become a feared personification of the urban underclass in this country.

The riots in South-Central L.A. subsided, but gang violence goes on. Incidents like the shooting death late last year of a gang rival outside the church memorial service for another youth illustrate how grim life and death can be in gang communities. While Los Angeles continues to have the most disturbing amount of gang crime, cities across the country now report the existence of gangs and accompanying violence.

The number of juvenile gang members and how much crime they commit are subject to debate. Different definitions of gangs and gang crime are used in tracking and research. Record-keeping systems also vary, as does the way the data are interpreted.

Gang experts say that cities and especially police departments go through distinct stages of acknowledgment of and response to gang problems. The first recognizable stage often is "de-nial"—an unwillingness to tarnish the city's image and cause public fear by acknowledging their existence. On the other hand, where serious crimes have spurred reaction, officials may put many youths and youth crimes under a blanket definition of gangs, comparatively overstating the problem.

A national survey of law enforcement jurisdictions tallied nearly a quarter of a million gang members and more than 46,000 "gang incidents" in 1991. Of the 72 largest cities reporting, almost 20,000 violent offenses were attributed to gangs, including 974 homicides. The study, conducted by West Virginia University for the U.S. Department of Justice, said gang members predominantly are black and Hispanic. The numbers of white and Asian-American gang mem-

Gang association and crime become attractive options where legitimate economic opportunities are lacking and social order is weak.

bers were reported as far fewer, but on the rise.

A growing body of knowledge about gangs, including why they exist, who belongs to them, how they operate and how to solve their associated problems, is like the numbers, subject to varying interpretations. There is considerable consensus that gangs are tied to poverty and related social problems. The availability of drugs and especially weapons seems to increase gang members' propensity for crime and violence.

Symptom of Poverty

Gang members overwhelmingly belong to an urban minority underclass. Research suggests that gangs and gang crime increase as economic opportunities decline. Ronald Huff, who directs the Criminal Justice Research Center at Ohio State University, has documented the fact that as manufacturing jobs were lost and unemployment rose in "rust belt" cities, low-income areas became fertile ground for juvenile gangs.

"An economically and socially marginal youth, who has dropped out of school or been expelled and is without job skills, is in deep trouble in Cleveland or Columbus," Huff reports. He and other researchers have noted that where neighborhoods, schools and families have decayed or dispersed, youths look for other means of esteem-building and social idenfity. Gang association and crime become attractive options where legitimate economic opportunities are lacking and social order is weak. Typical gang activities mirror the need for economic and social identity.

"Gang traditions have been crafted to satisfy precisely those needs which ache most powerfully in the souls of outcast adolescent males," writes Los Angeles District Attorney Ira Reiner in a 1992 report on gang crime and violence. Such traditions include

From *State Legislatures*, May 1993, pp. 28-31. © 1993 by The National Conference of State Legislatures. Reprinted by permission.

passing a tough physical initiation, strong group identity and camaraderie, and a readiness to defend honor and turf.

Contrary to popular image, most gangs are rather loose associations of crime-prone young men forming a "surrogate family," according to Huff. They may wear colors and other insignia of Crips or Bloods, but they tend to be small, autonomous cliques. In Los Angeles, Reiner says, cliques average around four or five members—"roughly a car-load."

Gang members spend a good deal of their time engaging in exaggerated versions of typical adolescent behavior, according to Huff, who is interviewing gang members in six cities for the National Institute of Justice. Rebelling against authority, listening to loud music, hanging out and drinking alcohol or getting high are typical gang activities. Being a good, aggressive fighter also is an important reputation-builder for young gang members. "Fighting and partying" are the main occupations of gang members, says the Los Angeles district attorney.

It is no misconception, however, that gang members commit many and often serious crimes. Experts distinguish members' drift into serious crime according to several gang types—distinctions that have policy implications as well.

"Predatory gangs," as identified by researcher Huff, commit the kinds of violent street crimes often associated with gangs—muggings, carjacking, rape and murder. These gang members often use drugs like crack cocaine, which contribute to violent, assaultive behavior. They also are likely to sell drugs, which pay for the sophisticated weapons they carry. Gang members often are readily available street dealers for organized cocaine cartels. Huff notes that lines start to blur between gangs and organized crime depending on the extent of involvement in organized drug trade. For some gang members, he says, "Color no longer is red or blue, but green."

Susan Pennell, who is directing a study of drug-involved gang members for the San Diego Association of Governments, says that while about three-quarters of gang members there sell drugs as a regular means of making money, only about one-third have sold drugs outside the county, a sign of higher-level involvement in the drug trade. It is not uncommon for older gang members to graduate into such drug-related criminality, researchers say. This trend appears to be accelerated by a weak economy and scarcity of legitimate jobs for young minority men.

"Instrumental gangs" tend to commit property crimes for money. Many members use drugs, including crack, and some sell drugs but not as an organized gang activity.

Finally, what Huff calls "hedonistic gangs" focus primarily on hanging out and getting high. Members commit minor property crimes, but not necessarily as a gang activity. Such gangs are not routinely involved in violent crime.

Almost any gang association carries with it the need for excitement and protection; therefore the propensity for violence is ever-present, says Pennell. "It should not surprise us that a group of young men who have drugs and guns and nothing to do would eventually wander into violent crime," she says.

Gang-related homicides usually are not random shootings or drug disputes, but rather the escalation of fights over turf, status or revenge, according to Reiner's analysis for the Los Angeles County district attorney's office. Drive-by shootings typically are committed by small sets of gang members, not entire gangs, and often are part of a chain reaction of vengeful events. Reiner says that one long-time gang battle among Crip factions in Los Angeles, to which he attributes two dozen deaths, started over a junior-high romance.

Pennell blames this kind of "ad lib violent crime" on the feeling of hopelessness that comes out of poverty paired with the availability of weapons. Interviews with some 200 gang members in San Diego reveal the same low regard for human life that other gang research has spoken of, Pennell says. "Many of these kids don't think they'll be alive at 25," she says. "And they accept that."

Gang Policy and Legislation

State legislation aimed at the gang problem has increased in recent years as gangs show up in cities and towns far from urban centers like Los Angeles and Chicago. Experts say that policy to deal with gangs needs to be centralized and comprehensive, pulling together all the systems involved and balancing the need for enforcement with prevention.

"A criminal justice response is very important, but by itself is not very effective," says Winifred Reed, who manages gang research projects for the National Institute of Justice. Prevention, intervention and suppression all are necessary for controlling the impact of gangs, Reed says.

Huff recommends a two-pronged approach: 1) aggressive enforcement against hard-core "predatory" gang members; and 2) prevention directed at marginal and would-be gang members. Examples of both approaches are found in state laws.

Enforcement legislation in states like California, Nevada, Florida, Georgia and Illinois enhances penalties for crimes carried out in participation with or at the direction of gangs. The California "Street Terrorism Enforcement Act" of 1988, which other states have since emulated in name and spirit, makes it illegal to participate in a criminal street gang. It provides for an extra two or three years' imprisonment at the court's discretion for felonies committed in association with a gang. If the felony is punishable by life imprisonment, a minimum of 15 years must be served before parole is granted. Misdemeanor offenses committed in association with gangs also carry mandatory jail time.

Florida's Street Terrorism Enforcement and Prevention Act also upgrades felonies or violent misdemeanors committed as street gang activity. Illinois' "gang transfer" law permits adult criminal prosecution of forcible felonies that are gang-related.

Some state laws, including a 1992 Oklahoma enactment, criminalize gang recruitment. Other state laws seek to address certain gang activities or equipment—most notably weapons. California law provides for confiscation of firearms or dangerous weapons that are owned or possessed by members of criminal street gangs for the purpose of committing crimes. Virginia state law allows localities to prohibit juveniles from possessing loaded firearms except in certain situations. Virginia also suspends driving privileges of delinquent youth found by a court to have unlawfully used or possessed a handgun.

Gang fondness for graffiti is addressed mostly at the local level. Some cities have adopted measures to restrict juvenile access to spray paint, and require perpetrators to restore or replace vandalized property. Huff says such graffiti laws give young gang members the right no-tolerance mes-

Coming to a Community Near You

Gangs are "coming to a community near you," warns an expert who says gangs are moving into communities less prepared to deal with them. This prediction, and recommendations for fighting gangs on all fronts, are compiled in *The Gang Intervention Handbook*, edited by Ronald Huff and Arnold P. Goldstein. The handbook offers these and other intervention and prevention strategies:

What Schools Can Do

Schools should begin with a "gang assessment" that looks at factors like graffiti, drugs, weapons and racial conflict to determine how much of a gang problem they have. From that starting point, other school tactics include:
• Develop a gang prevention and gang awareness curriculum, and implement it in the early grades. Focus on nonviolence, conflict resolution and peer mediation. Present the consequences of gang involvement. In Orange County, Calif., for example, anti-drug and anti-gang information has been added to regular course work for third, fifth and seventh grades.
• If gang problems are serious, consider dress codes that forbid gang apparel or paraphernalia. This will protect students who aren't in gangs as well as help curb flagrant gang association. Such a policy has to be carefully crafted to strike the right balance between students' right to free expression and the school's responsibility to provide a safe environment.
• Graffiti tells a story of what is happening with gangs. School administrators should read and understand graffiti, and remove it.

What Communities Can Do

Researchers believe that family factors strongly influence aggressive behavior that can lead to gang involvement. Social service agencies and community groups can:
• Provide services and support to address family stress, including unemployment, marital conflict, divorce and single parenting. Substance abuse problems require specialized, direct intervention. Family intervention also can include parenting classes. In Hawaii, police and schools jointly offer parent classes about gang activity and for diversion.

Many experts believe that when young people have "nothing to do" they are more apt to become involved in a gang. Examples of programs that help fill the void include:
• YouthBuild in San Francisco and elsewhere has at-risk youth doing neighborhood construction and renovation. Funded by state, local and private money, young people learn job skills and also receive counseling and job-readiness training. Involved adults act as mentors.
• GANG PEACE/FIRST Inc. in Boston uses mostly volunteers to provide youths with day and evening tutoring, job assistance, counseling and recreational activities.
• Project Match in Chicago, supported in part by state social services, uses one-on-one case management to teach self-sufficiency to kids who have seen little except joblessness and welfare.

What Police, Prosecution Can Do

Huff recommends that police departments establish central gang-control units to improve intelligence-sharing and reduce turf problems. A database on gangs and gang members, such as those in Los Angeles and Broward County, Fla., also aids enforcement efforts. In states with legislation defining criminal street gangs and setting penalties for gang-associated crime, a database helps in prosecution by tracking and documenting gang involvement.

An Operation Safe Streets program of the Los Angeles County sheriff's department helped tie together investigation and prosecution of gang crime. Gang prosecutions are among the toughest, often combining elements of career criminals, crimes committed by groups and fearful witnesses. Specific policy on gangs and specialized gang prosecution—especially "vertical prosecution" where the same prosecutor or team handles a case from start to finish—can improve success with these cases.

Effective gang prevention and suppression requires collective action, experts say. It's important to recognize that gangs are not just a law enforcement problem and for schools, social services, police, prosecutors, parents and others to plan and respond as a team.

The Gang Intervention Handbook is published by Research Press, Champaign, Ill., (217) 352-3273.

sage and may keep them from taking gang activity to the next, more dangerous level. Many state vandalism statutes also cover graffiti.

Other gang-related laws include a Colorado measure that defines the notion of "drive-by crime." At least five states passed laws in 1992 having to do with throwing objects from roadways, bridges or overpasses, said to be a gang activity or ritual.

Increasingly, states also are trying to prevent gangs. In addition to its enforcement act, Florida created gang prevention councils in 1990 whereby judicial circuits develop plans to reduce gang activity and other juvenile arrests. In 1991, Washington enacted a "Youth Gang Reduction Act" to establish gang prevention and intervention programs for elementary and secondary age youth through cooperation of

schools, local groups and government.

A 1991 Hawaii law has what some experts say is the best balance of juvenile gang enforcement and prevention. The Hawaii act allocated $3.2 million to coordinate law enforcement, public awareness, community and school-based intervention and prevention, and gang research and evaluation. A statewide law enforcement task force on youth gangs, an information system and clearinghouse on gangs, prosecution efforts that focus on gang members on the career-criminal track, school-based education and intervention programs, and parks and recreation programs have been well worth the money, according to the act's sponsor, Representative Annelle Amaral of Honolulu.

Hard-core criminal gang members are being targeted for prosecution while education and prevention with younger kids has interrupted the growth of gangs in Hawaii, Amaral says. Continued funding of $1.8 million was approved in 1992 as part of the executive budget.

An evaluation of Hawaii's gang act for the Legislature in 1992 said that the most notable success has been better communication among law enforcement personnel in various counties and collaboration of law enforcement with social service and youth agency workers. Gang prevention curricula and truancy prevention programs show promising effects on youths' attitudes and behavior, and better youth service and recreation programs have increased participation by typically hard-to-recruit, at-risk youngsters, according to the report. The Gang Reporting Evaluation and Tracking (GREAT) computerized system, said by the evaluation team to be too complex and cumbersome, is being redesigned to make it more practical and usable.

California also followed up on its street terrorism act with a law that uses asset forfeiture funds for a Gang Risk Intervention Pilot (GRIP) program. The program includes individual and family counseling, cultural and recreational programs, job training and other activities to get at-risk kids interested in something other than drugs and gangs, according to Assemblyman Richard Katz, who represents the San Fernando Valley.

Future funding for 14 GRIP programs operating in L.A. County is uncertain,

It should not surprise us that a group of young men who have drugs and guns and nothing to do would eventually wander into violent crime.

however. A governor's veto removed GRIP funds from last year's budget. The current asset forfeiture law used to fund the programs is due to sunset in 1994 with a number of new bids for forfeiture funds likely to be heard, according to California Assembly staff.

Katz has introduced a bill this year to keep forfeiture funds flowing into the types of gang-prevention programs the pilot project showed to be most effective. Efforts to rebuild state economies and revitalize cities cannot overlook crime prevention, Katz says. There were more than 800 gang-related homicides in Los Angeles last year, a city heavily affected by the loss of 800,000 jobs in the state since 1990.

States are finding other specialized means for funding gang prevention efforts. A "gangbuster bill" proposed by the Wisconsin Senate's assistant majority leader, Chuck Chvala, would create surcharges on weapon violations. These would fund police and gang prevention programs, including jobs programs that offer youths an incentive to get out of gangs, Chvala says. The Wisconsin bill also creates new penalties for drive-by shootings and gang recruitment, and enhanced penalties for gang-related crime.

Cities like Milwaukee, Madison and Green Bay are reporting gang problems that were unheard of 10 years ago, Chvala says. Loss of manufacturing jobs in the area has diminished economic opportunity for many of the state's young

people. "We cannot eliminate gangs unless we address the reasons they exist—hopelessness, joblessness and economic despair," he explains.

Huff suggests that states can get the most benefit for their prevention dollars by pinpointing areas with the most at-risk youth. He says a zip-code analysis identifying areas with the most gang-associated crime, public assistance, juvenile incarceration and mental health commitments will help states begin to prevent gang crime involvement.

The spread of gang crime to comparatively affluent suburbs and towns is a disturbing trend. Pennell says such "acculturation" occurs when gang association is made appealing even to youths who have average or better economic opportunity.

"Gangs are chic," Huff says. "Madison Avenue is hip to this," he explains, noting that billboards and other advertisements for cigarettes and alcohol have sprung up depicting gang gear or insignia. Los Angeles District Attorney Reiner agrees that gang music, language and clothing have made a big impact on popular youth culture, even though the stark reality of gang life is anything but glamorous.

Violent TV images help to anesthetize most people to crime and violence that increasingly has a youthful face. The FBI reported recently that the violent crime rate for juveniles reached a new high in 1990 with increases evident in all geographic regions of the country. The arrest rate of black youths for violent crimes was especially alarming. Certainly, the prevalence of juvenile gangs is not a phenomenon separate from crime and violence in general.

Gangs basically are made up of dangerous, alienated young men, who, individually, are likely to commit crimes. "After all," Reiner says, "if gangs disappeared tomorrow, there is no reason to believe their members would join the Boy Scouts."

Honey, I warped the kids

Hollywood still doth protest too much, while the stats on video violence pile up.

Carl M. Cannon

Carl M. Cannon is the White House correspondent for the Baltimore Sun.

Tim Robbins and Susan Sarandon implore the nation to treat Haitians with AIDS more humanely. Robert Redford works for the environment. Harry Belafonte marches against the death penalty.

Actors and producers seem to be constantly speaking out for noble causes far removed from their lives. They seem even more vocal and visible now that there is a Democrat in the White House. But in the one area over which they have control—the excessive violence in the entertainment industry—Hollywood activists remain silent.

This summer, Washington was abuzz with talk about the movie *Dave*, in which Kevin Kline stars as the acting president. But every time I saw an ad featuring Kline, the movie I couldn't get out of my head was *Grand Canyon*. There are two scenes in it that explain much of what has gone wrong in America.

Kline's character has a friend, played by Steve Martin, who is a producer of the B-grade, violent movies that Hollywood euphemistically calls "action" films. But after an armed robber shoots Martin's character in the leg, he has an epiphany.

"I can't make those movies any more," he decides. "I can't make another piece of art that glorifies violence and bloodshed and brutality.... No more exploding bodies, exploding buildings, exploding anything. I'm going to make the world a better place."

A month or two later, Kline calls on Martin at his Hollywood studio to congratulate him on the "new direction" his career has taken.

"What? Oh that," Martin says dismissively. " . . . that. That's over I must have been delirious for a few weeks there."

He then gins up every hoary excuse for Hollywood-generated violence you've ever heard, ending with: "My movies reflect what's going on; they don't make what's going on."

This is Hollywood's last line of defense for why it shows murder and mayhem on the big screen and the little one, in prime time and early in the morning, to children, adolescents, and adults:

We don't cause violence, we just report it.

Four years ago, I joined the legion of writers, researchers, and parents

Passing the buck in Tinseltown

MICHAEL KRASNY

Michael Krasny is currently the host of San Francisco radio station KQED's "Forum," a weekday talk show. Priscilla Yamin of Mother Jones and Karen Daar contributed research to these interviews.

For seven years, Michael Krasny hosted a successful West Coast radio talk show widely recognized for discussing serious issues and showing respect for callers. Krasny left his commercial program to move to public radio in February 1993. Many saw Krasny's departure from commercial radio as symbolic of the industry trend toward sensationalism and controversy—and away from public trust and responsibility.

Mother Jones commissioned Krasny to explore the trend toward excess, particularly excess violence, in the entertainment industry. Film and TV producers, directors, and writers claim that they want to create works of artistic and social value, yet too often what we—and our children—see is only blood and gore. How can we reconcile the First Amendment with the cost to society of viewing such violence? And to what extent are these individuals responsible for the repercussions of their violent movies and television shows? Krasny asked a few players for their thoughts:

Reprinted with permission from *Mother Jones* magazine, July/August 1993, pp. 16-21. © 1993 by The Foundation for National Progress.

2. CRIME, DELINQUENCY, AND VIOLENCE

who have tried to force Hollywood to confront the more disturbing truth. I wrote a series of newspaper articles on the massive body of evidence that establishes a direct cause-and-effect relationship between violence on television and violence in society.

The orchestrated response from the industry—a series of letters seeking to discredit me—was something to behold.

Because the fact is, on the one issue over which they have power, the liberals in Hollywood don't act like progressive thinkers; they act like, say, the National Rifle Association:

Guns don't kill people, people kill people.

We don't cause violence in the world, we just reflect it.

THE FIRST CONGRESSIONAL HEARINGS INTO THE EFFECTS OF TELEVISION VIOLENCE took place in 1954. Although television was still relatively new, its extraordinary marketing power was already evident. The tube was teaching Americans what to buy and how to act, not only in advertisements, but in dramatic shows, too.

Everybody from Hollywood producers to Madison Avenue ad men would boast about this power—and seek to utilize it on dual tracks: to make money and to remake society along better lines.

Because it seemed ludicrous to assert that there was only one area—the depiction of violence—where television did not influence behavior, the television industry came up with this theory: Watching violence is cathartic. A violent person might be sated by watching a murder.

The notion intrigued social scientists, and by 1956 they were studying it in earnest. Unfortunately, watching violence turned out to be anything but cathartic.

In the 1956 study, one dozen four-year-olds watched a "Woody Woodpecker" cartoon that was full of violent images. Twelve other preschoolers watched "Little Red Hen," a peaceful cartoon. Then the children were observed. The children who watched "Woody Woodpecker" were more likely to hit other children, verbally accost their classmates, break toys, be disruptive, and engage in destructive behavior during free play.

For the next thirty years, researchers in all walks of the social sciences studied the question of whether television causes violence. The results have been stunningly conclusive.

"There is more published research on this topic than on almost any other social issue of our time," University of Kansas Professor Aletha C. Huston, chairwoman of the American Psychological Association's Task Force on Television and Society, told Congress in 1988. "Virtually all independent scholars agree that there is evidence that television can cause aggressive behavior."

There have been some three thousand studies of this issue—eighty-five of them major research efforts—and they all say the same thing. Of the eighty-five major studies, the only one that failed to find a causal relationship between television violence and actual violence was paid for by NBC. When the study was subsequently reviewed by three independent social scientists, all three concluded that it actually did demonstrate a causal relationship.

Some highlights from the history of TV violence research:

• In 1973, when a town in mountainous western Canada was wired for television signals, University of British Columbia researchers observed first- and second-graders. Within two years, the incidence of hitting, biting, and shoving increased 160 percent in those classes.

• Two Chicago doctors, Leonard Eron and Rowell Huesmann, followed the viewing habits of a group of children for twenty-two years. They found that watching violence on television is the single best predictor of violent or aggressive behavior later in life, ahead of such commonly accepted factors as parents' behavior, poverty, and race.

"Television violence effects youngsters of all ages, of both genders, at all socioeconomic levels and all levels of intelligence," they told Congress in 1992. "The effect is not limited to children who are already disposed to being aggressive and is not restricted to this country."

BRIAN GRAZER, Ron Howard's partner, has produced more than twenty movies. "Most of my films have been sweet-spirited: *Parenthood. Splash. My Girl.* I'm proud of them. Others I'm not so proud of. I learned a big lesson with *Kindergarten Cop.* No one objected to the violent confrontation scene, and there was no problem with it in our focus groups. Then I showed it to my five-year-old, and all of a sudden, reflexively, I put my hand over his eyes. I knew at that point that we'd made a mistake. It was too late to cut the scene, but I would cut it now.

"Usually bad movies aren't hits. I don't see Freddy Krueger [*Nightmare on Elm Street*] movies, and I wouldn't want my kids to see them. I don't know why people make such movies. They're sick."

BOB SHAYE, chief executive officer of New Line Cinema, is responsible for the *Nightmare on Elm Street* horror films. "There's an almost sardonic or dour humor to Freddy Krueger [the *Elm Street* killer], especially to fantasy horror buffs. The tales are useful and cautionary. They suggest that evil and harm are everywhere and that we need to be prepared. They're not intended for kids.

"We create a product. People buy it or they don't. It pains my aesthetic judgment, but I often feel a good movie is one that makes money. My interest is in entertaining people. *The Killers* and *Batman?* Too much for kids. I can draw my lines. Not everyone can."

SAM HAMM shares screenwriting credit for *Batman* and *Batman Returns.* "It was probably a bad idea to excite small children to see *Batman Returns.* The tie-in to McDonald's was the idea of marketing people.

"But I'm ambivalent about all of this. I can remember being scared as a kid at horror films and developing a craving for that sort of thing, but that's what may form imagination in a strong way and that's what creates narrative and inner life. It teaches you to look for stuff that's not safe in the art you enjoy later on.

"I'm not arguing to expose kids to *Friday the 13th* movies or porno, but I feel there's too much caution about what kids see. Gravitating toward the forbidden is a natural part of growing up.

"I'm dubious of stimulation and effect, wary of speaking of anyone's experience but my own. I knew as a kid very clearly the distinction between real violence and cartoon or film violence. I'm waiting for the legions of those affected by what they see to give testimony."

VIVIENNE VERDON-ROE directed the documentary film *Women For America, For The World.* "I can't go to most popular movies without checking them out with friends first, because I can't physically sit through [violent ones]. My body will not allow it. People really ought to think about the effects. They

• Fascinated by an explosion of murder rates in the United States and Canada that began in 1955, after a generation of North Americans had come of age on television violence, University of Washington Professor Brandon Centerwall decided to see if the same phenomenon could be observed in South Africa, where the Afrikaner-dominated regime had banned television until 1975.

He found that eight years after TV was introduced—showing mostly Hollywood-produced fare—South Africa's murder rate skyrocketed. His most telling finding was that the crime rate increased first in the white communities. This mirrors U.S. crime statistics in the 1950s and especially points the finger at television, because whites were the first to get it in both countries.

Bolder than most researchers, Centerwall argues flatly that without violent television programming, there might be as many as ten thousand fewer murders in the United States each year.

• In 1983, University of California, San Diego, researcher David P. Phillips wanted to see if there was a correlation between televised boxing matches and violence in the streets of America.

Looking at crime rates after every televised heavyweight championship fight from 1973 to 1978, Phillips found that the homicide rate in the United States rose by an average of 11 percent for approximately one week. Phillips also found that the killers were likely to focus their aggression on victims similar to the losing fighter: if he was white, the increased number of victims were mostly white. The converse was true if the losing fighter was black.

By the age of eighteen, the average child has witnessed eighteen thousand simulated murders on TV.

• In 1988, researchers Daniel G. Linz and Edward Donnerstein of the University of California, Santa Barbara, and Steven Penrod of the University of Wisconsin studied the effects on young men of horror movies and "slasher" films.

They found that depictions of violence, not sex, are what desensitizes people.

They divided male students into four groups. One group watched no movies, a second watched nonviolent, X-rated movies, a third watched teenage sexual-innuendo movies, and a fourth watched the slasher films *Texas Chainsaw Massacre*, *Friday the 13th Part 2*, *Maniac*, and *Toolbox Murders*.

All the young men were placed on a mock jury panel and asked a series of questions designed to measure their empathy for an alleged female rape victim. Those in the fourth group measured lowest in empathy for the specific victim in the experiment—and for rape victims in general.

THE ANECDOTAL EVIDENCE IS OFTEN MORE COMPELLING THAN THE SCIENTIFIC studies. Ask any homicide cop from London to Los Angeles to Bangkok if television violence induces real-life violence and listen carefully to the cynical, knowing laugh.

Ask David McCarthy, police chief in Greenfield, Massachusetts, why nineteen-year-old Mark Branch killed himself after stabbing an eighteen-year-old female college student to death. When cops searched his room they found ninety horror movies, as well as a machete and a goalie mask like those used by Jason, the grisly star of *Friday the 13th*.

Ask the families of thirty-five young men who committed suicide by playing Russian roulette after seeing the movie *The Deer Hunter*.

Ask George Gavito, a lieutenant in the Cameron County, Texas, sheriff's department, about a cult that sacrificed at least thirteen people on a ranch west of Matamoros, Mexico. The suspects kept mentioning a 1986 movie, *The Believers*, about rich families who engage in ritual sacrifice. "They talk about it like that had something to do with changing them," Gavito recalled later.

may not faint, like I do, but they're getting desensitized to violence, and it contributes to the social violence of gangs and the like.

"It's incredibly difficult when there are so few alternatives. Teens go to movies because there's often nothing else for them to do, and if they are gruesome or bad movies, no one in society seems to be saying so.

"I'm not an insider. I'm not living down there. But I know enough. It's all money. Everything's money. It's horrible."

RICHARD DONNER directed the *Lethal Weapon* movies, *Superman*, *The Omen*, and *The Goonies*, among others. "If people see gratuitous violence in any of the *Lethal Weapon* movies, I wonder if they've seen the same movie. It's entertainment. That's my obligation. I brought social issues into the *Lethal Weapon* movies, like when Danny Glover's family comes down on him for eating tuna, or the 'Stamp out the NRA' sign up in the LA police station. In the last one the daughter wears a pro-choice T-shirt.

"You've got to prove [a connection between film violence and real violence] to me. Movies do provoke. I won't do gratuitous or animal violence. We went a little too far in the first *Lethal Weapon*, but I wanted to move more after that toward a less real and more comic-book effect, despite the great reaction we had.

"Public trust comes into filmmaking. The filmmaker is ultimately accountable. I can defend my own work only on personal grounds. If I'm a provocateur of anything, I hope it's good emotion and humor. Censorship is in the ratings system. It works."

CALLIE KHOURI won an Academy Award for her screenplay of *Thelma and Louise*. "I have a hard time with violence just to entertain, but I believe it can be very effective in getting a point across. I resorted to it in my film, but there was a conscience to it. Thelma and Louise felt they had done something wrong, and there were big consequences—including psychic consequences.

"Outlaw movies have always been a catharsis for men, but denied to women. I was extremely frustrated with the literal interpretation of *Thelma and Louise*. Doesn't anyone read anymore or understand metaphor? The film was supposed to be complex, without easy answers, and with flawed characters. I thought when Louise shot that guy that there'd be dead silence in the theater. That scene was written carefully: it was an attempted rape, and I wanted to make what she did wrong. And yet people cheered. I was stunned."

LESLIE MOONVES is head of Lorimar Studios, often called the fifth network, which produced the TV movies "Jack the Ripper" and "Deliberate Strangers" (about serial killer Ted Bundy), as well as shows that Moonves has considerably more pride in, such as "I'll Fly Away" and "Home Front." "I'd love to do another 'I'll Fly Away,' but the corporate bosses won't let me.

2. CRIME, DELINQUENCY, AND VIOLENCE

Ask LAPD lieutenant Mike Melton about Angel Regino of Los Angeles, who was picked up after a series of robberies and a murder in which he wore a blue bandanna and fedora identical to those worn by Freddy, the sadistic anti-hero of *Nightmare on Elm Street*. In case anybody missed the significance of his disguise, Regino told his victims that they would never forget him, because he was another Freddy Krueger.

Ask Britain Home Secretary Douglas Hurd, who called for further restrictions on U.S.-produced films after Michael Ryan of Hungerford committed Britain's worst mass murder in imitation of *Rambo*, massacring sixteen people while wearing a U.S. combat jacket and a bandoleer of ammunition.

Ask Sergeant John O'Malley of the New York Police Department about a nine-year-old boy who sprayed a Bronx office building with gunfire. The boy explained to the astonished sergeant how he learned to load his Uzi-like firearm: "I watch a lot of TV."

Or ask Manteca, California, police detective Jeff Boyd about thirteen-year-old Juan Valdez, who, with another teenager, went to a man's home, kicked him, stabbed him, beat him with a fireplace poker, and then choked him to death with a dog chain.

Why, Boyd wanted to know, had the boys poured salt in the victim's wounds?

"Oh, I don't know," the youth replied with a shrug. "I just seen it on TV."

NUMEROUS GROUPS HAVE CALLED, OVER THE YEARS, FOR CURBING TELEVISION violence: the National Commission on the Causes and Prevention of Violence (1969), the U.S. Surgeon General (1972), the Canadian Royal Commission (1976), the National Institute of Mental Health (1982), the U.S. Attorney General's Task Force on Family Violence (1984), the National Parents Teachers Association (1987), and the American Psychological Association (1992).

During that time, cable television and movie rentals have made violence more readily available while at the same time pushing the envelope for network TV. But even leaving aside cable and movie rentals, a study of television programming from 1967 to 1989 showed only small ups and downs in violence, with the violent acts moving from one time slot to another but the overall violence rate remaining pretty steady—and pretty similar from network to network.

"The percent of prime-time programs using violence remains more than seven out of ten, as it has been for the entire twenty-two-year period," researchers George Gerbner of the University of Pennsylvania Annenberg School for Communication and Nancy Signorielli of the University of Delaware wrote in 1990. For the past twenty-two years, they found, adults and children have been entertained by about sixteen violent acts, including two murders, in each evening's prime-time programming.

They also discovered that the rate of violence in children's programs is three times the rate in prime-time shows. By the age of eighteen, the average American child has witnessed at least eighteen thousand simulated murders on television.

By 1989, network executives were arguing that their violence was part of a larger context in which bad guys get their just desserts.

"We have never put any faith in mechanical measurements, such as counting punches or gunshots," said NBC's Alan Gerson. "Action and conflict must be evaluated within each specific dramatic context."

"Our policy," added Alfred R. Schneider of ABC, "... makes clear that when violence is portrayed [on TV], it must be reasonably related to plot development and character delineation."

Of course, what early-childhood experts could tell these executives is that children between the ages of four and seven simply make no connection between the murder at the beginning of a half-hour show and the man led away in handcuffs at the end. In fact, psychologists know that very young children do not even understand death to be a permanent condition.

But all of the scientific studies and reports, all of the wisdom of cops and grief of parents have run up against Congress's quite proper fear of censorship. For years, Democratic Congressman Peter Rodino of New Jersey chaired the House Judiciary Committee and looked at calls for some form

When you get burned with quality programming you get gun-shy—you feel you need to stick to the shows that make money. You know what the problem is? Network change. Somebody like Bill Paley [former chairman of CBS] used to say that he didn't care if he got a twelve share, because there was a public trust and social responsibility to put on an 'I'll Fly Away.' GE buys a network, and you've got a different agenda.

"Network presidents don't keep their jobs based on the number of Emmy awards. Let's face it: there is more sensation and violence because it works. The movie of the week has become the killer of the week story.

"Do we have a responsibility to our public? Of course. I honestly don't know what to do about it. How's that for an answer?"

JOE ESZTERHAS has written the scripts for such major Hollywood films as *Betrayal*, *Jagged Edge*, *Basic Instinct*, and *Sliver*. His work has been criticized as sexist and homophobic. "I don't like to be a Monday morning quarterback on my own work."

DAWN STEEL became the first woman to head a major studio when she was made president of Columbia Pictures in 1987. During her career, she has worked on such films as *Top Gun*, *Beverly Hills Cop II*, *Casualties of War*, *When Harry Met Sally*, and *Look Who's Talking*. She now runs her own production company. "I believe I've never made a movie in bad taste or with excessive violence. But for profit, I've had to make movies not from my soul. If I want to make a film for passion, I have to make it for less money.

"I'm more cynical about the violence in LA than about violence in our business. It's unanswerable whether movies reflect the culture or vice versa. I monitor my kid's movies and won't let her see what's not appropriate for her. There's no way you can censor any movie in this country that's being made. That's our First Amendment."

MATT GROENING is creator and executive producer of the TV hit "The Simpsons." "Anytime you visualize something, it's difficult not to glorify it. Every anti-war film is prowar, because its violence is stylized and an audience can be removed from it and enjoy it. Stylistically, violence is almost invariably glorified, even when you have an antiviolent point of view. Look at *Platoon*. Violence is invariably used in movies and TV as punctuation, and it does have a numbing effect on people after a time.

"Most TV, most movies, really, are less pernicious than tedious and boring. What's bad for kids is bad storytelling. Tell better stories."

BARRY DILLER, ex–chief executive officer and chairman of Fox and Matt Groening's former boss, now heads QVC Network. He couldn't disagree more with Groening about television's being mostly bad. "I can't imagine why he would say that. Pound for of censorship with a jaundiced eye. At a hearing five years ago, Rodino told witnesses that Congress must be a "protector of commerce."

"Well, we have children that we need to protect," replied Frank M. Palumbo, a pediatrician at Georgetown University Hospital and a consultant to the American Academy of Pediatrics. "What we have here is a toxic substance in the environment that is harmful to children."

Arnold Fege of the national PTA added, "Clearly, this committee would not protect teachers who taught violence to children. Yet why would we condone children being exposed to a steady diet of TV violence year after year?"

Finally there is a reason to hope for progress.

Early this summer, Massachusetts Democrat Edward Markey, chair of the House Energy and Commerce subcommittee on telecommunications, said that Congress may require manufacturers to build TV sets with a computer chip so that parents could block violent programs from those their children could select.

He joins the fight waged by Senator Paul Simon, a liberal Democrat from Illinois. Nine years ago, Simon flipped on a hotel television set hoping to catch the late news. "Instead," he has recalled many times, "I saw a man being sawed in half with a chainsaw, in living color."

Simon was unsettled by the image and even more unsettled when he wondered what repeatedly looking at such images would do to the mind of a fourteen-year-old.

When he found out, he called television executives, who told him that violence sells and that they would be at a competitive disadvantage if they acted responsibly.

Why not get together and adopt voluntary guidelines? Simon asked.

Oh, that would be a violation of antitrust law, they assured him.

Simon called their bluff in 1990 by pushing through Congress a law that allowed a three-year moratorium on antitrust considerations so that the industry could discuss ways to jointly reduce violence.

Halfway through that time, however, they had done nothing, and an angry Simon denounced the industry on the Senate floor. With a push from some prominent industry figures, a conference was set for this August 2 in Los Angeles.

This spring, CBS broadcast group president Howard Stringer said his network was looking for ways to cut back on violence in its entertainment, because he was troubled by the cost to society of continuing business-as-usual.

"We must admit we have a responsibility," he said.

Jack Valenti, the powerful head of the Motion Picture Association of America, wrote to producers urging them to participate in the August 2 conference. "I think it's more than a bunch of talk," Simon said. "I think this conference will produce some results. I think the industry will adopt some standards."

The federal government, of course, possesses the power to regulate the airwaves through the FCC, and Simon and others believe that this latent power to control violence—never used—has put the fear of God in the producers. He also thinks some of them are starting to feel guilty.

"We now have more people in jail and prison per capita than any country that keeps records, including South Africa," Simon says. "We've spent billions putting people behind bars, and it's had no effect on the crime rate. None. People realize there have to be other answers, and as they've looked around, they have settled on television as one of them."

Maybe Simon is right. Maybe Hollywood executives will get together and make a difference.

Or maybe, like Steve Martin's character in *Grand Canyon*, producers and directors from New York to Beverly Hills will wake up after Simon's antitrust exemption expires December 1, shake off the effects of their holiday hangovers, and when asked about their new commitment to responsible filmmaking, answer:

"What? Oh that. . . . that. That's over. We must have been delirious for a few weeks there."

pound, the hour and half-hour television series are very good. There's a lot of junk, but much more in the movie business, the record business, even legitimate theater. It's snobbery to call a show like 'Roseanne' lowbrow or vulgar. It's funny and interesting and has a good moral value and tone.

"TV movies are crummy. 'Hard Copy' is a lying, thieving, lowlife program of hideous, cynical purpose. It's not serious television. There are only a few tabloid shows, but they speak loudly.

"I think you look at society, and you see what is reflected on television in terms of violent action. Absolutely, [there is too much violence]. But we can be thoughtful and reasonable and change that, reduce it. I think plans over the last few years will help. Senator Simon's work with the networks will help."

PHILIP KAUFMAN co-wrote and directed *The Wanderers, The Unbearable Lightness of Being,* and *Henry and June,* and wrote and directed *The Right Stuff.* "There is a fascist edge to a lot of the violence we see. I'm in favor of pushing the envelope, but when you push it in romance or eroticism you get an NC-17 rating. It's easier to get an R rating if you use senseless violence, because the ratings board is largely conservative and embraces violence before sex."

JOSH BRAND, along with his partner, has produced the TV hits "St. Elsewhere" and "Northern Exposure." "If something gets a high rating, say, 'The Amy Fisher Story,' then advertisers pay more money. Now, did the networks create the audience for it, or do they pander to what the audience wanted? Is it okay to pollute the emotional and spiritual environment?

"Now there are studies [that show] that violent images don't affect people, just as the tobacco industry has studies showing that cigarette smoking doesn't cause cancer. And they use the First Amendment to evoke their rights and get into this study versus that study, and the whole thing becomes a wash, a miasma of moral mud. But I think that there is absolutely no question that the profusion of these kinds of images has a negative effect, not only on children but on human beings in general.

"But regulations are dangerous, particularly when dealing with the free expression of ideas. I do believe that some of those ideas are like pollutants, but there isn't one thing you can do. A panacea doesn't exist."

Although there may be no panacea, we must still look for solutions. How would you resolve the conflict between excessive violence in entertainment and the protections guaranteed under the First Amendment?

Write to *Mother Jones*, 1663 Mission St., 2nd Floor, San Francisco, CA 94103. Or fax us at (415) 863-5136.

When cities run riot

Loïc J. D. Wacquant

Loïc D. Wacquant is a French sociologist affiliated with the Society of Fellows of Harvard University. He has conducted extensive research on racial inequality in the United States and on comparative urban poverty. His recent publications include: The Zone: le métier de "hustler" dans le ghetto noir américain *(1992), and "Redrawing the Urban Color Line: The State of the Ghetto in the 1980s" (in C. Calhoun, ed.,* Social Theory and the Politics of Identity, *1993). He is currently writing a book about the culture and economics of professional boxing.*

OCTOBER 1990 in Vaulx-en-Velin, a quiet, depressed working-class town in the suburbs of Lyon, France: several hundred youths, many of them second-generation immigrants from the Maghrib, take to the streets and confront police after a neighbourhood teenager dies in a motorcycle accident caused by a patrol car. For three days, they clash with law enforcement officials and riot troops hastily dispatched by the government, stoning police vans, ransacking stores and setting 200 cars on fire. When calm finally returns, dozens of injured are counted, damage is estimated at some $120 million, and the country is in shock. The long-simmering rage of the *banlieues*—declining peripheral areas with high densities of degraded public housing—tops the political agenda.

July 1992 in Bristol, England: a nearly identical chain of events triggers several nights of rioting on the Hartcliffe estate, a poor industrial district on the southern edge of town. Violence breaks out after two local men joyriding on a stolen police motorcycle are killed in a collision with an unmarked police car. Later that night, some hundred youths go on the rampage through the local shopping centre. When police counter-attack, they are showered with bricks and stones, steel balls, scaffolding and petrol bombs. Over 500 elite troops have to be called in to restore order to a one-square-kilometre area temporarily turned urban guerrilla zone. Similar disturbances break out that summer in Coventry, Manchester, Salford, Blackburn and Birmingham.

April 1992 in Los Angeles: the acquittal of four white police officers in the brutal videotaped beating of Rodney King, a defenceless black motorist arrested after a car chase, sets off an explosion of civil violence unmatched in American history this century. In the black ghetto of South Central, white motorists are snatched out of their cars and beaten, stores vandalized, police cars overturned and set aflame. The Korean-owned licquor outlets, swapmeets and markets that dot the area are targeted for systematic destruction. So overwhelming is the eruption that neither firefighters nor the police can prevent the torching of thousands of buildings. Rioting promptly mushrooms outwards as scenes of mass looting multiply. A state of emergency is proclaimed and 7,000 federal troops, including 1,200 Marines, are drafted in. Sniper fire and

From *The Unesco Courier,* February 1993, pp. 8-12. Reprinted by permission.

shootings between rioters, police and store-owners who take up arms to defend their shops bring the death toll to forty-five. By the end of the third day of upheaval, nearly 2,400 have suffered injury and 10,000 are under arrest; a thousand families have lost their homes and twenty thousand their jobs. Total destruction is estimated at a staggering one billion dollars.

These outbursts of collective violence are but three drawn from a list of urban disturbances too long to enumerate. For the past decade has witnessed a spectacular increase in public unrest and rioting at the heart of the large cities of the First World. Most of the disorders, big and small, that have shaken up the French *banlieues,* the British inner cities and the ghettos and *barrios* of America have involved chiefly the youth of poor, segregated and dilapidated urban neighbourhoods and appear to have been fuelled by growing "racial" tensions in and around these areas. Thus the dominant interpretation in media accounts and political debates has been that they are essentially "race riots" expressive of animosity against, or between, the ethnic and/or immigrant "minorities" of these countries.

There is much to support this view. The Europe of the 1980s has indeed been swept by a seemingly unstoppable wave of racist sentiment. In France, long-covert "anti-Arab" hostility has burst out into the open and fuelled an increase in racist assaults, and it has found its political expression in the xenophobic populism of the National Front. In the United Kingdom, antagonism between black West Indians, Asians and whites has flared up in repeated street confrontations and grown more acrimonious, so much so that public unrest and violence are increasingly perceived as essentially "black" problems. Meanwhile in the United States a society-wide backlash against the gains made by so-called minorities (mainly African-Americans but also Latinos and some Asian groups) in the wake of the civil rights movement of the 1960s has led to a sharp deterioration of race relations revealed *inter alia* by an escalation in racially motivated or "hate" crime, a generalized fear of black males on the street, inter-ethnic incidents on university campuses, and the blatant exploitation of anti-black feelings by some politicians.

Yet the urban riots of the 1980s are not a simple extension of traditional uprisings such as the United States has experienced throughout this century. A closer look at their anatomy suggests that these disorders have, in varying proportions, combined two logics: that of protest against racial injustice and that of the poor rising against economic deprivation and widening social inequalities with the most effective, if not the only, weapon at their disposal, namely direct forcible disruption of civil life.

The 1980s may be the decade of the slow maturing of *mixed riots*—mixed in terms of their causes or goals as well as by virtue of their multi-ethnic composition. For, contrary to media portrayals, neither the French *banlieues* nor the British inner cities are solely or even predominantly populated by immigrants, and those who partook in unrest there were more often than not recruited across ethnic lines. Moreover, their demands are the demands of working-class youths everywhere: jobs, decent schools, affordable or improved housing, access to public services, and fair treatment by police. Similarly, in South-Central Los Angeles, the thousands who pilfered merchandise from burning supermarkets and mini-malls during the riot were far from being all blacks: over half of the first 5,000 arrests were Latinos and another 10 per cent whites. The uprising was not exclusively an Afro-American outcry against gross racial discrimination; it was also a revolt against poverty, hunger, and the severe material aggravation brought on by economic recession and cutbacks in government programmes. As one of the city's most astute observers puts it, "the nation's first multiracial riot was as much about empty bellies and broken hearts as it was about police batons and Rodney King."

VIOLENCE FROM ABOVE

It is tempting to view outbreaks of collective violence "from below" as symptoms of moral crisis, pathologies of the lower class, or as signs of the impending societal breakdown of "law and order". But close comparative analysis of their timing, makeup and unfolding shows that, far from being irrational, recent public unrest by the urban poor of Europe and America is a (socio)logical response to the massive *structural violence* unleashed upon them by a set of mutually reinforcing economic and political changes. These changes have resulted in a polarization of classes which, combined with racial and ethnic segregation, is producing a *dualization of the metropolis* that threatens not

downwardly-mobile families of the native working class and immigrant populations of mixed nationalities who are young, economically fragile and equally deprived of skills that are readily marketable in the core of the new economy.

Such an accumulation of social ills explains the oppressive atmosphere of drabness, ennui and despair that pervades poor communities in

Eruptions of big-city violence in the West are symptoms of a malaise that needs treatment in depth

simply to marginalize the poor but to condemn them to outright social and economic redundancy.

This violence "from above" has three main components: mass unemployment bringing in its wake pervasive material deprivation, relegation to decaying neighbourhoods, and heightened stigmatization in public discourse, all of which are the more deadly for occurring against the backdrop of a general upswing in inequality. Unlike previous phases of economic growth, the uneven expansion of the 1980s, when it occurred at all, failed to "lift all boats" and instead led to a deepening schism between rich and poor, and between those stably employed in the core, middle-class sectors of the economy and uneducated individuals trapped at the margins of an increasingly insecure low-skill labour market.

For the residents of flagging working-class areas, the reorganization of capitalist economies—visible in the shift from manufacturing to education-intensive services, the impact of electronic and automation technologies in factories and offices, and the erosion of unions—and the reduction of government outlays in the areas of welfare and low-income housing have translated into unusually high rates of long-term joblessness and a regression of material conditions. Simultaneously, advanced countries have had to absorb a fresh influx (or the definitive settlement) of immigrants from the Third World who are typically channelled into these very neighbourhoods where economic opportunities and collective resources are already diminishing. Such spatial segregation intensifies hardship by concentrating in degraded and isolated enclaves

many large Western cities. Residents of these cramped neighbourhoods feel that they and their children have little future other than the life of misery and exclusion to which they seem consigned at present. Added to this is the rage felt by poor urban youths as a result of the cultural discrimination and stigmatization imposed on residents of decaying urban areas.

Lastly there is the curse of being poor in the midst of a rich society in which active participation in the sphere of consumption has become a *sine qua non* of social dignity—a passport to citizenship even among the most dispossessed. As testified by the proliferation of "mugging" in the British inner city, *la dépouille* (the stripping of fancy clothes under threat of force) in the estates of the *banlieue,* and gold-chain snatching and drug dealing on the streets of the American ghetto, violence and crime are often the only means that working-class youths with no employment prospects have of acquiring the money and the consumer goods indispensable for acceding to a socially recognized existence.

THE DILEMMAS OF POLICING

If direct forms of infra-political protest by way of popular disruption of public order, direct seizure of goods and destruction of property have spread, it is also true that formal means of pressure on the state have declined along with the decomposition of traditional machineries of political representation of the poor.

The widening gulf between rich and poor, the growing self-closure of political elites, the increasing distance between the lower class and the dominant institutions of society all breed distrust and disaffection. They converge to undermine the legitimacy of the social order. In the vacuum created by the lack of political linkages and the absence of legitimate mediations between poor urban populations and a society from which they feel excluded, it is no wonder that relations with the police have become both salient and bellicose, and that incidents with the "forces of order" are invariably the detonator of explosions of popular violence in the cities. Trends in all countries converge to show that, whenever the police come to be considered as an alien force by the community, they become unable to fulfil any role other than a purely repressive one and can only *add* to further disorder and violence.

Political responses to urban violence and to the civil disruption it causes vary significantly from country to country depending on national ideologies of citizenship, state structures and capacities, and political conjuncture. They span a continuum between outright criminalization and repression at one end, and politicization of the problem via the collective renegotiation of social rights at the other.

The recent upsurge in popular violence at the heart of advanced urban societies has deep roots in the epochal transformation of their economy, cities, and state policies. The governments of rich nations have, to varying degrees, been unable or unwilling to stem the growth of inequality and to prevent the social and spatial cumulation of economic hardship, marginality and stigmatization in deteriorating working-class enclaves of the changing populace. The continued conjugation of ethnic iniquity and class exclusion in the same fragile areas promises to produce more unrest and to pose a daunting challenge to the very idea of citizenship in Western cities for years to come.

THE LOS ANGELES RIOTS: CAUSES AND CURES

Given the conditions present in Los Angeles and other American inner cities— economic disparity, physical isolation, failed social service and educational systems, and general hopelessness—the more appropriate question to ask regarding urban unrest last spring may be "Why don't such riots erupt more often?" Desperately needed are new forums for the resolution of conflicts and restructuring of failed systems.

Richard E. Rubenstien

Richard E. Rubenstien is a member of the faculty of the Institute for Conflict Analysis and Resolution at George Mason University, Fairfax, Virginia.

To some politicians and academic analysts, the devastating May riots in Los Angeles, California and several other cities, which took more than 60 lives and caused close to $1 billion in property damage, came as a complete surprise. Others, however, had predicted that an explosion of violent rage would soon ravage some major American city.

What few foresaw was that these disturbances would be *multi-ethnic,* involving Hispanics, whites, and Asians, as well as blacks,and that they would spread so quickly from inner-city to suburban areas, as well as to college campuses across the country.

Virtually every condition identified by national riot commissions as causes of the violence of the 1960s was not only extant but worsening more than two decades later.

For the past three years, scholars at George Mason University's Institute for Conflict Analysis and Resolution (ICAR) had warned that, unless dramatic changes in national policy were made and implemented, America's urban areas very likely would experience a return to the violent rioting of the 1960s and perhaps to more widespread and virulent forms of political violence.

The question we have attempted to answer at ICAR is not "Why do urban riots occur?," but "Why are they not taking place constantly?" Virtually every condition identified by national riot commissions as causes of the violence of the 1960s was not only extant but worsening more than two decades later.

Unemployment, poverty, shattered families, failure of the public schools, decaying housing and health systems, political powerlessness, abuse of power by the police, de facto racial segregation: All statistical indicators show these conditions becoming more aggravated from the mid-1970s to the present. Two statistics are particularly horrifying. The United States now imprisons a larger percentage of its population than any nation in the world, including South Africa. *Forty-two percent* of black men between the ages of 18 and 35 are under some form of police or court supervision.

Indeed, a new term came into popular usage in the 1980s to describe minority groups in the inner cities: the "underclass." In fact, this "underclass" comprises the lower levels of the American *working class,* whose standard of living has been declining since the mid-1970s. The racial or ethnic distinctiveness and more intensive impoverishment of urban minorities led many commentators to draw a sharp line between, say, unemployed blacks in Los Angeles and unemployed whites in South Chicago, Illinois, or Youngstown, Ohio. But it was the downward pressure on the class as a whole that plunged its lower stratum under water. The same economic conditions and decisions that de-industrialized urban areas across the United States, driving former workers in basic industries into poor jobs or "early retirement," turned the youth gangs of Los Angeles and Detroit into *lumpen* criminal organizations.

Reprinted with permission from *National Civic Review*, Vol. 81, No. 3, Summer/Fall 1992, pp. 319-324. © 1992 by The National Civic League, Inc. All rights reserved.

INHIBITORS OF VIOLENCE

Why, then, did urban minorities not renew the rioting of the 1960s? We identified several temporary inhibitors of renewed violence:

• The intensity of inner-city poverty, which had turned daily life into a scramble to survive and lowered expectations of political or economic improvement.

• The rapid growth of the trade in illegal drugs, which pumped significant amounts of money into poor neighborhoods, diverted aggression into intragroup struggles over control of the business, and temporarily "pacified" drug users.

• The development of a black or Hispanic "political class," which inhibited violent protest against incidents like the 1981 fire-bombing of the MOVE house by Philadelphia police—an atrocity that killed 11 people and destroyed an entire urban neighborhood.

While identifying these inhibitors, however, we pointed out that they were highly unstable, transient, and weak compared with the irrepressible drive to satisfy basic human needs. Black political leaders—as Mayor Tom Bradley of Los Angeles has now discovered—could not maintain their credibility as community representatives while presiding over the social and economic destruction of their communities.

. . . The disorders in Los Angeles and several other American cities were not caused only by police brutality or a malfunctioning criminal justice system.

The narcotics trade was not likely to be suppressed, but it might easily become better organized, with the most lucrative business opportunities migrating (as they have done) outside the inner cities. And, despite deepening poverty, the rage produced by thwarted expectations could easily be aroused—for example, by a recession that threw formerly employed minority workers into the ranks of the jobless, or by a jury verdict like that in the Rodney King case, finding that visibly brutal policemen were *not* guilty of assaulting a helpless black man.

In the wake of the recent rioting, familiar voices are calling for reforms in the administration of police and court systems. But the disorders in Los Angeles and several other American cities were not caused only by police brutality or a malfunctioning criminal justice system. The root cause of rioting is not even racism, in the sense of prejudice against blacks or Hispanics, but the systematic failure of the American system to satisfy basic human needs for economic security, individual and group identity, and human development.

The Los Angeles riot is America's Chernobyl: the catastrophe that reveals a more general crisis of the political and economic systems.

SYSTEM FAILURES

In order to identify and solve the problems that generate urban conflict, new conflict resolution processes are needed that involve the parties most directly affected. Preliminary analysis, however, points to three primary system failures that are responsible for creating a host of secondary (but extremely severe) social problems:

• **Insufficient and inadequate jobs.** American capitalism has thus far proved unable to provide meaningful jobs, with decent incomes and hopes of a brighter future, for minority men and women of working age. (Indeed, it has proved unable to provide such jobs for a much larger number of white workers.)

Contrary to a popular folk-prejudice, unemployment and underemployment are not the result of unwillingness to work hard. The United States media regularly report incidents in which hundreds and sometimes thousands of minority workers appear at job sites, standing in line day after day in hopes of securing a chambermaid's position in a new hotel or a checkout job at a supermarket.

For almost 30 years, American government and business have promised to provide economic opportunities to inner-city residents, but in practice they have relied on the free market to do the job. As a result, the most significant new business established in American cities during the past two decades has been the market in illegal drugs.

. . . The best educators are convinced that, with sufficient political will, imagination, and money, most public schools can do the job that a few "model" schools are now doing . . .

• **Educational collapse.** Public schools in the inner cities (and in many communities elsewhere) have proved unable to train their students for the jobs that do exist, many of which require "white collar" or technological skills. As Jonathan Kozol points out in his brilliant study, *Savage Inequalities* (1991), America's underfunded, mismanaged, and neglected school systems, which now rank near the bottom on the list of industrialized nations, both reflect and aggravate existing social inequalities.

Once more, popular prejudice has it that minority youth are uneducable, either because of low IQ scores, lack of family support for education, or personal instability. Yet the best educators are convinced that, with sufficient political will, imagination, and money, most public schools can do the job that a few "model" schools are now doing to prepare young people for survival and advancement. Unfortunately, few American leaders have so far been willing to make a serious commitment to radically upgrading urban education.

• **Political impotence.** Despite some innovative efforts made in the 1960s and early 1970s to regenerate local politics,

2. CRIME, DELINQUENCY, AND VIOLENCE

American democracy has proved unable to empower inner-city communities—and working-class communities elsewhere—to control their collective lives.

In part, this is the result of an impoverished definition of "politics" that leaves most major decisions to the private sector. In part, it is the result of institutions that limit mass participation to voting periodically for candidates offered by two "politics as usual" political parties. As the Los Angeles riot demonstrates, the symbolic satisfaction of putting "one of us" in office has obviously worn thin.

Virtually **every** *group subjected over several generations to intense poverty and oppression has found its family structure collapsing . . .*

Especially crippling to residents of the inner cities has been a large-scale migration of employed minority workers and professionals *out* of the cities and into nearby suburbs. Clearly, these problems will not be solved without a significant revitalization and restructuring of America's political institutions, particularly at the local and metropolitan-regional levels.

These failures bring in their train a host of desperate social problems, from the shattering of impoverished families and a rise in criminal behavior to police violence and gross miscarriages of justice.

One current view reverses this causal sequence by portraying the "declining black family" as the core problem—but this is a serious error.

Virtually *every* group subjected over several generations to intense poverty and oppression has found its family structure collapsing, its social institutions in disarray, and its children turning to crime. Among Jews, for example, family solidarity is legendary; but the Polish-Russian Pale of Settlement, where Jews were forced to live for almost one century under conditions not dissimilar to those of American ghettos, was an inferno of broken families and broken dreams, violent crime, prostitution, illiteracy, and disease.

Urgently required at present are analytical, conflict-resolving forums that bring together representatives of the groups most affected by urban violence . . .

One suspects that the current focus, amounting almost to a fixation, on the problems of black family life reflects a fashionable intellectual despair. A similar despair underpins current efforts in United States government circles to attribute black "criminality" to biochemical or genetic factors.

What, after all, can be done to restore a gravely wounded culture to health? This question is answerable, but not within the confines of "politics as usual" and conventional thinking.

Given these sources of continuing oppression and violence, what remedies *will be* effective? A prior question, however, is this: *How will effective remedies be discovered and implemented?*

We must begin to answer with the understanding that the failures described above are systemic and that limited, well-intended reforms—a community board charged with supervising police behavior, or a plan to promote ownership of individual dwellings in blighted urban areas—will not get to the root of the problem. It will prove impossible to solve inner-city problems by abstracting these regions from the rest of the nation, by focusing exclusively on problems of race and ethnicity, or by adopting policies for the "underclass" that do not also respond to the crisis of the working class as a whole.

CONFLICT-RESOLVING FORUMS

Urgently required at present are analytical, conflict-resolving forums that bring together representatives of the groups most affected by urban violence to consider how decayed systems may be restructured or replaced. Such forums might help create a new agenda for American politics in the inner cities and elsewhere.

Conflict resolution workshops and conferences are now being used in several arenas of deep-rooted social conflict, including Northern Ireland, the Basque regions of Spain, the Middle East, and South Africa. Their great advantage is that by focusing on basic human needs rather than immediate interests, they permit "unmentionable" options for systemic change to be identified, discussed, and evaluated in terms of their costs and benefits to the parties.

For example, current government proposals to solve the problem of joblessness in American cities are severely constrained—indeed, throttled—by self-interested, conventional approaches. For the fourth or fifth time in the last three decades, Washington has revived the "enterprise zone" plan to subsidize private corporations to invest in the ghettos. The defects of these schemes have long been recognized. They take too long to work. They are too expensive. They set black and white communities against each other. They do nothing to overcome the weaknesses in the American economy that are responsible for the problem. While enriching certain investors, they tend to create a new stratum of low-paid workers who are expected to be grateful to have any employment at all.

While such solutions to urban economic decline as enterprise zones merit attention, other alternatives urgently require identification and evaluation as well. For example, should we consider creating publicly owned industries whose managers would be politically responsible to the communities in which they operate?

Most American politicians and business leaders tend to dismiss this sort of idea out of hand; too "socialistic," they declare. But the Tennessee Valley Authority, which helped restore a large part of the South to economic health, was similarly decried.

SYSTEM-CHANGING ALTERNATIVES

Any idea with the potential to revitalize the American economy (and with it the inner-city economy) deserves careful consideration. The most pressing need at present is to broaden the discussion of system-changing alternatives beyond the narrow limits that have crippled discussion so far, in order that a real national dialogue can begin.

Similarly, rebuilding America's public school systems—not just in the inner cities but in urban areas across the country—requires the sort of fresh ideas that conflict resolution forums are designed to generate. How can the United States draw the best-qualified, most-dedicated young people from all races and classes into the teaching profession? Can teachers' salaries be doubled or tripled to reflect the true value of their work to society?

Without a political process that holds out hope for significant change, violence will surely escalate and spread to other urban areas . . .

How can we revolutionize the basic structure of the classroom to provide a more interactive and effective learning environment? Can the schools provide basic services (e.g., child care) that working-class parents are unable to afford? A number of promising educational models both in the United States and abroad await evaluation in conflict resolution workshops and conferences.

As in the case of new economic ideas, however, models capable of transforming the current systems of education and local politics are unlikely to be implemented without significant popular mobilization for change. The circumstance that will solve the problems which have subjected inner-city residents to a low-grade holocaust is a combination of new, system-transforming ideas and mass-based political action.

CONCLUSION

Without a political process that holds out hope for significant change, violence will surely escalate and spread to other urban areas, involving other aggrieved groups. It is notable that several disturbances triggered by the Los Angeles riot, in particular those in Seattle and Toronto, involved predominantly *white* rioters, and that riots in the inner cities were immediately followed by disorders on several college campuses.

In the 1960s, mass rioting in Los Angeles, Newark, Detroit, Chicago, and Washington D.C. generated a movement for "black power" in the streets and precedent-breaking legislative efforts in Washington. We do not yet know what political energies may be unleashed in the wake of the most recent disorders.

Still, we can take a first step toward eliminating the conditions that breed urban violence. We can create conflict-resolving forums locally, nationally, and internationally that are hospitable to new ideas. We can search systematically for urban programs that seem to work, publicize them, and evaluate their effectiveness.

Finally, we can and must advance a perspective that sees rioting—like crime, communal warfare, police violence, and other forms of antisocial behavior—as the result of unsatisfied basic human needs.

Aging: Problems New and Old

Whether or not the later years of life are going to be the "golden years" they can look forward to is becoming increasingly doubtful for many Americans. Health, the economy, and other factors may make retirement and the lives of older Americans far from what they had expected. Even organizations that were created to help the elderly may not have the best interests of the elderly at heart.

"Old Money" illustrates the fact that the largest non-profit organization in the United States, and perhaps the world, is more interested in its corporate holdings and image than in providing services for the elderly.

"The New Faces of Aging" attempts to break through the stereotypes surrounding aging and show that "conscious aging" can make the latter years productive and that the experience and wisdom of the oldest generation can help solve many societal ills.

"Unplanned Parenthood" deals with the growing problem of grandparents being forced to take over active parenting when their own children fail as parents. In addition to the stress of active parenting in their older years, the elderly have to cope with feelings of failure because their children failed as parents as well as worry that death or severe illness might prevent them from seeing their grandchildren through to adulthood.

"The Story of a Nursing Home Refugee" recounts how an intelligent, creative, and persistent 91-year-old woman managed to deal with insensitive nursing home staffs, poor living conditions, and a lack of privacy.

Looking Ahead: Challenge Questions

Why is it so crucial that today's young people focus on the problems of the elderly?

What would you say are the most significant problems and issues facing those over age 65?

What should be done to ensure that organizations that were created to represent the needs and interests of the elderly really do so?

What steps must those approaching retirement take if they want to be sure that their later years will be the golden years of life? What steps must our society take to help them?

In what ways would the symbolic interactionists', functionalists', and conflict theorists' approaches to the study of the problems of aging differ?

What values, rights, duties, and harms seem to underlie the issues and problems covered in this unit?

Old Money

Why the mighty AARP spends as much furnishing its offices as it does on programs to help the elderly

Christopher Georges

Christopher Georges is an editor of The Washington Monthly. *Research assistance was provided by Greg Bologna.*

The American Association of Retired Persons (AARP) receives approximately $75 million annually from the federal government to run a pair of job training and placement programs for older Americans—two of the largest of their kind. A recent phone call to AARP's Washington, D.C., headquarters to inquire about enrollment in the programs led to the following:

The caller, after unsuccessfully attempting to explain the programs to two befuddled receptionists, was bounced to Jack Everett, an official in the organization's Senior Employment Office, who cheerfully explained that AARP offers no federally funded job placement or training programs. Everett suggested calling the Department of Labor (the agency that pays AARP $52 million to run one of the programs) for help. He also offered other ideas, like, "Try the phone book under the senior citizens section," and suggested contacting the National Council on Senior Citizens, another, smaller advocacy group for older Americans. He even threw in some job-training advice: "You'll need a resumé. That's always a good first step. . . ."

Everett's not alone. Similar inquiries at AARP offices in major cities in 16 states turned up like responses: Only six of the offices were aware that these programs even exist, although AARP literature boasts that they're offered at 108 sites across the nation. One office suggested calling Elder Temps, a privately run job-placement firm. Another advised calling the Jewish Council for the Aging. Several others suggested enrolling in an AARP job search workshop and seminar—for a fee of $35.

In a way, those phone calls distill what's wrong with AARP, one of America's largest and most influential nonprofit organizations: In its brochures, it's dedicated to helping seniors work, play, and wield power. In real life, however, helping itself seems to be Job One. "It's no more than a big business," grumbles Virginia Fine, who until last year was an officer of a California AARP chapter. "The whole Washington operation is simply geared toward making money." A close look at the mammoth nonprofit's Washington command central offers a fair amount of evidence to back Fine's charge. In 1990, for example, AARP spent about as much on office furniture and equipment as it did on programs to help its 33 million elderly members.

The world according to AARP

Why should you care? If you're over 50, odds are you're a member: More than half the over-50 population has paid the $5 dues to belong. Next to the Catholic Church, it's the largest membership organization in America. But even if you're not an AARP card-carrier, you're paying for the organization's extravagance anyway, because AARP receives, in addition to its federal grants, a federal subsidy equivalent to nearly $20 million a year.

Reprinted with permission from *The Washington Monthly*, June 1992, pp. 16-21. © 1992 by the Washington Monthly Company, 1611 Connecticut Avenue, NW, Washington, DC 20009. (202) 462-0128.

Of course, AARP's nonprofit status also grants it something money can't buy—the trust of millions of older Americans: trust to represent their interests in Washington, to sell them worthy products, and to use their dues and fees in their best interest. For most of the organization's 34 years, the media and AARP members have accepted that trust at face value. But a peek at AARP's finances and lobbying efforts suggests that this trust may not always be well-earned.

AARP describes its mission as threefold: to lobby on behalf of seniors; sell them products and offer them discounts on other goods and services; and provide them with the chance to both volunteer their services and benefit from the volunteer work of others. For their $5 investment, members get an assortment of goodies: a subscription to *Modern Maturity*, AARP's bimonthly magazine (far and away America's largest, with a circulation five times that of *Time*); discounts from car rental companies, major hotel chains, airlines, and on American Express travel packages; and, of course, the opportunity to save money on health insurance, prescription drugs, and other products sold by AARP.

And sell it does. AARP's nine business enterprises sustain a cash flow of about $10 billion annually and revenues of nearly $300 million, with the greatest portion coming from AARP's centerpiece enterprise: group health insurance. With more than 5 million policy holders, it's the largest of its type. Last year, AARP profited nearly $100 million from this business alone. AARP's only role in selling the policies is as a middleman: AARP's partner, Prudential Insurance, offers the policies, which are promoted through AARP publications and direct mail solicitations. For every policy sold, AARP receives a 4 percent administrative allowance simply for collecting the premium and passing it on to Prudential.

AARP'S mail-order pharmacy, one of the nation's largest, brings the organization about $3 million per year. Its direct mail operation is so massive that AARP sends more than 1 percent of the entire nation's nonprofit third-class mail. Add to this the $100 million it collects each year in membership dues and the interest on about $50 million from Treasury bills, and total annual revenues add up to about 10 times the take of the United Way.

The United Way: Come to think of it, the comparison doesn't end there. AARP devoted about $30 million last year, and just $14 million in 1990, to programs aimed at directly assisting the elderly—a pittance compared to the funds it lavished on itself. Perhaps the most conspicuous symbol of AARP's use of resources is its new 10-story Washington headquarters. Leased for about $16 million a year, the 500,000-square-foot building is one of Washington's most alluring. Fellow lobbyists refer to the structure as the "Taj Mahal"; *The Washington Post*'s architecture critic described it last year as "a knockdown surprise, a classical package whose odd vigor is at once apparitional and relentless."

It's little wonder he was impressed: The structure, crowned with a medieval-style turret, boasts a state-of-the-art radio and TV broadcast studio, a fitness center, and a beautifully appointed marble lobby. Office lights are guided by motion sensors; even the stairwells are wallpapered and carpeted.

Nor was expense spared in furnishing the thing. Dozens of mahogany bookcases costing $1,800 each, for example, are built in throughout, and stained-glass windows adorn every floor. Total costs for furnishings and equipment came to $29 million in 1990.

"Even people here wonder if it's proper for a nonprofit for the elderly to be housed this way," says one

---

The AARP pays out nearly $2 million annually in lawyers' fees, which is more than it devotes to all but four of its more than a dozen elderly assistance programs.

AARP insider. As for the old furniture, it now sits idle in a Virginia warehouse rented at AARP expense. AARP officials defend the costs, saying that they sought to construct a building that would last for years to come. Also, they say, internal calculations showed that moving the old furniture to the new building would have cost just as much as the new decor.

Still, the decor is chump change compared to the $43 million spent on salaries for the 1,100 headquarters employees. "There are layers of people here, many of whom have little or nothing to do," says one D.C. insider. Busier, apparently, are the organization's lawyers. AARP pays out nearly $2 million annually in lawyers' fees, which is more than it devotes to all but four of its more than a dozen elderly assistance programs. AARP, in fact, retains two sets of lawyers: an in-house counsel and a team of lawyers from the New York firm of Miller, Singer, Raives, and Branden. The two lead attorneys, Alfred Miller and Lloyd Singer, have been closely associated with AARP since 1971, when the firm was formed specifically to provide legal counsel to the organization. Former AARP executive director Jack Carlson, who was fired after a 15-week tenure in 1987 following a dispute with the board of directors, explains that the lawyers' roles range from overseeing the business enterprises to monitoring committee meetings. "They permeate the whole organization," Carlson says. "There's a heavy-duty orientation to the commercial side and they didn't want anyone to come in and sabotage it."

Overseeing the empire today is executive director Horace Deets, a former Jesuit priest who joined

AARP in 1975. He is described as a low-key leader who travels frequently and who views his mission as decentralization of AARP and "intergenerational expansion" (that is, recruiting younger members). His salary is $200,000—not in the Aramony stratosphere, but at the high end of the spectrum of nonprofit executives' salaries. Deets reports to a 15-member board of directors and six national officers—all of whom are unpaid volunteers with roles limited mostly to making ceremonial appearances at functions representing AARP, attending conventions, and sitting on various committees that oversee AARP's commercial enterprises. Board members and about 250 other top-level volunteers scattered throughout the country enjoy expense accounts, free travel, and other perks that were worth about $11 million in 1990 alone.

Back in Washington, the 1,100 paid staffers are apparently not enough to get the job done at AARP-central. Every year, nearly $10 million is doled out to an army of consultants brought in to write public opinion polls, newsletter copy, and radio scripts and to perform other odd jobs, like providing "media training" to top-level volunteers preparing for radio and television appearances. AARP officials say they are unsure how many consultants are hired each year, but insiders place the number in the hundreds. Last spring, AARP paid nearly *$2 million* to a consulting firm to run an in-house workshop called "communicating with co-workers." Another consulting firm, Synectics of Cambridge, Massachusetts, was called in to instruct AARP employees on how to better provide input on projects and set priorities in the office. The amount Synectics received is unknown, but it was enough to prompt the firm to set up a satellite office in Alexandria to serve AARP. And last July, as staffers prepared to move from the old AARP building to the new headquarters, more hired guns were ushered in—in this case to help train employees in how to pack their belongings into boxes for moving.

Hot for profit

While the Washington crowd enjoys the riches of the organization, the level of support that flows back to members is rather paltry. Of the approximately $30 million spent assisting the elderly in 1991, $4 million went to coordinate programs such as educational forums and diet and exercise activities, $4 million was spent on the biennial convention, and $3.7 million was devoted to "education of older workers and employers in matters of obtaining employment . . . keeping employment and retirement planning." With respect to the last program, what AARP neglects to mention in its public financial records is that it also *charges* members $35 to enroll in such courses.

AARP has a penchant for charging members for services. One of the organization's most popular assistance programs is its 55/Alive driving education course for seniors. It is, of course, an important and useful service, but while AARP spends about $2.8

million to run it, it also *collects* an $8 fee from most of the 450,000 enrollees.

Leaders of local AARP chapters across the country also charge that the national office, despite its bulging bankrolls, does little to support them beyond printing pamphlets and offering moral encouragement. Many chapters hold bake sales or fundraisers to scrape up money for meetings or events. The scant support shows. So disorganized were local chapters that when phone inquiries were made regarding three of AARP's most vaunted volunteer programs (legal aid, services, Medicare/Medicaid advice, and a widow support ser-

> *Its 33-million-name list is the heart of AARP's financial empire; alone its worth millions of dollars, since direct mail solicitations are the corner stone of its fortunes.*

vice), only about a third of the offices contacted had any idea that the programs exist.

The response wasn't much better when similar inquiries were made to the Washington headquarters about its Medicaid/Medicare assistance program and the Financial Information Program (offering advice on money-related topics). In each case, callers were told that no such programs exist. But inquiries about purchasing health insurance and prescription drugs were handled promptly.

Another example of AARP's emphasis on profits over service occurred last year when chapter officer Virginia Fine of the Sacramento, California, AARP asked AARP's national office for a list of all AARP members in her region in an attempt to encourage members to become more active in the local chapter. AARP refused to release the list, saying it was confidential. Eventually she and other local leaders petitioned the state attorney general to force AARP to release the names. Why the hesitancy from Washington? Its 33-million-name list is the heart of AARP's financial empire; alone it's worth millions of dollars, since direct mail solicitations are the corner-stone of its fortunes. So protective of this list is AARP that its bylaws call for expulsion or suspension of any member who releases "a complete or partial list of members" without written permission from AARP's president.

Capitol crimes

Of course, direct services to the elderly aren't

AARP's only game, as officials there are quick to tell you. AARP's real forte is helping its members on Capitol Hill. AARP's legendary lobbying arm, which absorbs about $18 million of its budget, includes a team of 18 lobbyists and researchers in its policy shop, the Public Policy Institute. As expected, chief among AARP's causes are averting cuts in benefits for the elderly, protection of pensions, and various health care initiatives. AARP's lead lobbyist, John Rother, describes his team's lobbying style as "low key," presenting carefully researched data rather than holding press conferences or issuing "damning reports."

AARP has in past years been charged with neglecting the elderly poor in favor of the well-to-do, who are more likely to buy its services. More and more congressional aides and lobbyists, however, now credit AARP with placing greater emphasis on issues like low-income housing, as well as reemphasizing long-time causes like age discrimination, Social Security, and consumer-related issues. Yet some congressional AARP watchers still argue that the lobby has been conspicuously silent in several recent battles over bills designed to assist the elderly that could, coincidentally, also threaten AARP's financial empire.

➤*Medigap insurance reform:* In 1990, after investigations into Medigap insurance (policies designed to offer seniors coverage in areas not covered by Medicare), Congress, convinced that insurance sellers were swindling many seniors into buying protection they didn't need or already had, moved to clean up the mess. The reform legislation, which called for a fairer system for seniors but a less profitable one for insurance providers, won the hearty support of all seniors groups—except, according to congressional aides involved in enacting the legislation, AARP. AARP officials today insist that they fully backed the legislation. But one senior-level aide to a congressman who sponsored the measure disagrees. "They met with us and gave some suggestions, but most of these were on how to *soften* the bill."

➤*Prescription drug prices:* After congressional hearings in 1990 found that drug companies were overcharging Medicare for pharmaceuticals, legislation was introduced to force lower fees. The bill aimed not only to save the government billions of dollars, but also to help people insured through Medicare, who often faced out-of-pocket costs of 50 cents to a dollar per prescription, limits on the types of medications covered, and in some cases restrictions on the number of times they could refill those prescriptions. The losers were, of course, the drug sellers, who'd see their profit-margins diminish. Again, full support came from almost every seniors group except—you guessed it. While Rother insists that AARP worked hard to enact the bill, Hill staffers close to the legislation again disagree. "Sure, we wished AARP would have supported it, but they weren't involved," says a senior Senate staff aide instrumental in the bill's enactment.

➤*National health insurance:* Instead of endorsing any of the nearly one dozen plans introduced in Congress, AARP recently released a preliminary draft of its own health insurance plan, one it claims is best for all Americans, not just the elderly. While it includes a few "Canadian-style" features like universal long-term care coverage, the plan is, first and foremost, a "play-or-pay" model that calls for employers to provide insurance to employees or pay into a public fund. Employer-based programs have received criticism from other elderly groups because they do less for seniors than Canadian-style systems. As a result, elderly advocates question AARP's motives in eschewing any of the proposed Canadian-style plans, noting that an employer-based model, unlike nationalized health care, would allow AARP's $100 million insurance-selling enterprise to survive.

If the profitmaking impulse occasionally affects AARP's lobbying efforts, it also sustains the group's flagship publication, *Modern Maturity*, which the organization considers a crucial tool in its mission to educate seniors. While the magazine is filled with innocuous service pieces, there is a seamier side to the publication: its thinly masked mission to promote AARP's business enterprises. A survey of recent issues showed that on average more than a third of the advertising inches promoted AARP-sponsored products or services offered by its discount partners. In fact, about one in every 10 pages featured an ad pushing an AARP product. (Competing products and services almost never appear in the magazine.)

Of course, *Modern Maturity* doesn't run articles that outright endorse any of AARP's products or services. Instead, what you'll find on, say, the page opposite the health column is a full-page ad for the organization's insurance plan. And while articles offering advice on how to wisely invest money don't make specific mention of AARP's investment service (and of course omit mention of other plans, no matter how highly rated), they do appear close to ads for AARP's Scudder investment plan. "They wouldn't write a piece on a trip to the Second Coming unless it was operated by American Express tours," says Leonard Hansen, a New Orleans-based syndicated columnist on elderly affairs.

You might think some of AARP's members would get wise to self-promotion like this and do something about it. But while there are nearly 4,000 local AARP chapters across the nation, each with its own elected leadership, members have little voice in setting AARP policy. Washington keeps a tight grip on the selection of both regional and state leaders. State directors, area vice presidents, and state coordinators are all appointed by AARP's Washington-based executive committee. In the past, members attempting to assert their own opinions on political issues have faced the wrath of the Washington office. Ted Ruhig, who served several terms as an officer of AARP's Carmichael, California, chapter, was a regional director of AARP's voter education drive in 1989. Unhappy with AARP's position on catastrophic care legislation, Ruhig spoke out publicly against the lobby. A few weeks later, he received a letter from the Washington headquarters thanking him for his years of service to AARP and dismissing him from his leadership post.

"Occasionally we have to terminate people," Rother explains, "although it's not a pleasant thing to do."

Elder hostile

From the headquarters to the magazine, AARP seems a lot more of a business than a charity or grassroots lobby. In fact, the organization has in many respects evolved into a giant merchandising company that taxpayers subsidize to the tune of millions of dollars. "If I could, I'd walk into AARP and immediately shift the money around," Kurt Vondran, a lobbyist with the National Council on Senior Citizens, says enviously, thinking of the services and programs that could be created with that glorious $300 million budget.

Of course, Vondran's wishes aside, AARP doesn't *have* to chuck the mahogany bookcases, the box-packing consultants, the $11 million executive perks, or the selling obsession. It doesn't *have* to start functioning as a nonprofit, running programs on behalf of the seniors it's chartered to serve. There's another reasonable option. AARP can keep on peddling those products and living as baroquely as it likes —just as long as it drops the charitable cover and pays its taxes like other American businesses. That'd mean, hmmm, millions of dollars saved every year by the federal government—probably a bigger help to America's older people than the AARP will ever be.

The New Face of Aging

From intergenerational friendships to elder activism, the "conscious aging" movement offers a new concept of what's possible in the second half of life.

Jonathan Adolph

Jonathan Adolph is New Age Journal's *senior editor.*

Even after all these years, the memory still haunts Barry Barkan. It was his first visit to the nursing home where his grandmother had recently been placed, one of several such institutions that lined the beach front in Long Beach, New York. The place was "smelly, dark, dirty, and unfriendly," Barkan recalls. As for his grandmother, "nobody knew her for who she used to be, as a parent, as a mother, as a wife, as a person with a life and a vision, with a spiritual life. She had no identity." It was two in the afternoon and his grandmother lay on a hospital bed wearing a nightgown. Her teeth were not in her mouth.

"As a boy, I used to spend hours on end sitting in Grandma's rocker, talking with her about family and world affairs, especially as they related to the Jews, and about the old days—just chatting," he would later write. "Now there wasn't much to say. I couldn't find a way to transcend the sorrow that now became a barrier between my grandmother and the rest of us. She didn't want to live anymore. She said it again and again. Not as a person letting go of the sweet gift of life and preparing for a mysterious connection to the God to whom I remember her frequently praying, but as a person betrayed."

As the years passed, Barkan would recall that image of his grandmother—and see himself. And he realized that if he was going to age in a more humane world, change had to begin now. Drawing upon the empowerment and consciousness-raising techniques he had learned as a civil-rights and anti-war activist in the '60s, Barkan took his work right into the belly of the beast—the nursing homes themselves. Through what he came to call the Live Oak Project, he and his partners began establishing "regenerative communities" among residents and staff. "What we did, essentially, is we went in and organized a culture, a life, among the people in the home, by bringing them together at the same time every day and talking about what was going on in the home, in their lives; what was meaningful." In March 1986, the group took the work a step further and became owners of a nursing home of their own: the Live Oak Living Center at Greenridge Heights in El Sobrante, California. Today, the center's eighty-five residents use the regenerative-community model to take an active role in their own affairs, gathering regularly to plan meals, help produce books of poetry, or memorialize members who have died.

Old age. No issue touches more people and stirs less public debate. In a culture so enamored of outward appearance, aging is a reality many of us would simply rather not face. But, say Barkan and others working to redefine what is possible in our later years, by closing ourselves off from this integral stage of life we also deny ourselves a crucial opportunity for self-understanding. For along with wrinkled skin, gray hair, and sagging flesh, they argue, old age can also bring the wisdom, insights, and inner peace that often prove elusive in younger years. "All the emphasis on aging tends to be negative, because we tend to look at people from an external, material point of view," notes Rick Moody, deputy director of Hunter College's Brookdale Center on Aging and a leading thinker in the field. "If you just define people that way, you're never going to look at what the strengths of aging are, because the strengths really are inner."

From *New Age Journal*, March/April 1992, pp. 62-66. Reprinted by permission.

Breaking Stereotypes
EXTRAORDINARY, ORDINARY OLDER AMERICANS

Twelve years ago, public radio reporter Connie Goldman posed a question to a group of kindergartners for a supposedly light feature for Mothers' Day: What is old? The young students' answers—innocent reflections of cultural stereotypes—would set Goldman on a professional quest that continues to this day: to explode the myths and misconceptions about aging.

"There were an overwhelming number of negative responses," recalls Goldman, whose subsequent interviews with "extraordinary, ordinary older Americans" became the series "Late Bloomer" heard on National Public Radio and whose most recent work, a book of interviews with forty prominent older Americans titled *The Ageless Spirit,* will be published by Ballantine this May. "The children said, 'Old people, they fall asleep a lot,' or 'They keep saying the same thing over and over,' or 'They sit around, they don't do nothing.' "

In her interviews for NPR and elsewhere over the years, Goldman has been presented with quite another picture of aging: people who were using their old age—and the greater self-knowledge that comes with it—to explore new pursuits, learn new skills, give back some-thing to their communities. The stories Goldman's work has brought to light can be powerful inspiration: The recent retiree, say, who at his wife's suggestion dug out the accordion he hadn't played since their courting days and eventually found himself with a new volunteer career—playing for gleeful kids at nursery schools. Or the man who tutored kids in reading (even though he was legally blind) and was welcomed into a whole community of teachers and students in the process. "I sat in while he was tutoring these two little boys, and I said, 'How can you do that when you can't even see what they're reading?' And he laughed and said, 'Listen, I read for plenty of years before I lost my sight. I can tell if a sentence is being read right.'

"It's a matter of attitude," Goldman concludes. "It's how you deal with what life gives you. It's how you integrate it into your life. It's how you keep it from taking charge of your life. I mean, there *is* sadness. There is loss that comes with age—loss of mates and friends and family and often loss of mobility and loss of health. It isn't all freedom and it isn't all fun. But it also isn't all sadness and loss and grief and wrinkles."

Activism
GATEKEEPERS TO THE FUTURE

They meet in living rooms or gather around kitchen tables operating under the provocative nom de guerre Gatekeepers to the Future. Most often, they come together to simply discuss a topic of local significance—water issues, say, or the fate of the rainforests—but almost inevitably the talk leads to action. Soon, they're supporting a referendum or organizing a letter-writing campaign. As they become more and more informed about the problem," explains group founder Martin Knowlton, "they tend to become activists."

Wide-eyed teen-agers out to change the world? Not quite. Knowlton's Gatekeepers are almost exclusively of retirement age, people who are using their spare time and life experience to, in his words, "become active representatives of the people of the future." So far, the five-year-old group has some 450 members, roughly 150 of whom take part in the informal discussion/activism groups that the organization helps form and supports with background papers, a quarterly newsletter, and other resources.

Knowlton—a teacher, research engineer, world traveler, and social activist—is no stranger to the concept of organizing elders. In the mid-'70s, together with his colleague David Bianco, he founded Elderhostel, the hugely popular international travel and study program that now serves more than 200,000 over-fifty-five student-adventurers. If Elderhostel was Knowlton's "think globally," Gatekeepers to the Future is his "act locally." He is quick to note, however, that the organization does not have any political agenda other than encouraging elders to represent the interests of the generations to come. The individual discussion groups choose what they want to study and how they want to follow up on what they've learned.

The power of Gatekeepers, Knowlton explains, lies in "having an informed body of people who are influential dealing with these things." Under the group's watchful eye, the slow process of social change is given new importance. "We're doing things as a society today that we're probably not going to see the results of in our lifetime," Knowlton notes. "But they are going to have a possibly profound effect on the lifetime of our grandchildren's generation."

Intergenerational Relationships
THE MEETING OF PAST AND FUTURE

Nothing breaks down fears and misconceptions about aging, Nancy Henkin believes, quite like face-to-wrinkled-face contact. As head of Temple University's Center for Intergenerational Learning, Henkin has seen firsthand how our society's segregation of the ages strips both young and old of vital roles, and how restoring those roles—through intergenerational programs such as the ones she offers—can bring remarkable results. "There's nothing as special as going into a nursing home and seeing a kid who may be pretty wild at school wheeling a frail old woman around or feeding her lunch," she says. The old woman gains a companion, but just as important, "this kid feels terrific, because he's really helping someone who's worse off than he is."

But the Center's programs (there are now eleven) are not just about the young helping the infirm. One of Henkin's most successful—Linking Lifetimes—is a mentoring program, now in place in nine cities around the country, that matches adults aged fifty-five and older with kids beginning to slip through the social service cracks. The program specifically looks for men

tors who can share a common bond of experience—men who faced the same pressures growing up on the same neighborhood streets, say, or women who themselves were teen-aged mothers. "They can connect with the kids," notes Henkin, "in a way other people can't."

Uniting all the Center's programs—from Homefriends (in which high school students help house-bound elders) to Project WRITE (in which college students teach reading and writing to elders) to ECHO (a training program for elders interested in child care)—is the idea that both the young and the old are often untapped resources whose various skills and knowledge can be mobilized to meet community needs. At the same time, the meeting of past and future can have consequences that are even more far-reaching.

"If we start at a young age realizing that we're all connected," Henkin says, "and that someday I'm going to be like Grandma and that years ago Grandma was like me, then maybe we won't fear the aging process so much and maybe we'll be able to reach out to each other in more meaningful ways."

Housing
FINDING COMMUNITY

In her frequent talks around the country, gerontologist and housing expert Jane Porcino has been hearing an increasingly common complaint: People tell her they don't feel connected to other people. They feel alone. They miss a sense of community. And they worry about becoming even more isolated in their old age.

Fortunately, Porcino has some solutions. In *Living Longer, Living Better: Adventures in Community Housing for Those in the Second Half of Life*, she outlines dozens of innovative housing options now available that blend the privacy of home ownership with the companionship of group living. Ultimately, she says, housing is not simply a matter of shelter. "What we're doing here in a sense is developing a new form of family."

The options for older people vary widely, from informal collaborative arrangements (where one person may have a large house and another needs a place to stay) to intergenerational small-group living (where as many as a dozen unrelated people share a large house or apartment building) to larger intentional communities (which

attract people who share a common interest, often a spiritual perspective). Still, Porcino says, when it comes to elder housing, "people think its only a nursing home, retirement community, or living alone."

One of the most promising new ideas to Porcino is cohousing, an arrangement imported from Denmark in which members buy their own units within a larger housing or condominium complex but share meals, activities, and space in a common building. These intergenerational settings would seem to offer an ideal environment for an older person—with friends, entertainment, meals, and people of all ages nearby. As many as one hundred cohousing groups (including one started by Porcino's son) are now in various stages of formation in the United States, and Porcino predicts that many more will be created as people see the satisfaction that community living can bring. "It's healthier to live with others," she says. "Not only will we live longer, but we'll live better.

Spiritual Eldering
SAVING YOUR LIFE

For Rabbi Zalman Schachter-Shalomi, founder of the Spiritual Eldering Project at Philadelphia's P'nai Or Religious Fellowship, the key to gaining the wisdom and self-understanding that make one a true elder lies in the willingness to face death head-on.

"People who don't want to look ahead as they grow older *back* into the future rather than walk into the future," explains Schachter-Shalomi, who in his "From Aging to Sage-ing" seminars uses a range of self-exploration, imaginal, and group-discussion exercises to help older people confront their fears of aging. "When they back into the future, they look at the past. And when they look at the past, they see their failures."

Only by making peace with mortality, he says, can we keep open a path to the future. And with the future before us, we can then review our past in a more healthy light. "One sees that the painful memories aren't necessarily failures," he says, "but that the memory is like the grain of sand in the oyster that grows the pearl."

This process of life review—of exploring, in Schachter-Shalomi's words, "the obstacles, the emotional hot spots, the freak-outs and anxieties that shut down consciousness"—can be difficult for many people. But it can be made easier, he says, by viewing our lives as having a greater purpose than our Earthly existence

may suggest. "When a person finds out, I have been a cell in the global brain, I have made Earth become conscious of herself, this was my privilege—to be conscious and to be alive and to have loved and shared—that gives a different ambience to the person. It shows that the later years can be delightful rather than sad."

Maintaining a forward-looking attitude becomes all the more important as we head into the "October, November, and December" of the lifetime—the crucial period in our social and spiritual development when we can assess what our lives have taught us. "When you are working on a computer, sometimes you type a whole page and then the power goes out," Schachter-Shalomi observes. "If you have not saved your work to disk it is all lost. A lifetime asks the same question, 'Are you saved?' You must write into the global awareness what it is that you have accumulated in your lifetime and who you have become."

In Schachter's cosmology-a rich blend of Eastern spiritual ideas and Western transpersonal psychology as well as Jewish mysticism—the "saving" of each life has tremendous significance. "I believe there is more good in the world than evil—but not by much," he says. "The task of each of us is to help tip the scale. Every life matters immensely and every well-lived and completed life helps in *tikkun olam* (healing the world)."

That limited view of old age may be ready to give way, however, say Barkan, Moody, and other advocates of what is being called "conscious aging." Perhaps the greatest force behind this shift is demographic: The baby boom, that generational bulge that has shaped so much of cultural life in the late twentieth century, is now inching toward fiftysomething—and finding itself face-to-face with aging parents, failing health, and other hard-to-rebut evidence of human mortality. At the same time, this "age wave" of older Americans threatens to put new pressure on already overburdened health care systems and social services. In short, we have seen the elderly, and they are us—and our uncertain future is giving us pause. Notes Mark Gerzon, author of the forthcoming *Coming Into Our Own: Understanding the Adult Metamorphosis:* "There is this age group that is trying to say, 'Wait a minute. We lived our youth differently than our parents did. How do we live the second half of our life differently than our parents did?' "

That such concerns are on the rise is further evidenced by the creation of a three-day conference dedicated entirely to the alternative aging movement. Titled "Conscious Aging: A Creative and Spiritual Journey," the first-of-its-kind gathering, to be held in New York City May 1 through 3, will bring together more than two dozen prominent teachers, researchers, doctors, and spiritual leaders—from Yale surgeon Bernie Siegel to Rabbi Zalman Schachter-Shalomi to Gray Panthers founder Maggie Kuhn—all of whom are working to give old age new meaning. Hosted by the Omega Institute, a holistic education center in Rhinebeck, New York, the conference is being seen as something of a watershed event, a signal that the generation that once hoped to die before it got old may be ready to change its tune. "As it is now, we look on the elder years as worthless and even contemptible," notes Omega cofounder Elizabeth Lesser. "That kind of thinking robs so much from so many of us, no matter how old we are. We need a new way of looking at and experiencing aging."

For many people, however, thinking about growing old is still about as pleasant as contemplating extensive dental work. The reasons for this, notes University of Texas scholar Thomas R. Cole, author of *The Journey of Life: A Cultural History of Aging in America*, are often as much cultural as personal.

RESOURCES

Live Oak Living Center at Greenridge Heights
2150 Pyramid Dr.
El Sobrante CA 94803
(415) 222-1242

Spiritual Eldering Project
P'nai Or Religious Fellowship
7318 Germantown Ave.
Philadelphia PA 19119
(215) 242-4074

Center for Intergenerational Learning
Temple University
1601 N. Broad St.
Philadelphia PA 19122
(215) 787-6836

Gray Panthers
6342 Greene St.
Philadelphia PA 19144
(215) 438-0276

Gatekeepers to the Future
Fort Cronkhite, Building 1055
Sausalito CA 94965
(415) 331-5513

Omega Institute
RD 2, Box 377, Lake Dr.
Rhinebeck NY 12572
(914) 338-6030

Living Longer, Living Better: Adventures in Community Housing For Those in the Second Half of Life by Jane Porcino (Continuum, 1991); $15.95.

Coming Into Our Own: Understanding the Adult Metamorphosis by Mark Gerzon (Delacorte Press, 1992); $19.

The Journey of Life: A Cultural History of Aging in America by Thomas R. Cole (Cambridge University Press, 1992); $27.95.

"Aging and the Human Spirit Newsletter"
The University of Texas Medical Branch, M-11, Institute for the Medical Humanities
Galveston TX 77550-2764

"It never has been fun to grow old and frail and sick," Cole notes. "But before the middle of the nineteenth century, people had a sense, rooted in their religious traditions, that aging was part of a natural process that one could not change. One *could*, however, transform its meaning—depending on one's religious convictions—and live it as a journey to salvation."

That existentially comforting philosophy, however, was soon replaced by the scientific and medical views of growing older—ideas that are still with us today. "People consider aging as a problem that can be solved just as any other disease can be solved," says Cole. "You have an endless number of tummy tucks, eat the right foods, or run enough, and you'll be able to avoid the debilitating aspects." That idea, however, is only half true. What's more, Cole notes, by believing we can "solve" aging, instead of coming to terms with it, we lose a powerful opportunity for gaining self-knowledge. Our mortality, once accepted, he says, "can become the existential ground for compassion, solidarity, and spiritual growth." And it's not just the StairMaster set that may have trouble accepting aging. Explorers of self-development may get hung up as well, says Rick Moody. "In many ways the whole new age sensibility has often been centered

around issues of personal control—being in charge of your life, mastering your destiny, acquiring higher states of consciousness, that sort of thing," he says. "And in many ways aging represents the antithesis of that. It represents coping with finitude, loss of control, coming to terms with limits, but not necessarily in a negative way."

Moody, in fact, sees a close parallel between the difficulty we as individuals have in coming to terms with the limits of aging and the difficulty our society now has in coming to terms with the ecological limits of the planet. "In both cases," he says, "we're witnessing the collapse of the idea of unlimited growth."

For Barry Barkan, the task of breaking through denial and honestly facing issues of aging represents nothing less than the central social challenge of our time. In his latest project, Barkan intends to show his peers exactly why this is so. The book he is writing—"a wake-up call to the '60s generation" entitled *Live Oak Reveille*—will lay out the future as it might occur if action isn't taken: a future in which the baby boomers find themselves aging amid dwindling government resources; substandard health care, housing, and transportation; and unprecedented intergenerational strife. "For the first time in history we have the potential to turn over a world that's less good than the one we got from our parents," he cautions. "There's going to be a lot of anger about this."

That's the bad news. The good news is that we may have time to change things—to reprioritize the way our government spends its money, to resolve long-denied social problems, to create a society that respects its elders as we would like to be respected when we reach that age.

"We've got a very small window of opportunity," Barkan says. "And we have to work on a number of levels. We have to become conscious about the way we're relating to this generation of elders. We need to develop a vision of our own sense of elderhood, about what it means to be an elder, so we can age toward that vision. And we need to promote and develop a pro-elder public policy agenda."

"On a macro level," he continues, "we need to pacify the world. Because if we don't do it now, if we don't move from a militaristic world to a world that uses its resources for peace, then we're not going to have the kind of world that we can age into."

Barkan believes that the same demographic forces that are helping to create the approaching aging crisis can help head it off, if the baby boomers recognize what they stand to gain—and lose. "Many of my peers think back to the '60s and '70s as having been the heyday of our generation," he says. "But that's not the best day of our generation. The best day of our generation has got to be ahead of us.

"What we need to do now is gather our energies and our attention, thinking about ourselves, our lives, our future, and the lives of future generations," he continues. "We have to reorganize ourselves as a generation so that we can take power. Those of us who are now in our forties and fifties—this is the period in life when people ordinarily have become the movers and shakers of society and taken over the institutions of society. This is our power period."

Still, the task seems daunting: How can we break through our denial and confront aging in a more healthy way? More specifically, how can we learn to become not simply old people, but societal elders—people whose years on the planet are seen not as a burden to be borne but as a source of wisdom? And how can we create a society that will respect and honor that wisdom? The programs profiled on these pages—developed by advocates of "conscious aging"—suggest some first steps we can take toward that goal.

UNPLANNED PARENTHOOD

David Larsen

The author recently retired after many years as a reporter/writer with the Los Angeles Times.

Raising your grandchildren is a lot different than raising your own kids," says Mary Etta Johnson of Anaheim, California. "We hadn't had children in our home for years; suddenly they were there almost 24 hours a day."

Johnson and her husband, Albert, took their two grandchildren into their home after their daughter and son-in-law became involved in drugs and the marriage broke up. They've had the youngsters, now nine and seven, for five years now; in 1986, they got permanent custody.

In Media, Pennsylvania, Diane Warner decided she'd had enough and told her drug-addicted live-in daughter to move out. Her little grandson stayed.

Three years ago Melody Hudgins' daughter left her two-year-old son in a Hollywood motel room and went out to buy drugs. The tot was found by police, who turned him over to his grandmother. The boy's father? As in most of these cases, he simply isn't in the picture.

At an age when they least expect it, when they had other plans for their later years, an increasing number of grandparents nationwide are finding themselves being recycled as parents—to their children's children.

There are many reasons: death, abandonment, incarceration, mental illness, physical and/or sexual abuse. But the main cause is drug or alcohol addiction. And the burden, ironically, falls on a generation that played virtually no role in the drug scene.

There are no statistics to define the scale of the problem, which affects families in middle-class suburb and inner-city alike. But social-service agencies agree the number is rising.

Barbara Kirkland, an activist grandmother in Colleyville, Texas, says talks with family counselors nationwide lead her to conclude that about 5 percent of American families comprise a grandparent raising a grandchild.

Kirkland and husband Gerald are raising their ten-year-old granddaughter. Their son was killed in an industrial accident; their former daughter-in-law (the couple were divorced) has made no attempt to contact her child. "Friends suggested we attend parenting courses," says Kirkland of those first anxious months in her new role. "But this is different from being a young parent. That's why I founded a support group of my own: Grandparents Raising Grandchildren."

Across the country other grandparents in similar situations are using support groups to help them cope with the special challenges they face.

In a neon-lit conference room in Long Beach, California, visitors find a scene Norman Rockwell would never have painted. Nine grandmothers sit on couches and chairs facing each other. They aren't swapping recipes or travel tales. They're attending their weekly meeting of Grandparents As Parents. Sylvie de Toledo, the licensed clinical social worker who runs the sessions, started GAP three years ago after seeing firsthand the trials her own parents went through when her sister died and they took in her eight-year-old son.

"Older people in this situation feel cheated out of the traditional doting-grandparent role," she says. "And the children are also deprived of the relationship. The word 'grand' has been taken out of the experience for both generations."

De Toledo leads GAP groups at the Psychiatric Clinic for Youth in Long Beach and at the Reiss-Davis Child Study Center in Los Angeles; in between, she spends a lot of time on the phone helping grandparents in other states start their own organizations.

Judy Kingston and Peggy Plante started GAP in Quincy, Massachusetts, in November 1989. Judy and Larry Kingston are raising a nine-year-old grandson; Peggy Plante and husband Frank are raising their four-year-old granddaughter. The Plantes have permanent guardianship of their granddaughter and are in the process of adopting her.

Their group meets once a month in a nearby seniors' hall with anywhere from seven to 17 people attending. Sessions often feature guest speakers such as psychologists, social workers and attorneys who offer professional insights into members' problems. Between meetings, group members call each other when things get rough; there's also a monthly newsletter.

"I was surprised at how many of us there were," recalls Kingston. "I'm sure there must be even more people out there in this situation who aren't aware we exist."

In Shreveport, Louisiana, Betty and Ralph Parbs had already raised their own four children when they found themselves with three live-in grandchildren—all under age ten. One day Parbs remarked to her husband, "You know, honey, we can't be the only people in this position."

All it took to find the others was a small ad in the local paper.

"We got four responses," says Parbs. "Then it kind of snowballed." Now, five years later, GAIN (Grandparents Against Immorality and Neglect) draws some 50 people to meetings held twice monthly in the community room of a nearby mall.

Diane Warner founded her Pennsylvania group, Second Time Around Parents, in anger. "I'd been watching yet another television show about the drug problem," she recalls, the frustration rising in her voice. "They were talking about the millions of dollars the government is pouring into the war on drugs and into building new rehabilitation centers. And I *know* some addicts use rehab centers as a way to avoid jail—almost as a vacation—I've seen it in my own home! And I thought, 'God! Why isn't any of this money going to the victims—to the children of these drug addicts and their caregivers? What about *us?*' "

Second Time Around's weekly meetings attract some 20 grandparents. But Warner doesn't intend to stop there. Says she: "We've got a lot of political work to do. There isn't one law in this country that protects people in our position."

In Milwaukee, Wisconsin, child psychotherapist Carole Stewart started From Generation to Generation after noticing how many of her young clients lived with their grandparents.

"A lot of these people thought this would be their time in life," says Stewart. "And though they love their grandchildren, they didn't expect this responsibility. Raising children is the most stressful job in the world. Here, grandparents give each other advice on how to cope."

"For sure it helps us—we've learned how to laugh again," agrees Paula Browne of GAP in California. "But it also helps the kids. They'll ask why they don't have a normal family like other children. Then they go to our outings and realize they aren't the only ones living with their grandparents."

Support-group meetings fulfill the same general purpose. They're especially helpful, says de Toledo, because members are often in different stages of acceptance and draw emotional support from those with more experience.

Florence Gilmore, who flew to Washington state to collect her three young grandsons after their parents, both drug addicts, were declared unfit, was overwhelmed by practical matters: "When I first came to GAP I was emotionally and spiritually exhausted," she recalls. "I didn't know what shots the boys had had, where to find a good doctor. Eddie [my husband] and I spent all our time changing diapers. It was terrible. And for several months Eddie worked nights then babysat while I worked during the day. He was really wonderful."

"I was angry when I first came to these meetings," admits Melody Hudgins. "I resented having to raise a child again and I was angry at my daughter for putting me in this position."

Grandparents also feel guilty. "They say to themselves, 'What did I do to cause this?' " says Barbara Kirkland of GRG. "They have to acknowledge these feelings and that it's okay to have them. The fact is," she stresses, "probably nothing they did caused the situation."

That familiar lament, "Where did we go wrong?" hits hard at these times, especially when the adult children grew up in stable, loving homes. "The kids see some terrible things," says Diane Warner, whose home was wrecked when her daughter was beaten up by a companion—in front of the daughter's child.

Their own anxiety aside, recycled grandparents have to cope with the reactions of others: "People tell me I'm too old to be doing this," says Elinore Simmons, who's raising a seven-year-old boy and a four-year-old girl. "I tell them I have no choice."

As a result, social lives suffer.

"Other older people don't want to see you come around with little kids," says Johnnie Mae Short, who's raising three grandchildren. "They don't stop being your friends—they just don't have you over like they used to."

"Your social circle does change," agrees Kirkland. "Friends whose kids are in college don't understand when they phone and you have to put them on hold while you get Tommy a glass of water. Or they'll call you at 6 o'clock and invite you over, not realizing it's too late for you to get a sitter or that you're just too tired to make the effort. Soon the phone calls and the invitations stop."

Some grandparents are active in Girl or Boy Scouts, attend PTA meetings or do their part toward school events. "But they don't fit into that younger, more energetic group of parents who are confident they're going to change the world," says Kirkland. "They've already been there."

Though often it is widowed grandmothers who take in the children, there are many actively involved grandfathers. Frank Plante, for one, sees only opportunity in the situation. Says he: "It's like starting over again."

Other grandfathers, however, may feel neglected. Albert Johnson confesses to some resentment: "We'd just learned to play golf and were planning a trip to New England," he says. "But it won't happen now. Maybe a little later—with the kids."

Few grandfathers attend support groups; when they do, it's usually out of curiosity.

"The burden of raising a child at this stage of life and also coping with the loss of an adult child—for whatever reason—often causes problems between couples who've spent most of their lives together," says de Toledo. "It's important that grandparents share the responsibility. But it's imperative they set aside time for themselves away from the grandchildren; a time to give to each other."

That can be hard. All agree they don't have the energy they once had.

In Wisconsin, Virginia Walker, a regular at From Generation to Generation sessions, has good reason to be tired. As nursing secretary at a Milwaukee hospital her shift doesn't end until 11:30 P.M., she usually doesn't get to sleep before 2 A.M., and less than five hours later she's laying out clothes for the eight-year-old grandson she's raising as a single grandparent.

"He stays with the babysitter weeknights and she brings him over before she leaves for work in the morning," Walker says. "He and I see each other mostly on weekends, when we go to the library or the movies or maybe the park."

Says Charlotte Ellison, who is up before 7 A.M. and usually still doing laundry late at night, "I don't know whether it's killing me or keeping me alive."

Then there's the financial drain. Some grandparents have adult children as well as grandchildren dependent on them. Some have had to stop working, since the cost of child care negates their earnings.

Ellison gave up her highly successful career as a commercial artist, and she and her husband were forced to dip into savings they'd planned to use for retirement. Johnnie Mae Short and her husband have no savings left. Says Short: "We eat a lot of spaghetti and meatloaf." Diane Warner lost her $42,000-a-year job while trying to help her daughter fight her drug addiction. "But then she'd take off with my car and leave the boy at home," Warner recalls. She and her grandson are on welfare: now she's afraid she'll lose her home, too. For those like Warner who have custody of their grandchildren, there's the extra burden of court costs.

Unlike foster parents, grandparents raising their natural grandchildren receive minimal federal or state support. Some may qualify for Aid to Families With Dependent Children, but this is not as comprehensive as foster-care benefits. Foster-care payments are higher, include a clothing allowance, and increase as the child grows older. However, not all states allow relatives to be eligible for the foster-care program; some argue that "grandparents already have adequate incentive to care for their grandchildren." Social Security assistance is limited, available only when natural or adoptive parents have died or are disabled.

Senator John Heinz* (R-Pennsylvania), ranking Republican on the Senate Special Committee on Aging, is studying the impact of the nation's drug epidemic on America's families, and in particular on older citizens. He is exploring legislation that would help grandparents who must intervene to protect their grandchildren. One possibility: That when working grandparents have legal custody of one or more grandchildren, employers be required to extend group health insur-

[*Senator John Heinz died in a plane crash, April 4, 1991.—Ed.]

ance coverage to those children. Heinz is also looking at the foster-care program with an eye toward creating a new assistance category to accommodate the special circumstances that exist when a grandparent assumes the role of parent.

Says Heinz: "I plan to examine this issue closely for the sake of grandparents who have put their lives on hold to parent a second family, and for the children—the hidden victims of drug abuse. We should reward grandparents for stepping in to care for a needy child. They deserve the same support and respect foster parents receive."

And if all that weren't enough, the grandparents worry about their grandchildren's social and academic well-being. Some of the kids are embarrassed by their situation, particularly by the age gap. Their peers may tease them, thus emphasizing the difference between their families and those of their friends.

Betty Parbs likes to tell other grandparents who are raising their grandchildren not to dwell on ages. "That'll kill you, right there," she maintains. But sometimes the youngsters are the first to point it out. When Parbs accompanied her granddaughter to a school carnival, the girl remarked brightly, "You're a *lot* older than the other mommies."

Schoolwork itself proves a challenge. "Quite a lot of these children are behind academically because they missed school while living with their parents," says de Toledo. "They have difficulty learning and require special programs. They may have a hard time concentrating because they're constantly worrying about their parents"—to whom they still feel a strong attachment regardless of how badly they were treated. They're reluctant to give up hope their parents will change and return to take care of them.

Unfortunately, this fantasy is often shared by grandparents, who become easy targets for emotional and financial exploitation by their adult children.

The relationship that develops between grandparents and grandchildren in these situations is unique, resulting in a dependency on the part of the child that can be quite touching.

Johnnie Mae Short had a heart attack five years ago. "My granddaughter worries about me," she reports. "At school she uses the excuse that she's sick so she can call home—to see how *I'm* doing."

"Kids worry, consciously or unconsciously, that they'll be abandoned again, this time by their grandparents," says de Toledo. "They feel insecure when the grandparent taking care of them becomes sick. They think: If this grandparent dies, who will take care of me? It's a scary thought for a youngster."

In these dramas, all the players who are old enough recognize the alternative is usually a foster home, and few consider that acceptable.

For the grandparents it's a labor of love, but all reach a point where they need time out for themselves. Paula Browne takes a painting class at a nearby college. Simmons plays bingo once a month. Johnnie Mae Short takes refuge in Nintendo video games. Patricia Westfall, who had seven grandchildren living with her at one time, used to get up at 4 A.M. to crochet "because it was the only time when I had peace and quiet."

"Take time out for such things as exercise," advises Peggy Plante of GAP in Massachusetts. "Go to the hairdresser's. It will make you more fun to be with. When you're good to yourself, you can be good to others."

"It's important to have someone to talk with who is in the same situation," says Kirkland. "Most of the time your own family will tell you it's not your responsibility. And it's devastating to take your kid to court and have him or her declared an unfit parent. That's when you really need another grandparent for support."

It's not hard to find support if you're prepared to take the initiative.

"When you go to your grandchild's school, watch to see who's accompanying the other kids," says Paula Browne. "You'll see some grandparents and you can strike up a conversation." Other grandparents suggest similar tactics in supermarkets, malls and buses.

"We won't be hard to spot," says Hudgins. "We all look stressed."

Yet with all the tribulations and heartbreak, re-parenting does have its rewards, says Browne: "These kids give you so much more love than your own kids because you've taken them out of the depths they've been in."

Hudgins says grandparents put more into their new role than they did the first time around. "I had my own child in my 20s," she says. "I'm older and wiser now."

"When I come into the room and get a big hug," says Johnnie Mae Short, "it makes up for a *lot*."

It's no picnic—but, as Ellison says earnestly, "We don't want to see our grandchildren turn out the way our kids did."

Perhaps these grandparents' feelings are best summed up by Short. "I'd rather have them," she says, "than worry about them."

The story of a nursing home refugee

KATHARINE M. BUTTERWORTH
WHOLE EARTH REVIEW

Taking care of the elderly is not something we do very well in our society. Most older people prefer to live out their last years on their own or with loved ones rather than in a nursing home, so the burden of caring for them falls squarely on their family and friends. But because there is little public support—either in financial help or in tangible services—for those caretakers, sometimes that burden becomes too great and a nursing home becomes the only option. That's what happened to 91-year-old Katharine Butterworth, and this is her spirited account of that time. Dollars & Sense magazine describes the mixed-up financial picture of aging policy in the United States and reminds us that with our rapidly growing population, the problem is only going to get worse.

Young families who have the responsibility of caring for old people find it hard to tuck them in the chimney corner, mainly because there is no longer a chimney corner in which to tuck them.

A bulletin from my college proudly lists 10 graduates who lived to be 100, but every one of them is in a nursing home. A nursing home used to be a halfway house between hospital and going home. Now too often it is the permanent home, the last resort for a family desperate to handle an elderly invalid. Nursing homes are expensive and to receive any financial aid from the government, such as Medicaid, one must be destitute, but that is another story.

I know about three nursing homes, two for my husband, one for myself. My husband and I had had a good and healthy life when in our mid-80s he became ill, a bladder operation leaving him in need of a permanent catheter, the infection sometimes affecting his mind. I became ill and had to enter a hospital myself, so our children insisted he go into a nursing home.

When I recovered and returned home, I visited him. He had been given a small room opposite a noisy laundry room, and a woman patient next door was moaning all night. He said he was going to jump out the window, and I told him he was on the ground floor and could walk out. I sat with him in the dining room with three men who didn't talk; they had Alzheimer's disease. The trays were metal, and noisy when handed out. He was served a huge sausage, the kind he particularly disliked, no knife, and a little dish of stewed fruit with a limp piece of cake on top. No fruit juice or water, liquids he was supposed to have plenty of. In addition he was tied in a wheelchair, making it difficult for him to reach the table. It depressed both of us.

At a meeting with the head nurses and an accountant, in which I was asked to sign many papers to make my husband's acceptance in the nursing home permanent, plus pay a $3,000 deposit in case we got behind in our payments, I burst out, "He's coming home." The nursing home had started out as a solution to a problem but it had turned into a nightmare. We would both be home in our apartment, would manage some way and die together.

Our help at home was erratic and our children again insisted my husband be placed in a nursing home. He needed more care and often wandered at night, waking me up. Once he fell out of bed at 2 a.m., which entailed my calling the police because I could not lift him or help him to climb back in.

This second "home" was much more elegant, with Georgian-style architecture, trees, garden, the room itself large and pleasant, but help here was short and he was often left in bed most of the morning. The dining room had none of the clatter of metal trays and the varied food was attractively served, each person seated at an individual table or in a wheelchair with a tray. It seemed quietly civilized until one patient shoved his tray with everything from soup to dessert and it shot with a crash across the floor, requiring that some poor soul clean up the mess. The patients looked normal but, one could guess, often were not.

Then we found Sandy and a nursing home was no longer necessary. Sandy was with us part time for

From *Utne Reader,* January/February 1991, pp. 42-49. Excerpted from *World Earth Review,* Fall 1990. *World Earth Review,* Box 38, Sausalito, CA 94966-9924.

over a year until my husband died. She was going to college, wanted to earn extra money, and we paid her above the minimum wage. Never have I known a more dedicated, hard-working, cheerful, intelligent young girl. She likes old people, and plans to run her own nursing home some day. May her dream come true. She was ideal for us, permitting my husband to stay home where he was happiest. She was strong enough to give him a tub bath, for example, and because she was cheerfully persuasive there was little friction, and I began to relax. He died at home, which in itself was a comforting end.

Six months after my husband died I came down with pneumonia, and my son and daughter-in-law took me to the emergency room in the nearby hospital. Slowly I recovered physically. There were many complications, X-rays, medicines, a speech therapist and psychologist (which confused me, but apparently I had had a slight stroke that I didn't realize until later). The best medicine was my roommate, Ruth, a rollicking, cheerful woman who was seriously ill, but made everyone who came to our room—cleaning woman, nurse, or doctor—smile.

Eventually a physical therapist got me out of bed and walking, leaning on a walker. I was shocked at how wobbly I had become. I had been in the hospital two weeks and it was time for me to move out. My son, ever helpful and concerned, phoned, "Be ready, Ma, at nine, packed and dressed. The nursing home has a room for you." We decided that this was necessary because my son and daughter-in-law were away all day, and I could never manage alone.

This home was brand new, elegant and very expensive. The girl at the entrance desk was attractively dressed and gave the impression that we were being welcomed to some country estate although the two checks my son made out, one for a large deposit, the other for a week's stay in a double room, provided hard reality.

My first impression was that a great deal had been spent on decor—charming wallpaper, heavy pink bedspread, modern lamp at the bedside table, and a modern picture on the wall. All I wanted was to get undressed and into bed, and I promptly went to sleep.

Who cares for our elders?

"Why should a woman in her 60s feel she must use up her life savings—even sell her home—to keep her mother in a nursing home for less than two years?" asked American Association of Retired Persons vice president Robert Maxwell. "Why should a couple married for 30 years be forced to get a divorce in order to protect the wife's income and assets, while the husband impoverishes himself to qualify for Medicaid-funded nursing home care?"

They shouldn't, of course. These are consequences of government inaction on an issue that affects nearly all people at some time in their lives. Mention long-term care of older citizens to most Americans, and the first image that comes to mind is the nursing home. While nursing homes constitute a thriving industry in the United States, they are not where most care for elders takes place.

For elders who can no longer fully care for themselves, most care is provided at home by family members and friends. An estimated seven million older Americans require some sort of assistance—from once-a-week shopping help, to once-a-day meal preparation, to round-the-clock nursing care.

For incapacitated elders and their families, the choices are hard. Nursing home care is costly and of poor quality. Home care services are virtually non-existent in many states, and where they are available they are expensive. For most who quit their jobs to care for their parents, there is little income support. The lack of long-term

care is indeed a national crisis.

Though most surveys of elders indicate they would rather not be institutionalized in nursing homes, institutionalization is precisely what our present system of long-term elderly care encourages.

Given the demographics of the United States, nursing homes are a growth industry. Roughly 1.6 million nursing home beds were in use in 1986. Because the number of elders in the U.S. population is projected to rise through the year 2030, the demand for nursing home beds is expected to increase to over two million in 2000, and to nearly three million by 2030.

Nursing homes are now a $38 billion industry with more than 19,000 homes. Once dominated by "mom-and-pop" operators and charitable organizations, the industry is increasingly composed of large, for-profit chains.

For nursing home residents, absentee ownership brings negative consequences. The Massachusetts Department of Public Health, charged with monitoring nursing home care, reports that absentee-owned homes have significantly more code violations than locally owned and non-profit homes.

For the patient or the patient's family, nursing home care is extremely costly. Average costs per day run as high as $100. Annual costs range from $25,000 to $40,000. Unless residents are extremely poor—or until they reach that point—most of the cost of nursing home care is borne by elders and their families. Medicare will pay only up to 100 days of acute medical and rehabilitative services in a nursing home, leaving people needing long-term care completely uncovered. Medicare pays only 2 percent of the nation's nursing home bill.

Looking back I can see why I have been critical of my elegant surroundings. One loss was not having a telephone. In the hospital I could lie in bed and gossip with all my friends. My son usually called every day. Eventually I could use the nurses' phone down the hall, but I had to have the phone handed to me across the desk, stand up, and naturally the call had to be short.

I shared a room with Rose, a woman who had been there for some time and who was a favorite with all the nurses. Her dressing often needed changing at 2 a.m., a process that involved a great deal of nurse chatter, lights, and curtain noisily pulled for "privacy." That I was awoken was unimportant to everyone but me.

Rose had a telephone that her son had had installed. I asked Rose if I could use hers and would pay her and she agreed. I used her phone just once, when she was taken for some test and I thought my conversation would not bother her. With my address book in hand I went to her bedside table to make the call. As I was dialing, a tall head nurse stalked in, accused me of using Rose's property when she was out, and snatched my address book, saying that I must have taken it from Rose's drawer. I was startled by this false accusation and angry that this woman could think I would use the phone without Rose's permission. Later I made a scene with a superintendent but nothing came of it. Rose laughed when she returned, and all that really happened was I couldn't sleep that night and was given a sleeping pill. It was a good example of the old and the weak versus the young and the strong.

Was I doomed to spend the rest of my life in this nursing home? For one thing I felt it was too expensive. How long would my money last, spent in this ridiculously extravagant fashion? It was up to me to get up and return to normal life. Weak, I got dressed and with my walker managed to make it to a big living room, where I had breakfast off a tray. There I found a dozen other more active people doing the same. The next day I

Medicaid, known as the long-term care insurance policy that requires impoverishment for a premium, is the major public payer for long-term care services. For the poor and those older Americans impoverished by the high costs of long-term care, Medicaid covers nearly all nursing home expenses. Medicaid pays nearly half the nation's nursing home bill, making it—by default rather than by design—the country's long-term care insurance policy.

Once on Medicaid, older people needing care are hardly free of worry. Medicaid sets a fixed payment rate for nursing home care that is on the average 15 to 20 percent lower than the rates charged private payers. This gives nursing home operators a strong incentive to discriminate against those on public assistance. Medicaid-supported elders seeking nursing home care typically wait four times as long for a bed in a nursing home as privately paying elders.

With all of the problems associated with nursing home care, it is perhaps not surprising that older people overwhelmingly prefer to be cared for in their own homes. Yet government spending for long-term care is heavily biased in favor of nursing homes. Neither Medicare nor Medicaid covers any significant part of home care services. As a result, 85 percent of home care is provided by friends and family members without institutional support. Of the 15 percent who receive care from paid providers, 60 percent pay the entire bill themselves. High turnover among home care workers, who are overworked and underpaid, further hampers the availability of adequate home care.

Not surprisingly, most of the caregivers—paid and unpaid—are women. Women frequently care for their infirm husbands, whom they outlive by six years on average. The burden of care also falls on adult children, usually daughters and daughters-in-law, who give up paid work to care for frail family members. The vast majority of paid home care workers are also women.

Ironically, although home care tends to be much cheaper than nursing home care, cost containment is one of the major reasons for the government's bias toward institutional care. Public officials, recognizing that the number of elders currently going without publicly supported services far exceeds the number receiving support, fear a surge in demand for home care if the government were to provide it.

According to a recent survey commissioned by senior advocates, the U.S. public is greatly concerned about the inadequacy of long-term care. Sixty percent of respondents said they had direct experience with family members or friends needing long-term care, and more than 80 percent said nursing home costs would be a major hardship on their families. Most significant, over 70 percent said they wanted a government program providing universal long-term care and would be willing to pay higher taxes to support it.

—*Dollars & Sense*

Excerpted with permission from Dollars & Sense *(Jan./Feb. 1988). Subscriptions: $19.50/yr. (10 issues) from Economic Affairs Bureau, 1 Summer St., Somerville, MA 02143. Back issues: $3 from same address.*

carried in the portable radio my son had brought me and I came back to the world and listened to the news and my favorite classical music station. At lunch, again with my walker, I went to the dining room despite the 20 minutes it took me to travel the short distance down the hall. I began to feel that with determination I could grow strong.

The staff of this particular home worked hard to make things easy and pleasant for the patients—one could say they ought to for the price. There was an exercise class every morning, and I joined this. We sat in a big circle, some in wheelchairs, others in regular chairs. A young, peppy woman led us. She brought a huge lightweight ball that she would roll to each in turn and we would kick it back with right then left foot. Many of us were weak but one could see an improvement. There were exercises with arms, "pick the apple out of the tree, then put it down in the basket"; silly, but it got one's muscles moving.

The staff organized movies and an ice-cream party for those of us who could walk or get someone to push our wheelchairs to the parlor. I began to walk the corridors for exercise, and to explore different areas. There was one much more expensive-looking area that had a living room arranged with couches and easy chairs as in a private home. Here the public library had installed a wide choice of books in large print and this attracted me. Just by signing my name and room number I could help myself. I realized for the first time that my illness had been severe enough for me to give up reading. I took out a novel that looked lightweight and easy to follow, and this room became my favorite.

In my own area there was a music room that was not used much, and I would take my book here, pretending there were no hospital beds around the corner. This room had an expensive grand piano made in China. Here on Sunday afternoon there was a concert for piano and harp. A young lady brought in her harp, an undertaking that took more time than the concert itself. Unfortunately there were barely more than a dozen people who attended.

As I walked around more I became acquainted with more patients. There was one pleasant woman with one arm paralyzed, who was always in a wheelchair. She explained to me that when she and her husband found they had physical problems they could not solve, they sold their house and both entered this nursing home with the idea of ending their lives here. They had enough money to pay for the most expensive suite, brought their own furniture, and often had special meals ordered. I never met her husband, but she was such a cheerful realist she was a pleasure to talk to.

There was another alert old gentleman whose son visited him every Sunday, and he was eager to talk. He knew the area, had been in business all his life, and would have preferred to stay home. His wife had died, and he needed too much care for his daughter-in-law to handle. Again there was enough money for him not to worry.

Many of these old people grumbled and complained and were dull to talk to. The patients whose minds were affected I found depressing. One attractive woman beautifully dressed in different outfits was like a flitting bird. She explained that her children had left her here, and she wanted to escape but she didn't know how to get out. Then she would jump up and run down the hall. There was one man with Parkinson's disease who would walk endlessly up and down the hall never meeting one's eye, looking vaguely for someone, something, perhaps his own identity.

There was a dumpy little woman with Alzheimer's disease, and she too was a wanderer with fluttering hands. She liked my room and once tried to get into my bed, to my horror. Another time she stole a book I had carelessly left on my bed. I had a nurse search her room, but we never found it, and I wrote the public library apologizing, hoping someone would return it.

Unlike the pleasant woman and her husband who planned to make this their permanent home, my attitude from the beginning had been to get strong and to leave the nursing home as soon as possible. I was lucky that I had no debilitating disease, that I could walk, and that my mind was normal. My finances were not great enough to pay for this "hotel" (for a bed and meals were what it amounted to, with little mental stimulation). In a little over three weeks I persuaded my son and daughter-in-law to take me in.

When I got to their rather cold house (the nursing home had been overheated), and had to get my own breakfast and lunch, and be alone all day, I realized I had been too impatient. I was not as tough as I had thought I was. I often would crawl back in bed and sleep an uneasy sleep, but soon I would force myself, warmly dressed, to walk around the back yard or go out for the mail. There was plenty to read, too much, but the most endearing feature was the family cat, Brandy. She too was lonely during the day, and she and I would lie down together on my bed, or she'd sit in my lap, and we'd talk and purr and were close company. Evenings and weekends were wonderful, with the stimulating company of my son and daughter-in-law, and delicious meals where all I did was set the table. The nursing home seemed far away. The next jump was to my own apartment, but this was cushioned by the arrival of my daughter, who cooked for me and spoiled me. Without the help of my children could I have recovered so quickly?

Now, two years later, at 91, I live alone. How long can I hope to keep moving about with family and friends, to take walks around the pond in the neighboring park? Can I hope to escape the permanent nursing home?

Elder care: How the U.S. stacks up

The United States isn't the only nation scrabbling to meet the needs of a growing elderly population. Our limited federal health insurance for the old and lack of a comprehensive respite-care program for caregivers puts us behind some countries. But our commitment to Social Security sets us ahead of others.

	UNITED STATES	JAPAN	CHINA	SWEDEN
PEOPLE 65 OR OLDER	30 million (12%)	13.3 million (11%)	53 million (5%)	1.5 million (18%)
WHERE THEY GET CARE	About 95% care for themselves or are cared for by family and friends. Some get assistance from in-home caregivers and adult day-care centers. The rest live in nursing homes.	About 65% of the elderly live with their children. The rest live in state-sponsored hospitals, geriatric health facilities, and nursing homes.	Adult children are subject to criminal penalties if they don't support their parents. State-supported services care for the 10% of elders who can't work and have no spouse or grown children.	More than 90% live alone or with their families and receive such services as delivered meals, transportation, and weekend care; 7% live in nursing homes; and 2% live in apartments with 24-hour nursing staffs. Adult day-care centers are available.
WHO PAYS	Less than 2% of long-term care and just 42% of nursing home care is paid for by the federal government. Home-delivered meal services and some day-care centers receive federal and state funding.	The national and local governments provide free or very-low-cost health care to older people including medicine, hospitalization, and transportation, as well as day care.	Work units (factories, farms, schools, etc.) provide all social services, including health and respite care.	All institutional care and social services are paid for by the municipal governments, with help from the national government, which also pays all pensions.
HOW THE GOVERNMENT HELPS	About 33% of the federal budget goes to Social Security, Medicare, and Medicaid.	In 1986, it spent about $29.6 billion on elder-care programs.	The government underwrites part of the cost of various welfare programs, including homes for the aged, community-based long-term care, and hospitals.	This year, $1.5 billion will be spent on elder care.
AVERAGE TAX RATE	34%	28%	Not available	51%
FUTURE PLANS	Congress is considering extending Medicare coverage of long-term health care, as well as the Family and Medical Leave Act, which would guarantee unpaid leaves for employees whose parents need care.	The government hoped to increase the number of adult day-care centers from 96 in 1989 to 3,000 by 1990.	By 2030, about 24% of China's population will be elderly, and there will be fewer young adults because of a current requirement that couples have no more than one child.	The government is increasing subsidies that will allow elders to stay in their own homes.

Reprinted by permission. Copyright © 1989 Special Report: On Family, *Whittle Communications, 505 Market St., Knoxville, TN 37902.*

Health and
Health Care Issues

To be happy, productive, and active, individuals must also be healthy. But at some point, nearly everyone has problems with health and requires help. For some, this help is readily available, affordable, and effective. But to a growing number of Americans, becoming sick is frightening and devastating because these individuals cannot afford or are not eligible for health insurance. Any illness requiring hospitalization will destroy them financially. For a society that boasts one of the highest standards of living in the world, it is paradoxical that we cannot provide adequate health care for all of our citizens regardless of their ability to pay. In the United States, health care is not a right but a privilege, and the numbers of privileged individuals are rapidly shrinking.

"Wasted Health Care Dollars" examines the factors that are accelerating the costs of health care and what must be done to contain them.

"Risky Business" has moved into the health insurance industry. To maximize earnings for its investors, managers of health insurance companies have engaged in questionable business ventures that are placing their companies in financial jeopardy. Thus, thousands of individuals could find themselves facing significant increases in their health insurance premiums or even without health care coverage at all.

"Deadly Migration" discusses the result of extensive health and environmental regulations in many industrialized nations. To escape these regulations with their associated high costs, major industries are relocating in less developed countries. This unregulated migration is spewing massive amounts of sewage and pollutants into the air and the groundwater, causing long-term suffering for the residents of these countries.

"Confronting the AIDS Pandemic" looks at the toll in lives, resources, and economic costs AIDS will take by the year 2000. Entire societies will be decimated, causing significant repercussions around the world. The problem of AIDS necessitates a coordinated worldwide effort, which is not occurring because many industrialized nations are electing to tackle "their" problem independently.

Looking Ahead: Challenge Questions

Is adequate health care in the United States a right or a privilege? In your estimation, which should it be?

What are the major factors contributing to the dismal health care statistics of the United States?

What activities of the health insurance industry might be threatening your health?

What reforms, if any, should be imposed on the health insurance industry?

How might AIDS impact on the world's economy? What threat does the AIDS epidemic pose for the rights and freedoms of those with and without AIDS or the HIV virus?

What can each individual do to contribute to the solution and control of AIDS?

From a global perspective, what can and must be done to control and eradicate AIDS?

How might you benefit and/or be harmed by the migration of large industrial companies to Third World countries?

In what major ways would the approaches of the three major types of sociological theorists differ in relation to the study of health issues?

What conflicts in values, rights, obligations, and harms seem to underlie the issues covered in this unit?

ARE YOU FOOLING YOURSELF?

If you have sex with other men, no matter how infrequently,
always use latex condoms.
Because once is all it takes to transmit the AIDS virus.
So protect yourself…and your partner. For more information, call:

AIDS Hotline 718 485-8111.

AIDS
Rubber Up For Safety

City of New York, Edward I. Koch, Mayor   Stephen C. Joseph, M.D., M.P.H., Commissioner, Department of Health.

WASTED HEALTH CARE DOLLARS

The U.S. is spending enough to bring every citizen high-quality, high-tech medical care—if we stop squandering our resources.

Of the $817-billion that we will spend this year on health care, we will throw away at least $200-billion on overpriced, useless, even harmful treatments, and on a bloated bureaucracy. We are no healthier than the citizens of comparable developed countries that spend half what we do and provide health care for everybody. In fact, by important measures such as life expectancy and infant mortality, we are far down the list.

If the wasted money could be redirected, the U.S. could include those now shut out of the system—without increasing the total outlay for health care and without restricting the availability of $100,000 bone-marrow transplants or $40,000 heart operations to those relatively few who need them.

"I can't imagine a system that's more dysfunctional than the one we have now—more expensive, not doing the job, with more waste," says Dr. Philip Caper, an internist and medical policy analyst at Dartmouth Medical School. Although the total amount of waste in our health-care system is difficult to estimate, researchers have now examined many of the system's components, with consistent results. For a wide range of clinical procedures, on average, roughly 20 percent of the money we now spend could be saved with no loss in the quality of care. By restructuring the system, we could also save almost half of the huge amount we now spend on administrative costs (see "The $200-Billion Bottom Line"). A more efficient system would also make it much easier to detect health-care fraud—a problem that the U.S. General Accounting Office has estimated to cost tens of billions of dollars a year.

While these facts are well known to students of the health-care system, they've been remarkably absent from the debate that's developing over health care in this election year. Politicians and lobbyists for health-care providers have presented the public with a daunting choice: If we want to provide every American with access to health care, they say, we'll either have to pay much more into the system or accept lower-quality medical services.

However, such scenarios assume that the current price structure for medical care, and the current patterns of treatment and hospitalization, will remain fixed. They needn't, and they shouldn't. Our health-care system is so inherently wasteful and inefficient that a complete overhaul is an option worth contemplating. It may, in fact, be the only option that makes sense.

The waste in the system comes from many sources. We receive a great deal of care that we don't need at all. The care we do need is delivered inefficiently. And the futile effort to control a runaway system has created a huge bureaucracy that by itself sucks up more than a hundred billion dollars a year.

30 years of increases

By now, it's hardly news that health costs have spiraled out of control. Health care now consumes about 16 percent of state and local tax revenues. In the years since 1986, private businesses have spent about as much on health care as they earned in after-tax profits. For small businesses, insurance has become unaffordable; three of four concerns employing 10 or fewer people simply don't provide health bene-

Less waste, longer lives

"Look at the rest of the industrial world. On average, they spend half as much as we do on health care. They cover everyone and live longer. It's waste. There's no other explanation."
—Alan Sager, health economist, Boston University School of Public Health

This report [Part 1 of a 3-part series] examines the forces behind the current crisis in health-care costs. The next two reports in this special series will look at the possible solutions [see *Consumer Reports,* August and September, 1992].

One approach to cost control, pioneered by health maintenance organizations, is to "manage" medical care in detail. The management can include such practices as restricting patients to a single primary-care doctor who must approve all specialist referrals; penalizing doctors who order too many tests or procedures; and preapproving elective hospitalizations. In our next report, we'll rate HMOs and examine how well managed care actually contains costs.

Another approach is to set overall spending limits and stick to them, while otherwise leaving doctors and hospitals to practice as they see fit. That's what other industrialized countries, including Canada, do in various ways. Part three of our health-care series, [in] the September issue, will take a close look at the Canadian system, among others, and will analyze the criticisms that have been leveled against it by U.S. health-care providers and insurers.

Finally, we'll outline the health-care reform proposal that Consumers Union favors as providing the best combination of universal access, quality care, and cost containment.

Reprinted with permission from *Consumer Reports,* July 1992, pp. 435-448. © 1992 by Consumers Union of United States, Inc., Yonkers, NY 10703-1057.

fits. At any given time, roughly 35 million Americans—most of them employees of small businesses or their dependents—have no health coverage at all.

Over the last 10 years, Government and private business, appalled to see health care absorbing an ever-growing portion of their revenues, have tried to get a grip on its costs in various ways. But costs have risen as fast as ever. "As quickly as payers patch the system up, the providers find the spaces between the patches," says Maryann O'Sullivan, director of Health Access, a California consumer coalition.

Our health-care system doesn't just allow prices to rise—it practically demands that they do. Although some recent reforms have had a modest effect, the system has traditionally allowed doctors to order whatever procedures they want, and has paid both doctors and hospitals whatever they think they should get.

In both respects, the American system stands alone in the developed world. Though the particulars of their systems differ, Canada, Japan, and the Western European countries all have adopted universal, standard payment schedules set by direct negotiation with doctors and hospitals. In addition, most have set an overall ceiling on national medical expenditures. As a result, not a single developed country other than the U.S. devotes more than 10 percent of its gross national product to health care. The U.S. broke that barrier in 1985; this year, the nation will spend 14 percent of the GNP on health.

It wasn't always so. Back in 1960, the U.S. spent a modest 5.3 percent of its GNP on health care, about the same as other industrialized nations like Canada or Germany did at the time. What changed everything was the advent in 1965 of Medicare, which ultimately had implications far beyond the over-65 population it served.

Before Medicare, private insurance companies covered the population less extensively than they do today. All the insurers left treatment completely to the doctor's discretion and provided reimbursement for any test or treatment a physician ordered. But because a large percentage of people had only hospital coverage, and no insurance to cover doctors' bills, physicians tended to keep fees at affordable levels.

In 1965, Congress enacted Medicare, the vast, Government-financed

THE $200-BILLION BOTTOM LINE

To date, no one has come up with a comprehensive price tag for the cost of unnecessary medical care, overpriced procedures, and inefficient administration in the U.S. health-care system. After extensive review of the literature, however, we believe that $200-billion is a conservative estimate of the amount the health-care system will waste this year. Here's why.

Of the $817-billion projected to be spent on health care this year, about one fifth—$163-billion—will go for administrative costs. Except for a fraction of a percent spent on research, the rest—roughly $650-billion—will go to actual patient care. Physician and hospital services together make up most of that total, with the rest going to dentists, nursing homes, drugs, and various other expenses.

By our estimates, at least 20 percent of that $650-billion, or $130-billion, will be spent on procedures and services that are clearly unnecessary.

Many researchers have now attempted to quantify the rate at which specific procedures are used unnecessarily. Twenty percent represents a rough average of the rates found in major studies, and is a figure that several leading researchers in this field told us was a good approximation for the rate of unnecessary care.

Twenty percent also seems to be a conservative estimate of the rate of unnecessary hospital days, even though changes in Medicare and private-insurance policies make it difficult to estimate that number precisely.

Finally, as Dr. John Wennberg of Dartmouth and his colleagues have demonstrated repeatedly, the rate at which physicians use a given procedure can vary four- or five-fold between one location and another. The supply of hospitals and physicians also varies greatly. Except in extreme cases where people lack access to basic medical care, people living in low-use or low-supply areas seem to be just as healthy as those in high-use or high-supply areas.

Dr. Wennberg and his colleagues argue that areas with abundant doctors and hospitals could provide significantly fewer health-care services without

harmful consequences. Similarly, the high rates of procedures done in many areas could be cut back without overall harm. This sort of adjustment happens automatically, they note, in industrialized countries that control costs by capping the amount of money available for health care.

If overuse of medical services wastes $130-billion a year, administrative inefficiency adds about $70-billion. Projecting from 1991 estimates by the General Accounting Office, the U.S. could save roughly $70-billion this year by switching from our fragmented and inefficient insurance system to a single-payer system—one in which all citizens receive health care from private doctors and hospitals that are paid by a single insurance entity. The savings would come roughly equally from insurance-company overhead and hospital and administrative costs.

Adding those two figures together—$130 billion plus $70-billion—gives an estimate of $200-billion for the annual waste in the U.S. health-care system. This estimate, however, leaves out several important elements: Physicians' fees and the cost of technology, drugs, and procedures. If those costs were brought into line with reimbursement standards in other countries, the savings would be greater.

Moreover, we have not added in the cost of outright fraud—a factor that the General Accounting Office estimates could eat up a full 10 percent of the total health-care budget.

Some physicians cheat the system by ordering unnecessary tests and procedures—a type of fraud that is included in our estimates of unnecessary care. Other types of fraud, however, would not have been caught in the studies of unnecessary care that have been done. These include billing for services never rendered, falsifying reimbursement codes to collect more than the usual payment for a service, and submitting inflated bills for supplies and medical devices.

Since we have not counted the cost of these fraudulent practices—or of the high price scale for health-care providers in the U.S.—our $200-billion figure is truly a minimum estimate.

High-tech without high costs Although they control health-care costs much more effectively than the U.S., other developed countries still provide high-tech care to those who need it. Between 1988 and 1990, Canada, France, Australia, and Israel all did more bone-marrow transplants per capita than the U.S.

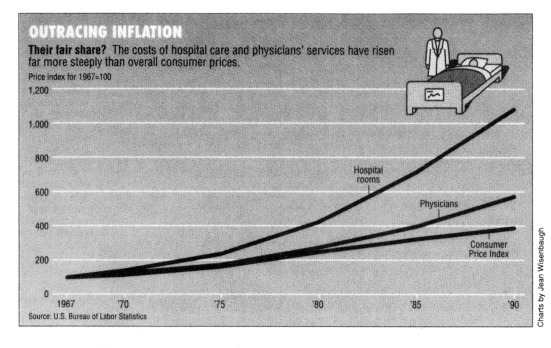

OUTRACING INFLATION

Their fair share? The costs of hospital care and physicians' services have risen far more steeply than overall consumer prices.

Price index for 1967=100

Hospital rooms

Physicians

Consumer Price Index

1967   '70   '75   '80   '85   '90

Source: U.S. Bureau of Labor Statistics

Charts by Jean Wisenbaugh

A freeze or a meltdown? In 1986, in the midst of a Medicare freeze on physicians' fees, doctors increased their services enough to collect 15 percent more from Medicare than they had the year before.

program of social health insurance for the elderly, along with the less extensive Medicaid program, in which the Federal Government shares costs with the states. In order to overcome the powerful, sustained opposition of doctors and hospitals to what they called "socialized medicine," Congress made a fateful—and, in retrospect, very expensive—decision. Under Medicare, all doctors were paid on the basis of their "usual and customary" fees for a given service (the system that Blue Shield was already using).

This approach, which allowed each individual physician to name his or her own price, soon became universal throughout the insurance industry. So as more and more employers began offering major-medical plans that covered doctors' bills, they bought into a system with no effective constraints on costs. Predictably, doctors' fees began a rapid upward climb.

Hospitals profited as well. Under Blue Cross, which had dominated hospital insurance, hospitals were paid only a daily room charge, plus additional fees for various services, tests, and supplies. Under Medicare, however, the hospitals were not only able to collect their actual charges; for the first time, they were allowed to build the cost of capital improvements into their rates. Hospitals, which had been receiving Federal subsidies for growth since the late 1940s, now got another incentive to expand.

After Medicare, U.S. health-care expenditures turned more sharply upward. For a time—perhaps a decade or more—no one seemed to notice or care. But over the past 10 years or so, as costs have become truly staggering, the system has begun to change. Medicare has set limits on physicians' fees for several years, and private insurance companies have begun reviewing many procedures doctors perform before they will pay for them. Medicaid budgets have been steadily cut back, to the point where many states now pay doctors and hospitals less than the cost of delivering care.

Experience has shown, however, that attempts to manage the health-care system a piece at a time are likely to fail. Physicians and hospitals can charge their privately insured patients more to make up for Medicare's fee restrictions. And doctors and patients alike have resisted efforts by insurance companies to determine what is appropriate and necessary treatment, having grown used to a system that has provided as much medical care—to the insured population, that is—as anybody wants.

No sense of limits

Having operated for years under a system that sets virtually no limit on what can be done or what can be charged, both doctors and patients have been seduced by the idea that, when it comes to treating sickness, it's necessary to do "everything."

"We want more. We want more time with the doctor. We want more procedures. We want more pills," says Randall Bovbjerg, a health-

policy analyst at the Urban Institute in Washington, D.C. "We can't sit and watch the course of a cold; we go and buy tons of things we aren't even certain will make it better."

"Imagine if we sold auto-purchase insurance and said, go and buy whatever car you want and we'll pay 80 percent of it," says James C. Robinson, a health-care economist at the University of California, Berkeley. Under those conditions, a lot of people would go buy a Mercedes.

Much of the time, physicians will order more tests and procedures out of a genuine desire to do whatever they can for their patients. "Doctors look at one patient at a time and think, 'If I've done one thing, what else can I try?' " says Ann Lennarson Greer, a medical sociologist at the University of Wisconsin. "They're not inclined to think about overall costs." Several studies, in fact, have asked doctors if they knew the costs of hospital tests and services they routinely ordered—and found many had only a vague idea at best.

But while extra tests and treatments drive up the cost of medical care, they may do so with no real benefit to the patient. New diagnostic technologies, in particular, are especially likely to be overused; unlike surgery or invasive procedures, they "don't require the clinician to take any real risk," Greer says. Thus, the use of computerized tomography (CT) and magnetic resonance imaging (MRI) scans, two expensive, relatively new imaging technologies, has grown explosively in recent years. Yet no one has clearly defined when they are useful and when they are a waste of time and money.

"The original CT scanner proved to be an absolute revolution in the treatment of patients with head injury," says Dr. Mark Chassin, a physician who is senior vice president of Value Health Sciences, a private firm that analyzes the use of health-care services. "We produced hundreds of these things and they got out in the community. They were used for people with head trauma— terrific—but they also were used for people with headaches, dizziness, and all sorts of other vague symptoms." Diagnostic imaging, says Dr. Chassin, is a prime example of how "we continue to invest in technology in an absolutely irrational way."

The law of induced demand

Medical care is totally unlike services delivered by other professionals. When clients hire an architect or a lawyer, they generally know what they need and roughly how much it's going to cost. But in medicine, physicians make virtually all the decisions that determine the cost of care. The patient, ill and uninformed, is in no position to do comparison shopping—nor motivated to, if insurance is paying the bill.

And the more doctors do, the more they get paid—a situation that's tailor-made for cost escalation. "It's the easiest thing in the world to increase the volume [of things a doctor does]," says Dr. Philip Caper, the Dartmouth internist. "Just do a few more tests. There's always a rationale. Schedule three doctor visits instead of two, and reduce the time you spend on each visit."

The creation of medical "need" by those who then profit from it is called induced demand, and it's rampant. Most obvious is the problem of "self-referral," in which physicians will refer patients for treatment at facilities in which they have a financial interest. In Florida, where at least 40 percent of physicians have such investments, a study by professors at Florida State University found that physician-owned laboratories performed twice as many tests per patient as independent labs. Similarly, in a study of private health insurance claims records for more than 65,000 patients, University of Arizona researchers found that doctors who had diagnostic imaging equipment in their offices ordered four times more imaging exams than doctors who

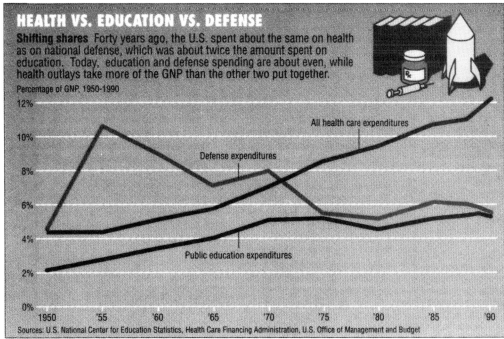

HEALTH VS. EDUCATION VS. DEFENSE

Shifting shares Forty years ago, the U.S. spent about the same on health as on national defense, which was about twice the amount spent on education. Today, education and defense spending are about even, while health outlays take more of the GNP than the other two put together.

Percentage of GNP, 1950-1990

All health care expenditures

Defense expenditures

Public education expenditures

Sources: U.S. National Center for Education Statistics, Health Care Financing Administration, U.S. Office of Management and Budget

referred patients elsewhere for the tests.

Occasionally, self-referral can turn into actual fraud. A recent report by the General Accounting Office— which estimated that fraud may account for as much as 10 percent of all health-care costs—cited several examples in which self-referral had been abused. In one California case, the owners of mobile medical laboratories allegedly gave kickbacks for referrals to physicians who sometimes used phony diagnoses. The case, which is still being investigated, involves an estimated $1-billion in fraudulent billings.

In other cases, however, physicians may increase the demand for their services without even being aware of it. When it comes to American medical care, supply seems to create demand almost automatically. Actuarial studies have shown that in areas with the greatest supply of physicians, people simply go to the doctor more often.

If more physicians create more demand for medical care, we can look forward to a flood of it in the near future. The per capita supply of practicing physicians is expected to increase 22 percent between now and the year 2000.

The phenomenon of induced demand applies to hospitals, too. Dr. John Wennberg, a physician who is professor of family and community medicine at Dartmouth Medical School, was curious as to why people in Boston went to the hospital more

frequently than people in New Haven. When he studied the problem, he found a simple answer: Boston has more hospital beds to be filled—one-third more than New Haven on a per capita basis.

Surprisingly, Dr. Wennberg found that physicians in Boston and New Haven were completely unaware of the discrepancy. When he asked doctors in New Haven whether they felt their area was short of hospital beds, they said they didn't. In fact, at any given time, about 85 percent of hospital beds in New Haven were filled—precisely the same percentage as in Boston.

The likely explanation, according to Dr. Wennberg, is that physicians almost unconsciously will refer their patients to the hospital if space is available, stopping only when the local hospitals' capacity is nearly used up. If many beds are empty, doctors will be more likely to refer patients with borderline conditions, such as gastroenteritis or acute low back pain, for which hospitalization is optional but not imperative. By doing so, of course, they drive up the cost of care.

An unnecessary burden

With so many incentives to overtreat patients, it seems inevitable that a sizable fraction of American medical care must be simply unnecessary, if not downright harmful. But how large a fraction? In the late 1970s and early 1980s, researchers at the Rand

Growth without limits
The Health Industry Manufacturers Association, a medical-equipment trade group, predicts a 7.4 percent annual growth rate for health technology throughout this decade—unless "negative scenarios," such as more safety regulation and cost containment, take effect.

MEDICAL RED FLAGS

IS THIS TREATMENT NECESSARY?

Over the past decade or so, an entire industry has sprung up to identify overused and unnecessary medical treatments. The players range from academic researchers to policy analysts to private entrepreneurs that have insurance companies as their clients.

Some treatments, by virtue of their cost or their ubiquity, have attracted particular attention from the watchdogs. These treatments, listed below, are hardly the only sources of unnecessary care in the system. Nor, of course, does a procedure's presence on the list mean that it is always used unnecessarily—or even that that is usually the case.

Nevertheless, if your physician does suggest that you have one of these procedures, you'd be well advised to think twice. You might want to seek a second opinion, if possible, or question your doctor closely on the possible alternatives to the suggested treatment.

Cesarean section. About one in four U.S. births is completed surgically, a rate that may be twice the ideal. In this country, obstetricians routinely perform cesareans when the baby is breech, or for the vaguely defined diagnoses of "prolonged labor" or "fetal distress." Hospitals that have systematically set out to eliminate unnecessary cesareans have cut their rate at least in half without any apparent risk to mothers or babies. (See CONSUMER REPORTS, February 1991.)

In recent years, the electronic fetal monitor, a device for tracking the fetal heart rate during labor, has come to be used routinely in American hospitals—and has contributed to the high cesarean-section rate. Since abnormal fetal heart rates

Redlined jobs
Many health-insurance companies won't sell policies to people working in barbershops, car washes, convenience stores, grocery stores, hospitals, nursing homes, doctors' offices, law offices, parking lots, or restaurants.

are associated with oxygen deprivation, it was assumed that prompt, automatic detection would enable doctors to intervene early enough to prevent fetal brain damage—for example, by performing a cesarean section on the mother.

But since the fetal monitor's introduction, no fewer than nine comparative studies, involving tens of thousands of women, have failed to demonstrate the hoped-for benefit. Monitored women do have a higher rate of cesarean sections and other costly interventions. But their babies fare no better than those of women monitored by the traditional means, in which a nurse simply checks the fetal heartbeat periodically with a stethoscope.

Hysterectomy. After cesarean section, this is the second most common major surgery in the U.S. Value Health Sciences, a firm that applies the Rand Corp.'s methodology for insurance-industry clients, calls 27 percent of hysterectomies unnecessary, the highest percentage of all procedures it evaluates. Rates of hysterectomy also vary greatly throughout the country, an indication that physician practice and preference play as much of a role as objective need in the decision to perform the operation. Many gynecologists still routinely recommend hysterectomy for fibroids, uterine prolapse, and heavy bleeding; alternative treatments are available for all three conditions. (See CONSUMER REPORTS, September 1990).

Back surgery. Value Health Sciences has reported that 14 percent of proposed laminectomies, the most common type of back surgery, are unnecessary. Occasionally, some material from a ruptured disc will press on spinal nerves and cause

disabling or painful symptoms that require surgical correction, says Dr. Charles Fager, a neurosurgeon at the Lahey Clinic in Burlington, Mass. But usually, back pain yields to bed rest, the passage of time, physical therapy, or a combination thereof. "I only operate on one out of every 25 or 30 people I see," says Dr. Fager. Some surgeons aren't so finicky. Dr. John Wennberg of Dartmouth Medical School has traced sudden "epidemics" of back surgery to the arrival of a new neurosurgeon in a locality.

Magnetic resonance imaging. This powerful new imaging technique, which produces detailed pictures of internal organs without exposing the patient to radiation, is still so new that doctors are working out its best uses. In the process, they'll inevitably use it when they don't need to. Some groups of physicians have invested in MRI machines, creating the added temptation to profit by referring their patients for the test. Also, because MRI is virtually risk-free, it's especially likely to be overused as a defensive measure.

Experts stress that MRI procedures, which cost about $1000 apiece, should be ordered only when a patient's symptoms suggest he or she may have a condition that cannot be diagnosed definitively in any other way.

Prostate surgery. Dr. Wennberg and his colleagues at Dartmouth have shown that surgery for noncancerous enlargement of the prostate is among the most variable of procedures. They have also looked closely at what happens to men who get the surgery and those who don't. For many men, medical therapy can relieve symptoms. For

Corp., a think tank in Santa Monica, Calif., began to find out.

Using an elaborate process for developing a consensus among nationally recognized medical experts, the Rand team came up with an agreed-upon list of "indications" for various procedures. They then checked the actual medical records of thousands of patients who had

received the procedures, to see whether they had been treated appropriately. The definition of "appropriate" care was starkly simple: Based on the patient's condition and expert opinion, the likely benefit of the procedure must have been greater than the risk involved in doing it.

Even with their elaborate analysis,

the Rand researchers were not able to tell in every case whether a given procedure had been appropriate or not. They divided their cases into three groups: Those where the procedure had been "appropriate," those where it was "inappropriate," and those where its use was "equivocal," the largest group. Despite this degree of uncertainty, however, others, putting off surgery isn't particularly dangerous, though the urinary obstruction caused by the condition can be uncomfortable.

When patients in a health maintenance organization were fully informed in advance of the risks and benefits of surgery, in a study that Dr. Wennberg designed, 80 percent of men with severe urinary symptoms chose to postpone the operation.

Clot-busting drugs. These drugs, when administered within four to six hours of the onset of a heart attack, can break up the blood clot blocking the coronary artery and thus greatly reduce the damage to the heart muscle. The largest comparative study done to date, of 41,000 patients worldwide, has found that all currently available clot-busting drugs are about equally effective in preventing fatal heart attacks—but one, streptokinase, has the lowest incidence of the most dangerous side effect, cerebral hemorrhage.

Of the two drugs used in the U.S., streptokinase also happens to be by far the cheaper—about $200 per dose compared to $2000 per dose for its genetically engineered competitor, tissue plasminogen activator (TPA). Nevertheless, TPA commands a majority of the U.S. market, apparently thanks to aggressive marketing by its manufacturer, Genentech.

For a person having a first heart attack, there's no reason to be treated with the more costly drug. Second treatments with streptokinase, however, are unsafe, since the first treatment can set up the mechanism for an allergic response to any future injection.

Rand found clear evidence of inappropriate overtreatment. Among the results:

■ Of 1300 elderly patients who had an operation to remove atherosclerotic plaque from the carotid artery, nearly one-third—32 percent —didn't need it.

■ Of 386 heart bypass operations, 14 percent were done unnecessarily.

■ Of 1677 patients who had coronary angiography—an X-ray examination of blood flow in the arteries nourishing the heart—17 percent didn't need it.

So striking were the results that Rand's methods for determining appropriateness have since been put to commercial use. Value Health Sciences, which now employs some of the original Rand researchers, has extended the methodology to several dozen high-volume medical procedures. A number of major insurance companies and health maintenance organizations now use this program to flag unnecessary procedures.

Value Health's results confirm the original Rand findings. Its review system has found very high rates of unnecessary usage for certain procedures: hysterectomy, 27 percent unnecessary; surgery for an uncomfortable wrist ailment called carpal tunnel syndrome, 17 percent; tonsillectomy, 16 percent; laminectomy, a type of back surgery, 14 percent. Similar results have come out of studies done by other investigators, who have examined procedures from preoperative laboratory screening (60 percent unnecessary) to cesarean section (50 percent unnecessary) to upper gastrointestinal X-ray studies (30 percent unnecessary).

The uncertainty principle

Physicians can inadvertently contribute to the cost of unnecessary medicine even when they have only their patients' best interest in mind. Lay people tend to think of medical care as a straightforward proposition: For Disease A, prescribe Treatment B. That's not the way it is in real life. To practice medicine is to be afloat in a "sea of uncertainty," says Dartmouth's John Wennberg.

Every symptom can be investigated by a huge array of tests; for many diseases, physicians have a wide range of treatment choices. And doctors often base their choices as much on folklore and intuition as on science.

"Doctors really hate risks," says Ann Lennarson Greer, the Wisconsin sociologist. "They have certain procedures that seem to work for them, and they'd prefer to keep doing them, especially in areas where there's a lot of uncertainty."

This innate conservatism is reinforced by the isolation in which most doctors practice, says Greer, who has spent more than a decade studying why doctors and hospitals behave as they do. A physician can

spend his or her entire career within a single referral network, based at a single hospital. These local colleagues, Greer has found, are the principal influence on a physician's decisions about how to diagnose and treat diseases or whether or not to adopt new technology. But they may not be the most reliable source.

A phenomenon called "small area variations," which was discovered by Dr. Wennberg early in his career, is a striking demonstration of just how unscientific medical practice really is. In the late 1960s, he had moved to Vermont to work as a health administrator and educator. Once there, he soon stumbled across a curious geographic pattern to a common operation, tonsillectomy.

"In Stowe, the probability of having a tonsillectomy by age 15 was about 70 percent," Dr. Wennberg recalls. "If you lived in Waterbury, over the hill from Stowe, it was about 10 percent." Indeed, there turned out to be a 13-fold difference in the local rates of tonsillectomy between the most and least surgery-happy Vermont communities he studied.

Medical uncertainty and the isolation of doctors largely explain those bizarre disparities. Dr. Wennberg discovered that doctors in Stowe, who talked mostly to each other, believed that if you didn't take tonsils out early, they'd become chronically infected and cause no end of trouble. Doctors in Waterbury, who didn't talk to the doctors in Stowe, held the opposite (and, as it turned out, correct) viewpoint: If left alone, most kids with frequent sore throats would eventually outgrow them.

This phenomenon turned out to be true of a lot more things than tonsillectomies. In Portland, Me., Dr. Wennberg found, 50 percent of men had prostate surgery by the age of 85; in Bangor, just 10 percent did. The rate of heart surgery was twice as high in Des Moines as it was in nearby Iowa City.

Subsequent studies by a number of researchers, working throughout the country, have shown that the use of all kinds of medical procedures varies dramatically from region to region. In fact, Dr. Wennberg has found the only procedures that *don't* show such variations are those few for which there is basically only one accepted treatment, such as hospitalization for heart attack or stroke.

Inefficiency experts

The waste in the system goes far beyond the provision of unnecessary

Serving the rich In 1988, Beverly Hills had one internist for every 566 people. Compton, a poor Los Angeles community, had one internist per 19,422 people.

care. Even when medical treatments are necessary, they're frequently done with no regard for efficiency.

Milliman and Robertson, a Seattle-based consulting firm, advises hospitals and other health-care organizations on ways to cut costs without compromising the quality of care. The firm's actuaries and physicians have examined thousands of individual medical records to develop guidelines on how long patients should stay in the hospital for such common conditions as childbirth or appendectomy—provided they're in generally good health and have no complications. Applying those guidelines to actual current records from a dozen urban areas across the country, the firm's actuaries concluded that 53 percent of all hospital days weren't necessary, including all the days spent in the hospital by the 24 percent of patients who didn't need to be there in the first place.

As a private, commercial firm, Milliman and Robertson is in business to identify overuse for its clients, and might have a bias in favor of finding what it's paid to find. However, other studies by academic researchers have also found high rates of inappropriate hospitalization. A recent Rand Corp. review of published studies, most of which used data from the early and mid-1980s, estimated that 15 to 30 percent of hospital use was unnecessary.

The current rates of unnecessary hospitalization are difficult to estimate, since the system is in flux. The overall number of hospital days per thousand Americans—a standard measure of hospital utilization—has dropped over the last decade, in response to efforts by Medicare, health maintenance organizations, and private insurers to contain costs. But there are still large regional variations in hospital use, suggesting that waste still exists in the system.

Past experience shows it's possible to lower the number of days people spend in the hospital with no ill effects. In 1984, Medicare created financial incentives for hospitals to discharge patients as soon as possible, and not to admit them at all unless strictly necessary. The incentives worked; in two years, the average number of in-patient days per Medicare recipient fell 22 percent.

That sharp decline apparently had no real impact on the health of the patients involved, according to several statistics. The rate at which discharged patients need to be readmitted to the hospital shortly after

leaving—an important index of low-quality care—has actually gone down for Medicare patients since 1984. Some care that used to be provided in the hospital can now be done at home, at much lower cost.

A medical arms race

Despite the efforts over the past decade to keep the costs of hospitalization down—by limiting hospital admissions, length of stay, and in-patient costs—our national hospital bill continues to rise. In 1990, hospitals soaked up 38 percent of national health expenditures (twice as much as doctors) and collectively earned a profit of $7-billion. Hospital administrators have proven how nimble health-care providers can be in getting around virtually any effort to rein them in.

For many years, hospitals expanded at a rate well beyond the national need, with the Government's help. During the 1950s and into the 1960s, the Federal Government provided subsidies to build new hospitals, and a decade later, Medicare allowed hospitals to pay for their capital improvements by charging higher fees. The result was a spate of hospital-building that had little relationship to clear community needs. New facilities and new wings were built, beds needed to be filled, and the law of induced demand kept them occupied—imposing a high cost on the health-care system and providing a high profit for the hospitals themselves.

When Medicare started to crack down on costs in 1984—paying hospitals a fixed fee to take care of each patient, based on his or her diagnosis—the hospitals reacted swiftly. Fewer Medicare patients were admitted, and those that were admitted stayed in the hospital for a shorter time. But the hospitals compensated by boosting their outpatient, psychiatric, and rehabilitation services, for which Medicare had set no cost limits. Although charges for hospitalization dropped, the costs for those other services ate up those savings, and more.

Hospitals also stepped up their efforts to attract privately insured patients to make up for the money they were losing on Medicare and Medicaid. Having built the capacity for many more beds than the nation needs, hospitals now tried to fill them—and to fill them with patients who had generous insurance policies and needed lots of medical services. "Hospitals make money by deliver-

ing services," explains William Erwin, who is a spokesman for the American Hospital Association. "If you don't need much done to you, the hospital isn't going to make money on you."

Attracting patients to a hospital isn't the same as attracting customers to a new restaurant or hardware store. Consumers decide on their own when and where they want to eat out or buy some drill bits. When they're sick, their doctors decide when and where to hospitalize them. So hospitals must market on two fronts: They must appeal directly to privately insured patients, and they must keep their admitting doctors happy.

To induce physicians to admit patients, hospitals resort to everything from first-year guaranteed incomes to subsidies for initial practice expenses. The effort pays off. In 1990, according to an annual survey by Jackson and Coker, an Atlanta physician-recruiting firm, the average doctor generated $513,000 in in-patient hospital revenue.

Another way to keep doctors happy is to provide them with state-of-the-art medical equipment. As a bonus, hospitals can then tout their up-to-date technology directly to consumers. Uwe Reinhardt, a Princeton University health economist, likes to paint the following scenario in his lectures:

"Imagine that you're a young couple in Chicago, stuck in a traffic jam in the Loop, and you see a billboard that says: 'Mount Sinai: The Cheapest Place in Chicago, Have Your Baby Here.' Then you go on and you see another billboard that says, 'Holy Mercy: The Only Place with a Glandular Schlumpulator, Have Your Baby Here.' Where are you going to go?"

Some regulatory efforts were made in the 1960s and 1970s to restrain hospitals from acquiring excessive amounts of expensive technology, with mixed success. In any case, Federal support for that effort was discontinued during the Reagan years. The rationale was that "unleashing competition" among hospitals would allow the free market to operate and help keep the cost of medicine down.

The irony, though, is that competition actually drives costs *up* where hospitals are concerned. The hospitals gain no competitive advantage by controlling costs, since their customers—doctors and patients—don't pay for their services anyway. In-

---

Where readers placed the blame Asked to name the biggest contributor to the cost of health care, 23 percent of our readers incorrectly picked malpractice suits (see the box at right). An equal number named hospital costs, which *are* the biggest factor. Doctors' fees and health-insurance companies came in third and fourth in the survey.

THE 'CRISIS' THAT ISN'T

MALPRACTICE: A STRAW MAN

Ask physicians to explain why the cost of health care goes up continually, and you're likely to hear complaints that the U.S. malpractice system encourages unnecessary "defensive" medical care. The public seems to have bought this argument. In a recent survey, CONSUMER REPORTS subscribers guessed that malpractice tied with hospital costs as the biggest factor driving the cost of health care.

Is malpractice such a villain?

It's true that malpractice costs are higher in the U.S. than in other countries. And in the mid-1980s, malpractice claims—and, accordingly, insurance premiums—did take a sharp upward swing. There was much talk then of a malpractice "crisis." But that crisis now seems to have abated, as have previous ones. Malpractice is a cyclical phenomenon: Periodically, the incidence of claims rises, then falls back.

At the moment, malpractice claims have been in one such downswing. The rate of claims has declined steadily since the peak of the last "crisis" in 1985. So have malpractice insurance premiums. In 1990, according to Medical Economics magazine's annual survey of physicians, doctors' malpractice premiums on average consumed only 3.7 percent of their practice receipts—although the percentage may be double that for high-risk (and high-paid) specialties, such as obstetrics, surgery, and anesthesiology. The U.S. Department of Health and Human Ser-

vices puts the total cost of malpractice at less than 1 percent of total health outlays.

But then, no one argues that the direct cost of malpractice insurance is the main factor driving up the cost of care. Instead, it's assumed that physicians, fearing malpractice suits, are forced to practice "defensive medicine" just to protect themselves in the event of a lawsuit.

Defensive medicine undoubtedly exists, and doctors themselves feel that the threat of malpractice forces them to do more tests than are truly necessary. But quantifying the cost of defensive medicine is a slippery matter. The American Medical Association made a stab at it in the 1980s, and decided that the total cost of medical malpractice, including premiums and defensive medicine, was about 17 percent of physicians' earnings.

However, the AMA estimate was based on physicians' own reports of what they considered defensive practices, such as doing more diagnostic tests, sticking with the safest possible treatments, telling patients more about treatment risks, and keeping more complete records.

As that list suggests, one problem with defining defensive medicine—let alone measuring it—is that it's difficult to distinguish from care delivered for other reasons. Is a doctor doing an unnecessary test out of fear of a lawsuit, or because the medical culture values doing "everything," or simply to reassure an anxious patient? Did an obstetrician perform an

unnecessary cesarean for legal protection, for scheduling convenience, or to earn a higher fee?

"You mostly get anecdotes when you're talking about defensive medicine," says Randall Bovbjerg, an analyst at the Urban Institute in Washington, D.C., who has worked on several malpractice studies.

That's not to say there isn't a malpractice crisis, however. "The greatest single problem about malpractice is that there's a lot more of it out there than anyone is dealing with," says Bovbjerg. "Patients are getting avoidable injuries and no one is stopping it."

Documentation for Bovbjerg's claim comes from a study conducted by Harvard University researchers for the state of New York. The researchers reviewed a random sample of New York hospital records in 1984 and found that 3.7 percent of patients suffered "adverse events," slightly more than one-quarter of which could be attributed to actual negligence.

Of those who suffered negligent injuries, only about one-eighth ever filed malpractice claims, and only about one-sixteenth ever recovered any damages. Conversely, the study found many cases in which patients filed malpractice suits with no clear evidence of negligence.

Costs aside, the current malpractice system is at best only an imprecise means of controlling the quality of medical care.

stead, hospitals compete only on the basis of perceived quality, and end up vying to see which one can secure and promote the newest well reimbursed technology, whether the technology is needed or not. Several hospitals in an area may have their own neonatal intensive care units, MRI machines, or cardiac care centers, when only one would serve the population equally well. This year, despite the recession, hospitals plan to increase spending on new equipment by 15 percent, according to a survey by Shearson Lehman Brothers.

To attract the well-insured population, hospitals also provide amenities that have nothing to do with actual health care but add to the bill, includ-

ing cable TV, private rooms and baths, gourmet menus, and the like. Baylor University Medical Center in Houston spent $18-million on the Tom Landry Sports Medicine and Research Center, complete with 7000-square-foot dressing rooms lined with oak lockers, and a 10-lane pool with underwater computerized video cameras used to analyze its patrons' swimming strokes.

Hospitals have also become more and more consciously concerned with projecting an upscale image that they hope will bring in an affluent clientele. Entries in a recent contest held by the Academy of Health Services Marketing, an organization of hospital marketing executives, reveal the new focus. For instance, the Southern Regional Medical Cen-

ter in suburban Atlanta got Rosalynn Carter to endorse its maternity service after her grandchild was born there—as part of a successful campaign "to increase gross revenue . . . by marketing to a target market of insured, higher-income women, ages 25-49," according to the contest submission.

The trend is troubling, because there's clear evidence that the total cost of health care rises in areas where many hospitals begin to compete for the same pool of well-insured patients. Health economists James C. Robinson and Harold S. Luft of the University of California, Berkeley, examined data from 5732 hospitals nationwide, and found that costs per admission were 26 percent higher in hospitals that had more

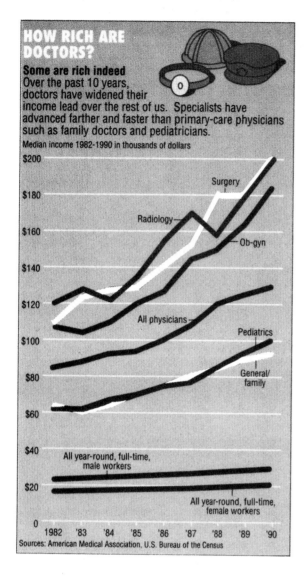

HOW RICH ARE DOCTORS?

Some are rich indeed
Over the past 10 years, doctors have widened their income lead over the rest of us. Specialists have advanced farther and faster than primary-care physicians such as family doctors and pediatricians.

Median income 1982-1990 in thousands of dollars

- Surgery
- Radiology
- Ob-gyn
- All physicians
- Pediatrics
- General/family
- All year-round, full-time, male workers
- All year-round, full-time, female workers

1982 '83 '84 '85 '86 '87 '88 '89 '90

Sources: American Medical Association, U.S. Bureau of the Census

than nine competitors within a 15-mile radius. In a smaller-scale study of 747 hospitals, they found that those in competitive areas allowed patients to stay in the hospital longer after surgery—something that tends to please both patients and doctors, but with a high cost and no clear medical benefit.

More specialists, high costs

Just as American hospitals lead the world in high-priced technology, American physicians are heavy purveyors of expensive treatments and diagnostic tests—and reap great personal rewards for using them. Doctors in the U.S. earn much higher incomes relative to their fellow citizens than do doctors in other countries. According to figures from the Organization for Economic Cooperation and Development, in 1987 U.S. doctors earned 5.4 times more than the average worker. In Germany, the multiple was 4.2; in Canada, 3.7; and in France, Japan, and the United Kingdom, 2.4.

Historically, the highest fees have gone to doctors who perform concrete procedures, such as surgery, endoscopy, or diagnostic imaging. So-called evaluation and management services—in which doctors may examine and question the patient and prescribe a treatment, but don't actually do a specific procedure—haven't paid nearly as well.

In 1990, for instance, internists charged a median of $110 for a comprehensive office visit for a patient they hadn't seen before, according to a survey by Medical Economics magazine. Such a visit involves taking a medical history, doing a physical examination, and talking with the patient about his or her current condition. It can take up 45 minutes of the doctor's time. By contrast, the same survey found internists charged a median fee of $126 for spending 10 minutes to examine the bowel with a flexible fiberoptic device called a sigmoidoscope.

While individual physicians have great leeway in deciding what they will charge for a given procedure, insurance companies have established computerized databanks that help them determine whether or not the fee is "usual and customary" for that procedure. By this standard, a doctor whose fees are at the very top of the local scale may not receive full reimbursement. But there's no track record of cost for new procedures. With the help of medical specialty societies and the AMA, physicians have secured very high rates of reimbursement for new treatments.

"When something is in development, it's new, it's experimental, only a few physicians use it, there's some risk involved, and the price gets set accordingly," explains Joel Cantor, a program officer at the Robert Wood Johnson Foundation. "Then the technology diffuses and gets easier to use. More physicians get good at it. But the price never goes down."

The classic example is the extraction of cataracts and implantation of artificial lenses in the eye. This undeniably useful technology was introduced in the early 1980s and became a standard procedure by the end of the decade. During that time, however, many ophthalmologists became wealthy by charging $2000 or more for a cataract extraction that could be done in about an hour.

Primary-care physicians, such as general internists, family practitioners, and pediatricians, don't do procedures like that. Instead, they spend their days in office visits, which have long-established, and thus lower, "usual and customary" fee profiles.

As a result, their incomes are much lower than those of specialists. In 1990, the median income for general family practitioners was $93,000, and for pediatricians, $100,000, according to the American Medical Association's annual survey. Median income for surgeons and radiologists, on the other hand, was $200,000. Senior specialists can earn much, much more. Cardiovascular surgeons in group practice averaged about $500,000 in 1990, according to a study by the Medical Group Management Association.

Medical-school students, who must pick a residency program in their senior year, are painfully aware of these economic distinctions. In addition, they're trained in an academic environment that has long rewarded specialists with prestige and research grants. Young physicians, who leave medical school with a huge debt load, are increasingly turning to specialization. Overall, about one-third of U.S. physicians are in primary care. But among 1987 medical school graduates who have now completed their internships and residencies, only one-fourth have gone into primary care, according to data from the Association of American Medical Colleges.

A fed-up Ohio family doctor, responding to a survey by his professional society, the American Academy of Family Physicians, summarized his feelings this way: "Why bother with 60- to 70-hour work weeks, constant phone calls, all night emergency room visits, poor reimbursements, demanding patients, the need for instant exact decisions . . . concerning a million possible diseases, when you can 'specialize' in one organ, get paid $500 for a 15-minute procedure, only need to know a dozen drugs and side effects, and work part time?"

Do we really need our luxurious quantities of cardiologists, dermatologists, neurosurgeons, and urologists? Other countries get along fine with about a 50-50 ratio between primary-care doctors and specialists. The evidence is that we could, too.

A team from the New England Medical Center recently looked at patients who got their usual care from primary-care physicians (internists or family doctors) or from specialists (cardiologists and endocrinologists). The groups were not identical; the specialists tended to have older patients with more medical problems. But even after that difference was factored in, the specialists ran up higher bills, on average, than the primary-care doctors. They put more patients in the hospital, prescribed more drugs, and performed more tests. Yet an analysis still in progress appears to show that the two groups of patients had similar health outcomes.

The medical profession itself acknowledges the imbalance. The principal professional journal for internists, the Annals of Internal Medicine, said in a 1991 editorial: "Given the number of subspecialists already in practice, there are not enough highly specialized cases to go around. . . . We cannot continue to practice this way when cost containment is the dominant health policy issue of our times."

This year, Medicare began an effort to even out the economic imbalance between primary care and specialty physicians. The new program, known as the Resource-Based Relative Value Scale (RBRVS), is essentially a standard, national fee schedule, adjusted for geographic variations in the cost of practice. It increases the reimbursement for evaluation and management services, and greatly reduces the reimbursement for procedures. Physicians, however, may find a way around this constraint, as they have around others. For one thing, doctors can always simply raise their fees for privately insured, non-Medicare patients—although some private insurance companies may eventually adopt a version of the RBRVS fee schedule.

Since the mid-1980s, doctors have also manipulated the reimbursement system by "unbundling" services— that is, charging for two or more separate procedures instead of one. For instance, instead of billing $1200 for a hysterectomy, a doctor can collect $7000 by billing separately for various components of the operation. Commercial services conduct seminars to teach doctors how to maximize reimbursement in this way. But unbundling can cross the line into outright, prosecutable fraud, according to the General Accounting Office's health-care fraud report.

Supplier-side economics

Just as the providers of care have profited hugely over the years, so have those who supply the providers—the pharmaceutical com-panies and the makers of medical equipment and devices. They can charge top prices for their products, secure in the knowledge that the system will reimburse them. The pharmaceutical industry has been one of the nation's most profitable industrial sectors; it operates with an average profit margin of 15 percent and has given an average annual return to investors of 25 percent over the last decade.

Companies that latch on to new medical technologies can also earn huge profits. In spite of the current hand-wringing over health-care reform, health-care stocks as a group increased in value by fully 50 percent in 1991.

"A lot of people in health care are making a lot of money," says Stephen Zuckerman, a senior research associate at the Urban Institute in Washington, D.C. "They're not unhappy with the current system."

Curiously, the debate over health-care costs in the U.S. tends to assume that the cost of drugs and medical technology is immutably fixed. But international comparisons demonstrate that this needn't be so. In Japan, for example, the national fee schedule pays $177 for a magnetic resonance imaging (MRI) exam, compared with an average charge of about $1000 in the U.S. Pharmaceutical prices, which vary widely from country to country, are also significantly higher in the U.S. than anywhere else.

Nothing for something

As costly as it is, our health-care system might be worth its price if it somehow ended up making us healthier than people in other countries. But it doesn't.

Of the 24 industrialized nations making up the Organization for Economic Cooperation and Development (OECD), the U.S. spends more than twice as much on health per capita as the average. And it devotes a far greater percentage of its gross national product to health care than any other country. Yet the other OECD countries—with the exception of Turkey and Greece, by far the poorest of the group—all have roughly as many doctors and hospitals per capita as we do.

As for health status, of the 24 OECD countries, the U.S. ranks:
- 21st in infant mortality.
- 17th in male life expectancy.
- 16th in female life expectancy.

Dr. Barbara Starfield of the Johns Hopkins School of Public Health compared the U.S. with nine industrialized European nations in three areas: the availability of high-quality primary care, public-health indicators such as infant mortality and life expectancy, and overall public satisfaction with the value of health care. In all three areas, the U.S. ranked at or near the bottom.

The problem, simply put, is that the system is geared to providing the services that can earn physicians and hospitals the most money—not the ones that will do the public the most good. The U.S. has four times as many $1.5-million magnetic resonance imaging devices per capita as Germany does. But at the same

The uninsured aren't welcome **From a hospital marketing consultant's brochure: "To promote cardiology services, savvy marketers select all those at higher risk for heart disease, who are between the ages of 35 and 65, privately insured . . . it's target marketing at its best."**

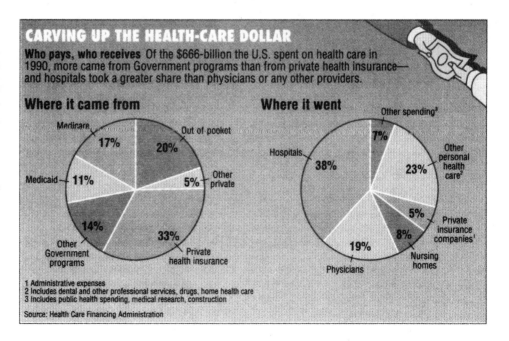

CARVING UP THE HEALTH-CARE DOLLAR

Who pays, who receives Of the $666-billion the U.S. spent on health care in 1990, more came from Government programs than from private health insurance—and hospitals took a greater share than physicians or any other providers.

1 Administrative expenses
2 Includes dental and other professional services, drugs, home health care
3 Includes public health spending, medical research, construction

Source: Health Care Financing Administration

time, the U.S. system short-changes the basic, low-tech care that has, over the years, proven effective at preventing disease.

The poor and uninsured are most likely to suffer from the imbalance. During the 1980s, while American hospitals were falling all over themselves to add costly, high-tech neonatal intensive-care units, the number of mothers unable to get basic prenatal care climbed, as did the incidence of premature births.

In most states, Medicaid now pays nowhere near the actual cost of delivering care; hospitals lose money on their Medicaid admissions. As a result, many doctors and some for-profit hospitals refuse even to accept Medicaid patients.

People with no insurance at all fare even worse. A group from the University of California, San Francisco, for example, looked at the hospital care given to sick newborn babies in the state's hospitals in 1987. Even though the uninsured babies were, on the average, the sickest group, they left the hospital sooner than insured babies and received fewer services while they were there. The Rand group has also shown that when California cut back on Medi-

Costs exposed, prices cut After a state government survey revealed it was charging $14,000 more for heart bypass than a local competitor, St. Vincent Health Center in Erie, Pa., dropped its bypass price by $10,000—the first rate reduction in its 116-year history. Estimated annual savings: $5-million.

caid coverage a decade ago, the health of people who lost their coverage declined dramatically.

"We've been sucked into believing that if we have a national health program, we're going to have rationing," says Dr. Philip Caper of Dartmouth. "The answer is, we have rationing already. Ask somebody who lost their health insurance, or can't get a bone-marrow transplant because they're on Medicaid. If that isn't rationing, what is?"

Hospitals that serve the poor and uninsured are suffering as well. The success of private hospitals in attracting well-insured patients has put an increasing burden on the public and not-for-profit hospitals still willing (or required) to accept all comers. A 1990 survey of 277 public and teaching hospitals found that 38 percent sometimes held patients overnight in the emergency room because no regular beds were available; 40 percent had turned away ambulances because of overcrowding.

Hospitals in California have even shut down their trauma centers as a way of barring the door against uninsured patients. "Hospitals find themselves jockeying for geography," says Bettina Kurowski, a vice president of St. Joseph Medical Center in Burbank, which closed its trauma center when its annual losses hit $1.5-million and threatened the financial survival of the hospital as a whole. "If you can be promised service areas that include freeways, and therefore get trauma cases covered by auto insurance, you can break even. If you don't include freeways, mostly you get penetrating [gunshot and stab wound] trauma, and those patients by and large don't have insurance."

Red tape and red ink

Ultimately, our cumbersome, inequitable system of reimbursement raises the costs for all of us—insured and uninsured alike—and causes problems for physicians as well. "In order to preserve the mirage of a private system, we've created the most bureaucratic, regulated system of any in the world," says David Mechanic, director of the Institute on Health Care Policy at Rutgers University.

A key characteristic of the U.S. system is its obsession with making sure that patients get only what their insurance entitles them to, and nothing more. That means, for instance, that hospitals must keep meticulous

track of everything used by a particular patient, down to individual gauze sponges or aspirin tablets—all adding to administrative costs. More important, the burden of dealing with multiple forms from a huge number of insurance companies requires a lot of clerical manpower.

Increasingly, too, doctors and hospitals have to answer to Government and private review panels that evaluate many aspects of the care they offer. Government reviewers work to ensure that Medicare and Medicaid patients are not being undertreated, while private insurers want to make sure that their patients are not being overtreated.

Hospitals in the U.S. spend fully 20 percent of their budgets, on average, on billing administration—compared to only 9 percent for Canadian hospitals. To run a health plan covering 25 million people, Canada employs fewer administrators than Massachusetts Blue Cross, which covers 2.7 million.

Our nation's more than 1200 private health-insurance companies add to the red tape by the necessary maintenance of their underwriting, marketing, and administrative staffs. This overhead consumed an average 14 cents out of every premium dollar in 1990, according to the Health Care Financing Administration.

Private physicians, too, have been forced to hire extra office help to cope with the ever-enlarging demands of third-party review, regulations, and paperwork. Drs. David Himmelstein and Steffie Woolhandler, internists at Harvard Medical School who are prominent critics of the U.S. health-care system, have calculated that the average office-based U.S. physician employs twice as many clerical and managerial workers as the average Canadian doctor. Dealing with the bureaucracy has become so intrusive that doctors have developed a name for it: the "hassle factor."

Dishonest physicians have also taken advantage of the system to bilk insurance companies. According to the General Accounting Office report: "This complex system itself becomes an impediment to detecting fraud and abuse. . . . a physician who bills for more office visits than can reasonably be performed in a day, for example, may not be detected if the billing is split among several payers."

Drs. Woolhandler and Himmelstein, who favor a Canadian-style system, have calculated that about 20 percent of U.S. health-care spending

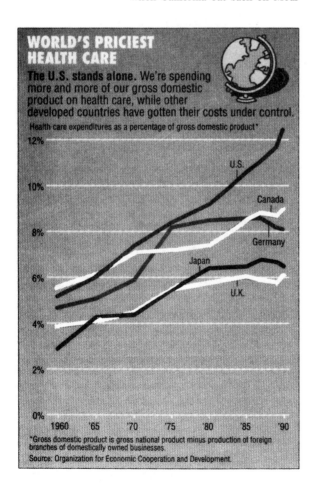

WORLD'S PRICIEST HEALTH CARE
The U.S. stands alone. We're spending more and more of our gross domestic product on health care, while other developed countries have gotten their costs under control.

Health care expenditures as a percentage of gross domestic product*

12%
10%
8%
6%
4%
2%
0%

U.S.
Canada
Germany
Japan
U.K.

1960   '65   '70   '75   '80   '85   '90

*Gross domestic product is gross national product minus production of foreign branches of domestically owned businesses.
Source: Organization for Economic Cooperation and Development.

goes for administrative costs: insurance overhead, hospital and nursing administration, and physicians' overhead and billing expenses. Not surprisingly, the private health-insurance industry says this estimate is too high. However, industry representatives decline to offer their own figure.

Universal coverage and uniform fee schedules enable other countries to avoid most of the administrative expense of the U.S. system. The single-payer Canadian system, where all health-care costs are ultimately paid by the Government, devotes about 10 percent of expenditures to administration. The General Accounting Office calculates that if the U.S. were to adopt a single-payer Canadian-style system, we would save about $70-billion a year in insurance overhead and the administrative costs to doctors and hospitals.

Enough for all

No matter what corner of the health-care system is examined—hospital costs, clinical procedures, administrative expenses—at least 20 percent seems to represent waste or inefficiency. If the system could be redesigned to get rid of this excess, it could, in effect, provide 20 percent more necessary service without costing any more than it does now.

Granted, devising a totally efficient system would be difficult, if not impossible, to accomplish. However, there is easily more than enough excess spending in our current system to take care of the roughly 14 percent of the population who are not currently under any public or private insurance plan.

In [the August and September 1992] issues of CONSUMER REPORTS, the different options for health-care reform [are examined]. But it's already clear that the ideal health-care system for American consumers, whatever it turns out to be, will have to be radically different from the wasteful, patchwork system that governs our health care today.

Dissatisfied Americans
Pollsters asked citizens of 10 developed nations to rate their health-care systems. U.S. respondents were the unhappiest of the lot. Fully 60 percent said our system is in need of "fundamental changes."

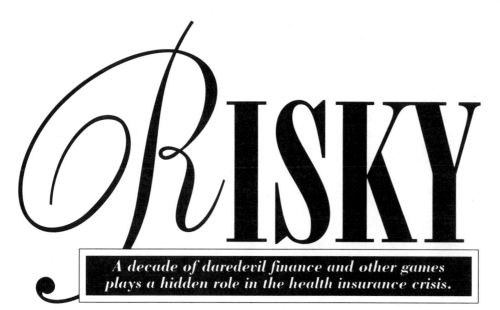

RISKY BUSINESS

A decade of daredevil finance and other games plays a hidden role in the health insurance crisis.

Jeffrey Denny

Jeffrey Denny is executive editor.

Like many small-business proprietors, Jan and Phil Fenty of Washington, D.C., fret constantly about the cost of health insurance. Owners of Fleet Feet, a running shoe and clothing franchise, the Fentys pay dearly to cover themselves and their two full-time employees under the Washington-area Blue Cross/Blue Shield Health Plan. Just recently Blue Cross gave notice that Fleet Feet's premium would be increased 28 percent, bringing their monthly payment to $1,800.

So the Fentys were outraged to read in the *Washington Post* that Blue Cross had raised rates partly because of some $100 million in losses from various for-profit business ventures, many unconnected to medical coverage. For example, one of its subsidiaries reportedly now owns Cape Cod beachfront property and a

rock-and-roll recording studio on a 145-acre New England farm—the unintended result of having loaned $11.1 million to a student travel agency that defaulted.

"It made me angry to see those big shots wasting our money and our rates going up and up and up," says Jan Fenty.

The Fentys are among the untold number of health insurance policyholders nationwide who may have suffered higher rates, reduced coverage, unpaid bills or cancellation because of a little explored factor in the nation's health insurance crisis: The same kind of 1980s-style go-go investment practices, questionable business dealings, lavish spending and help-yourself ethics that brought down the savings and loan industry also have undermined the insurance industry.

Under a tattered patchwork of state laws and virtually no federal oversight, health insurance underwriters have lost billions of dollars investing in high-yield, low-grade "junk" bonds, real estate and other dubious ventures. Sporadic cases of fraud have compounded the losses.

"It's been a well-told tale here," says Lester Dunlap, a consumer advocate for the Louisiana Department of Insurance. "You find this in almost every state."

Until recently, there was little concern about how health insurers invested their assets as long as they provided an efficient system for spreading out the cost of medical care. But increasingly their financial management is a matter of public policy.

"I don't think the public is aware of what could happen to their health insurance because of some of these problems," says a congressional aide who investigated life/health insurance company failures.

A review of insurance industry reports, ongoing congressional investigations, newspaper articles and pending lawsuits, as well as interviews with insurance regulators, financial analysts and other industry observers reveals a disturbing picture: **GAMBLERS' MENTALITY.** A 1990 paper by Investors Diversified Services (IDS) named "imprudent investment management" among the "major factors" in the

From *Common Cause* magazine, Spring 1993, pp. 9-15. Reprinted with permission from *Common Cause* magazine, 2030 M Street, NW, Washington, DC 20036.

failure of the 48 largely health and accident insurers it studied. "Over half...had an investment portfolio significantly different from the industry norm," the report noted.

AILING INSURERS. The number of life/health insurer insolvencies tripled during the 1980s "and this trend appears to be continuing," the U.S. General Accounting Office (GAO) concluded in a recent report. And 14 of the 72 Blue Cross health plans nationwide, the country's largest health insurer with 94 mil-

COST TO ADMINISTER MEDICARE, PER BENEFITS PAID: 1.4%...

...TO ADMINISTER PRIVATE HEALTH INSURANCE: 17%

Source: Congressional Budget Office

lion policyholders, are in "weak" or "very weak" financial condition, according to an independent analysis.

POLICYHOLDERS STUCK. In addition to facing higher rates or cancelation, policyholders also may be saddled with unpaid medical claims because the system of state "guaranty funds" designed to clean up after insurance company failures is full of holes, according to the GAO. And with rare exception, the guaranty funds do not cover Blue Cross policyholders, members of health maintenance organizations (HMOs) or employees of self-insured businesses — more than 120 million policyholders.

On top of that, the rash of failures has contributed to the increase in health insurance premiums because the guaranty fund system is financed by insurance rate increases, as well as tax revenues. The cost of covering unpaid life/health insurance claims from insurers that failed between 1976 and 1991 is expected to reach $4.2 billion, according to A.M. Best, an insurance rating agency.

The health insurance industry insists that it's financially stable on the whole, arguing that most of the 1,500 medical underwriters in business today are healthy and that fraudulent operators are rare. And executives with the nation's largest health insurers reject the notion that investment losses have harmed policyholders. "Absolutely nothing else contributes to [the health insurance crisis]

other than...the explosion in health care costs," says John Maginn, chief investment officer at Mutual of Omaha, the nation's premier underwriter of individual health plans.

But logic dictates that when an insurance company's overall financial picture is weakened by investment losses, it leaves less room to hold back rate hikes or keep risky policyholders. "Everything that affects the bottom line" affects health policies, says a National Association of Insurance Commissioners (NAIC) official.

This is particularly true for Blue Cross plans and small health insurers operating near the margin, according to Robert Hunter, president of the National Insurance Consumers Organization (NICO), a leading industry watchdog. "If you're already having trouble, and then your investments start to go bad, then it puts critical pressure on you to get rid of people [and] raise rates," Hunter says.

THE PARTY'S OVER

The health insurance business is fairly straightforward. Companies take in premiums based on policyholders' medical histories, set aside reserves to cover expected claims and "surplus" for unexpected claims, and keep a share for overhead and profit.

Surplus and reserve accounts are invested. Companies that sell several lines of insurance — most health policies are sold by life insurance companies, for example — typically sink their money into a mixture of investments of various risk, maturity and payoff.

Life/health insurance companies try to carry some low-risk, liquid investments, such as money market securities, that can be converted quickly into cash to reimburse the continuous stream of medical claims. These tend to offer low returns. They also try to carry as many high-return investments as possible, which tend to be riskier. That's where the trouble began.

During the 1980s many insurance com-

panies started selling financial services, competing with S&Ls, banks and brokerages to give customers top returns. This encouraged insurers to sink their assets into high-yield ventures. By the end of 1990, the average life/health insurance company had a quarter of its assets in junk bonds, real estate and mortgage loans, according to A.M. Best. Life insurance companies in fact held about 30 percent of the outstanding junk bonds, a separate 1990 analysis estimated.

By then the roof was falling in. Between 1988 and 1990 the junk bond default rate (the portion rendered worthless) tripled from 3 percent to 10 percent. The real estate market also collapsed, littering the landscape with vacant office buildings, unfinished subdivisions and unmet mortgage payments.

The collapse in 1991 of two major life insurance companies—Executive Life of California and New York (because of junk bond losses) and New Jersey's Mutual Benefit Life (real estate losses)—focused national attention on the insurance industry's investment woes. But little attention was paid to the impact on health insurance, even though life insurers are the largest underwriters of health policies.

For example, Travelers and CIGNA each reported reductions in health division net income because of sharply devalued real estate investments. A third of Travelers' mortgage and real estate holdings—$5.2 billion worth—were "underperforming" as of last fall while 6.3 percent of its investment portfolio was in junk bonds. Aetna Life & Casualty posted an 18 percent decline in net income overall for 1991 largely due to commercial mortgage losses. Aetna had $1.5 billion in junk bonds and $1.6 billion in problem mortgages last fall.

Company officials deny that their health policyholders have been hurt as a result. But critics say the same investment strategies that helped to sink the S&L industry are playing an indirect role in the health insurance crisis. "First they take our money with a false promise of safety," Martin Weiss, a Palm Beach, Fla., financial adviser who analyzes the health insurance industry, maintains. "Then they invest it in junk bonds and speculative real estate, and now they're trying to make us, the consumers, pay for their blunders."

E.F. HUTTON SPOKE

While Blue Cross health plans are non-profits, many still couldn't resist the go-go investment game.

One eager participant was Blue Cross of West Virginia. In early 1987, Shearson Lehman Brothers, the big Manhattan brokerage house, and E.F. Hutton, the financial adviser, offered to loan the Blue Cross plan $25 million to buy 30-year U.S. Treasury bonds on credit and make futures and options trades at the Chicago commodities exchanges, according to a pending lawsuit filed in state court by the West Virginia insurance commission.

Convinced, the Blue Cross plan bought the Treasury bonds and over the next 10 months undertook a frenzy of high-risk commodities trades, at times making a dozen or more transactions a day. It stopped only after it had lost $2.3 million — plus $150,000 it had paid Shearson and Hutton for their financial services. Shearson Lehman (which later acquired Hutton) refused to comment for this article.

Partly because of its losing investments, West Virginia Blue Cross became the first in the Blues network to collapse, stranding 51,000 policyholders with unpaid medical claims and others with reduced or canceled coverage. Local doctors have defied court orders and ignored pleas from state officials not to dun patients. Some policyholders' credit ratings have been ruined. One medical group with $114,000 in unpaid claims reportedly insists that patients needing non-emergency surgery pay half their bill in advance. "I lost a total of over $23,000 myself," one policyholder told Congress. "How could a health insurance company simply go bankrupt and leave over $41 million worth of claims unpaid?"

West Virginia Blue Cross also hemorrhaged an undetermined sum of money through a number of for-profit subsidiaries and affiliates, some of which were set up for the personal gain of the health plan's executives, a Senate investigations subcommittee chaired by Sen. Sam Nunn (D-Ga.) found in a 1992 probe. An offshoot of one subsidiary set up to invest in real estate and travel agencies sold computer equipment back to the health plan at mark-ups of 80 to 130 percent, the state insurance commissioner found later.

Nationwide many Blue Cross plans have financed the creation of for-profit ventures, some health-related and some not, in an effort to earn extra money to hold down premiums. The Blue Cross

national association in Chicago defends this practice and argues that subsidiaries altogether cleared some $195 million in profits in 1991 (although a Blue Cross spokesperson could not say how it affected premiums).

But the Nunn subcommittee's ongoing probe of the Blues has revealed a "tendency...to devote inordinate amounts of time, monies and resources on subsidiaries not directly related to their primary task of providing low cost, quality health care coverage," a staff report notes. For example:

INSURANCE FAILURES DUE TO UNDERPRICED PREMIUMS: 23%...

...DUE TO INVESTMENT LOSSES AND ALLEGED FRAUD: 45%

Source: A. M. Best Company

■ Washington, D.C.'s Blue Cross plan operated 45 subsidiaries, including a group of far-flung companies that provided travel services such as evacuating ill travellers, finding lost luggage and selling trip-interruption insurance. It lost $32 million; the health plan was close to failing when a neighboring Virginia plan agreed to take it over.

■ The Maryland plan is in trouble partly because of $120 million in subsidiary losses. One subsidiary did make money: In 1989 (the same year health premiums rose more than 25 percent), the health plan invested $14.7 million to set up BCBSM Finance, which bought and sold stock. Before shutting down in December, BCBSM Finance cleared $500,000 in profits — but that was far less than the $2.4 million it could have cleared had the $14.7 million been sunk into a passbook savings account paying 4 percent interest.

BRANDO'S LIFE MASK
It's not always risky ventures that hurt health policyholders. According to industry studies, alleged internal fraud has played a noticeable role in the rash of insurance company insolvencies.

Consider allegations involving George Washington Life of West Virginia, a $40 million commercial life/health insurer that state regulators seized more than two years ago. Regulators charge that John Wilbur of Jacksonville, Fla., and other

executives of the insurer and its parent company skimmed $14 million in premiums from George Washington for their private enrichment and conspired to mislead examiners about their activities.

"GW Life's money and assets were systematically looted...from 1981 through at least 1991," West Virginia's insurance commissioner charged in a $45 million fraud and civil racketeering lawsuit filed in September. That, as well as "systematic fraud and breaches of fiduciary duty" by company officers, directors and lawyers, caused the company to fail, the suit charges. Wilbur did not respond to requests for comment.

That's nothing compared to what emerged from the rubble left by the collapse of World Life and Health of Pennsylvania in 1991. It was licensed to sell health, life and accident insurance in 18 states, had 64,000 policyholders — and will cost $28 million to clean up. Here's what Senate staff investigators and state regulators found:

Some of World Life's policyholders actually were covered by two reinsurance companies whose principal assets were laughably bogus. Among them were so-called "treasury bills" issued by something called "Sovereign Cherokee Nation Tejas." State regulators contacted the purported Indian tribe's office in Atlanta, Ga., to check out the treasury bills. They wound up speaking with the treasurer, who called himself "Wise Otter" and spoke with a pronounced British accent.

Wise Otter turned out to be Dallas Bessant, a British citizen and owner of the two companies. "Cherokee Nation Tejas is neither sovereign, Cherokee nor a nation," Nunn subcommittee investigators later reported. "It is a sham, run by a group of 'white' or 'Anglo' Americans for the sole purpose of financial self-enrichment."

And what backed the Cherokee Nation Tejas treasury bills? Items included a "life mask" of Marlon Brando the company claimed was worth $1.5 million; titles to movies such as *Computer Beach Party*, *Distant Drums* and *My Girl Tisa*; gold mineral leases, valued at nearly $100 million, for a site under a municipal parking lot in Central City, Colo.; and certificates of deposit from nonexistent financial institutions. The "tribe" was in such sorry financial shape that at one point its officers were denied credit to rent rooms at the Motel 6 in Dallas.

Small-business owners Jan and Phil Fenty were outraged that their Blue Cross plan spent $44,000 on golf outings.

WASTING AWAY

The years of financial mistakes and misdeeds are playing out with a vengeance.

According to Blue Cross national association spokesperson Julie Boyle, an internal "watch list" of endangered plans includes six: Maryland, New Hampshire, New Jersey, Empire of New York, Vermont and Washington, D.C., which together cover some 15 million people. (Only the Washington, Maryland and New Jersey plans are reported to have suffered large subsidiary losses.)

But health insurance analyst Martin Weiss says that number may be too low. According to his financial rating system, which was submitted in testimony to the Nunn subcommittee, 14 Blue Cross plans were still "weak" or "very weak" as of early December. "Weak" means that policyholders could be at risk, Weiss says; "very weak" means they already are. Another 14 received only "fair" ratings.

Because the Blues are nonprofit and often required to insure people whom commercial insurers refuse as too risky, they tend to be hit harder by rising medical costs and operate close to the edge.

But many commercial, for-profit health

insurance companies haven't fared much better. The incidence of life/health insurer failures has increased sharply since the mid 1970s; more than 140 failed between 1989 and 1991. On top of the failed firms, "a significantly greater number of insurers had affiliate or overstated asset problems resulting from overexposure in low-quality assets, typically, [junk] bonds, commercial mortgages or commercial real estate projects," A.M. Best notes.

The health segment has been hit hardest. The cost of covering unpaid medical claims left by failed insurers far exceeds that of other insurance claims — $190 million in 1989 and 1990 alone, according to the GAO.

OUT IN THE COLD

Often health insurers that suffer investment losses play games with policyholders, challenging claims, delaying payments and refusing to cover portions of medical bills deemed beyond "usual or customary" costs, which become increasingly arbitrary, state regulators say. "The net effect on the consumer is he doesn't get the response he expects," says Lester Dunlap of the Louisiana state insurance department.

And while health insurers downplay any connection, investment losses have been linked to rate increases when company books are laid bare. Examining the Washington and Maryland Blue Cross plans in the wake of their financial woes, insurance regulators found that both increased their premiums to help cover subsidiary losses. "The only way you can get [the money] back is through rates...," John Picciotto, the Maryland plan's chief legal officer, told the *Washington Post*.

When banks fail, the federal government covers depositors' money. When health insurers fail, the only place policyholders can take their medical bills is to the system of state-administered guaranty funds, which are designed to pay bills the failed insurance company had promised to cover. Unfortunately, the system is full of holes (see box, next page).

And for some policyholders, there's the ultimate nightmare if their insurance company fails: cancelation. When World Life and Health was seized by Pennsylvania insurance regulators in 1991, the firm had already spun off its 30,000 individual health and accident policies to another Pennsylvania insurer. But most group health plans were terminated. "[Policyholders] had to go find another

health insurer," says a Pennsylvania insurance commission spokesperson.

State insurance liquidators often try to find another insurer to take over policyholders of failed companies. "We've been pretty successful at selling off these blocks," Oklahoma Insurance Commissioner Cathy Weatherford says. Indeed, it can be relatively easy to find new carriers for healthy policyholders, especially large employee groups.

But many insurers will not assume those with poor medical histories, preexisting health conditions or contracts that limit rate hikes. And "nobody wants the little groups," says a Pennsylvania insurance department spokesperson. When Michigan's HMO West failed in 1988 the state liquidator had to twist arms to get other health plans to accept two women left stranded days before they expected to give birth. "Under these conditions, a significant number of individuals...may be unable to obtain new health insurance," the GAO noted.

There is practically no protection when an insurance company decides to cancel or sell off health policies before it goes under. As California's Great Republic Life Insurance Co. suffered financial problems that led to its liquidation in 1991, it canceled a health plan with 14,000 policyholders, including Stan Long, 38, of Los Angeles, who had been diagnosed with HIV, the AIDS virus.

Long went more than a year without coverage, but "lucked out" because his condition was stable, his doctor was a close friend and his pharmacist refused to charge him. Now Long is covered under California's health insurance risk pool, which is financed by cigarette taxes. But he's still angry.

"My business has more regulations than health insurance does," says Long, a partner in an interior design firm.

ASLEEP AT THE SWITCH

Who let the insurance industry gamble with people's medical security? Perhaps it's not surprising to find many of the same players from the S&L debacle:

THE ACCOUNTANTS. Recently, the Big Eight accounting firm Ernst & Young agreed to pay $400 million to settle federal lawsuits charging the firm with failing to adequately audit four large thrifts that subsequently failed (costing taxpayers $6.6 billion) and to call off any more federal suits.

Ernst & Young currently is being sued for $55 million in damages by the West

Virginia Blue Cross liquidator in connection with its auditing of the local Blue Cross plan. "Ernst & Young repeatedly told the department that the plan would not fail, but that its problems were only cyclical," West Virginia Insurance Commissioner Hanley Clark testified in July. Ernst & Young says the suit is "totally unfounded and will be dismissed."

On the whole, the Nunn subcommittee investigation found, accountants "played a significant role for [the] sham deals" that resulted in insurer failures.

FLAWED OVERSIGHT. The insurance industry has fought any reform of the 1945 McCarran-Ferguson Act, which flatly outlaws federal regulation, leaving an uneven state-by-state system.

An insurance company licensed in a dozen states may be subject to a dozen different state laws and regulatory approaches. NAIC, the state regulators' association, attempts to set nationwide standards and in the last two years has recommended tougher laws and regula-

tions to head off insurance failures — and federal regulation. But until recently the association did little about the problem because it was primarily concerned with keeping ailing insurers afloat, critics say.

"Monday morning quarterbacking in the regulation of financial interests is really quite easy," a NAIC official responds. "Look at federal regulation of banks and thrifts. We think our regulation stacks up quite well against these."

Many state insurance regulators continue to lack the legal power, political backing or resources to oversee the industry, however. "Current U.S. insurance regulations are replete with a number of significant loopholes," the Nunn subcommittee noted. Most states' investment regulations have been passive, allowing insurers "to invest in virtually any type, quality or concentration of asset without limitation," Minnesota insurance regulator Thomas Borman testified in 1990. And regulators had an average of only $250 to investigate each complaint they receive and $4,000 to ex-

amine each company they regulate, according to a 1990 study by an insurance agents' association. Until last September, the federal charter of Washington, D.C.'s Blue Cross plan actually limited the local insurance commissioner's authority to regulate the health plan; the District government has never audited its books.

The Blue Cross system has been accused of stonewalling and thwarting regulators "by either putting politically powerful individuals on their boards or by making contributions to certain campaigns," according to a Nunn subcommittee staff report. West Virginia's Blue Cross spent $102,000 between 1987 and 1990 "in lobbying and attorneys' fees …primarily to fight the department's attempt to strengthen the state's laws and jurisdiction over" the health plan, according to state Insurance Commissioner Clark. "Not included in this figure," he added, "is the salary for current and former state legislators who were also on the plan's payroll."

CO-OPTED REGULATORS. Some regula-

NO GUARANTEE

ABOUT A YEAR AGO, the American Council of Life Insurance placed a large advertisement in the *Wall Street Journal* proudly announcing that all 50 states had established life and health insurance guaranty funds, which are designed to protect policyholders from getting stuck with unpaid medical bills or death claims should their insurer fail.

Noting that the funds are financed by assessing insurers a percentage of their income from life and health insurance premiums, the council proclaimed, "The fact that life insurers have to help pay for the mistakes of other companies gives them a powerful incentive to maintain the financial strength of the industry."

Nice try. Insurers actually contribute little to the funds. Who really pays? We do. In all but a handful of states, insurers are permitted to recover their guaranty fund payments by raising premiums or filing for tax breaks. Eighty-six percent of the guaranty fund assessments in 1990 will be reimbursed by the public.

"The guaranty funds are used as a massive tax benefit for the companies," a Missouri state senator told the *St. Louis Post-Dispatch*. "People should know that they are the ones paying...for the insolvent insurance companies."

Another problem: The guaranty system isn't as airtight as the ad implied. "The term 'state guaranty fund' is a misnomer masking the system's faults," Mary Lynn Sergeant, a General Accounting Office (GAO) researcher, testified last spring.

As the GAO noted in a 1992 report, "Some policyhold-

ers of multi-state insurers may have no protection at all should their insurer fail," particularly if a policyholder moves to a state where his or her insurer is not licensed to operate. And 28 states place some limit on medical claims left by defunct health insurers; in 22 states, the cap is $100,000. In Utah, policyholders have to absorb the first $500. Guaranty funds have failed — or refused — to cover unpaid medical claims right away.

The insurance council's ad also didn't note that millions of health insurance policyholders aren't covered at all by the guaranty fund system. These include people covered by unlicensed, fly-by-night operators. Or employees of companies that insure themselves through third-party administrators, a growing but barely regulated trend in medical coverage. Most of the 94 million Blue Cross policyholders aren't covered either. And only four guaranty funds cover health maintenance organizations (HMOs), which represent some 38 million people and which the insurance industry sees as the future of health coverage in America. HMO coverage "is something the states ought to be considering," says Michael Surguine, a legal specialist with the National Association of Insurance Commissioners.

"With the rising number of failures of small insurers and the recent regulatory takeover of large life/health insurers, there is a growing likelihood that even more policyholders...will face the prospect of falling through the safety net and landing without the benefits promised by their insurers," the GAO reported. —*J.D.*

CRISIS? WHAT CRISIS?

JOHN WILBUR OF JACKSONVILLE, FLA., sure knew how to live. For years Wilbur charged his firm for several annual trips to Europe, dropping some $100,000 on travel and entertainment in one year alone, a state official who reviewed company documents confirms. At one point Wilbur spent 12 weeks at the Marriott Marquis hotel in Manhattan, which wasn't itemized but would cost about $12,000 today. Wilbur also charged virtually all his personal expenses to his firm — including laundry bills. All that on top of a $350,000 annual salary.

Generous perks aren't unusual in many blue-chip corporate suites. But Wilbur was chair of George Washington Life Insurance Co., a relatively small life and health underwriter chartered in West Virginia and headquartered in Florida. Until September 1990, that is, when George Washington folded — in part, state insurance examiners say, because of Wilbur's lavish spending habits.

The crisis in affordable medical coverage makes it hard to stomach the way some insurers spend money.

Take salaries, for instance. In 1991, CIGNA chair and CEO Wilson Taylor received $1.3 million in compensation, then-Aetna board chair James Lynn received $1 million and Travelers CEO Edward Budd got $923,000. Or political contributions: In 1991-92, Aetna made $46,000 in corporate contributions to various Republican committees.

And for a nonprofit entity, the Blue Cross network seems to have a lot of money to throw around, according to an ongoing probe by the Senate investigations subcommittee.

To begin with, Bernard Tresnowski, president of the Blue Cross and Blue Shield Association, which represents the nation's locally based Blue Cross health plans, drew $622,000 in salary, benefits and allowances in 1991. Tresnowski in fact was the second-highest paid executive of all 37 medical trade groups tallied by *National Journal*, besting even the affluent American Medical Association.

At policyholder expense, executives of the Washington, D.C.-area Blue Cross plan, which is in deep financial trouble, flew to exclusive international resorts to investigate restaurants, beaches and accommodations for future business meetings. Top executive Joseph Gamble spent $447,000 on travel from 1987 through 1992, including 22 trips to Europe aboard the Concorde. During a 1989 jaunt to London, Paris and Zimbabwe, which cost $7,900, Gamble attended a conference to give a speech on fraud in the insurance industry. When he retired last fall, Gamble was presented with a three-dimensional collage commissioned from a local artist. Cost: $29,000.

Salary and compensation for former Maryland Blue Cross president Carl Sardegna increased 284 percent between 1986 and 1991. And while the Maryland plan was seeking rate hikes and its "financial picture was dark," state insurance commissioner John Donaho testified, the health plan annually pitched hospitality tents at the Preakness horse race — at a cost of more than $65,000 in 1992 alone — "under the guise of being a good corporate citizen," Donaho said. To entertain guests, the Maryland Blue signed a $300,000, four-year lease for a 14-seat exclusive luxury sky-box suite at the Baltimore Orioles baseball stadium, complete with private elevator and bathrooms, wet bar, two color TVs and an internal telephone to order refreshments. Food and drink wasn't included — that came to an extra $588 per game, on average.

Before it collapsed in 1990, stranding 51,000 policyholders, the West Virginia Blue spent at least $102,000 in lobbying and attorneys' fees, mostly to fight regulators' attempts to strengthen state laws and oversight of Blue Cross. Policyholders paid $340,000 in settlement costs and attorneys' fees in connection with two cases of sexual harassment filed against two officers. They kept their jobs.

West Virginia policyholders also unknowingly bought the health plan's president a new Lincoln Continental. But when other executives decided it would look bad — after all, the health plan was in the middle of a financial crisis — the car was traded for a cheaper Pontiac. The president ended up "not really liking the Pontiac," however, so the plan re-purchased the Lincoln.   —*J.D.*

---

tors are too close to the industry. Many are former industry employees and vice versa. According to another study by the insurance agents' group in 1990, 49 percent of the insurance commissioners who left office between 1984 and 1989 went on — some immediately — to positions in insurance companies or provided legal, accounting or consulting services to the industry. In 1976, for example, West Virginia insurance department examiner Michael Davoli was assigned to audit George Washington Life. Three years later Davoli was hired by the insurer's parent company as assistant to the chairman of the board, according to the West Virginia insurance commission suit.

Insurance companies often pick up the tab for food, drinks and entertainment at regulators' quarterly meetings, sometimes because regulators ask them to, according to published reports.

A QUESTION OF TRUST

Sensing that change is inevitable, the insurance industry recently softened its opposition to any major reform of the health care system. The Health Insurance Association of America has endorsed a plan in which the government would require employers to buy a standard employee health insurance package and tax more generous health benefits.

"[F]orcing some employers to buy your product seems a helluva lot better than having your industry shut down by the government," a *National Journal* columnist noted.

But given the industry's stewardship of scarce medical resources, many people have a gut-level distrust of any health care reform plan that leaves insurance companies in control.

"If they decide to change and not concentrate on profits but on people's health, then it's possible I could trust them," says small-business owner Jan Fenty of Washington, D.C. "But for the past 12 years everybody had license to go crazy and forget the average person."

Deadly Migration

HAZARDOUS INDUSTRIES' FLIGHT TO THE THIRD WORLD

JOSEPH LaDOU

JOSEPH LaDOU, M.D., is chief of the Division of Occupational and Environmental Medicine at the University of California, San Francisco. As a director of the International Commission on Occupational Health, he has traveled extensively to investigate working conditions and to establish training programs in occupational and environmental medicine in newly industrialized countries.

In 1988, a California manufacturer of epoxy coating materials decided that it could no longer afford to make its products in the United States. The cost of complying with new emission standards for the solvents the products contained would simply have been too high. Yet the company learned that if it set up shop in Mexico, it not only could use the same solvents but could dump wasted solvents at no cost into the arroyo behind the plant.

It's no secret that the low cost of manufacturing in Third World and newly industrialized countries has prompted thousands of First World corporations and investment groups to set up manufacturing operations there. The biggest lure, of course, is cheap labor—factory wages in countries such as Thailand, Bangladesh, Ghana, Guatemala, and Bolivia are often as low as 5 percent of those in industrialized countries. Companies also manufacture abroad to be closer to foreign markets and to overcome trade barriers. In return, the host countries reap significant benefits. According to the U.N. Environment Programme, foreign companies and investors have provided 60 percent of all industrial investment in developing countries over the past decade. For many nations, such investment is the primary source of new jobs.

But the industrial migration has a perverse side, the extent of which the California epoxy case can barely hint at. As developed nations enact laws promoting en-

vironmental and occupational safety, more and more manufacturers are moving their hazardous and polluting operations to less developed countries, most of which have either no environmental and worker-safety regulations or little power to enforce those that are on the books. Hazardous industries have migrated to many parts of Africa, Asia, and Eastern Europe. Japan, for example, with its limited land and dense population, has a pressing need to export manufacturing industries such as electronics, chemical production, and metal refining. And many European nations have exported hazardous industries such as textiles, petrochemicals, mining, and smelting.

There is an ironic twist to the problem. Countries that spend little on things like sewage systems, water treatment plants, and enforcement of environmental and occupational safety can offer tax rates dramatically lower than those in the industrialized world. Foreign-based manufacturers take the bait and move in, polluting waterways and endangering workers. Yet the host government can't afford remedies because of the low tax rate.

Pollution and working conditions are so bad that, in effect, the Industrial Revolution is taking place all over again, but with much larger populations of workers and in many more countries. And many of the resulting deaths and injuries are taking place with the complicity of First World companies.

The Faces of Exploitation

The practice of using less developed nations as a dumping ground for untreated factory waste is but one of many forms the export of industrial hazards can take. Industries whose markets in developed countries are

 From *Technology Review*, July 1991, pp. 46-53. © 1991 by *Technology Review*. Reprinted by permission.

shrinking because of environmental concerns are vigorously promoting their products in the less health-conscious Third World. DDT is a compelling example. Its worldwide production, led by U.S. and European companies, is at record levels, even though it has been illegal to produce or use the pesticide in the United States and Europe since the 1970s.

Asbestos is another distressing example. To stimulate the development of companies that will produce asbestos products, Canada's government sends free samples of the material to a number of poorer countries, where many workers and communities are still unaware of the mineral's dangers. (Bangladesh received 790 tons, worth $600,000, in 1984.) Partly as a result of such promotion, Canadian asbestos exports to South Korea increased from 5,000 tons in 1980 to 44,000 tons in 1989. Exports to Pakistan climbed from 300 tons to 6,000 tons in the same period. Canada now exports close to half its asbestos to the Third World.

The First World also exports entire industries—including most lead smelting, refining, and product manufacture—that present occupational hazards. In developed nations, companies using processes that involve lead are required to take costly precautions to protect workers. U.S. lead workers must receive special training, have proper work clothes and changing facilities, and go on paid leave if tests reveal high lead levels in the blood. But in the lax regulatory climate of Malaysia, most lead-acid battery workers—at both foreign- and locally owned plants—have lead levels three times as high as allowed in U.S. workers. And lead plants exported to India continue operating even though 10 per cent of the workers have lead poisoning.

Even a migrating industry that doesn't involve toxic materials can be hazardous, because First World corporations often apply a double standard to worker safety. At home, they might comply rigorously with health and safety regulations. Abroad, the same companies let safety standards plummet to the levels prevailing in the less developed host country.

Those levels are miserably low. Worker fatality rates are at least twice as high in industrializing countries, and workplace injuries occur with a frequency not seen in the developed nations since the early years of the Industrial Revolution. Workers in poor countries—usually with limited education, skill, and training—tend to labor in small, crowded factories with old, unsafe machinery, dangerous noise levels, and unsound buildings. Protective gear is seldom available. The companies also tend to be geographically scattered and inaccessible to health and safety inspectors.

On learning of such conditions in India or Malaysia, we in the First World may wince but may also be tempted to put them out of mind—to regard them as a Third World problem from which we are comfortably remote. Yet Americans need look no farther than their own southern border to find some of the worst instances of migrating industries' disregard for human health and environmental safety. Many of the factories that U.S. and other foreign interests operate in northern Mexico freely pollute the water, the air, and the ground and subject workers to conditions nothing short of Dickensian.

The Siesta of Reason

In 1965, Mexico sought to overcome chronic unemployment through the Border Industrialization Program, designed to lure foreign manufacturing business—mainly from the United States—into Mexican border states. The country's government hoped that foreign capital would flow into the economy along with modern production methods that would help create a skilled workforce.

Under the program, manufacturers send raw materials and equipment to Mexico. If they agree to take back the finished products, they need pay taxes only on the value added in Mexico instead of on the value of the entire product. Another big draw is that factory wages average about $5.40 per nine-hour day, less than in Korea, Taiwan, Hong Kong, and other countries long favored for off-shore manufacturing. For U.S. investors, the cost of transporting goods and materials to and from northern Mexico is lower as well.

Today, nearly 1,800 factories operate under this program in northern Mexico, employing about half a million workers. The plants, known as "maquiladoras," extend from Tijuana in the west to Matamoros on the Gulf of Mexico. Their owners include some of the largest U.S. corporations: IBM, General Electric, Motorola, Ford, Chrysler, General Motors, RCA, United Technologies, ITT, Eastman Kodak, and Zenith. Japan's Sony, Matsushita, Hitachi, Yazaki, and TDK also run maquiladoras, as do numerous European companies.

Most maquiladoras are small plants with fewer than 100 workers. In the program's early years, they were largely clothing manufacturers and hand assembly operations, employing mostly women. Today maquiladoras manufacture or assemble a wide range of products, from automobile parts to high-technology electronic components. Men now account for close to 40 percent of the workforce.

No one disputes that the main goal of the Border Industrialization Program has been met. The estimated $3 billion in foreign exchange earnings that maquiladoras pump into the Mexican economy each year now exceeds revenues from tourism and is second only to Mexico's oil and gas exports. Virtually all the new manufacturing jobs created in Mexico in the past decade—and a fifth of the country's manufacturing jobs overall—resulted from the rapid growth of the maquiladoras.

Yet these benefits have come at a high cost. The Border Industrialization Program has created serious social and environmental problems in both countries, but especially in Mexico. The prospect of employment in maquiladoras has caused the populations of border towns and cities to swell. Since 1970, for example, Nogales (south of Tucson) has grown fourfold to 250,000, and Juarez (across the Rio Grande from El Paso) has grown from 250,000 to 1.5 million.

Overcrowding strains these municipalities beyond their limits. Tens of thousands of workers subsist in cardboard huts in squatters' camps without heat or electricity, and sewage is dumped into the arroyos, through which it flows to the nearest river or estuary. At least 10 million gallons of raw sewage from Mexico flows into the Tijuana River every day, polluting San Diego's beaches. The Mexican government is so hard pressed to deal with the problem that the U.S. government, the state of California, and the city of San Diego have agreed to pay most of the $192 million cost of a treatment plant on the border.

But maquiladoras do more than just overburden sewers. Many owners and managers—especially of small maquiladoras engaged in metal working, plating, printing, tanning, and dyeing—readily admit that they moved their operations to Mexico partly because hazardous processes are unwelcome in the United States and other developed countries, and that Mexico is not creating any serious obstacle to their activities. As one owner of a furniture factory explained to me, "I can find lots of Mexican workers in the United States. What I can't find here in Tijuana is the government looking over my shoulder."

Indeed, the very terms of the Border Industrialization Program seem to encourage recklessness. Many foreign companies or investment groups set up maquiladoras through the Mexican government's "shelter program," whereby the parent company—typically known only to the government—maintains control of production and a Mexican company forms to act as co-manager. This shelter firm recruits, trains, and pays all the Mexicans in the workforce. It also manages relationships with the local community and with the Mexican government. In short, foreigners run the business while their Mexican partners see to the social tasks. Because it is a Mexican corporation, the shelter operator shields the foreign company from liability in case Mexico ever cracks down on violators.

Consequently, the foreign operators have little incentive to make sure the 20 million tons of hazardous waste that maquiladoras generate each year is properly disposed of. No data are available on how much of this waste is deposited in rivers and streams, the air, or the ground, but the volumes are enormous. For example, the New River flows northward from Baja California into California contaminated by industrial wastes such as chloroform, benzene, toluene, xylene, and PCBs, and by agricultural runoff that contains various pesticides,

including DDT. The river also carries more than 20 million gallons of raw sewage each day.

California has evaluated numerous alternatives to protect community health and Imperial Valley agriculture. The cheapest solution is to provide the Mexican city of Mexicali with a wastewater collection and treatment system, following the approach proposed for Tijuana sewage. The U.S. Environmental Protection Agency may eventually have to take similar action for all the major cities and towns along the U.S.-Mexico border. In that event, the U.S. taxpayer would ultimately pay for the reduced cost to industry of manufacturing in Mexico.

Mexico's lax monitoring of industrial practices encourages dumping of hazardous waste. Under Mexican law, toxic materials brought in by plants for use in manufacturing—such as paints, cleaning solvents, oils, and acids—must be returned to the country of origin or recycled in Mexico. But according to the Texas Water Commission, only about 60 percent of these waste materials leave Mexico. The other 40 percent—much of it toxic, the commission reports—is disposed of illegally in Mexico's sewers, drainage systems, and landfills. When waste is returned to the United States, it is often transported in improperly packaged and labeled containers.

Dirty Work

Just as the amount of illegally dumped waste is difficult to pin down, so too is hard information on working conditions in maquiladoras. Not only do U.S. and Mexican maquiladora managers deny investigators access to their plants and their workers, but the Mexican government discourages inquiries and health studies. What's more, the U.S. Department of Commerce refuses to share its list of companies participating in the maquiladora program so as not to discourage them from complying with reporting procedures.

High worker turnover rates—6 to 15 percent per month in the states of Chihuahua, Sonora, and Baja California—also make it difficult to survey health effects in maquiladoras. Controlled studies are almost impossible with such an unstable employee population.

What investigators have been able to piece together is that while working conditions in the maquiladoras vary greatly, they are in most cases far inferior to those required in developed countries. Many plants are inadequately ventilated and lighted. Accidents resulting from inattention to safety procedures and the absence of safety equipment are frequent. Nogales maquiladoras reported more than 2,000 accidents in 1989—three times the accident rate of comparable factories on the U.S. side of the border. Sanitation is poor, production quotas are high, noise is often excessive, and machinery is often unsafe.

Workers also receive few rest periods and must perform long hours of microscopic assembly work. And even though many workers regularly handle hazardous materials—especially organic solvents—protective clothing, gloves, and other safeguards routinely required of U.S. industry are rare. To make matters worse, the workers lack safety instruction on the hazardous materials they are using—again a U.S. requirement.

Some plants even allow workers to take home empty contaminated steel drums that once contained hazardous chemicals such as pesticides, solvents, acids, and alkalies. Thousands of these containers are used to store water for domestic purposes throughout the industrial regions of Mexico.

Because of a dearth of studies, the amount of harm caused by such exposure is essentially unknown. But the case of Matamoros, the town where the former U.S. company Mallory Capacitors operated a maquiladora for many years, raises alarming possibilities. The Matamoros School of Special Education has identified 20 retarded children whose mothers were pregnant while employed by Mallory and required to work with PCBs, highly toxic chemicals used in the company's products. PCBs were banned in the United States in 1977 because of their toxicity.

The Matamoros exposures occurred for full workdays over many months. The women often had to reach into deep vats of PCBs with no protection other than rubber gloves. Many of the workers developed the chloracne rash these chemicals typically cause. Recent medical studies in Taiwan and Japan of pregnant women exposed to PCBs reveal the same sort of retardation as in the children of Matamoros. It is very likely that many more children damaged by their mothers' work at Mallory live in other Mexican towns that health researchers have not yet studied. And Matamoros may not be the only town in Mexico where PCBs have caused retardation.

Why does Mexico allow these environmental and occupational abuses to continue? One reason is a lack of resources to combat the problem. SEDUE (Secretariat of Urban Development and Ecology), Mexico's environmental oversight agency, faces financial constraints that limit its ability to regulate the maquiladora industry.

But political constraints play a role as well. The Mexican government enthusiastically supports the maquiladora program. Should SEDUE become too agressive in its efforts, the government might withdraw the meager environmental funds the agency does receive. Municipal governments also operate from a precarious position. If they complain about hazardous waste dumping or unsafe working conditions—or if they press for taxes to support better sewage treatment facilities, schools, and medical care—the owners might move the plants to other cities or even other countries.

Despite these problems, Mexico has made some progress in environmental regulation. In May 1989,

SEDUE required all plants to obtain water discharge permits indicating their compliance with Mexico's rather liberal laws on toxic waste treatment. They may then dump the treated water into the sewer system. Any plant violating this requirement can be fined up to $70,000, and those responsible face a prison sentence of six years. But like most environmental laws in developing countries, this threat is made by an agency that lacks the full backing of its government and the resouces to carry out its mission. So far, this effort has produced few results, although a number of companies are now consulting with industrial hygienists and safety engineers to ensure that they will not be fined.

The U.S. government, too, is inching toward cleaning up the border—likewise with few concrete signs of progress. The federal Rio Grande Pollution Correction Act of 1988 aimed at dealing with that river's problems. But its limited scope and lack of financial support led to widespread disappointment and an array of further legislative attempts. Congress is now considering legislation to set up a permanent U.S.-Mexican environmental health commission, in which the EPA and SEDUE would work jointly to evaluate the maquiladoras and explore ways of preventing or punishing environmental abuse along the border.

Unfortunately, none of these proposals addresses the fundamental flaws of the maquiladora program, such as its failure to raise enough taxes to improve infrastructure. Given both governments' acceptance of the present system, no law that would attack the problems at their roots has any serious likelihood of enactment in the near future.

An International Approach

The slowness of the United States in dealing with abuses by the maquiladoras is typical of the way First World nations have responded to the problems caused by the export of hazardous industries. Like the EPA, which devotes only about a tenth of a percent of its budget to its Office of International Affairs, the environmental agencies of other wealthy countries are just beginning to develop concern for the consequences of industry's actions abroad. Nevertheless, it is the exporting nations that need to take the initiative.

The host countries, hungry for jobs and foreign capital, cannot be expected to make the first moves to end unsafe and polluting practices—and they often resent outside pressure to do so. Poorer nations take the position that only after they have attained the standard of living that rich countries enjoy will they adopt the restrictive environmental policies of the First World. What's more, these countries generally lack large, well-funded environmental groups like those in Europe and the United States. Popular support for actions that may impede the growth of the job market and a rise in living standards is virtually nonexistent.

Thus the world's industrialized nations will have to work together to end the shameful practice of exporting obsolete and hazardous technologies and industries. International agreements must replace the perverse incentives that threaten the world's environment.

International environmental organizations could help stem many of these problems. The U.N. Environment Programme, for example, has been working with a number of Third World countries to introduce siting requirements for hazardous industries. UNEP is also developing information centers on hazardous materials. The U.N. World Health Organization (WHO) and International Labour Office (ILO) provide some guidance to developing countries on occupational health and safety. But the combined annual budgets of these agencies is only about $3 million, severely hampering their ability to fund environmental research and provide worker education and health inspections. And WHO and ILO have confined their activities mainly to larger employers, while the vast majority of worksites in developing countries are small.

Other global bodies have made laudable attempts to control industry's behavior. The OECD Guidelines for Multinational Enterprises, the U.N. Code of Conduct on Transnational Corporations, and the ILO Tripartite Declaration of Principles Concerning Multinational Enterprises and Social Policy attempt to provide a framework of ethical behavior. The ILO declaration of principles, for example, recommends that multinationals inform worker representatives about hazards and protective measures. But stronger medicine is needed.

When industry migrates to developing countries, governments and international lending institutions could require environmental impact assessments. The World Bank, along with other international lenders, now offers to produce such assessments when the host country can't. The bank has also taken steps toward requiring poor countries to put occupational and environmental protections in place as a condition for receiving development capital. Similarly, industrialized countries must insist that companies apply the same safety and environmental regulations to their manufacturing operations abroad as they do at home.

As part of this effort, countries need to cooperate to set global standards for occupational and environmental exposures to dangerous substances. Some newly industrialized countries have formulated lists of chemicals and metals that should receive priority regulation and enforcement. Yet these lists often contain laboratory reagents, rarely used chemicals, and other materials not likely to pose occupational and environmental problems, while omitting many highly toxic substances that see broad use. Industrialized countries therefore need to adopt one set of standards with which all companies manufacturing in poorer countries must comply.

So far, both rich and poor nations see the short-term advantages in the export of hazardous industries but turn a blind eye to long-term harm. In the Third World and the First World alike, the risk of future accidents like Bhopal, the cost of environmental cleanup, and pollution's toll on public health are seldom discussed with candor. But as the developed countries have found, the longer environmental damage and hazardous working conditions continue, the greater the cost of remedying these problems once regulations and enforcement are in place. By disregarding such concerns, First World industries are shifting substantial burdens to those least able to bear them.

ANALYSIS

Confronting the AIDS Pandemic

Daniel J. M. Tarantola and Jonathan M. Mann

Daniel J. M. Tarantola, M.D., is a lecturer in international health at the Harvard School of Public Health. Jonathan M. Mann, M.D., is director of the International AIDS Center of the Harvard AIDS Institute.

In 1986, the world undertook to mobilize against the AIDS pandemic in an effort that continued to grow until the beginning of this decade, when it began to stall. Today, the global HIV/AIDS pandemic is spinning out of control—its broad course has yet to be influenced in any substantial way by policies and programs mounted against it.

In 1991–1992, the Harvard-based Global AIDS Policy Coalition undertook a review of the state of the AIDS pandemic. The findings of this review, which appear in our new book *AIDS in the World* (Harvard University Press, December 1992), raise the alarm and call for an urgent revival of the response to AIDS.

The magnitude of the pandemic has increased over 100-fold since AIDS was discovered in 1981. From an estimated 100,000 people infected with HIV world-

wide in 1981, it is estimated that by early 1992, at least 12.9 million people around the world (7.1 million men, 4.7 million women, and 1.1 million children) had been infected with HIV. Of these, about one in five (2.6 million) have thus far developed AIDS, and nearly 2.5 million have died.

The spread of HIV has not been stopped in any community or country. In the United States, at least 40,000 to 80,000 new HIV infections were anticipated during 1992; in 1991, more than 75,000 new HIV infections occurred in Europe. In just five years, the cumulative number of HIV-infected Africans has tripled, from 2.5 million to over 7.5 million today. HIV is spreading to new communities and countries around the world—in some areas with great rapidity. An explosion of HIV has recently occurred in Southeast Asia, particularly in Thailand, Burma, and India, where, within only a few years, over one million people may have already been infected with HIV. HIV/AIDS is now reported from areas that, so far, had been left relatively untouched, such as Paraguay, Greenland, and the

Pacific island nations of Fiji, Papua New Guinea, and Samoa. The global implications are clear: During the next decade, HIV will likely reach most communities around the world; geographic boundaries cannot protect against HIV. The question today is not *if* HIV will come, but only *when*.

INCREASED COMPLEXITY

The pandemic becomes more complex as it matures. Globally it is composed of thousands of separate and linked community epidemics. Every large metropolitan area affected—Miami, New York, Bangkok, London, Amsterdam, Sydney, Rio de Janeiro—contains several subepidemics of HIV going on at the same time. The impact on women is increasing dramatically, as heterosexual transmission accounts for almost 71 percent of HIV infections. Worldwide, the proportion of HIV infected who are women is rising rapidly, from 25 percent in 1990 to 40 percent by early 1992. The epidemic also evolves over time: In Brazil, the proportion of HIV infections linked with injection

This article appeared in *The World & I*, January 1993, pp. 80-87. Reprinted by permission of *The World & I*, a publication of The Washington Times Corporation, © 1993.

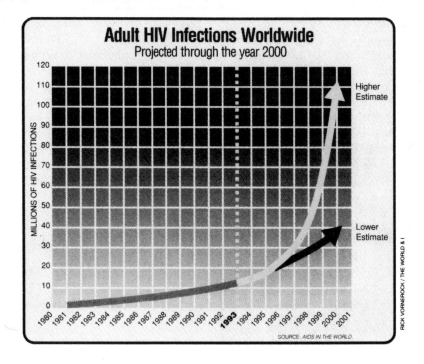

Adult HIV Infections Worldwide
Projected through the year 2000

SOURCE: *AIDS IN THE WORLD.*

RICK VORNEROCK / THE WORLD & I

drug use has increased over ten-fold since the early 1980s; in the Caribbean, heterosexual transmission has now replaced homosexual transmission as the major mode of HIV spread.

The pandemic's major impacts are yet to come. During the period 1992–95 alone, the number of people developing AIDS—3.8 million—will exceed the total number who developed the disease during the pandemic's history prior to 1992. The number of children orphaned by AIDS will more than double in the next three years: from approximately 1.8 million today to 3.7 million by 1995. The pandemic has not peaked in any country—no community or country can claim "victory" against HIV/AIDS. By 1995, an *additional* 5.7 million adults will become infected with HIV. Thus, from 1992 to 1995, the total number of HIV-infected adults will increase by 50 percent. During the same period, the number of children infected with HIV will more than double, from 1.1 million to an estimated 2.3 million.

By the year 2000, the Global AIDS Policy Coalition has projected that between 38 million and 110 million adults—and over 10 million children—will become HIV infected. The largest proportion of HIV infections will be in Asia (42 percent), surpassing sub-Saharan Africa (31 percent), Latin America (8 percent), and the Caribbean (6 percent). By the end of this decade, 24 million adults and several million children may have developed AIDS—or up to 10 times as many as today.

Only a few years ago, tuberculosis was considered a stable problem that was endemic mostly in the developing world. If it was also prevalent in certain socioeconomic groups in industrialized countries, there was a common belief that the situation was largely under control. This general sense of complacency, denounced by many who had been fighting the disease, led to a decline in resources allocated to surveillance, prevention, and treatment services. When HIV came on the scene, it found a vulnerable population.

There is a dangerous synergy between HIV and tuberculosis that makes the combined effects of both worse than their separate effects added together. HIV makes individuals and communities more vulnerable to tuberculosis; it increases the rate of reactivation of tuberculosis infection, shortens the delay between TB infection and disease, and reduces the accuracy of diagnostic methods. Recent outbreaks of multiple-drug resistant tuberculosis have occurred in New York City and in Miami, especially in hospitals and prisons. Combining its projections with estimates made by the World Health Organization, *AIDS in the World* estimates that, by early 1992, there were more than 4.6 million people with both TB and HIV infection

■

Geographic boundaries cannot protect against HIV. The question today is not *if* HIV will come, but only *when*.

■

worldwide, 81 percent of them in Africa.

TAKING STOCK

Confronting the growing pandemic are national AIDS programs. These actions may involve governmental institutions and agencies, nongovernmental organizations, and the private sector.

Almost invariably overseen by ministries of health, they are generally implemented through government agencies and health services.

The success of a national AIDS program involves the extent to which it helps curb the course of the HIV epidemic and provides quality care to those already affected. On this basis, no program in the world can yet claim success.

Of the 38 countries surveyed by the Global AIDS Policy Coalition, 24 reported having conducted an evaluation since the inception of their national program. In general, the evaluation findings can be summarized as follows:

• Once created, programs become operational rapidly.
• They were successful in raising public awareness on AIDS issues although they did not always prevent (and at times they even generated) misperceptions among certain communities.
• They raised appropriate human rights issues and in some instances managed to prevent violations of these rights.
• They exchanged information—and in some cases made funds and skills available—at the international level.

Industrialized countries were generally able to secure the financial, human, and technological resources required to increase drastically the safety of blood and blood products, and establish diagnostic and treatment schemes reaching most (but not all) people in need. The same could not be said, however, about developing countries, which are constrained by lack of resources, weak infrastructures, and multiple developmental or even survival issues.

Common criticisms of these programs are their lack of focus and priority setting, their weak management, their lack of inte-

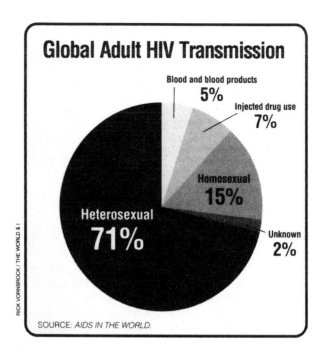

Global Adult HIV Transmission

Blood and blood products 5%

Injected drug use 7%

Homosexual 15%

Unknown 2%

Heterosexual 71%

RICK VORNBROCK / THE WORLD & I

SOURCE: *AIDS IN THE WORLD.*

gration with existing disease prevention and control services, and their inability to actively involve other health programs, sectors, and nongovernmental organizations. Denial persists about the pandemic's impact upon women; prevention and research efforts worldwide still inadequately involve them.

In its report, the Global AIDS Policy Coalition suggests indexes that can be applied at the national or regional levels. Similar indexes are being developed for the assessment of community vulnerability.

THE COST OF AIDS

AIDS policies and programs used to be guided by two motives misperceived by many as antagonistic: a human rights/humanitarian approach and a public health perspective. The economic argument was seldom raised because it was not politically advantageous to make the cost of AIDS a major public issue. It did not conform to the humanitarian agenda (cost is secondary to human rights) nor to the public health perspective (the population must be protected). But with

the rising number of people and communities affected by the pandemic, the cost of prevention and care and the general economic impact of AIDS have become critical issues.

The economic perspective considers the impact of AIDS in a decade that began in a worldwide recession. It can be argued that the impact of HIV/AIDS on young, productive adults and their children will jeopardize the national development of many countries. In July 1992, a study conducted by an American team estimated the economic impact of the pandemic by feeding epidemiological projection data into a computer model of the global marketplace. It concluded that by the year 2000, the pandemic could drain between $356 billion and $514 billion from the world's economy, and developing countries are expected to be the hardest hit.

The Global AIDS Policy Coalition estimated that money spent on AIDS in a one-year period during 1990–91 was in the range of $1.4–$1.5 billion for prevention, approximately $3.5 billion for adult AIDS care alone, and $1.6 billion for research, for an adjusted total of $7.1 to $7.6 billion (including costs for treating those persons with HIV before AIDS occurs). Interestingly, about 95 percent was spent in industrialized countries that have less than 25 percent of the world's population, 18 percent of the people with AIDS, and 15 percent of HIV infections worldwide.

For HIV prevention activities in 1991, about $2.70 was spent *per person* in North America and $1.18 in Europe. In the developing world, spending on prevention amounted to only $0.07 per person in sub-Saharan Africa and $0.03 per person in Latin America. Of the $5.6 billion spent on AIDS research since the discovery of AIDS in 1981, $5.45 billion, or 97 percent, has been spent in industrialized countries. The United States is the biggest contributor to global AIDS research spending, with $4.8 billion, or 86 percent of the world total. Domestic and international research have led to a considerable advancement of knowledge. Research funds benefited from annual increases in the late 1980s, but resources support-

The United States is the biggest contributor to global AIDS research spending, with 86 percent of the world total.

ing this research are reaching a plateau.

For AIDS care, 89 percent of world spending in 1990 was used to help less than 30 percent of the world's people with AIDS—those living in North America and Europe. And yet, the cost of medical care for each person with AIDS—roughly equivalent to annual per capita income in developing countries—is overwhelming individuals and households everywhere. Inequities in treatment and prevention are growing. The cost of one year's treatment with AZT is about $2,500, while per capita income in all developing countries averages $700—in sub-Saharan Africa the

figure is $470—or less than one-fifth the cost of AZT for one year. Individual studies have indicated that the annual cost of care for an adult with AIDS varied in 1990–91 from $32,000 in the United States to $22,000 in western Europe, $2,000 in Latin America, and a mere $393 in sub-Saharan Africa.

These figures translate into the harsh reality of length of survival and quality of life of people with AIDS. The need for AIDS care and the inequity in access to quality services will continue to grow: The number of AIDS treatment years for adults alone will increase from an estimated 433,000 in 1992 to 619,000 in

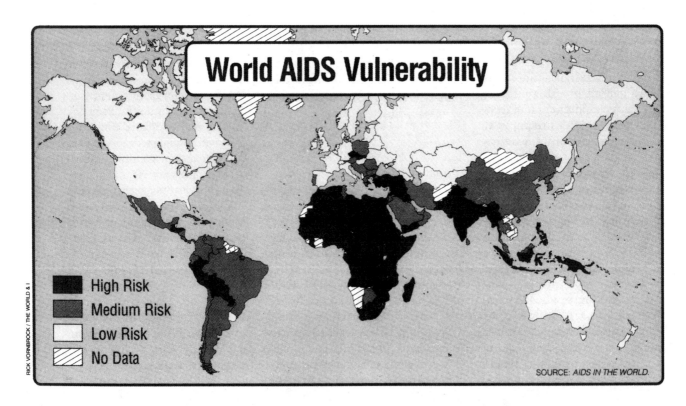

World AIDS Vulnerability

High Risk
Medium Risk
Low Risk
No Data

RICK VORNBROCK / THE WORLD & I

SOURCE: *AIDS IN THE WORLD.*

1995; almost 60 percent of these will be in Africa and 26 percent in the industrialized world. Built into these estimates, however, is the average duration of survival of an adult with AIDS, which in Africa is estimated at about one year after diagnosis, less than half of the survival duration of an adult with AIDS in the industrialized world.

Despite the introduction of HIV diagnostic tests over seven years ago, unscreened blood is currently responsible for at least 5 percent of global HIV infections. Most sub-Saharan African countries still cannot afford a safe blood supply. And even if an AIDS vaccine became available today, its impact on the world would be limited by inequities in access to it.

NEED FOR A GLOBAL VISION

Where efforts have been made to provide a coordinated response to the growing crisis, there are clear signs of positive individual responses. But where programs are confronted with weak national commitment, declining resources, and a growing sense of complacency, national AIDS programs are in jeopardy and, together with them, the people they are intended to serve. Many governments, constrained by their lack of resources, continue to avoid the reality of the pandemic: More people become infected because they do not have sufficient access to information and services; more individuals require care that they cannot afford; more families and communities are affected by the impact of a pandemic that has only begun.

Industrialized nations are turning away from coordinated efforts, showing a growing preference to work independently, on a bilateral basis, with chosen developing countries. Fragmentation of efforts by industrialized countries has led to competition among donors in some countries. It is clear that as the pandemic continues to worsen, AIDS programs will be forced to struggle with insufficient funds.

Global efforts have failed to motivate low-prevalence countries to act before the epidemic reaches them in force. India, Burma, and the Sudan are examples of a delayed response and a failure to learn from the experience of heavily affected countries.

Overall, the world has become more vulnerable to HIV and AIDS. On the basis of the societal factors that create vulnerability to spread of HIV, *AIDS in the World* has identified 57 countries as *high risk* for HIV spread—including countries that have thus far escaped the brunt of the pandemic, such as Indonesia, Egypt, Bangladesh, and Nigeria. An additional 39 countries are considered to be at *substantial* risk of a major HIV epidemic, including 11 Latin American countries, 8 in the southeast Mediterranean, 7 in Asia (including China), 4 in the Caribbean, and 9 in other regions.

We *are* at a critical juncture in the confrontation with AIDS, but we are not helpless. By revitalizing leadership, by addressing prevention and the needs of the affected, by formulating clear, international strategies, by accelerating effective, safe, and affordable treatments and vaccines, it *is* possible to stall the future spread of the pandemic.

At a time when many countries are undergoing major geopolitical transitions and are facing severe economic recessions, HIV/AIDS is not simply fading away. The world will continue to experience a rapid increase in the number of people developing AIDS until there is a cure. In the meantime, a troubled world population can unite together to fairly and equitably make available prevention and treatment programs until that day comes.

Poverty and Inequality

It is not clear whether poverty is the result or cause of inequality, but it is clear that where one is found, so is the other. Most individuals, regardless of how little or how much they have, would agree that poverty is bad, but they do not necessarily agree that inequality is bad. To those raised in capitalistic societies, inequality is seen as the driving force behind the American success story. The ability to improve one's economic position, the chance to move up corporate hierarchies, the opportunity to have access to the best that life offers are what has made America great. Conversely, the lack of upward mobility is the direct cause of the fall of communism. It is not inequality that is bad, but the degree of inequality. When the gap between the top and bottom becomes extreme, when the number of individuals at the bottom greatly exceeds those at the top, when the opportunity for improving one's self is removed, then questions of inequality as a social problem emerge.

"The Front Lines of Welfare Reform" examines the innovative programs initiated by the governor of Wisconsin and mayor of Milwaukee. These programs are being closely scrutinized by President Clinton as part of his "reinventing government." The Wisconsin programs have had impressive results, but the author believes that their costs might be so high that the nation as a whole could not afford them.

"Going Private" is seen as one way to reduce the cost of doing business. Businessman and presidential candidate Ross Perot and others argue that private industry can do almost anything better and cheaper than most government bureaucracies. This may be true in some cases, but cheaper is not always the best when the lives of poor, sick, aged, and extremely vulnerable people are involved.

"Manufacturing Poverty" explores the conditions of Third World workers employed in modern factories owned and operated by U.S. corporations. Since profit is the primary driving force of any corporation, humanistic concerns that reduce the profit potential tend to be minimized. This article raises some serious concerns about the potential effects of NAFTA for workers on both sides of the U.S.–Mexico border.

"No Exit" is what many individuals trapped in isolated urban ghettos discover. No matter what they desire, no matter how hard they work, they cannot escape unemployment, crime, violence, drugs, and the inadequate services of the inner city. This article examines the social conditions that have turned their American dream into a nightmare.

"The New Faces of Poverty" looks at the emotional devastation caused by unemployment through factory closures, company mergers, and failed businesses. This article features first-person accounts of middle-class people who were forced into welfare.

"When Problems Outrun Policy" examines the effects of economic growth and inflation on American lifestyles. While few Americans find their lifestyles unaffected, growing numbers are finding it difficult to stay above the poverty line. The author discusses why this trend is occurring and what difficult choices and changes must be made to reverse it.

Looking Ahead: Challenge Questions

How is the distribution of poverty changing?

What are the major problems facing a president who wants to eliminate or seriously reduce poverty?

What societal problems are ensuring that the poor stay poor?

What problems must President Clinton resolve if he seriously wants to "reinvent" government and win the war on poverty?

What effect might NAFTA have on the workers in both the United States and Mexico?

How might privatization hurt those it is designed to help?

Are private organizations always better than public ones?

Why are those at the bottom of the middle class increasingly falling into the lower class?

Why will many students find it difficult to rise above their parents in wealth, status, influence, and power?

How would sociologists differ in the ways they go about studying problems of inequality and poverty?

What are the conflicts in rights, values, obligations, and harms that seem to be underlying each of the issues covered in this section?

The Front Lines of Welfare Reform

William Tucker

Summary: Always-progressive Wisconsin has been no different when it comes to welfare reform. Both Milwaukee's mayor and the state's governor have introduced programs to reduce the welfare rolls, and the results have been impressive — enough so to gain the attention of President Clinton, who may use Wisconsin's ideas on the federal level. Still, there are questions about how much the programs will ultimately cost.

Welfare is an awful way to help poor people," says John Norquist, the 6-foot-7, boyishly affable mayor of Milwaukee. "We're going to get rid of it within the next three years. Milwaukee is going to be the first city in the United States to be free of the welfare system."

Norquist has already convinced President Clinton that he means business. On June 1, Clinton made a trip to Milwaukee to celebrate the city's New Hope Project, calling it a pilot effort for his administration's plans to "end welfare as we know it."

"The idea of giving people the tools they need to move off welfare, and calling a halt to it after two years — saying it has to come to an end and people who can should go to work — I think is a good thing," Clinton said before the Metropolitan Milwaukee Association of Commerce. "I think we ought to fund that experiment in Wisconsin and see if it won't work."

Remarkably enough, Norquist's project isn't the only game in town. Halfway across the state in Madison, Republican Gov. Tommy Thompson has been pushing his own welfare reform since 1987, introducing concepts such as Learnfare, Workfare and what has been dubbed "bridefare" to reduce welfare dependency. The results have been impressive: Wisconsin's welfare rolls are down 17 percent over the past six years, while those in the rest of the nation have increased about 30 percent.

David Ellwood, an assistant secretary of the Department of Health and Human Services who is heading the Clinton administration's reform efforts, says: "The Wisconsin efforts offer a model that fits in well with our reform effort. We are absolutely committed to making work pay, dramatically increasing child support enforcement, and creating a time-limited system followed by work."

Given Wisconsin's long history of willingness to embrace new and progressive ideas, it is no surprise to find the state out front in welfare reform.

Wisconsin was the first state to adopt workmen's compensation (1911), unemployment insurance (1931), health maintenance organizations (1947), job protection for the handicapped (1965) and statewide political primaries (1903).

Even so, the state's turnaround on welfare has taken many people by surprise. "Just a few years ago, we were getting a lot of criticism for our high welfare payments," says Thompson. "But the Republicans didn't want to do any of the heavy lifting to change the system, and the Democrats just wanted to throw more money at it."

Wisconsin still ranks 11th in the nation, or 27 percent above the national average, in the size of its Aid to Families with Dependent Children payments. A decade ago, the state was frequently cited as proof that welfare wasn't causing the nation's epidemic of poverty, family breakdown and teenage pregnancy, since the state's high welfare benefits were matched with one of the lowest rates of welfare dependency in the nation.

But then things began to change. In the mid-1980s, welfare recipients in Chicago "discovered" Milwaukee as a haven of high welfare payments (45 to 50 percent higher than in Illinois) and a relatively tranquil alternative to Chicago, with its violence-ridden housing projects. Soon there was an exodus of welfare recipients across the state line. As *Newsweek* reported in 1989: "The influx has cre-

By William Tucker. From *Insight*, August 16, 1993, pp. 6-11. © 1993 by The Washington Times Corporation. Reprinted by permission. All rights reserved.

ated serious problems. Growing numbers of welfare migrants have put a strain on schools, created a housing crunch, introduced street gangs and driven up the crime rate. . . . Longtime residents say that once-tidy yards now go untended and out-of-work men loiter on every corner."

Jim Miller, president of the Wisconsin Policy Research Institute, a Milwaukee think tank, says that "by the late 1980s, our polls showed a much higher level of anger with welfare in Wisconsin than in the rest of the country." Before anyone knew it, Milwaukee also had the highest rate of black teenage pregnancy in the nation.

Wisconsin residents, however, instead of wringing their hands or blaming everything on Washington, decided almost immediately to act.

"I talked with a lot of people on welfare and their refrain was always the same," says Thompson, who served in the state Assembly for 20 years. "They would say, 'Give us a program that will get us off welfare. We really don't like it.'"

Running on a platform of welfare reform in 1986, Thompson defeated the incumbent Democratic governor, Tony Earl, with 53 percent of the vote.

Within a year of taking office, Thompson instituted Learnfare, a program in which all teenagers in welfare families, whether parents or children, must attend school or have the family's benefits reduced. Next came Workfare, a program that requires able-bodied welfare recipients to take jobs, participate in job-training programs or have their benefits cut.

In 1990, the state implemented Children First, designed to make fathers delinquent on child support either pay up, report for unpaid community service jobs or go to jail. Now being tried as a pilot program in Racine, Children First is collecting child support from 23 percent of absent fathers, above the national average of 18 percent. Eight men are in Racine County Jail because of failure to make support payments.

Scheduled to begin in July 1994 is what the press has been calling bridefare, a program that will let unwed teenage mothers marry without losing any welfare benefits. Subsequent childbearing, however, will not be rewarded. Any welfare mother will receive only half the current benefit increase for a first child born while on welfare and no additional benefits for children thereafter.

Waiting in the wings is a program called Work Not Welfare. If it receives federal approval, it will limit the stay on welfare to two years. Says Jean Rogers, administrator of the Division of Economic Support in the state Department of Health and Social Services, "We will be first in the nation to have a moderately time-limited welfare program" like Clinton has proposed on the national level.

Thompson, a genial country lawyer, is a self-taught student of human nature. Asked where all his ideas on welfare reform have come from, he taps his forehead and smiles. "Right in here," he says.

"I'm a great listener. I spent a lot of time going around the state hearing people's opinions on the subject. Even people who are on welfare say they can't stand it. They're looking for something different. When I got into the office, I said, 'We're just going to try some of these ideas just to see if they work.' And that's what we're doing."

Since 1987, Wisconsin's welfare rolls have shrunk from 98,000 to 81,000 while the rest of the country's have ballooned from 3.8 million to 4.9 million. Only two other states — Iowa (down 8.8 percent) and Illinois (down 4.4 percent) — and the District of Columbia (down 1.5 percent) have also seen their rolls dwindle.

Is Wisconsin discouraging people from applying for welfare, or getting them into the working world more quickly? "The answer seems to be that we are getting them off the rolls faster," says Thompson. "We're getting people out of the dependency trap and into useful jobs."

In Milwaukee, by contrast, the accomplishments — although much ballyhooed by Clinton — are much slimmer. Far from being a full-scale experiment, the New Hope Project is little more than a pilot program — the kind that often produces notable results when the staff is small and enthusiasm high, but that turns into just another bureaucratic handout when duplicated on a large scale.

The New Hope Project operates out of a single office in a small shopping center. Begun two years ago, the program includes only 50 people — all carefully selected by community groups. Clients search for a private-sector job; if they can't find one in eight weeks, they are given a community service job and paid by the city. At the beginning, only eight worked full-time and 29 were on welfare. Within the first six months, 36 had moved to full-time jobs with private employers. But the number working full-time with private employers has since slipped to 30, while 13 participants are employed by community service groups. "The recession has hurt the job market," says Ameenah Muhammad, a former welfare recipient who now works on the program.

On the basis of these results, Mayor Norquist is asking the federal government to appropriate the amount it would save by getting 600 people off welfare and Medicaid — probably about $6.6 million a year — to expand the program to that many participants over the next three years.

The New Hope Project offers people below the poverty line four things: an earnings supplement to bring their income from work above the poverty line; guaranteed access to a publicly funded community service job if they cannot find work in the private sector; guaranteed child care, with payments scaled according to earnings; and guaranteed health care (membership in an HMO), with copayments also scaled to income.

David Riemer, the city's director of administration and author of *Prisoners of Welfare*, has been one of the principal architects of the program. "We calculate the New Hope Project will cost about $11,000 per year per participant," says Riemer. "That may seem like a lot, but it's no more than we're spending already. In 1988, the Wisconsin Policy Research Institute estimated that Milwaukee was spending $10,384 per poor person and $31,000 per family on all poverty programs."

But John Wagner, who wrote the research institute's report and now works in the Thompson administration on welfare reform, disputes this interpretation of the data. "When we calculated those numbers, we were trying to show how much money that gets spent on poverty *doesn't* reach poor people but gets consumed by service vendors," says Wagner. "We threw in Social Security, unemployment insurance, veterans' pensions and a lot of other things that won't be eliminated by a program that replaces welfare."

A more reasonable estimate of the cost of a program to replace welfare is found by calculating that each of Milwaukee's 36,000 mothers receiving Aid to Families with Dependent Children is getting about $6,000 in welfare payments, $3,000 in Medicaid premiums and $1,200 in food stamps, for a welfare bill of $10,200 per case and $367 million overall. But the ultimate goal of the New Hope Project is to serve many more people — all

65,000 heads of households and single people in Milwaukee below the poverty line. The bill would be closer to $715 million.

In addition, New Hope's projections assume that the number of participants who require government-funded community service jobs will remain constant at the 20 percent figure experienced with the first 50 participants. It is far more likely that as the program reaches further into the poor population, a much higher percentage of participants will prove unemployable, driving the costs of providing public service jobs higher.

"The problem with New Hope to this point has been that it's all volunteer," recruiting only people who want to be in the project, says the Policy Research Institute's Miller, a former aide to New York Gov. Mario Cuomo. "When you start expanding, the dynamics are going to be different. You're going to hit a lot of people who either won't work or don't have employable skills. At that point, New Hope is going to start costing a ton of money."

Ellwood of HHS says this would be true on the federal level, as well. Although he has backed the two-year limit on receiving welfare, he also says a $40 billion program of health care, child care and public service jobs must be in place before the limit is enforced. "Nobody's talking about saving money," says Ellwood. "We're talking about spending money."

When confronted with the costs, Norquist turns expansive. "You really can't measure the benefits in current savings," he says. "Once you've gotten rid of welfare, you can save all kinds of money. You can slow down prison construction, you can abolish the Department of Housing and Urban Development, you can cut out urban aid programs — you can wipe out just about every other poverty program."

At the same time, Norquist concedes that he is uneasy with the commitment to provide every person below the poverty line a government-funded job. "Any public service job should pay low wages, giving people an incentive to move over to private employment as quickly as possible," he says.

An even more nettlesome problem is what to do if welfare recipients don't want to participate. Norquist and Riemer talk bravely about cutting the allowable time on welfare to almost nothing. "Governor Thompson says he wants everybody off wel-

fare in two years," says Norquist. "Why wait that long? We're saying if you don't want to take advantage of job access, then you don't get welfare today." Yet welfare is still available to anyone who drops out of the New Hope Project, and the city is a long way from implementing any new policy.

Other commentators have noted the dilemma. Writing in the *Wall Street Journal*, Irving Kristol recently argued: "The neo-liberal response, advocated by Mr. Clinton during his campaign, which calls for 'two years and out' for all able-bodied welfare recipients, is a fantasy. It will not happen. We are not going to see state legislatures and the huge welfare establishment ruthlessly dumping welfare families onto the streets. Public opinion will not stand for it, liberal politicians will not be able to stomach it. It is merely a rhetorical diversionary tactic, and conservatives who are now attracted to it will end up distancing themselves from it as fast as they can."

On June 23, the *New York Times* noted that several Clinton administration officials are already backing away from the two-year limit. Commenting on this, Sen. Daniel Patrick Moynihan, a New York Democrat and father of the 1989 Family Support Act, said, "I fear that time limits mean very different things to people in the administration and the public at large." A Democratic congressman added, "It has the makings of a massive misunderstanding and recrimination when it comes out."

A visit to one of the state's Workfare pilot projects offers an interesting perspective on how things are going at ground level. At the Job Opportunity and Basic Skills, or JOBS, program run by Goodwill Industries in Racine, administrators have assembled a small group of successful female graduates of the program, all around 30. They sit around a table, each with an anxious social worker hovering at her side.

As the discussion proceeds, all the women have similar stories. At about age 20, each met a young man with whom she had an unsuccessful romance. They dated for a while, but the relationship didn't work out. Before the affair ended, however, each "accidentally" had a child. (One woman with two young children confesses that they were conceived by two different men. "It was almost the same guy," she says.)

Since that time, they have been bouncing in and out of the welfare system. One says she has been working steadily the whole time — which

doesn't correspond with welfare eligibility rules. After a little explanation, it's found that she has been working "off and on," timing her job-seeking efforts in order to retain Medicaid eligibility, which continues for one year after a recipient leaves the welfare rolls. "You really can't raise a child without that medical card," she says.

None of the women is a member of a minority. All are obviously embarrassed about their social status and "lack self-esteem" — as their social workers are quick to say after the women are gone. Were it not for their ill-fated romances, all would simply be young women finding their way through the working world.

Yet these women are also the cream of the welfare crop when it comes to employability. Beneath them lie layer upon layer of single mothers for whom the working world is a distant prospect and collecting a welfare check is as routine and unrewarding as paying taxes is for the rest of the populace.

The discussion session at the JOBS office raises a question: How did the federal government ever get into the business of subsidizing the romantic illusions of young women in the first place?

To be sure, there has always been a small percentage of young women who have illegitimate babies. But in the past, their parents had to bear the financial burden — one reason parents always counseled against unwed motherhood. Now, when a young single woman has a child, welfare is there to pick up the slack.

In cold, rational terms, having a child out of wedlock and at a young age can be seen as an admission ticket to the welfare state.

Where are the men in all this? Certainly not in the Racine jobs program, and as yet there are only a handful in the New Hope Project. In fact, Aid to Families with Dependent Children is devoted exclusively to single mothers and their children. The welfare system has to a large extent divided the underclass between aimless, violent men and "dependent" single mothers.

A different and apparently far more successful approach has been taken by Charles Ballard, founder of the National Institute for Responsible Fatherhood and Family Development in Cleveland. The private institute signs up young men who have fathered children and abandoned them to the welfare system. The men must first sign papers acknowledging their paternity, then pledge to support their children.

"The men take it from there," says Ballard, 56, a former paratrooper and social worker. "They find jobs, go to school, even make plans for college. We don't suggest anything. We just show them their responsibilities."

Although only 8 percent of the men had jobs when they entered the program — and many were living off crime and taking drugs — 60 percent now have full-time jobs and 11 percent have part-time jobs. Eleven percent are enrolled in college.

Ballard is convinced that the welfare system marginalizes young men and undermines family formation, creating a destructive underclass mentality. "All the programs are for young women," he says. "The message to fathers is, 'Get out of the way and don't interfere. You are the problem.' "

Both Thompson and Norquist say they have reached the same conclusions.

"The welfare system has substituted the government for fathers," says Thompson. "We're hoping our reforms can reverse that trend."

Says Norquist: "The key is family formation. The welfare system has been the biggest obstacle we have to forming families. That's why we want to get rid of it."

Going Private

States pawn off public services

CAMILLE COLATOSTI

As clinic workers protested, armed security guards forcibly evicted emotionally and mentally impaired patients from Detroit's Lafayette Clinic last October. Closed since then, the clinic was the only public psychiatric research hospital in Michigan.

"Patients were treated like cattle," according to the United Auto Workers' magazine *Solidarity*. "Ordered to pack their bags, they were herded into buses as friends and relatives called tearfully from behind fences."

"I'll never get over what I saw," says Deborah Dell'Orco, spokeswoman for UAW Local 6000, which represents 22,000 state employees. "It was a holocaust for the mentally ill."

The patients and workers at Lafayette Clinic were the latest casualties of privatization—the process of selling public services to private firms. Naming privatization as one of his guiding principles of government, Michigan Governor John Engler promised to "return to the private sector those state operations that can be more effectively and efficiently performed by the private sector."

Patient dumping, transferring state clients to corporate providers, saves the state the cost of running its own institutions. It also benefits the private facility, which accepts the patient's Medicaid and Supplemental Security Income. But it can prove dangerous for patients.

Stories abound of substandard care received at private institutions. Patients are neglected; they live in dangerous conditions and suffer physical abuse. Beverly Enterprises, for example, the nation's largest for-profit nursing-home chain, has been cited for 173 major patient-care violations and class-action suits alleging wrongful death are pending in Michigan, Georgia, and Florida.

But Governor Engler claims that Michigan, facing a budget deficit for the third year in a row, has no choice but to pare down. And Michigan is not alone in its decision to reduce state services and rely on the private sector instead. Trying to trim the size of state and local government is a national trend.

In part, this trend results from a severe economic crisis. In 1991, forty-seven states spent more than they took in. And 1992 wasn't much better: thirty-five states that had adopted balanced budgets again confronted deficits.

The reasons for the deficits include:

¶ The recession. "During tough economic times," says Mike Ettlinger of the Washington, D.C.-based Citizens for Tax Justice, "high unemployment means declines in personal income tax and increases in welfare and social-service costs."

¶ The decline in Federal aid to states and cities. Between 1980 and 1989, the real value of grants to state and local governments dropped by 38 per cent. In 1979, Federal aid accounted for 22 per cent of state and local budgets; in 1989, it made up only 16 per cent.

¶ Regressive tax systems. States raise revenue primarily from low- and middle-income people, not the wealthy and corporations. According to *A Far Cry from Fair*, a report by Citizens for Tax Justice, "Forty-four states and the District of Columbia tax the very rich at lower rates than they tax the poor. In five states—Nevada, Texas, Florida, Washington, and South Dakota—the poor pay five times as great a share of their incomes in state and local taxes as do the rich."

As Ettlinger explains, "Soaking the poor just doesn't raise enough money to support a modern economy, especially when you consider the current distribution of wealth in the United States. The richest 1 per cent of all families make more than the bottom 40 per cent. The top fifth make more than everyone else put together."

Still, budget crises alone don't explain the privatization trend. An ideology gaining popularity among policymakers—and articulated in *Reinventing Government*, by David Osborne and Ted Gaebler—holds that local governments need to be remade.

The authors cite conservative economist Peter Drucker, who wrote that "the purpose of government is to make fundamental decisions and to make them effectively. . . . Any attempt to combine governing with 'doing' on a large scale paralyzes government's decision-making capacity." In other words, governments should not provide services but instead oversee them.

Government works best, claim economists Michael Mills, Charles Van Eaton, and Robert Daddow of the Heartland Institute, a conservative research group in Detroit, "when it employs, under its oversight, someone else to do the doing."

So, beginning from the assumption that government is bureaucratic and ineffective, proponents of "reinventing government" focus not on increasing revenues but on two other areas.

Sometimes they eliminate services completely. *The States and the Poor*, by the Center on Budget and Policy Priorities, reports that the last two years have seen forty-four states cut or freeze benefits in the Aid to Families with Dependent Children program; twenty-two states eliminate or severely reduce general assistance ben-

Camille Colatosti, the author of "Stopping Sexual Harassment: A Handbook for Union and Workplace Activists," is a free-lance writer and a member of UAW Local 1981. She lives in Detroit.

From *The Progressive*, June 1993, pp. 29-31. © 1993 by Camille Colatosti, director of the Working Women's Project in Detroit. Reprinted by permission of the author.

efits; twenty-six states freeze or cut supplemental benefits to poor, elderly, and disabled recipients of Supplemental Security Income.

At other times, they propose transferring public services to private contractors and promoting competition. While this does not exactly mean running government like a business, it does involve introducing corporate concepts to public service.

"Government and business are fundamentally different institutions," explain Osborne and Gaebler. "Government is democratic and open. Hence it moves more slowly than business, whose managers can make quick decisions behind closed doors. Government's fundamental mission is to 'do good,' not to make money. . . . Government must often serve everyone equally, regardless of their ability to pay or their demand for a service; hence it cannot achieve the same efficiencies as business."

Yet, they conclude, "The fact that government cannot be run just like a business does not mean it cannot become more entrepreneurial."

While Osborne and Gaebler claim that "entrepreneurial" means "creative and flexible," the positive examples they ask politicians to emulate emphasize lean production techniques. The key to success involves finding ways to provide services at little cost. Usually, this requires paying workers low wages with no benefits.

Reinventing Government points to Frank Keefe, former secretary of administration and finance in Massachusetts, who argues: "Contracting with private vendors is cheaper, more efficient, more authentic, more flexible, more adaptive. . . . Contracts are rewritten every year. You can change. You cannot change with state employees who have all sorts of vested rights and privileges."

"The state can't fire anybody," is the way Alan Flory puts it. Executive director of the Community Organization for Drug Abuse, Mental Health, and Alcoholism Services, a private corporation managing $17 million in state contracts in Arizona, Flory continues, "My people—I can push 'em; I can make 'em work hard."

Employed on a year-to-year basis, contract workers are too vulnerable to expect "rights and privileges." Over 35 per cent of public-sector workers, on the other hand, belong to unions and demand certain compensation standards.

Detroit Mayor Coleman Young has put Flory's philosophy into practice. Blaming most of the city's fiscal crisis on overpaid public employees, he laid off more than a thousand clerks and typists and contracted their work to private firms.

But the laid-off workers, most of whom are African-American women, are among the lowest-paid employees in the city. They average only $22,000 a year—hardly an outrageous salary. Giving these jobs to private contractors meant forcing many workers onto the unemployment rolls, while compelling others to accept significantly lower wages.

Even with such wage and benefit cuts, it remains unclear that privatization really saves money. The costs of converting to the private sector and administering the contract can run high. For example, eleven out of twelve contracted services were more expensive than in-house costs, according to a 1992 study by the General Accounting Office.

"The actual savings gained in public contracting out are razor thin," says Elliot Sclar, a professor at Columbia University. "Studies suggest that when everything goes well, real cash savings are less than 10 per cent. However, things frequently do not go well."

Often, contractractors will 'low-ball' bids for the first year or two–until the government loses its ability to provide people with the service.

Often, too, contractors will "low-ball" their bids for the first year or two—until the government loses its ability to provide the service. Once the government has become dependent on the private sector, the contractor will raise its price.

Privatization also results in increased opportunities for corruption. "There's bribery, kickbacks, conflicts of interest, and charges for work never performed," says Bobbi Rabinowitz, vice president for publicity at AFSCME Local 371 in New York City. Local 371 recently won a victory against privatization. City administrators wanted to contract out an important health-care service: evaluating hospital patients as they are released to determine the need for home care.

"Our members were doing a fine job," says Rabinowitz. "There was nothing wrong whatsoever. Contracting wouldn't save money, stop waste, or improve efficiency. The service is already efficient."

So why switch? Workers believe that administrators wanted to return favors to individuals who stood to gain from the contracts.

Newsweek magazine reported similar cronyism in Massachusetts. One-fourth of the 1,300 firms the state contracts with each year turn out to be technically insolvent. "Some agencies do a fine job," concluded *Newsweek*. "Some—including a medical-services firm whose owner billed the state for his Lincoln Continental and his chauffeur—slip past official scrutiny."

On top of such abuses, services often suffer. Take the example of public hospitals. Today, the private management of public health facilities is a booming business. Contractors show profits of 15 to 30 per cent. But public accountability disappears, and the quality of patient care deteriorates.

Typically, public hospitals feel a budget crunch not because they are mismanaged but because patients lack insurance and funds to pay. Management can eliminate fiscal problems only by scrimping on service and limiting public access. Private management firms have been known to screen uninsured patients before admitting them, turning away those who cannot pay. Some require deposits before providing care. Others eliminate or reduce unprofitable services. All told, these tactics call into question the mission of public hospitals: to provide health care for the indigent.

When, ten years ago, Chicago's Cook County General Hospital hired Hyatt Medical Management Services, Inc., to consult on its budget and administration, public service began to suffer. Unconcerned about the hospital's mission, Hyatt began to charge the poor for inpatient and outpatient services. It increased room rates and intensive-care rates to obtain higher insurance reimbursements and turned away people who were ineligible for Medicaid.

"Within eight months after Hyatt came to Cook County Hospital to improve efficiency," says Geraldine Dallek of the National Health Law Program, "the situation had deteriorated. Under Hyatt's direction, the hospital regularly lacked such basic supplies as aspirins, paper towels, urine-specimen cups, syringes, blood culture bottles, and similar items. Then the entire computer recording system for hospital supplies broke down—supplies like insulin were rationed and wards began hoarding whatever they had, in fear of running out."

While services to the poor suffered, Hyatt profited and the hospital's deficit increased. A 1990 complaint that former Massachusetts finance director Peter Nessen made to then-Governor Michael Dukakis seems relevant: Of contracting out, he said, "We often made decisions when we knew nothing at all about the product, the outcome, and most important the effect of the program for the client."

"Privatization certainly isn't the wrong choice in every case," concedes Kathleen Gmeiner of the Michigan Fair Budget Action Coalition, a group of labor, community, and religious activists fighting to restore state services. "Doctors at public hospitals receive a fee for service, for example. And this works relatively well. But if public-health services themselves, or even the Medicaid system, were privatized, the government would lose its capacity to contain competition and to contain costs. The state would lose its capacity to provide Medicaid and would be at the mercy of the private sector."

For Gmeiner, the test of good government is how it treats its most vulnerable citizens. "Government must provide each citizen opportunities for self-sufficiency," she argues. "And for those citizens who are incapable of self-sufficiency, government must assume the role of permanent provider of economic support, social support, and protection to enable them to live with dignity."

Such a statement reveals, perhaps more than any other, the difference between those who favor effective and responsive public service and those who advocate privatization. To proponents of "reinventing government"—politicians like Governor Engler of Michigan, Governor William Weld of Massachusetts, former President Ronald Reagan, and, to some extent, President Bill Clinton—the number of people "incapable of self-sufficiency" appears extremely low. To some degree, all discuss the need to pare down government, to make it smaller.

"Politicians are selling off government services—and eliminating government it-self," says Bob Lathrop, Michigan political director of the Service Employees International Union. "Engler, for example, is shirking his responsibility to govern at the same time that he's trying to make government as small as possible."

Gmeiner agrees. "Proponents of privatization, politicians like Engler, aren't reforming government," she says. "They're not making it more efficient or more responsive to human need. They are simply slashing benefits without compunction. Engler, for example, has shown no creativity in making system changes. He's created no new jobs and no new job-training programs. He's simply denied people access to services they need."

Along with activists across the country, the Michigan Fair Budget Action Coalition is trying to move the debate from sheer economics to a people perspective. "We want people to decide what services they need," says Gmeiner. "Then we'll discuss funding."

Citing a 1992 Milbank Memorial Fund Report called *Hard Choices in Hard Times*, Gmeiner proposes that "the principles of fairness and liberty guide the choices that state and local officials make."

"Fairness and liberty have several meanings," the Fund reports. "Fairness includes taking care of the least advantaged, removing impediments to opportunity, and accommodating competing interests. Liberty connotes decisions about social needs that will have priority over individual decisions to dispose of income. Both fairness and liberty require that government be involved in assuring well-being. At times, government is the agent of first resort; sometimes, it is the guarantor of health and safety."

To fund the services that people need, the Michigan Coalition proposes cutting corporate tax breaks by 10 per cent to increase revenue for human services.

This would generate $700 million to $1 billion, which does not seem unreasonable to Gmeiner, who says Michigan has cut 20 per cent of its social-services budget since 1990. But businesses oppose it. In particular, General Motors, Ford, and Chrysler have implied they'll take their business elsewhere if their tax breaks are slashed.

Some states are taking other measures to balance their budgets, including increasing taxes on the wealthy. In 1992, for example, Ohio, a state whose cuts in general-assistance benefits were second only to Michigan's in 1991, actually raised income taxes for families earning over $200,000 a year. This helped fund small increases in Aid to Families with Dependent Children and in Medicaid.

Kansas made a similar income-tax change and, at the same time, reduced taxes for poor families. Unfortunately, these tiny increases in tax revenue are nowhere near enough. And says Marian Kramer, leader of Up and Out of Poverty, the national advocacy group for the homeless, people shouldn't settle for them.

"The people are losing," she says, "losing in the courts and in the legislature. When the government ceases to take care of its people, then the people have to do something to set things straight. We have to take matters into our own hands. It's time for us to fight back—and to fight now, as hard as we can for as long as it takes."

Manufacturing Poverty
The Maquiladorization of Mexico

Dan LaBotz

Dan LaBotz is a Cincinnati-based writer, teacher and activist. His most recent book is Mask of Democracy: Labor Suppression in Mexico Today.

Conditions in Mexican *maquiladoras* provide an insight into the frightening future — in many respects, NAFTA is the border industry program writ large.

IN JUAREZ, THE WORKERS, most of them young women, leave their homes at six in the morning to go to work. The best of these homes are three or four rooms made of concrete block and adobe; the worst are one or two rooms made of discarded lumber and tar paper. Many have no running water or toilets. The workers walk unpaved side streets which, depending on the season, are dusty, muddy or occasionally snowy to wait for the city bus or company van to pick them up and carry them to work.

Many of these workers labor in modern factories owned and operated by U.S. corporations. Equipped with the latest combination of electronic controls and robotic machines, these factories are located in well-paved and well-lit industrial parks served by superhighways and railroad lines. The plant managers and supervisors are usually U.S. men earning six-figure salaries who live in El Paso, Texas and drive their BMWs across the border to work. The lower-level supervisors are Mexicans who translate the employers' instructions into Spanish. In other cases, the workplace may be some subcontractor's hole-in-the-wall facility. There, conditions are worse: wages may be as low as $3.75 per day, and workers may not be covered by the national health program for workers.

This is life in Mexican towns and cities along the U.S.-Mexican border, where multinational corporations, drawn by low wages, have set up *maquiladoras*, or manufacturing and assembly plants, bringing dangerous environmental pollution and a host of social problems into desperately poor neighborhoods.

"There are a whole series of problems which are linked to the *maquiladora*," says Teresa Almada, a social worker with the Independent Popular Organization in Juarez. "There are problems with the urban infrastructure, such as the lack of water, sewers, electric light." Other problems, she says, include low wages, industrial pollution and pervasive sexual harassment of women workers. "The issue of the *maquiladora* isn't just the factory which comes here," she says, "but rather that in cities along the border in Mexico, the size of the *maquiladora* industry is so great in relation to the city, that the *maquiladora* limits and determines the entire social reality of the city."

Conditions in the *maquiladora* communities in cities like Tijuana, Juarez, Reynosa or Matamoros provide an insight to the frightening future, for, as Mexican Secretary of Commerce Jaime Serra Puche has stated, in many respects NAFTA is Mexico's *maquiladora* — or border industry — program, writ large. Mexico's *maquiladora* program allows foreign companies to set up factories that produce for export; NAFTA would allow foreign businesses to invest freely throughout Mexico. Just as multinational corporations have shifted production to Mexico's *maquiladoras* in order to take advantage of cheap labor and lax environmental regulations, so it can be anticipated that U.S. and Canadian corporations will find the main attraction of investing in Mexico to be the country's low social standards, some of which are dramatically inferior to those of its industrialized Northern neighbors.

The new frontier

In 1965, the Mexican government established a limited free trade zone along the U.S.-Mexican border through the Border Industrialization Program, which encouraged foreign corporations to build factories and create jobs in Mexico. Many U.S. corporations, including General Motors and Zenith, moved factories to Mexico to take advantage of low wages or to escape U.S. environmental or workplace safety regulations. The program mushroomed in the 1980s when repeated devaluations of the peso dramatically lowered Mexican wage rates. Today, 850 U.S. corporations operate one or more *maquiladora* plants, and more than 80 percent of the *maquiladora* companies are U.S.-owned. About 68 percent of all investment in the *maquiladora* zone comes from the United States.

The *maquiladoras* have drawn hundreds of thousands

From *Multinational Monitor*, May 1993, pp. 18-23. Reprinted by permission of *Multinational Monitor*, P.O. Box 19405, Washington, DC 20036, $25/yr.

of Mexicans to live in border towns and cities. Over half a million workers, two-thirds of them women, labor in over 2,000 such factories, for about 50 cents an hour or $4.50 a day. Cities like Tijuana and Juarez grew at the spectacular rate of over 7 percent a year, burgeoning to a population of over one million inhabitants today. Juarez now has about 340 *maquiladoras* employing 150,000 workers in a city of 1.3 million inhabitants. Many of these cities' residents live in shacks and hovels in neighborhoods without sewers, running water, electricity or paved streets.

"The *maquiladora* is the axis of the economy in cities like these," explains Almada. Local politics have come to be dominated by business consortiums, such as the Bermudes group or the Fuentes group, which build industrial parks for the multinational corporations. These Mexican business interests, closely tied to multinationals, become important forces not only in the local economy, but also at city hall and in the state legislature.

Given this sort of power structure, the city's economic resources are frequently diverted from the needs of the working class inhabitants to those of the Mexican and multinational industrialists. The domination of multinational corporations and Mexican real estate interests leads to the construction of highways, rail spurs, airports and other facilities, rather than to the building of homes or the paving of streets in working class neighborhoods. For example, according to Almada, Juarez officials are placing a budgetary priority on paving the streets and highways which connect the industrial parks. "Pavement is the priority," she says, "in a city where half the people have no sewer system."

> The resources of *maquiladora* communities are frequently diverted from the needs of working people to those of multinational industrialists.

Hazards of the *maquilas*

Work in the *maquiladoras* involves tasks such as assembling wire harnesses for automobiles or electronic circuit boards for computers, putting together stereo systems or sewing shirts and blouses. The pace of work is usually rapid and intense, lasting for nine-hour days, 45 hours per week. The turn-over of the workforce is extremely high.

Virtually all *maquiladora* supervisors and technicians are men, while more than three-quarters of the operatives are girls and women. In this situation — where most workers have no labor unions and the government does not protect workers' rights — sexual harassment is endemic. "Many of the girls are between 14 and 20 years old," says Almada, and, "[as] they leave the factories they are in a lot of danger. Rapes occur frequently, many of which go unreported. Many young women become pregnant with no possibility of a stable family life." Attorneys, social workers and women activists report that sexual harassment and rape often go unreported either because women fear reprisals in the form of firing or because a lack of resources to deal with rape and harrassment lead to a climate of shame and humiliation for the victims of these crimes.

"The majority of women workers in Mexico are not protected by the legal system as established by federal labor law," according to Patricio Mercado, a leader of Women in Labor Union Action (Mujeres de Accion Sindical). There are many reasons why women are not protected by the law. Young women workers, some coming from the countryside, may not know their rights, or may be afraid to assert those rights in the face of male authorities who represent employers, the government and unions. Simply put: they fear losing their jobs if they complain. Some have gone to work illegally at the age of 14 using forged documents and may be reluctant to attempt to exercise their rights. Others work in small shops or factories which have an ephemeral existence; Mexican workers call them *golondrinas* or swallows because they may fly away at any moment. These run-away shops often do not pay the *aguinaldo* or annual bonus, and they do not make the annual distribution of profits under the constitutionally mandated profit-sharing law. In other cases, the exhausting pace of work forces some women to leave the workplace before they are entitled to any benefits.

In the factory itself there are many threats to worker health and safety. A 1991 study of the Matamoros-Reynosa area by the Work Environment Program of the University of Massachusetts at Lowell concluded that "the working conditions identified in this study are reminiscent of the nineteenth century sweatshops of the U.S. industrial town." The study found "clear evidence that *maquiladora* workers are suffering from musculo-skeletal disorders related to working conditions, including rapid pace of work, poor workplace design and other ergonomic hazards. Acute health effects compatible with chemical exposures were also identified, indicating the potential for the future development of chronic diseases in the workforce."

According to the Mexican Secretary of Commerce, almost 40 percent of the *maquiladora* plants produce electronic equipment. While there are few good studies of occupational illness in the Mexican *maquiladora* industry, studies of electronic plants in North America and Europe have revealed problems among workers including increased rates of miscarriages and high rates of muscle skeletal disorders, such as carpal tunnel syndrome. Some solvents used in these plants may cause peripheral neuropathy, that is, numbness and tingling in the hands and feet. One Mexican study reported that some Mexican plants use benzene, a known carcinogen. Over 80 chemical plants operate on the border, including Stepan Chemical of Chicago, which has been accused of toxic dumping. In addition, metalworking plants use lead and zinc, both of which are also potential health hazards. Lead can cause reproductive and kidney problems and hypertension.

Mexican occupational health professionals such as Asa Christina Laurel, the author of several studies of Mexican health and safety laws, have long criticized the Mexican government for its failure to enforce occupational health and safety laws. In general, Mexican authorities have failed to collect information or carry out studies on workers' health problems.

The rapid industrialization and urbanization of cities like Juarez has also resulted in severe social problems. For example, neither the employers nor the government provides child care for workers' children. "Child care is a real issue now because both parents have to work" in order to earn a subsistence income, says Lilia Reyes, a labor lawyer who works with the Workers Center (Centro Obrero) in Monterrey, Nuevo Leon. She notes that single working mothers "may have to wait months before

Casualties of Free Trade— Workers' Loss in Watsonville

I live and work in the community of Watsonville, California, where I represent the 4,000 members of Teamsters Local 912. Watsonville is located between Monterey and Santa Cruz at the head of the great Salinas valley which has provided much of the United States with vegetables for many years. It was the setting for John Steinbeck's *In Dubious Battle*.

Our community's agricultural base has made it the home of many ethnic groups: Mexicans, Chinese, Filipinos, Italians and Yugoslavs, among others. These people all came to work the land, and, since World War II, to work in plants that process the fruits and vegetables that don't go to fresh market. This work is now leaving. Our community is being hurt by decisions being made in corporate board rooms thousands of miles from here. Small companies are closing or being taken over by huge transnational corporations that are running away.

Green Giant was first to head to Mexico. In 1983, Pillsbury bought the company and opened a vegetable processing facility in Irapuato, Mexico, eliminating 800 jobs in Watsonville. In 1989 Pillsbury was taken over by Grand Metropolitan, a giant English holding company which decided to use broccoli and cauliflower grown in Mexico. This eliminated another 380 Watsonville workers. Other companies have followed Green Giant's example. Today, about 9,000 fewer people in the Watsonville area are working in the food and related industries.

While the private sector has benefited from running away from our town, the public is paying for it. Workers pay with their livelihoods. Taxpayers pay to retrain them and provide them with extended unemployment benefits, medical care, food stamps and other forms of aid. More of the local tax burden is taken up by individual taxpayers as the corporations flee. The residents and the remaining food processors (who aren't big enough to move) pay an increased share of costs, for instance, for the $20 million sewage-treatment plant that was mandated by the EPA to clean waste water from Green Giant's and the other departing employers' former operations.

People in Irapuato pay in another way. Clean water there is in short supply. The rivers running through town are severely polluted by the untreated sewage of 500,000 inhabitants and by industrial wastes from factories and a nearby oil refinery. Green Giant, free of local regulation, is drilling more than 450 feet deep to pump out about a million gallons a day of potable water in order to clean and wash exported vegetables. They currently discharge the dirty water, untreated, back into the polluted river.

The children of Irapuato pay too. Because of their parents' declining wages, more of them are entering the workforce at an early age. Indeed, the Mexican public has seen a vast reduction in its standard of living since 1982, when foreign investment was liberalized. Foreign companies actually pay less in annual wages to their workers than Mexican employers do. To get around a constitutional requirement to pay their workers a share of the profits, multinational corporations juggle their books to show no profitability from Mexican operations.

This story is not unique to Watsonville, Irapuato or the food processing industry. We are seeing our communities throughout the United States and the world being degraded by private-sector decision-making. Given the diversification and resources of the corporate giants, it is difficult for isolated local struggles to be effective in combatting their abuse. It is becoming increasingly clear to those of us who have fought this kind of fight, that the tactics of taking on one employer at a time will not be effective in this "New World Order." To have some control over our communities, we must be able to change laws.

Now, just as this realization is being made, the transnational corporations with the help of their friends in government want to change the rules of the game. This is what free trade with Mexico is about. This is what the Generalized Agreement on Tariffs and Trade is about. Corporations want governments to make it easier for them to run away from environmental standards, worker protections, and any but the lowest standards of community responsibility. By virtue of trade agreements, they want the right to ignore the rules of fair conduct established by local, state and even national governments. They want a system, for instance, that would overrule Californians who pass tougher environmental initiatives.

I would suggest that anyone who is interested in maintaining or improving our standard of living or protecting the planet needs to understand what we are up against. To fight this "free trade" menace, we need a broad vision of community improvement that involves workers, environmentalists, human rights activists and other public-spirited persons in the United States, Mexico, Canada and everywhere else. The globalization of capital makes necessary a corresponding globalization of labor, whose "solidarity," however, must now include almost everyone. The transnational corporations are in a better position than before to take advantage of narrow self-interests and play us off against each other. We must resist those manipulations in concert with our brothers and sisters throughout the world. Economic forces seem to be creating a situation where, in order to change our communities, we now have to change the entire world!

Joe Fahey is president of Teamsters Local 912 in Watsonville, California.

Workers who have attempted to organize to address some of these maquiladora-created problems have met with harsh repression.

they can get a place. There just aren't enough child care centers."

The *maquiladoras* are also a factor leading to the proliferation of child labor, with children from desperately poor families often using forged birth certificates to begin working in the *maquiladoras* at 14 or 15 years of age.

Employers, social workers, women's groups and academics all agree that there are significant numbers of children working in the *maquiladoras*, although there are no concrete figures on their actual number. One employer speculates that 5 percent of *maquiladora* workers are underage.

Labor Crosses Borders

With U.S. and Canadian companies threatening to shift production to Mexican *maquiladoras* in ever greater numbers — and faced with the fact that labor competition will be heightened even further with the adoption of NAFTA — progressive unionists in all three countires have begun to emphasize international labor solidarity. A number of international labor coalitions have emerged from joint campaigns against particular corporations. The Communication Workers of America, for example, formed an alliance with Canadian and Mexican communication workers unions in the course of a dispute with Northern Telecom. Teamster Local 912 in Watsonville, California saw its canning plant close, costing 800 Mexican and Chicano workers their jobs. Local members joined with workers in Irapuato, Mexico in an effort to force Green Giant to build a waste-treatment plant in Irapuato and to provide extended job training for the Local 912 workers in Watsonville.

Another important nascent coalition is the North American Worker-to-Worker Network, which involves teamsters, autoworkers, electrical workers and service employees in making direct contacts between U.S., Mexican and Canadian workers. The goal of the program is to eventually build coalitions to use their economic and political power to counterbalance the power of multinational corporations, while protecting the rights and working conditions of workers.

Mexican and U.S. trade negotiators alike contend that NAFTA would improve workplace and community conditions in the *maquiladora* zones and throughout Mexico. But the evidence to support that assertion is weak. Mexican wages have plummeted during the period of the *maquiladoras'* rapid growth, falling from $1.38 per hour in 1982 to $0.69 per hour in 1988 to an estimated $0.51 per hour in 1991. And labor rights have been substantially restricted since the mid-1970s. Mexican officials tout these low wage levels in courting foreign investment, and it is undisputed that cheap, non-unionized labor and lax regulatory enforcement are the reasons foreign investors look to Mexico. Because foreign investors in the *maquiladoras* or in Mexico generally under NAFTA would overwhelmingly be export-oriented and relatively unconcerned with Mexican domestic consumption, guaranteeing labor rights, raising wages or enforcing environmental and health standards would undermine the basis of their investment: low costs.■

—D.L.

Repressing unionist

Mexican workers who have attempted to organize to address some of these *maquiladora*-created problems have met with harsh repression. A strong upsurge of labor activity occurred during the late 1970s among a youthful, militant workforce which joined labor unions, organized strikes and attempted to negotiate contracts for improved wages and benefits.

But the combined efforts of multinational employers, the ruling Institutional Revolutionary Party and the one-party-state's labor unions, the Confederation of Mexican Workers (CTM), the Regional Confederation of Mexican Workers (CROM) and the Revolutionary Workers and Peasants (CROC), soon succeeded in crushing the labor upsurge [see "Mexican Labor: The Old, the New and the Democratic," *Multinational Monitor,* January/February 1991].

Employers fire and blacklist union activists and other outspoken workers. These practices have gone on for years and continue today. Consequently, most *maquiladoras* are unorganized, and state-controlled unions represent workers in those that are organized.

These unions are of little use in improving conditions for the workers. Some are "ghost unions," that is, unions unknown to the workers. These phantom unions negotiate "protection contracts" that protect the employers by giving workers contractual wages and conditions inferior to those guaranteed by labor law. Others are what Professor Jorge Carrillo Viveros of the College of the Northern Border in Tijuana calls "low profile unions," or unions with no presence on the shop floor.

In April 1993, workers at the BESA plant in Juarez petitioned for the right to form a "coalition" which under Mexican labor law would give them the right to bargain with their employers. All 113 workers who signed the petition were immediately fired, the employer preferring to pay them their severance rather than have a union in the plant. One worker, who must remain anonymous, explains that because the labor authorities give the activists' names to the employers, those who sign such coalition petitions are always fired.

Union dissidents who demand democracy and insist that their unions fight for economic and social justice are fired with the collusion of management, the union and the government. The Mexican Boards of Conciliation and Arbitration and the labor courts are notoriously worthless in the defense of workers' rights. Activists are blacklisted by the employers and the unions, and in some cases threatened and beaten. Today workers and independent unions like the Authentic Labor Front (FAT), and some leftist parties like the Revolutionary Workers Party (PRT) are forced to organize by building secret union cell structures within plants and corporations.

No Exit

In isolated urban ghettos, a better life seems a world away

Barbara Vobejda

Washington Post Staff Writer

CLEVELAND

Five years ago, Adrienne Walker set out to work at the Stop N Shop. It was a shining moment for her. She was a single, inner-city mother living on welfare who had applied for a job in the suburbs, interviewed and been hired, easy as that. All she had to do was get there.

That wasn't so easy. She convinced a friend to drive her, but it took 45 minutes, and after a few days her friend "got lazy," she says. She took the bus, but to make the right connections she had to leave home 3 1/2 hours before her shift began.

In the meantime, her grandmother was struggling to take care of Walker's 1-year-old son. And then the final straw: she found out she was pregnant with a second child.

It all just seemed too much, and after 10 days on the job, she quit.

Now that suburb, that job and the fleeting promise of deliverance seem a world away from Walker's neighborhood, a battered landscape of public housing projects and boarded-up factories.

For Walker and those who live around her, escape seems impossible. They are isolated from jobs and services, surrounded by poverty and threatened by crime. They pray that a troubled, overburdened school system can lift their children out.

"I would like to move," says Walker, now married and the mother of three. But even with that $5-an-hour job in the suburbs, she says, "it would not be easy."

Neighborhoods like Walker's reflect a new dimension to urban life in America: Never before have inner-city residents been so isolated from mainstream society.

Scholars argue that this isolation is at the heart of the worst ills of the inner city, a tangle of crime, unemployment and stubborn poverty, all of which President Clinton has pledged to attack.

But repairing the cities, which have come to embody the nation's most intractable problems, could prove to be more complex and difficult for Clinton than fulfilling any other campaign promise. It entails overhauling health care and welfare, improving schools, curbing the drug trade and revitalizing the economy.

And in big cities, those daunting tasks are made even more complicated by the chasm—psychological, physical, economic and social—that separates the urban ghetto from virtually all other facets of American life.

"Getting in there with programs is more difficult" because of this chasm, says Health and Human Services Secretary Donna E. Shalala, who will oversee many of the Clinton programs aimed at urban problems.

"The issue is not just that people have moved, but the jobs have moved," she says. And for this and other reasons, inner-city residents "don't have the resources to deal with these issues."

In neighborhoods from Cleveland and Detroit to Chicago, New York, Washington and Los Angeles, inner-city isolation takes many forms.

It is economic. Cities have lost millions of manufacturing jobs, leaving urban residents like Walker with few work opportunities. They are unprepared for the white-collar jobs downtown, and service jobs outside the city are far away and pay too little to allow a move to the suburbs.

It is physical. Urban sprawl has moved more of the population, employment, shopping and services farther from the urban center. Middle-class suburbanites have less reason to drive into the central city, leaving neighborhoods distinctly separated by class, with little interaction or empathy among their residents.

For residents of the inner city, the new glass towers downtown and the suburban brick houses sit beyond reach, like elusive visions of prosperity.

It is racial and social. The flight of the middle class—black and white—from the inner city has left a population that is overwhelmingly black and poor, devoid of healthy businesses, strong schools or other institutions that contributed to stability in the past. This concentration of poverty means that children grow up with little exposure to steadily employed adults, making it easy for them to see unemployment as a way of life.

From *The Washington Post National Weekly Edition*, March 15-21, 1993, pp. 6-7. © 1993 by The Washington Post. Reprinted by permission.

"In short, the communities of the underclass are plagued by massive joblessness, flagrant and open lawlessness and low-achieving schools, and therefore tend to be avoided by outsiders," wrote University of Chicago sociologist William Julius Wilson in his 1987 book, "The Truly Disadvantaged," which first laid out in detail the increasing concentration of poverty in the inner cities.

The result, he argued, is that those who live in these neighborhoods, "whether women and children of welfare families or aggressive street criminals, have become increasingly socially isolated from mainstream patterns of behavior."

Walker is not personally isolated; she has a supportive, extended family. Many of those around her have strong ties to their churches. But they have virtually no social interaction with suburbanites or middle-class society. And as a group, they exist in a stunningly hopeless and solitary milieu.

"I knew about this neighborhood, but I never thought I'd be living here," says Francie Tate, who lives a few doors from Walker in the same public housing complex. "When I told everybody I was moving to 79th [Street], everybody said that's really bad."

Tate, the single mother of two sons, Martel, 1, and Robert, 6, was frightened at first. Television violence, she says, pales in comparison to what children here see in the parking lot. Walker tells of her husband discovering a woman's strangled and beaten body in a car just outside their front door.

Another time, she woke to the sound of a burglar smashing her picture window. She still is not sure whether he made it into the apartment or was frightened off by her screams.

As she tells the tales of daily life in the ghetto, one of her sons listens impassively, the TV flashing in the background.

The isolation of the community makes even the most prosaic chores more difficult. There are no supermarkets nearby, only expensive corner stores, so shopping requires a long bus ride.

Tate waits for a "jitney," an unofficial taxi service, to bring her home with her groceries. She shops once a month when she gets food stamps, hauling home six gallons of milk, four of which she freezes.

She now feels comfortable in the neighborhood, she says, "but I don't want my kids to grow up here." Tate dreams of moving to North Carolina, living in a "gorgeous" house, with a country kitchen and a big back yard where her sons can run.

In her neighborhood, she says, "it's going to get worse before it gets better. There are people on the street. More jobs are closing now. And there's going to be more people on the streets."

The daily trials of inner-city residents like Tate and Walker are well known to Housing and Urban Development Secretary Henry Cisneros, who as former mayor of San Antonio was forced to grapple with urban ghettos. "People have nothing—nowhere to go for food or services," he says.

The new administration may explore some policy proposals, he says, including conversion of the first floors of high-rise buildings into supermarket and shopping complexes to create a place "of common activity and contact." In the meantime, he says, "isolation is a very serious problem."

Cleveland's inner city has spiraled down quickly and dramatically over the past decade, largely the result of the collapse of the area's manufacturing base.

Since 1979, metropolitan Cleveland lost 88,000 manufacturing jobs, a phenomenon that has left long stretches of city geography dotted with abandoned factories, crumbling shells that were once the economic heart of the community.

Even in metropolitan areas where the number of jobs has increased, virtually all of the employment growth has been not in the city but in the suburbs, says Mark Alan Hughes, an urban geographer and coauthor of a recent Urban Institute study on the subject. This is true in Washington, D.C., Chicago, Los Angeles, Philadelphia and Detroit, among others.

At the same time, population moved out of many cities and inner-city poverty rates grew. In Walker and Tate's neighborhood, known as "Central," the poverty rate is 63 percent.

Cleveland's neighborhoods are among the most segregated in the nation, according to University of Michigan demographer William Frey. And the city is much worse off than its surrounding suburbs. When "dissimilarity" between suburbs and city is measured in terms of unemployment, income, poverty and other statistics, the contrast is greater here than in most of the nation's other major metropolitan areas. The division between city and suburbs is true across America, accompanied by a sharp alienation between suburbanites and the inner-city poor.

Lewis West, who runs a social service agency near King-Kennedy Estates, a notorious public housing project, says the Cleveland suburbs are full of people who are "scared to death" of Central. "The public perception is that it's a bad place to be. The local paper described it as 'Dodge City,' " he says.

But many of those who live in Central say it is not the high crime rates, but the lack of jobs that has inspired the deepest desperation.

"There were times when I just lost hope. I got a trade as a machinist but I can't get a job," says Robert Bey, who was laid off from his factory job in 1982. "Big industry doesn't care about the people they leave in the inner city."

Robert Agnew, a recovering addict who has been unable to find work, remembers when auto and machine factories were vital here, along with huge bakeries and a General Electric plant. "The steel mills was happening," he says. Today, "we live in a jungle. This is a war."

At Vocational Guidance Services, a job training facility in Central, a project is underway to encourage employers in the neighborhood, among them a metal stamping factory, storage business and print shop, to hire local residents. But officials at the training center warn that they face an enormously difficult task.

The loss of jobs and the soaring rates of unemployment are most to blame for the isolation of the inner city, says Claudia Coulton, director of the Center for Urban Poverty and Social Change at Case Western Reserve University here.

Neighborhoods elsewhere in the city that were stable only a short time ago, she says, are facing the same prospect: As factory workers have lost their jobs and have less money to spend, property values have declined, housing stock has deteriorated and drug trafficking, especially in crack cocaine, has moved in.

"That's when you began to see areas losing their more middle-class population and a rise in other problems, delinquency, crime, infant mortality," she says.

In Central, a black neighborhood that has been impoverished for a generation, economic segregation worsened considerably over the 1980s, she says. While just a quarter of poor people in Cleveland were living in impoverished areas—neighborhoods in which there are virtually no middle-class people—in 1980, that figure doubled to half by 1990.

Poverty rates increased in many big cities over the 1980s: in Detroit, from 22 percent to 32 percent; in Los Angeles, from 16 percent to 19 percent; in Milwaukee, from 14 percent to 22 percent.

And even in cities where the poverty rate fell—including Washington, D.C., where it slipped from 19 percent to 17 percent—the rates declined more in the suburbs, meaning that poverty became more concentrated in the central cities, according to urban geographer Hughes.

The concentration of poor people makes it even harder to find jobs, sociologists argue. In nonpoor neighborhoods, people often find work through neighbors, friends and relatives. But when an entire community is impoverished, those who are looking for work have no connections to help get jobs.

Coulton contends that children suffer too when they are outside the mainstream. Unlike their peers in middle-class neighborhoods, they are exposed to behavior, from dress and attitudes to delinquency and teenage childbearing, that keeps young people from getting ahead.

Tracie Glenn, a single mother who has been struggling to find steady work, says she was struck by a sad contrast recently when she was cleaning the suburban house of a professional couple.

The house, says Glenn wistfully, "was beautiful. All these awards and certificates were hanging there. . . . I heard the daughter talking to her mother, and I knew she was going someplace."

WATCHING THE MAINSTREAM MOVE

Over the past decade, the inner cities have become increasingly isolated as population and jobs have moved out.

In some places, the number of jobs inside the city declined, to the benefit of the suburbs:

The result has been a significant increase in inner-city poverty, especially in:

METRO AREA	SUBURBAN JOB GROWTH 1980-86	CITY	POVERTY RATE 1980	POVERTY RATE 1990
Chicago	100%	Detroit	22%	32%
Cleveland	100	New Orleans	26	32
Dayton	100	Cleveland	22	29
Detroit	100	El Paso	21	25
Greensboro	100	Milwaukee	14	22
Louisville	100	Houston	13	21
Seattle	99	Los Angeles	16	19
Newark	97	Dallas	14	18
Los Angeles	95	Fort Worth	14	17
Providence	95	Denver	14	17
Youngstown	93	Oklahoma City	12	16
Washington, D.C.	91	Phoenix	11	14

SOURCE: U.S. Census Bureau and Urban Institute

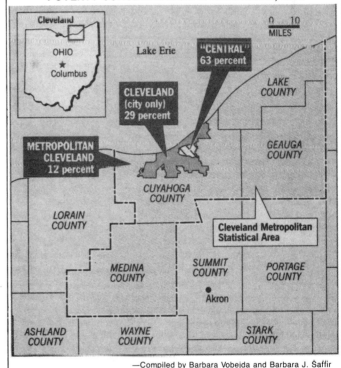

POVERTY CONCENTRATION IN CLEVELAND, 1990

—Compiled by Barbara Vobejda and Barbara J. Saffir

BY JAY LIEBENOW FOR THE WASHINGTON POST

But then she thought of her own neighborhood. "Kids 12 and 13 are selling drugs. And a lot of [the parents] have their kids doing it."

Of her own 11-year-old son, she says, "I don't know what he'll grow up to be. . . . I'm in a lot of fear."

For children, says Harvard University sociologist Gary Orfield, the effects of being sequestered in a ghetto are worse than for adults.

5. POVERTY AND INEQUALITY

Those children "most dependent on education are concentrated in places with the most rotten education," he says. "When you concentrate poverty, you concentrate health problems, family problems, school populations are very unstable, kids are exposed to criminal problems."

At George Washington Carver Elementary School in Cleveland's inner city, the children need only look out the classroom window to see gang fighting, prostitution and drug dealing, principal Theodore Carter says.

He says he has watched as the community around the school crumbles, literally and figuratively. Across the street, for example, just one structure stands on a block that once had 10 houses.

Carter tries to get the parents involved, but at his monthly parent-teacher meetings, he is lucky to get a dozen parents in a school that enrolls 460 students.

He has come to a bleak conclusion about his students, 80 percent of whom live in poverty. "If they can't get out of the projects, I don't think there's much hope. Some will be productive, but when it's generation after generation in the projects. . . ."

Their parents may know they should move, but they are stuck, he says. "They don't have the resources."

The hope of leaving the ghetto dances constantly before Adrienne Walker.

Her mother, a clerk with the federal government, fled to the Cleveland suburbs 13 years ago after Walker fell into a troubled high school crowd and began skipping classes. Walker says she excelled in her new suburban school, earning a high school diploma with A's and B's.

But Walker did not stay in the suburbs. When she was forced to find her own place six years ago, the easiest option seemed to be a public housing unit in the same complex with her grandmother, back in the inner city.

The road into the ghetto was easy. Leaving, she knows, will not be. It will require a much higher income, enough to cover rent on an unsubsidized apartment. And it will take savings, for security deposits and other moving expenses.

And then there are the well-known bureaucratic traps: If she or her husband, Dwayne Jennings, finds work, she loses Medicaid coverage and welfare benefits. If they amass savings, her assistance is jeopardized.

When Walker and Jennings were married last year, he was getting $6 an hour as a cook at a downtown restaurant. Her resident manager learned of the marriage, and the monthly rent on the apartment rose from $55 to $300. Walker's welfare check fell from $359 to $296.

Jennings was laid off and has been out of work since July. He heard of a good job at a factory in Twinsburg, a suburb to the south, but there was the same hitch.

"How was I going to get there? How was I going to get back?" he says.

Like most residents here, Walker and Jennings have an escape plan, however abstract and tenuous. They say they will buy a small apartment building when Jennings receives an $8,000 settlement for a work injury. Walker plans to sign up for courses at the local community college.

In the meantime, they live in a world circumscribed by boundaries middle-class Americans never face: avoiding corner markets where residents say prices shoot up the day food stamps are issued; waiting until relatives can drive them Christmas shopping, so their packages don't get stolen on the bus ride home; letting their children play in parking lots because the playground next door has been overrun by drinking, gambling teenagers; facing a $5 fine if their children play on the housing project grass.

Walker thinks she knows what it feels like to be freed from the trap. For a short time this year, when her husband was working and she was receiving benefits, they caught up with the bills. For the first time, they went to the grocery store once a week.

"People would say, 'Dang, didn't you just go to the grocery store?' " she says. "I could take the kids downtown, buy them blue jeans, buy them a meal at McDonald's."

For some reason, the liberty of buying that Happy Meal seems to haunt her. She says now when she takes her children shopping, her oldest son, Greggory, inevitably pleads with her: "Mommy, can we get this? Can we go to McDonald's?'

"I'll say, 'No! Don't ask me that. . . .' He'll look at me like, 'I just asked you for McDonald's.' "

It is that exchange, more than anything else, that she dreads. It is then, she says, that she feels stuck.

Washington Post staff writer Guy Gugliotta contributed to this report.

The New Faces of POVERTY

A STARTLING REPORT ON WHY THE SOLID MIDDLE-CLASS FAMILIES OF THE '80s ARE BECOMING THE WELFARE RECIPIENTS OF THE '90s

Claire Safran

Sherry Mahmens, 37, picks up her family's groceries at a busy supermarket in Pleasant Hill, Iowa. Though she owns a wardrobe of stylish clothes (leftovers from her days of dressing for success as a computer specialist), she's pushed them to the back of her closet. Today, the smart thing is to dress down for the unemployment line, the welfare office, and the supermarket.

Still, she feels conspicuous. Five-foot-two, a fragile 105 pounds, Sherry senses the eyes of strangers on her as she pushes her cart up to the checkout counter. She knows that they're listening when she raises her voice, above the clatter of cash registers, to tell the clerk she'll be paying with food stamps.

"And I know what's going through their minds," she says. "My old coat is still 'too nice' for someone on welfare. My basket is loaded with bargains, but they always spot the six-pack of cola. They think, So that's where my tax dollars are going. Just over a year ago, when I was working, it's what I thought, too."

In the 1990s, you can forget about the whale, the spotted owl, and the dolphin; this decade's endangered species is the middle class. In 1992, hard times have commuted out of inner city ghettos and Appalachian hollows and arrived in the suburbs. In the past two years, more than two million people have joined the welfare rolls. And like the Mahmenses, many of them are standing on unemployment and food stamp lines for the first time.

Overnight, poverty has become personal. Approximately one in ten Americans survives on food stamps, and most of us know at least one family member, friend, or neighbor who isn't making it. And though some may rant about "welfare cheats" out for a free lunch, little more than half of all Americans who are eligible for food stamps actually receive them. Pride stops some; red tape stops others.

But statistics tell only part of the story. Women like Sherry Mahmens tell the rest. In early 1991, Sherry was earning $27,500 as a computer specialist. Her husband, Ron, was putting in long hours as a car salesman and, even in a sluggish market, racking up $30,000 a year. Then, in March, they learned how precarious their comfortable lifestyle could be.

On his way to work, Ron was rear-ended by a truck and sustained internal head injuries. Since then, he has suffered from splitting headaches, blurred vision, blackout spells, and memory loss. Because he was injured just as he was switching from his own health insurance policy to a family plan, Ron was caught in benefits limbo. He's not eligible for unemployment benefits because, technically, he still has a job. When we talked with them, his disability claim had been turned down. And there was no settlement yet from the trucking company.

Two months after Ron's accident, with the economy still in decline, Sherry was laid off. They've lived on her unemployment benefits: $800 a month plus $200 in food stamps. Out of that, they've paid $400 for rent, $200 for utilities, and bought gas for the car, medication for Ron, and food for themselves and Megan, their five-year-old daughter.

To survive, Sherry and Ron have sold some of their belongings—their almost-new bicycles, Sherry's few bits of jewelry, "keepsakes" like Megan's playpen and toys. At Christmas, they sold Megan's present from last year, an electric Barbie car, in order to buy her a new gift. "Maybe we should've used the

The MORENOS

"At work, they tell me I should dress more professionally. I'd love to. But how? I buy my clothes secondhand at the Bargain Basket. 'What good is going to work, Mom?' my six-year-old keeps asking. 'We still don't have anything.'"

Lisa Moreno, 32, of Des Moines. A single mother of three, she earns $6.07 an hour as a customer-service representative.

money to pay something on our electric bill," Sherry says, "but a kid has to have a little bit of happiness."

Now and then, Sherry pulls out one of her smart outfits and goes job hunting. "But if I find something, what then? Who'll take care of Megan? And who'll be there if Ron has one of his spells?"

An independent woman, she now has to count on the kindness of others. Ron's sister has helped with the rent and loaned them a car when theirs was repossessed. Toward the end of the month, when the food stamps run out, the local community center provides a carton of free food.

"But some nights, we're close to sending Megan to bed without dinner," Sherry says, sighing. "Some nights, the only thing left to eat is stale bread and some cheese."

That's when Sherry tries to remember that some people are even worse off than she. "At least we have a roof over our heads," she says. "But I don't know for how long."

I n this election year, the plight of the ex-middle class and about-to-be poor will certainly be an issue with voters. Valerie Palmquist, 31, keeps a careful eye on the news. She's "hoping that Bush will do something, praying that somebody will come up with a plan to stop this country from going downhill."

Valerie runs a licensed day-care center out of her home in the rural town of Foreston, Minnesota. She has two children, five and six. With a paid helper, she used to look after 14 others. "But every time one of my customers lost a job, I lost a part of my business. Other people switched to unlicensed care, which is cheaper, or they'd leave their kids with relatives, which is the cheapest of all."

As the number of children dwindled, Valerie had to let her helper go, adding one more name to the unemployment rolls. As her center shrank to four chil-

dren, her husband Robert's income was falling, too. He's a trucker, but with the construction industry in hard times, he's hauling fewer and fewer loads. Today, the Palmquists are struggling on about $17,000 a year, but that makes them too rich for food stamps; the income limit for a family of four is $16,512.

Once upon a happier time, the Palmquists had health insurance through Robert's former job. Early in the recession, that company closed down, and Robert signed on with a new employer that doesn't provide those benefits. Now, like 34 million other Americans, Valerie and Robert do without. "A routine checkup?" she says. "A Pap smear? Forget it." The Palmquists can't afford the $375 a month that private insurance would cost them. If Valerie's not climbing the walls, it's because the chil-

The BALDWINS

"I never dreamed I'd turn 40 and still need help from my parents. They're sending my husband to graduate school to learn a new profession. But who knows if a man in his midforties will be able to find a job?"

Pam Baldwin, 45, of Meridian, Idaho, with husband Robert and their three children. Their family farm was foreclosed in 1990.

dren qualify for Minnesota's children's health plan, which—for $25 a year—covers almost everything. "It's funded by a smokers' tax. Actually, I've quit smoking," Valerie says with a grin,

"because I can no longer afford it. That's my only good news."

Valerie grew up in an affluent suburb of Minnesota, and as she remembers, "I never went without *anything*." Today, her toughest moments are saying no to her children. "It seems like that's my only answer to them these days. They're supposed to get an allowance, 50 cents each, but some weeks I just don't have it. Every three months they come home with lists of inexpensive books, two dollars each, that they can order through school. I used to let them buy two or three. Now it's just one, and that hurts. Because it's not enough for children to go to libraries. If they're going to love reading, they need to own books."

At times, feeling the tension, she and Robert snap at each other. "He thinks that being a real man means taking care of your family. That bothers both of us because, in a way, I think it, too. This recession is different from earlier ones. It's long, so very long. And I can't even see the end of it."

Valerie shops for the children's clothes at garage sales and does "a lot of hinting" to grandparents. Her mother places long-distance phone calls, to save Valerie the expense, and she's paying the tuition for Valerie's home-study college courses in interior decorating.

Once a month, Valerie drives to a nearby town to pick up staples from a food program—MAC (Mothers and Children), which helps families whose children are too old to qualify for WIC (Women, Infants, and Children). For each child every month, she gets five cans of evaporated milk, a big box of powdered milk, instant potatoes or macaroni or rice, two boxes of cereal, two six-ounce packages of powdered eggs ("not bad if you add cheese to them"), peanut butter or dried beans, canned meat or stew, four cans of fruits and vegetables, five 46-ounce cans of juice, two pounds of butter, four pounds of cheese, a jar of honey, and a bag of cornmeal.

"I'm not ashamed to take it," she insists. "It's not charity, even if some people think so. After all, we still pay taxes. Right now, maybe we're getting back more than most people. But as soon as we don't need it anymore, we'll be there to help others."

For extra cash, Robert repairs furniture, and the two of them are trying to start an upholstering business. "We're not sitting around," says Valerie. "We're working our butts off, and it's still not enough these days."

That means torn work boots for Robert, with plastic bags on the inside when it rains. It means frequent dinners

The RUSSOS

"My children are the ideal age for their parents to be unemployed. We don't have to pay for college yet, and they're too old to need day care. We try to be honest with them. I tell them, 'Disneyworld will still be there a year from now.'"

Kerry Russo, 39, of Ridgefield, Connecticut, with husband Vito and their three children

FRIGHTENING FACTS

- Nearly one tenth of all Americans, or 25 million*, use food stamps, an all-time high since the program began in 1961 and a startling jump of 29 percent since 1990. Every month, up to 400,000 Americans join the program.
- The number of people who require government help to buy their meals in Connecticut, the country's wealthiest state, has risen by 20 percent since 1991.
- Approximately 4.8 million American families live on welfare—an annual increase of 380,000 individuals between March 1991 and March 1992. Nine million of our country's neediest are children.
- In the past year, 12.9 million children required free or subsidized school lunches, 700,000 more than last year—and the largest jump in a decade.
- The ranks of the unemployed have swelled from 6.8 million in July 1990, when the recession began, to 9.2 million as of April 1992—a 35 percent increase.
- 13.5 percent of the nation's population—or 33.6 million—live below the poverty line (an annual income of $13,359 for a family of four). More than half (19.4 million) are women.

*Statistics are the most recent available at press time. Sources: Department of Agriculture, Department of Health and Human Services, Connecticut Department of Income Maintenance, and U.S. Bureau of the Census

of pasta (which Robert doesn't like) and rice (of which none of them are fond). "But we eat it anyway," she says. "At school, the children get lunch, and that's an important part of their nutrition. 'Like it or not,' I tell them, 'eat as much as you can.'"

In one-income families, unemployment is an even ruder awakening, "like being mugged," says Kerry Russo, 39, of Ridgefield, Connecticut. In the booming eighties, Kerry and Vito Russo could afford every luxury on his income as a successful commodities broker. They lived in a comfortable house in a stylish suburb with their three children—now ages 11, 9, and 7. In the slumping nineties, the last shudder of the Wall Street crash, Vito's been out of work for a year.

Though Kerry felt "helpless" at first, she refused to act it. "I'd been a stockbroker, too. But I'd been at home for at least ten years, and it was a humbling experience to try to get back into the job market. I was competing with a hundred people for every job." Eventually, she began working part-time in a local shop and full-time as an aide in the Ridgefield school system. But the school job—and the health insurance that came with it—ended this school year. "Budget cuts," she explains with a sigh.

Luckier than most, this family tumbled out of affluence and landed on a cushion, their savings from better times. Out of that, they pay their hefty mortgage. "But," Kerry worries, "we're close to the end of those savings."

A lifelong Republican, she's looking to Democrats this election year. "Bush is blind. He doesn't see what's happening. He doesn't realize how many people are losing their homes." She's nostalgic for an idea that goes back to Franklin Delano Roosevelt and the Depression of the thirties—a moratorium on bank foreclosures. "We need something like that now, because if you lose your home, that's it. You're done."

For Kerry, the worst of it is watching her husband suffer. "I look at a successful businessman going through this absolute torture. I can hold him. I can tell him it's going to be okay. But it's out of my hands. And that's the frightening part, how little control we have over our lives."

With other women in Ridgefield, Kerry is part of a new support group for the spouses of the unemployed. "Sometimes it's a big crying session. Some-

The FRIEDMANS

"Some of our friends have passed along hand-me-downs for the children, but others have stopped calling. Maybe they don't know what to say."

Marjorie Friedman, 33, a Brookfield, Connecticut, mother of two. Her part-time secretarial job has been her family's most steady income since January 1991, when her husband lost his job.

times we just sit and laugh. We're not used to having idle husbands around the house. I like it, but some don't. 'If he fixes one more thing, I'll scream,' a woman said one night. Everyone knew what she meant."

Kerry, as she knows, will survive. One day, life will be normal again but not exactly the same. "It used to be that if you followed the rules, you'd be fine. That doesn't apply anymore. They've changed the rules."

When Problems Outrun Policy

Returning to rapid economic growth and taming the market's tendency to create both wealth and poverty requires a new vision of domestic policy.

Robert Haveman

Robert Haveman is John Bascom Professor of Economics and Public Affairs at the University of Wisconsin-Madison and the Robert M. La Follette Institute of Public Affairs.

Recent events have brought many Americans face to face with a series of harsh realities. While economic life for many of us remains prosperous, a growing number—and an increasing proportion—of adult Americans are living below the poverty line.

For this group, especially for those on the bottom rungs of the nation's income ladder, conditions are especially severe. Their incomes have, in unprecedented fashion, failed to rise with economic growth. Their neighborhoods have become crime-infested and drug-dominated. The schools which their children attend are able neither to sustain order nor maintain educational standards. The social institutions that were vital to them in their youth—their churches, clubs, neighborhoods—seem irrelevant today. Their families have been broken up (or never put together) and the values with which they navigate life have little resemblance to those dominant in earlier times.

Unresponsive government

In addition to these economic, social, and value changes, poor people and minorities have experienced others as well. Many now perceive one of the fundamental institutions in their lives—the government—to be inimical to their interests. In the past,

they viewed the government as being protective. They depended on it to maintain minimal standards of physical and social order. They felt assured it would be responsive in time of crisis.

Welfare was considered a "safety net" by poor people and minorities. They had faith that the police would sustain order, the parks department would maintain parks, the roads department would fix roads, the sanitation department would clean the streets, and that public employment would offer job opportunities. This view by poor people—that government was an ally in improving their lot and making their neighborhoods habitable—may often have been more an apparition than a reality, but it was their belief.

One reason for poor people's past affirmation of government was that public officials then seemed clearer in their statements about the responsibilities of the public sector. What government was all about, according to the words of the political leaders, was the setting and enforcement of acceptable standards of income, education, sanitation, safety, and access to services.

Moreover, government people backed up their words with actions and money. Programs designed to meet people's needs—for development of skills, legal counsel, safety, mental and physical health services, and access to shelter—were visible. And the civil servants within these public programs either cared or pretended to care, and, more often than not, believed that they and their programs mattered.

From *Challenge*, May/June 1993, pp. 28-35. Reprinted with permission of the publisher, M. E. Sharpe, Inc., 80 Business Park Drive, Armonk, NY 10504, USA.

Even if there was often little real evidence that economic security was increasing, or that neighborhoods were safer and schools better, or that there were more job opportunities, or that housing conditions were improving, the press and community leaders regularly cited efforts by government to make things better. The services provided may not always have been cost-effective, but they were palpable, and announced that government was trying.

Many of today's poor no longer perceive government in this way. Few political leaders offer clear statements about government's responsibility and its role. Indeed, the main theme of many government leaders is that government has little, if any, responsibility for personal and community well-being. Few budgets providing services to the poor have increased, and rarely do news stories report government's attempts to improve the lot of the poor. Increasingly, public institutions once viewed as protective appear punitive and threatening.

Perhaps equally important, private standards have also changed for the worse. Family values, judgments about individual responsibility, perceptions of appropriate personal behavior and appearance, and expectations of the good will of neighbors have all eroded. The roots of these changes are not clear. Has it been a more permissive environment led by public acceptance of changed personal standards? Can it be the availability of cheap drugs and weapons, and the opening of "markets" in drugs and other illicit goods, generating substantial returns to criminal activity? We can only guess. We cannot really know.

The role of the economy

My thesis here is that the performance of the U.S. economy should not be omitted from any list of the causes of our problems. A further thesis is that this poor economic performance did not occur in a vacuum; more precisely, that governmental policy contributed significantly to its failure. If these two theses contain truth, then it follows that government has a responsibility to change its course, and I offer some suggestions for such a redirection.

The future of the American economy is high on everyone's list of concerns. While there are some encouraging signs regarding macroeconomic performance—a dwindling trade deficit, low inflation, a "solved" savings and loan crisis—other signs are less favorable. Unemployment remains stubbornly high. Saving, investment, and economic growth remain at historically low levels. The public deficit rises. The health of the banking and insurance sectors seems increasingly fragile. The macroeconomic future is surely not rosy.

This macroeconomic scenario is relatively well known, but another set of facts regarding the American economy is less clearly perceived. They involve the performance of the "micro" parts of the economy—the labor market, income flows and their distribution, the changing composition of jobs, and the changing character of the requirements and delivery of education.

I offer a few microeconomic perspectives about the American economy in order that we may understand more clearly whence we have come and where we should be going. They suggest that social problems have indeed overwhelmed policy. Moreover, I contend, much of federal government social policy—welfare, Social Security, health policy, and tax policy—has contributed to these developments. And I shall take the opportunity to indicate several fundamental policy changes that might contribute to narrowing the gap between problems and policy.

Decline in productivity growth

The median worker in the U.S. economy has experienced no increase in his or her real wage and salary earnings since the mid-1970s—a period of almost twenty years. Only when fringe benefit increases are included does real median worker compensation appear to have held approximately even. Moreover, capital per worker—plant, machinery, and equipment—has also sagged.

Why this dismal performance? While we cannot identify the causes with certainty, many have been suggested, often bearing supporting evidence. At its crux, this dismal earnings and investment performance is linked to the changes that have occurred in the rate of productivity growth—the rate of increase in the ratio of output to labor inputs—in the American economy.

In the 1950s, productivity grew annually by 2.64 percent. It remained at a high 2.5 percent in the 1960s. In the 1970s, however, the bottom dropped out, and the productivity growth rate fell to 1.24 percent. The 1980s were even worse, recording a dismal 1.09 percent annual growth.

But identifying the slowdown in productivity growth as the culprit only masks the root cause. What has caused the decline in productivity growth, a decline that most analysts mark as having begun about 1973? Again, several factors seem to be at work, arguably the most important being the oil price shocks that occurred in 1973 and again in 1976. Among other things, the radical change in the price of this input rendered obsolete a significant share of the U.S. capital stock designed, as it was, for an energy-intensive production process.

But, other factors contributed as well. Among them were the tilt in the composition of U.S. workers toward the less experienced (women, youth, and immigrants); the impact of environmental and other regulations diverting some capital investment funds from normal plant and equipment toward emissions reduction; and the declining quality of the education of an ever younger work force relative to the needs of industry. While one can compile a catalogue of potential factors with ease, assigning a specific share of the blame to any one is more difficult.

Owing to the stagnation of productivity and wages, American families have secured rising incomes almost exclusively by working more. Women's labor-force participation has increased, resulting in some growth in total family income. But even this income growth has not been significant, and what expansion we have experienced should properly be attributed to increased work effort and increased work time. There is clearly an upper limit to this source of family income growth.

One fact stands out ominously: American families no longer look forward to increasing standards of living, or to a world in which sons and daughters live better than their parents.

Growing gap between rich and poor

The gap between rich and poor has greatly increased over the past twenty years. The wages of a high school graduate, relative to those of a college graduate, have fallen by 15 percent since 1980. Since 1975, the income of the top 20 percent of the nation's households has risen from 41 percent to 44 percent of the total income pie—an historic increase. What lies behind this unsettling trend? As before, there is no sure explanation, but a few of the most important factors seem clear.

New jobs in the American economy have appeared with technical requirements beyond the abilities of an increasing share of the nation's job entrants to meet them. Those with little or inadequate education have done very poorly, both relative to their earlier experience and relative to others with more education and skills. These workers—some

new entrants to the job market and others being recycled from other jobs—have been forced into low- or minimum-wage slots requiring little skill. The wages of many of these jobs are insufficient to lift a family of four out of poverty. By any standard, the living standard of the families of these workers has shrunk.

On the other hand, those with substantial education or skills have experienced relatively high demand for their services, and their wages have been bid up, their family income following close behind. The result has been a growing gap between the economic status of families headed by high school graduates and those headed by college graduates.

A second factor is related to changes in the structure of American industry. The manufacturing sector has long been in decline, and the distribution of jobs has become tilted toward that part of the labor force where wages are typically lower—the service and trade sectors. The decline of manufacturing is also associated with the fading numerical strength and negotiating power of American trade unions. As a result, a pool of physically difficult (but high-paying) jobs has disappeared and has been replaced by part-time, seasonal, and low-paying jobs.

A third factor lies in important changes in U.S. tax laws that have made financial transactions extremely lucrative, with or without any clear view that they represent real efficiency gains. These tax law provisions have encouraged leveraged and hostile takeovers capable of generating huge returns to those who have engineered them. They have reduced the effective tax rate on high-income people while allowing it to creep upward for middle- and low-income people. Not only did this process generate huge incomes for those involved in arranging these corporate reorganizations, they often resulted in business failures, plant closings, and the shift of production capacity to other countries with lower labor costs. It is this shift that lies behind the stories of workers who, despite long experience in and dedication to firms and plants, have lost their jobs, exhausted their unemployment benefits, and been forced into either early retirement or low-paying, unskilled work.

Because of this widening of the nation's income distribution, we have seen a decline in social cohesion among America's diverse groups. More people with sagging living standards and little hope for future prosperity have come to see the enormous accumulation of income and wealth by others as having occurred at the expense of their own lagging prospects.

One manifestation of diminished social cohesion

is the increase in officially defined poverty, rising from about 12 percent in the 1970s to 14 percent in the 1980s. Another example is the growth in minority youth unemployment rates to the 40 percent range, resulting in alienation, frustration, hopelessness, and anger. Yet another manifestation, though far more difficult to document, is the apparent ability of the rich to convert their income and wealth into economic power and political influence.

As a result, the nation is showing signs of polarization stemming from this growing inequality. We see dissolution and frustration among the losers, and position and power among the winners. The analogy between the structure of some our large cities, encumbered with abject poverty enclaves isolated in and surrounded by palatial wealth, to those of some third world countries has been suggested with increasing frequency.

The "New Poor"

Those who have filtered to the bottom of the income distribution include some of the nation's most economically vulnerable citizens. These households contain a disproportionate share of the nation's children, on whose shoulders the nation's economic future depends. The groups of "new poor" that now populate the bottom of the income distribution include families headed by unwed mothers, children, minority youth, and families headed by young workers with little education. While other groups, notably the elderly and older workers, have bubbled up from the bottom of the distribution over time, the new groups have sunk down into it.

What factors account for this pattern of gainers and losers over the past several decades? Again, several factors are at work, and again, the precise role played by any of them remains in doubt. One indisputable factor is the growth in single-parent families, due in large part to the explosion in divorce rates and the increased number of women choosing to give birth although unmarried. Today, over 350,000 children are born each year to teen unmarried mothers, up from less than 200,000 per year in 1970. A typical pattern for the majority of these mothers is to join the welfare rolls within a few years of giving birth. Indeed, from 1970 to 1989, mother-only families grew from about 10 percent of all families to about 21 percent.

A second factor is the declining relative economic status of single-parent families during the past 20 years. While intact families registered income gains due to the advantage of having two working mem-

bers, the primary sources of income support for single parents—government assistance programs and the low-skill labor market—eroded significantly. The per capita income of single-parent families fell from 67 percent of that of intact families to 55 percent.

A third factor can be found in the elevated rate of childbearing among younger people, especially those with low education, low skills, and low earnings. Not surprisingly, the nation's population of children has become concentrated in young families, often economically disadvantaged. The children's poverty rate has increased from a par with other age groups in the nation in 1965 to about 150 percent of that level today. The children's poverty rate today stands at over 20 percent.

Finally, due to the rapid rise during past decades in the real level of Social Security benefits, government entitlement resources have become increasingly skewed toward the older population and away from children. By most estimates, the level of public support to children has fallen in real terms. As a result of this shift, the poverty rate of the elderly, which was much higher than the general poverty rate in the 1960s, now stands below that of the rest of the nation's citizens.

Because of this widening gap between children of younger families and members of the older population, the level of intergenerational animosity has increased. The elderly fight tenaciously for the maintenance of governmental Social Security and medical-care benefits. Younger families observe the publicly supported prosperity of older people and they resent it. Citizens, more generally, have come to recognize the declining level of investment in America's children, and have begun to face up to the serious implications of this trend for the future economic performance of the nation.

Can anyone doubt the increasing evidence that the nation is seriously misallocating resources among generations, being provident to older citizens whose working days are largely done, while skimping on young people whose later productivity will determine the nation's economic future? The implications of this for the nation's continued prosperity and for continued harmony among its different generations are serious.

The present versus the future

Consistent with the elderly having done well relative to youth and children, the nation has become more consumption-oriented and less investment-oriented, more concerned with the present than with the future, and increasingly ready to pass along the costs of our current living standards to future generations.

Manifestations of the nation's present-mindedness are ubiquitous. Nearly all the most prominent issues currently on the nation's agenda reflect a concern with neglected investments in our future. The enormous and persistent deficits and the growing debt imply a public sector willingness to borrow from the future in order to support consumption today. The concern with the quality of education at all levels suggests a perception that we have not been paying enough attention to the preparation of our children and youth for participation in a technologically advanced economy. Our savings and investment rates have, in recent years, fallen substantially relative to earlier levels.

From 1950 to 1979 the nation's saving rate averaged between 8 percent and 9 percent of GNP. Since 1980, it has averaged 4.2 percent. We clearly have been unwilling to forgo consumption in order to save and invest in future productivity and output gains. We decry the reduction in the quality of our roads, bridges, and parks. And we marvel at the ability of other nations to construct rapid rail systems and advanced technology communications networks, while we apparently cannot. We collectively judge that environmental degradation has gone too far, a numbing realization that here too we have used our legacy to support current living standards, apparently discounting the implications for our future.

Perceiving the problem, however, is easier than identifying its causes. Tastes—indeed, changing tastes—no doubt play an important role in this overconsumption and misuse of our inheritance. Perhaps we are passing through an era in which self-gratification dominates concern for our children and the world in which they shall live. Patterns of delayed marriage and low birth rates are consistent with this. The desire of women for an established career prior to childbearing, high divorce rates (often carrying painful lessons on the risks of early marriage), and a bleak horizon for income gains in middle age have made early childbearing and family-forming less attractive than it once was. For a variety of reasons, young people have reserved time to fulfill their own desires before entering into more enduring work and personal relationships.

Affluence, too, has played a role. Those at the top of the nation's income ladder, who have done well despite a slow-growing economy, have tended to

engage in more leisure activities than when their incomes were lower. A choice of this nature, almost by definition, involves satisfying immediate desires at the expense of work, diligence, and productivity.

Observers of recent developments in Japan report the dissatisfaction of young people there with a life of long work hours and self-sacrifice in the interests of production. The call for more leisure and consumption grows louder there too. And perhaps perversely, a predictable concomitant of increased leisure is that it is consumed jointly with a variety of goods and services ranging from cars to campers to cruises to cottages. The likelihood that the increased demand for them has squeezed out both saving and investment is strong.

Moreover, the present-oriented nature of our private choices has probably influenced choices made in the public sector. One can see the increasing generosity of Social Security benefits over the past decades as being driven by just such a desire for more consumption in old age.

The implications of this drift toward "present orientation" are not difficult to see. Because investment is the "engine" propelling economic growth, the prospects for rapid future growth are not good. Few analysts forecast a return to growth rates of the sort we experienced in the two decades after World War II. With slow economic growth comes a lower rate of technological change and continued sluggish patterns of productivity improvement. If our performance on these fronts is inferior to that of our competitors, we will continue to prejudice our competitive economic position and our ability to participate in the production of those goods and services that lie on the cutting edge of technological change. Perhaps most discouraging is the fact that our profligacy will tend to saddle our children today, and those yet to be born, with the costs of our consumption.

A recent study estimates that the continuation of our current public-sector policies will require the typical child born next year to sacrifice at least $50,000 of his or her future earnings (in present-value terms) to pay for the present- and consumption-orientation of existing policy.

There can be no doubt that the consumption binge in which we participate will inhibit our future growth and prosperity, erode our international competitive position, and leave a legacy to our children which includes poor prospects for increases in economic well-being. It will leave responsibility for the support of a large and growing pool of nonworking dependents to our children as well as a large bill for the unpaid-for consumption which we have enjoyed.

What role has the federal government played?

In part, the direction taken by the American economy reflects the impact of demographic changes in our own society and international developments beyond our control. However, some of these disturbing trends are our own fault. A significant portion of the responsibility for them must be allocated to decisions made by U.S. citizens, either personally or collectively through the public policies they have implicitly supported. There is little doubt that the federal government by its policies, and the U.S. citizenry by its support of those policies, have been major contributors to the economic malaise we are now experiencing.

In essence, government policy has served as an engine of consumption—not of investment, nor work, nor productivity. It has been a primary source of the intergenerational conflicts in which we now find ourselves embroiled. And it has contributed to the growing inequality in income and wealth.

These are strong assertions, and have to be buttressed with some facts. To support these propositions, I offer a number of examples of policies that, in my judgment, have played an important role.

• The increasing generosity of Social Security benefits and medical-care coverage through Medicare has improved the standard of living of older citizens and stimulated consumption spending by them. A major chunk of this spending has been on health-care services. There is little doubt that the incentives in these programs have encouraged the rapid increase in the demands of older people for health care. These demands must bear part of the responsibility for the uncontrolled rise in the price of medical care. Moreover, these cost increases burden younger working citizens more than older citizens. And since the living standard of the retired elderly has risen by more than that of wage earners, is it any wonder that we see more serious conflicts between the generations?

• The financing of rising Social Security benefits by means of a payroll tax penalizes work and production, and rewards the consumption of leisure. Moreover, the payroll tax is a very regressive tax, burdening middle- and lower-income persons more than those with higher incomes. In sum, it penalizes

work, encourages the consumption of leisure, and increases the spread between the rich and the poor in our society.

• The exemption of fringe benefits from income taxation, in the case of health insurance, subsidizes its provision—in all likelihood, its overprovision—which in turn fosters the use of health-care services beyond the efficient level. In turn, the excess health-insurance coverage so stimulated by this provision increases business labor costs, thereby reducing employment, production, and productivity. Moreover, the exemption primarily benefits higher-income workers, again increasing the spread between the highest and lowest earners in the country.

• The neglect of infrastructure investment (highways, roads, sewers, parks, libraries, community public facilities), and the slowdown in public support for R&D contribute to torpid economic growth and sluggish gains in productivity in the same way that low levels of investment by private firms in plant and equipment inhibit output and growth. The government's neglect of these forms of public investment is part of the packet of policies that neglects investment and fosters consumption.

• The failure to maintain environmental quality has at least three major implications. It means that the prospect of our future enjoyment has been mitigated, that we have been overusing the environment in past production activities without paying its inevitable cost, and that future generations will have to foot the bill for improving the quality of the environment, if this basic aspect of life is to be sustained, let alone improved.

The failure to implement efficient environmental policies implies a public unwillingness to invest in our collective future well-being, to require production activities to bear the costs of the environmental degradation for which they are responsible, and to impose on ourselves—rather than our children—the costs of our own enjoyment.

• Federal tax policy has also contributed to our social and economic problems. I refer, in particular, to capital gains preferences, the subsidies of home ownership, the treatment of some forms of interest expense as a cost of doing business, the enormous reduction in tax rates on high-income people, and the preferential tax treatment of income earned by U.S. companies producing in Puerto Rico and overseas. These measures have fostered the rash of leveraged buyouts which has radically boosted the incomes of financial transactors in the 1980s, subsidized the housing purchases and other consumption of already wealthy citizens, and encouraged the relocation of production facilities to other countries, thereby costing numerous middle-income jobs.

In short, these tax provisions—many of recent vintage—have stimulated inefficient investment, encouraged excessive consumption expenditures, contributed to growing inequality in after-tax income, wage rates and earnings, and have led to serious problems of job loss and displacement in the nation.

• Retrenchment of federal support for urban areas— especially within the central city—is exemplified by the erosion of training programs, housing assistance, support for school facilities, improvements in teacher quality, and education program enrichment. Cutbacks in these areas have contributed to the plight of this nation's worst-off and most vulnerable. It has fostered what some commentators call the "two-tiered" society—rich "mainstream" families living in neighborhoods that are isolated from the abject poverty, homelessness, and destitution experienced largely by racial minorities.

The lapse of governmental investment in central cities—their schools, their workers, their homes— has fostered the growth of urban ghettos, has eroded social cohesion, and has reduced the economic potential of the next generation's work force of minority people.

What sort of policy strategy is now in order?

I have argued that the nation is afflicted with a set of economic ills that involve both serious inequalities and growth-constraining inefficiencies. The nation's inequality problems are draconian, pitting younger workers against older workers, high school dropouts against college graduates, and the 30-year-old unemployed or minimum-wage worker against the 30-year-old living in the suburbs and driving a new car.

The efficiency problems are no less in evidence— slow economic growth, productivity and wage stagnation, deteriorating public infrastructure, an educational system the performance of which is being increasingly questioned, and a work force that must compete in world markets with workers whose pay is but a fraction of its own. Given this constellation of problems, is it even possible to think about designing a single policy program—one package of policies, one set of resource shifts—that could simultaneously contribute to the solution of the nation's

inequity problems, and make the federal government an engine for investment and growth rather than consumption?

While I do not have the answer, I believe that devoting substantial thought to this broad question is a worthy activity. My hunch is that there is a package that would accomplish this, and that it would have as its components some of the items I suggest below. While each component in this package may not, itself, contribute to all the equity and growth goals, I am convinced that the entire package would secure for us both more efficiency and more equity, a more rapidly growing society, and a more cohesive one.

My candidates for inclusion in a national program for growth and equity include the following:

• Increased resources for improved education and skills for today's children, perhaps involving increased attention to apprenticeships and school-work transitions for the non-college bound, in order that we may increase the human capital and productivity of the next generation's workforce, and better match its skills to the jobs created by business.

• A refundable tax credit (or expanded Earned Income Tax Credit) serving as a safety net to those at the bottom of the nation's income distribution, in order that we may reduce the worst of the nation's poverty.

• Increased resources for central city improvements in the areas of crime, drugs, job training, housing, mass transit and health, in order that we may encourage a more even start for today's poor and disproportionately minority children and youths.

• A universal capital account for youths—a fund set up in the name of each child who turns 18 and who graduates from high school—from which withdrawals could be made for purchases of approved education, training, and health investment, in order that we may promote those human capital investments that youths would voluntarily choose if they had the resources.

• A wage-rate subsidy providing higher work-related income to today's youth and younger workers than their current real productivity may warrant, in order that we may give this cohort incentive to work and a cushion against the adversities with which they are saddled.

• An investment tax credit and encouragement to domestic R&D spending, in order that we may provide the incentive for private-sector enterprises to engage in those activities that will promote more rapid economic growth—the main hope of today's younger working-age people.

• Incentives directed at working-age people for increases in private saving, in order that we may finance the additional capital investment required by private businesses, and require working-age people to assume increased responsibility for their own well-being in retirement years.

• A radical revision of the Social Security retirement income program which would turn it into a universal poverty-line benefit program covering all citizens older than, say, 65, in order that we may free up monies to support these other initiatives and to encourage citizens to save while working and to support their own well-being during retirement.

• A carefully crafted estate and inheritance tax, in order that we may recoup for the purpose of these other initiatives some share of the enormous wealth holdings generated in the 1980s and now held by those who will be retiring over the next decades.

• A streamlined federal income tax that would eliminate most of the remaining special provisions, in order that we may encourage efficient private savings and investment decisions, redirect behavior from present-oriented activities toward future-oriented activities, and finance the other resource reallocations included in the package.

• And, if this does not generate enough revenue, a value-added tax of modest proportions.

Unless my perception is inaccurate, a package of this nature would yield the nation a greater degree of equality, increased economic growth, and an investment-oriented public sector. It would also require a larger and more efficient public sector. This last is, in my view, an essential element in working our way out of our current malaise, a prerequisite for securing a productive and equitable society over the next decades.

For some, a larger public sector may be a bitter pill to swallow. Nonetheless, I simply cannot envision a return to rapid economic growth and a taming of the unbridled market's apparent tendency to simultaneously create great wealth and abject poverty without a radically different vision of U.S. domestic policy.

Such a vision requires a public sector that serves as an engine for investment rather than consumption, a public sector that nurtures children and poor people rather than the elderly and the wealthy. It also implies a policy sea-change requiring national political leadership and the public resources to go with it. It requires that those in government again declare that the public sector has a responsibility to foster both growth and equity, and that it act on that declaration.

Cultural Pluralism: Race and Ethnic Relations

America has been referred to as the melting pot of the world because individuals from radically different cultural and ethnic backgrounds have been melded into "Americans." They have largely abandoned their histories, unique cultural heritages, and languages, and they have acquired a common identity. Thus we have Irish Americans, Italian Americans, African Americans, and so on, with the focus being on their common identity as Americans. Thus cultural pluralism has been minimized.

Some argue that this lack of cultural pluralism is what made America strong and that this lack of divisive ethnic, religious, and racial differences promoted unity. As a result, people were not restricted to specific geographic localities by race or ethnicity: they could fit in any area. Even the Civil War was not fought over cultural factors as much as economic ones. The consequences of true cultural pluralism can clearly be seen in the ravaged countries of the former Soviet Union, South Africa, and North Africa.

But some people bemoan the fact that Americans expect new immigrants to become both assimilated and acculturated. Newly arrived immigrants, they argue, should be able to retain most of their ethnic differences without becoming second-class citizens. Diversity is the spice of life and ethnic tolerance the sign of social maturity.

"An American Melting Plot" supports the belief that ethnic and social class differences are divisive and should be actively discouraged. The author argues that volunteerism results in differing social camps, each with its own worldview and stereotypic perceptions of each other. Individuals with alternatives will gravitate toward those choices with the fewest risks and negative consequences. Other individuals will be forced to fight the wars, do the dirty work, and become guinea pigs for the novice physician. The author suggests ways in which ethnic and social class differences can be minimized. Rather than allowing people to volunteer for military service, attend schools they choose, or participate in community service projects, all citizens should be required to participate.

"America: Still a Melting Pot?" examines the impact that the existing immigration policies and immigrants have had and are currently having on the United States. With an economy that is slowing down, unemployment on the rise, overcrowded schools, and increasing demand for taxes to support education, health care, and crime control, can the United States continue to function as the world's safety valve? The emergence of racism, ethnic prejudice, and violence seems to be associated with fears that the new immigrants will take the few jobs that are available.

"Japan's Influence on American Life" has been both dramatic and traumatic. Our perspectives of ourselves, our ways of life, and the American mystique are being assaulted. The ways in which the Japanese have clustered in various communities have resulted in varying degrees of segregation, prejudice, and hostility.

"Is White Racism the Problem?" for all the social ills of black Americans? The answer is no! Focusing exclusively on racism as the source of all social problems for any minority is not only wrong, it is divisive and counterproductive.

Looking Ahead: Challenge Questions

Just what is meant by the concept "cultural pluralism"?

Should America still admit millions of people fleeing poverty, racism, and war?

What implications do our existing immigration policies have for citizens?

Is cultural pluralism a potentially divisive environment, a unifying situation, or an enriching phenomena?

What will be the implications for education when a majority of the residents of the United States do not trace their roots to western Europe? Should the educational curriculum of American schools be altered to reflect the unique makeup of specific communities?

What influence is the "Japanese success" having on the United States and on you? What can the "Japanese experience" teach us about prejudice, discrimination, and race/ethnic relations?

To what degree is white racism responsible for the problems of black Americans?

Just what is meant by "white racism," and what are its origins?

In what unique ways would the three major theoretical perspectives tend to view the issue of cultural diversity?

What major issues, values, rights, obligations, and harms are the basis of race and ethnic issues?

Unit 6

An American Melting Plot

Why whine about our increasing

class segregation? Let's end it

Mickey Kaus

Mickey Kaus is a senior editor of The New Republic
and a contributing editor of The Washington Monthly.
This article is excerpted from The End of Equality,
published by New Republic/Basic Books.

W hat really bothers liberals about American society? Is it that William Gates, the 35-year-old founder of a computer software company, is worth $4 billion, and that some people drive Mercedeses and Acuras while others drive Hyundais and used K-cars? Is it that the wealthiest 40 percent of families receive 67.3 percent of the national income?

Or is it that the experience of confronting degraded beggars is now a daily occurrence for Americans who live or work in our major cities? Is it that a whole class of Americans—mainly poor, black Americans—has become largely isolated from the rest of society and is acquiring the status of a despised foreign presence? Is it that the wealthiest 20 or 30 percent of Americans are "seceding," as Harvard's Robert Reich puts it, into separate, often self-sufficient suburbs, where they rarely even meet members of non-wealthy classes, except in the latter's role as receptionists or repairmen? And is it the gnawing sense that, in their isolation, these richer Americans not only pass on their advantages to their children, but are coming to think that those advantages are deserved, that they and their children are essentially not just better off, but better?

If I'm right, distaste for this second sort of inequality—social inequality—is at the core of liberal discontent. Yet the primacy of this value is only occasionally made explicit in our ordinary political conversations. It is "subliminal" in the sense that it forms the unacknowledged motive of liberal policies that are justified on more familiar rhetorical grounds. Specifically, liberals tell themselves they are for "more equality" of income and wealth, when if they asked themselves, I think, they would probably discover they're actually after social equality—equality of dignity, of the way we treat each other in everyday life.

The point is that money equality isn't the only factor that determines social equality, and it may not be the crucial one. More important, perhaps, are the social attitudes and institutions that determine how much weight the money variable has. But if that's true, why spend all our energies trying to twiddle the dial that produces greater or lesser money inequality? An equally promising approach would focus on changing those attitudes and institutions that translate money differences, however large or small, into invidious social differences.

This is the Civic Liberal alternative. Confronted with vast disparities of wealth, it attempts, not to redistribute wealth "progressively," but to circumscribe wealth's power—to prevent money inequality from translating into social inequality. The primary way it does this is through social institutions that create a second, noneconomic sphere of life—a public, community sphere—where money doesn't "talk" where the principles of the marketplace (i.e., rich beats poor) are replaced by the principle of equality of citizenship. As the pre-1989 Eastern European champions of "civil society" tried to carve out a social space free of communist domination, so Civic Liberals would carve out a space free of capitalist domination, of domination by wealth.

The foundation of this community sphere is the United States is, of course, the political institution of

From *The Washington Monthly,* July/August 1992, pp. 26-32. Excerpted from *The End of Equality* by Mickey Kaus. © 1992 by Mickey Kaus. Reprinted by permission.

democracy. There the marketplace stops, and the rule is not "one dollar, one vote" but "one citizen, one vote." The same principle applies to other important components of our community life, such as public schools, libraries, highways, parks, and the military draft. Each of these institutions attempts to treat all citizens, rich and poor, with equal dignity. They are especially valuable parts of the public sphere because, in contrast with the rather formal and abstract equality of voting, they require rich and poor to actually rub shoulders with each other as equals. So do many other, less obvious but important institutions such as museums and post offices, even parades and softball leagues.

Now, you can argue that money "talks" in our democracy, too, and that it talks even louder these days as politicians depend more and more upon rich donors to fund their increasingly expensive campaigns. Meanwhile, the affluent and the poor no longer rub shoulders in the public schools of even small cities, as the middle class flees to its suburban enclaves or else abandons public education entirely. In bigger cities, the everyday experience of public life in streets, parks, subways, and libraries has been ruined by crime, incivility, and neglect. The draft has been replaced by a volunteer army that the rich can simply avoid.

But these are precisely the sort of things with which Civic Liberalism concerns itself. Instead of worrying about distributing and redistributing income, it worries about rebuilding, preserving, and strengthening community institutions in which income is irrelevant, about preventing their corruption by the forces of the market. It tries to reduce the influence of money in politics, to revive the public schools as a common experience, to restore the draft. And it searches for new institutions that could enlarge the sphere of egalitarian community life.

Not all components of the public sphere have deteriorated in the late twentieth century. The jury system, for example, still brings disparate members of the community together, if only occasionally, in a way that often convinces those who serve that common sense isn't a function of income or race. More generally, the courts still treat a Michael Milken or Leona Helmsley with an inspiring lack of deference. But other institutions have not been so hardy. Let's start with the institution that has deteriorated most dramatically: the military.

There are perfectly good military reasons for replacing the current all-volunteer force (AVF). Some of these reasons are related to social equality. The Gulf war proved that the egalitarian objections to an AVF become loudest at the worst time, just as the prospect of combat and death looms. At the very moment we were trying to intimidate Saddam Hussein in the winter of 1990–91, our country was split by a debate over whether the rich would bear their fair share of the fighting. The only reason the controversy wasn't crippling may have been that the battle turned out to be short, with few casualties on our side.

There are other, more technical problems with the AVF that have less to do with egalitarianism, such as the fact that the pool of young men from which we must buy our volunteers is shrinking (from 8.6 million men aged 18 to 21 in 1981 to an estimated 6.6 million in 1995). But the main justification for a draft remains moral. Volunteer-army advocates rely on the logic of the private sphere, in which everything, even soldiers' lives, is convertible into cash. If some young Americans are freely willing to go into battle for $25,000 a year—well, it's a deal. ("You took the money, now shut up and die," as former Navy Secretary James Webb caricatured the argument during the Iraq crisis.) But it is one thing for society to pay people to pick up its garbage and drive buses. It's another to pay them to risk their necks in battle. If dying in combat isn't outside the economic sphere, what is? The draft is the most natural and—again, because it involves the risk of death—most potent, arena of democratic experience. It doesn't only break down class barriers for a couple of years; it breaks them down for life, in part by giving all who serve a network of military acquaintances that crosses class lines. Even Henry Kissinger used to hang out with his old Army buddies.

A democratic draft is hardly a bold, idealistic step into the future. It's something America has done before. To reinstate it, we don't need new taxes or new leaders—simply a new law.

True, thanks to communism's collapse, the military will only need about 11 percent of America's draft-age men by 1995. But, however modest the manpower needs of the military, a draft is the most socially egalitarian way of meeting them. Even if only 11 percent of men in the upper, middle, and lower classes served—and all the others had to think about serving—it would do more to promote social equality than all the "transfer payments" liberals might conceivably legislate.

Genuine draft

Yet it would be even more effective to involve more than 11 percent, and more than just men—to make the military part of a broader scheme of national service, including civilian service. Here is an idea that separates Civic Liberals from those with other priorities.

"At the age of 18, you should be focusing on your dreams and ambitions, not picking up cans in Yellowstone," sniffs Republican Jack Kemp. For social egalitarians, however, national service is valuable precisely because it would force Americans to pause in their disparate career trajectories and immerse themselves in a common, public enterprise. It is the draft in a weaker dose, more widely dispensed.

The notion of national service was revived in the eighties—to no apparent effect. Universal service was endorsed by Gary Hart, who predicted it "might be the biggest issue" of the decade. Senator Sam Nunn and Rep. Dave McCurdy introduced legislation that would have made federal student aid contingent on one or two years of service. (The Nunn-McCurdy bill went nowhere when the education establishment realized it would supplant existing loan programs.) William F. Buckley distinguished himself from most on the right by calling for a service scheme that would enroll 80 percent of America's youth by means of various "inducements" and "sanctions." Buckley's proposal, too, went nowhere.

For Civic Liberals the overriding goal, of course, is class-mixing. This helps clarify the sort of national service program we're talking about. For example, it excludes Job Corps-type programs designed to help salvage underclass kids through elaborate vocational training. The more national service "targets" the poor, the less it will be seen as a duty for all classes. Nor is the Civic Liberal test of success whether national service participants become less selfish. It's simply whether a large cross section of the population winds up serving together under conditions of equality.

Purely voluntary programs fail to meet this test; the ambitious sons and daughters of upper-class families simply don't sign up. Some national service advocates (like Buckley) nevertheless hope that "incentives" of various sorts might subtly induce participation by the rich. But such financial inducements can still be easily ignored by the wealthy. The only way to guarantee class-mixing is to make national service mandatory. That requires the threat of a penalty harsh enough to be coercive. It could be jail. It could also be a heavy monetary penalty that judges could tailor to fit the financial circumstances of any refuseniks—though it would have to be a potential fine of hundreds of thousands, perhaps even millions, of dollars if it were going to guarantee the participation of the truly wealthy.

A mandatory service scheme would enlist a lot of people—3 to 4 million a year, assuming the plan targeted young men and women of draft age. What would they be doing? Here again, it matters that social equality is the main goal. If we see national service mainly as an antidote to the "culture of selfishness," then the grungier the work, the better. Cleaning up mud slides is just the thing to teach incipient yuppies a thing or two. But the Civic Liberal imperative is to mix the classes, not to beat the selfishness out of them. National service jobs could be enjoyable, even career-enhancing. What's important is that they have a heterogeneous, communal aspect.

There are plenty of worthy tasks that fit this bill. Care for the infirm elderly is probably the most pressing need. Buckley notes that between 125,000 and 300,000 older Americans now living in nursing homes could move back into the "normal community" if there were enough workers to assist them with their daily chores. Those who are incapable of leaving nursing homes often lead lives of brutal loneliness—but the cost of professional attendants is simply too great for the vast majority of American families to bear by themselves.

In strict economic terms, national service is almost surely an inefficient way to help these lonely, old and ill Americans. It would be cheaper (once you count the "opportunity costs" of forgoing all the other things the servers could be doing with their time) to raise taxes to pay for a lot of nurses and handholders. But national service lets us do something in addition to providing services. It allows us to carve out a part of life where the market is negated, where common, nonmarket values that even conservatives like Buckley invoke—fellowship, solidarity, and social equality—can flourish.

There are other needs almost as critical: tutoring the illiterate and semiliterate, helping maintain or patrol public spaces, sorting library books, perhaps assisting in the care of preschool children in day care. As long as the tasks are class-mixing and valuable, a national service would be free to do whatever work the market, for one reason or another, cannot do—whether that work is grungy or exhilarating, and whether or not the government could do it more cheaply some other way.

Unfortunately, an emphasis on the most useful work puts national service on a collision course with public employee unions, which see young draftees as threats to their jobs (the same reason they also fear a WPA-style guaranteed jobs program). The more useful the work, the greater the chance some union member is already doing it.

One solution is to restrict national service to a few concrete tasks of proven utility and practicality. "There are four or five jobs we clearly know how to train kids to do," says Kathleen Kennedy Townsend, who runs a student service organization for the state of Maryland. Her list: teachers' aides, police aides, nurses' aides, a rural "conservation corps" to clean up the environment, plus a similar corps to repair and maintain urban public spaces. Put those together and you probably have enough jobs to keep several million young people usefully employed at a time.

The final question facing any mandatory national service scheme is how to integrate it with the military. That's trickier than you might think. The armed forces, as noted, need only a small fraction of those eligible to serve. What's more, they require stints of service lasting at least two years (otherwise training costs become too high). Requiring two years of civilian service seems a bit much. But one year of civilian service could hardly be treated as the equivalent of two years in the army.

Clearly, military service should count as the fulfillment of any service requirement. Beyond that, young Americans could be given a choice of military or civilian service—but the military's wages would have to be set much higher to compensate for the greater risks and longer tour of duty. Because the rich would be less tempted by such financial incentives than the nonrich, the result would probably be class division, with the military disproportionately poor and the affluent opting to avoid the perils of potential combat.

A better approach, for social egalitarians, would combine universal service with conscription. Teenagers would first be subject to a military draft, with no civilian alternative. If they escaped in the draft lottery, they'd have to do a year of civilian service. This hybrid draft/service setup might well be perceived as fairer than any attempt to allow more freedom of choice at the expense of universal exposure to military risks. Rich and poor teenagers would take their chances in the draft together. If chosen, they would serve together for two years. If they weren't chosen, they would still serve together as civilians for one year.

This sort of service scheme is the most intrusive Civic Liberal strategy; it would interrupt the lives of all Americans. But precisely because it is intrusive, it holds out the possibility of doing for everyone what Joseph Epstein, editor of *The American Scholar*, remembers the peacetime draft did for him: "[I]t jerked me free, if only for a few years, from the social class in which I have otherwise spent nearly all my days. It jerked everyone free. . . ."

Doctored results

Given the continuing threats to social equality, Civic Liberals can hardly be satisfied with restoring the public sphere where it has deteriorated. They need to seize on new possibilities to expand it. Of all the potential new egalitarian institutions on the horizon, the biggest involves the provision of health care.

Health isn't a good like other goods. If somebody can't afford a car, we're willing to say, well, he doesn't have a car. But if a man who can't afford medical care is bleeding on the sidewalk, we are going to provide him with it one way or another, at public expense if necessary. As with the draft, the issue is life or death.

Of course, saying health care should be available to everyone doesn't necessarily mean it must be available in equal measure, or that the experience of getting it will necessarily be one that mixes classes. But the goal of universal coverage offers a solid base for building a potent democratic institution. We know it cements social equality to have Americans attend the same schools and serve in the same army. What effect would it have if they used the same doctors? The experience might not be as intense as school or service, but it would be repeated throughout a person's life.

Certainly universal health insurance seems to play a major socially equalizing role in Western Europe, where every country has some sort of universal national health plan. In most of them, the plan's egalitarianism is a source of fierce national pride. When everyone uses the same system, it not only reinforces "solidarity," it also ensures the quality of care. Upper-middle-class Americans will not tolerate bad treatment for very long (just as they wouldn't have tolerated the Vietnam war if their sons had been drafted).

In the United States, we have a patchwork system that, rather than putting everyone in the same boat, puts different groups in different boats and lets some fall in between. At the bottom, Medicaid covers only about 42 percent of the poor, mainly those on welfare or other mothers with young children. At the top, the revenue code heavily subsidizes generous employer-paid health plans by not counting them as income (a $40 billion tax break). Falling between boats are those who are unemployed, self-employed, or whose employers don't have a company plan. They are left to fend for themselves, to buy private insurance (with after-tax dollars). Between 31 and 37 million people in this group aren't insured at all, and that number has been growing. But if Americans reach the magic age of 65, they can relax. They qualify for Medicare, which will cover most of their bills.

It's not necessarily true that the more "socialized" a system is, the better it satisfies the demands of social equality. The British, German, and Canadian systems all currently meet the goal. The "socialized" British system allows those with money to purchase private insurance, but that doesn't undermine class-mixing because most of the private insurance merely supplements the national health system, where the most advanced, high-tech medicine is still practiced. Only about 10 percent of the population uses the private system (though that percentage is growing).

Germany also manages to include about 90 percent of its population in a single system. The Germans do this by the simple expedient of requiring 75 percent of the population to join one of several "statutory sickness funds." Those with incomes above a certain threshold can opt out, but once they've done so, they can never opt back in. Not surprisingly, most remain with their assigned funds. The system's motto might be, "We have ways of making you stay." An even simpler, more effective strategy can be found in Canada, where it is flat-out illegal to buy basic private health insurance. Canadian waiting rooms mix virtually 100 percent of the population.

But less sweeping plans are less likely to achieve this objective. Senator Edward Kennedy's patchwork employer-based insurance scheme, in particular, looks like a loser for social equality. Medicaid and Medicare would still exist, probably with differential standards of care. Some employers would still provide lavish, fee-for-service insurance; some would consign their employees to spartan HMOs. Taxpayers (most of whom would already be covered, one way or another) probably wouldn't want to pay for much in the way of gap-filling last-resort insurance. We'd still have a system in which different classes report to different waiting rooms.

Even under the most promising plans, the crunch for Civic Liberalism will come when attempts to control the overall cost of health care force some method of rationing ever-more expensive medical procedures. What happens when affluent Americans—*increasingly* affluent Americans—are faced with this rationing? They will not calmly take their place in the queue for CAT scanners or proton-beam accelerators or artificial hearts. They will go outside the "universal" system and pay more money to get the expensive technology they want.

The temptation will be to let them, with the result of producing a two-tier health system of elaborate care for the affluent and basic care for everyone else.

A Civic Liberal strategy would require regulations, such as those in Germany, making it unappealing to opt out of the "universal" system. At the very least a heavy tax disincentive will be necessary. The goal would only be to make enough (say, 90 percent) of the populace use the public sphere's waiting rooms. It's one thing, Civic Liberals could argue, for the rich to be able to buy the nicest cars, or the houses with the nicest views. It's another thing to make it easy for money to buy life itself.

Kids or cash?

Health care isn't the only new public sphere possibility. Day care is another service with impressive potential for growth. The debate over day care has been between those (mainly Democrats) who want to encourage communal day care centers and those (like President Bush) who would simply give cash to parents with preschool kids and let the parents decide whether to use the money to buy day care. Civic Liberals would tend to favor communal centers. Indeed, day care is a public sphere institution offering a unique escape from the tyranny of suburban class-segregation. Unlike schools, day care centers can be conveniently located near places of work rather than near homes. And poor preschool children aren't nearly as threatening to upper-middle-class parents as, say, poor adolescents. Locate the day care centers near work, and let the toddlers of secretaries mix with the toddlers of bank presidents. Let their parents worry together and visit together.

A range of other government institutions—museums, post offices, libraries—at least potentially reinforce social equality by providing services to all citizens. There is an important distinction to be made here—one typically ignored by American admirers of European social democracies—between provision of such common services and the provision of cash. With "in-kind, universal" services, Robert Kuttner notes, people of all classes actually meet and interact with each other and with those doing the servicing. They wait together, flirt, swap sob stories and advice, save each other's place in line, keep an eye on each other's kids. The "middle class is . . . reminded that poor people are human," Kuttner writes. This is the stuff of social equality.

But none of these virtues is evident when all the government does is send out checks—even if, as liberals typically recommend, benefits go to the middle class and rich as well as the poor. Recipients receive their benefit checks in isolation. The cash is spent, and is intended to be spent, in the private, money sphere. No communal experience is involved. On the contrary, the recipient's attention is focused more intensely on the importance of money and what it can buy. How much solidarity is there in cashing a check? Rich and poor don't even cash them in the same places.

Out at third

Civic Liberalism would also recognize and protect the social-egalitarian power of class-mixing institutions that are technically in the "private sector." Particularly important are casual gathering places like taverns, coffee houses, and drug stores. Ray Oldenburg calls these "third places" because they offer an alternative to the other two main sites of our lives—home and work. One essential characteristic of a good third place is that it is accessible to people of all income levels; as Oldenburg puts it, "Worldly status claims must be checked at the door in order that all within remain equals." In the mid-seventeenth century, he points out, coffee houses were actually called "levelers" because they mixed the various classes in a way unheard of in the old feudal order.

It's easy to underestimate the significance of such unpretentious institutions. But they embody much of what Americans feel they've lost since the move from small towns—the general store, the pharmacy soda fountain of *It's a Wonderful Life*, the neighborhood bar romanticized on "Cheers."

The decline of those "private" democratic places is bound up in the process of suburbanization. Zoning changes that allow coffee shops, stores, and taverns to locate near residences, instead of in single-purpose commercial strips, would help. Still, it would be hard for even a nearby neighborhood tavern to mix classes in a neighborhood that is itself segregated by class. Fully restoring third places as class-mixing institutions will have to await the success of longer-term strategies to integrate the suburbs by income, as well as by race.

But some privately operated enterprises that are part of our public life don't rely on class-mixing at the neighborhood level. Organized professional sports are an obvious example. Going to a major league baseball game remains one of the few enjoyable experiences shared at the same time, in the same place, by people of various classes—one reason it's considered so precious. But even the democratic aspects of spectator sports are threatened by a number of recent developments. Attending a ball game has become a distinctly less egalitarian experience, for example, with the unfortunate invention of the tax-deductible corporate "skybox." Team owners now routinely demand stadium renovations that enable them to maximize the square-footage devoted to the rich. Another inegalitarian development is cable television, which allows broadcasters to restrict spectatorship to those who can afford to subscribe. In 1987, most New York Yankee home games were available only on cable. The result was a tremendous protest and a threat of congressional action, in part because large sections of New York—the poorer sections—weren't even wired for cable.

In general, the decline of network broadcasting (and the advent of demographically targeted "narrowcasting" on cable) should disturb social egalitarians. Network TV is often awful, but it once had the virtue of giving all Americans a common, classless set of cultural experiences. As the network audience share declines (it's fallen from 92 percent to 64 percent), that is increasingly no longer true. Instead of everybody watching Milton Berle, young professionals watch the Arts & Entertainment Network while the less cultured tune in to "Married with Children."

But once the egalitarian importance of these private institutions is acknowledged, Civic Liberals will be able to take steps to halt their deterioration. The tax deduction for stadium skyboxes and season tickets could be completely eliminated, for example—not on economic grounds, but on social-egalitarian grounds. Television coverage of sporting events could be regulated to keep it universal, preventing cable companies from buying the rights and then broadcasting only to the cable-ready affluent. If necessary, the sports franchises themselves could be regulated, purchased by municipalities, or even seized by eminent domain. If the TV networks collapse completely, the government could establish a BBC-style network, less snooty than the current Public

Broadcasting System, with a preferred spot on the broadcast spectrum nationwide. These may seem like relatively small things, compared with the draft or national health care. But they matter.

The point isn't that the Civic Liberal reforms suggested above would ensure social equality. That will require something more. The point is that once we set out to rebuild the public sphere, we can make fairly large improvements fairly expeditiously. It requires nothing we haven't done ourselves in the past—or that we can't copy, with appropriate modifications, from other democratic capitalist nations. We can frame our obligations so that rich and poor Americans serve the nation together. We did that in World War II. We did it in the fifties. We can have a society in which the various classes use the same subways and drop off their kids at the same day care centers and run into each other at the post office. We don't have to equalize incomes or make incomes "more equal" or even stop incomes from getting more unequal to do these things. We just have to do them.

America: Still a Melting Pot?

Tom Morganthau

Few Americans remember Israel Zangwill, but he was a transatlantic celebrity in the years before World War I. Poet, novelist, dramatist and political activist, Zangwill was a founding father of the Zionist movement and an ardent suffragist. He knew Theodore Roosevelt, Oscar Wilde and George Bernard Shaw, and he was a prolific, if preachy, writer. Here is a bit of dialogue from Zangwill's greatest hit, a four-act melodrama that opened in Washington in 1908. The speaker is David, a young composer:

America is God's Crucible, the great Melting-Pot where all the races of Europe are melting and re-forming. . . . Germans and Frenchmen, Irishmen and Englishmen, Jews and Russians— into the Crucible with you all! God is making the American!

The imagery comes from steelmaking, which was state-of-the-art technology then. The play is "The Melting-Pot," a phrase that has lived ever since. Zangwill, despondent at the eclipse of many of his political ideals, suffered a nervous breakdown and died in England in 1926. America had already turned its back on his optimism and, in an orgy of blatant racism, virtually cut off immigration. Two generations later, immigration is running full blast—and Americans once again are asking fundamental questions about the desirability of accepting so many newcomers and the very idea of the Melting Pot. They believe, with some justice, that the nation has lost control of its borders. They are frightened about the long-term prospects for the U.S. economy and worried about their jobs. They think, erroneously, that immigrants are flooding the welfare rolls and are heavily involved in crime. And

they are clearly *uncomfortable* with the fact that almost all the New Immigrants come from Latin America, the Caribbean and Asia.

The latest NEWSWEEK Poll reveals the public's sharply shifting attitudes. Fully 60 percent of all Americans see current levels of immigration as bad; 59 percent think immigration in the past was good. Fifty-nine percent also say "many" immigrants wind up on welfare, and only 20 percent think America is still a melting pot.

All this—an incendiary mixture of fact, fear and myth—is now making its way into politics. The trend is most obvious in California, where immigration is already a hot-button issue, and it is surfacing in Washington. Recent events like the World Trade Center bombing, the arrest of Sheik Omar Abdel-Rahman and the grounding of the

---

1600–1776
Seeking greater fortune and religious freedom, Europeans braved the Atlantic to settle in America before the Revolution

---

Golden Venture, an alien-smuggling ship crammed with nearly 300 Chinese emigrants, have revived the 10-year-old controversy about illegal immigration. "We must not—we will not—surrender our borders to those who wish to exploit our history of compassion and justice," Bill Clinton said last week, announcing a $172.5 million proposal to beef up the U.S. Border Patrol and crack down on

visa fraud and phony asylum claims. On Capitol Hill, the revival of an issue that many had thought dead is shaking both political parties, and Democrats such as Sen. Dianne Feinstein of California are scrambling to neutralize nativist backlash. "Some of the people who opposed me totally 10 years ago are now saying, 'What's happening to our country? We gotta do something!' " said Republican Sen. Alan Simpson of Wyoming, a perennial advocate of tougher immigration enforcement. "It's ironic beyond belief. Attitudes have shifted dramatically, and it's coming from the citizens."

This is not the 1920s—a time when most Americans regarded dark-skinned people as inherently inferior, when the Ku Klux Klan marched through Washington in a brazen display of bigotry and when the president of the United States could tell an Italian-American congressman, *in writing*, that Italians are "predominantly our murderers and bootleggers . . . foreign spawn [who] do not appreciate this country." (The president was Herbert Hoover and the congressman was Fiorello La Guardia.) The civil-rights revolution changed everything: it gradually made overt expressions of any ethnic prejudice into a cultural taboo. Almost accidentally, the moral awakening of the 1960s also gave the nation an immigration law that reopened the Golden Door. This law, passed in 1965 with the firm backing of Robert Kennedy, Edward Kennedy and Lyndon Johnson, has slowly led to a level of sustained immigration that is at least as large as that of 1900–1920. It inadvertently but totally reversed the bias in U.S. law toward immigration from Europe, and it created a policy so complicated that almost no one understands it. The policy, in fact, is a mess, whatever one thinks of the desperate Chinese on the

From *Newsweek*, August 9, 1993, pp. 16-22, 23. © 1993 by Newsweek, Inc. All rights reserved. Reprinted by permission.

The Economic Cost of Immigration

IMMIGRATION HAS ranked with corn and cars as a mainstay of American economic growth. The traditional theory is simple: energetic workers increase the supply of goods and services with their labor, and increase the demand for other goods and services by spending their wages. A benign circle of growth uncurls as a widening variety of workers create rising riches for each other. Two hundred years of U.S. history seem to confirm this theory. Yet the perception today is that immigration is a drag on the economy, not a lift. In truth, it's both. "The short-term costs of immigration today are much higher," says Michael Boskin, formerly chief economist to George Bush, "but in the long run, immigrants are still great news for our economy."

The NEWSWEEK Poll shows that 62 percent of those surveyed worry that immigrants take jobs away from native-born workers. That can be true in times of high unemployment. In California, where the jobless rate is 9 percent, immigration is soaring and native-born Americans are actually leaving to find work in other states, some temporary displacement may be occurring. But in normal times, any job loss is more than offset by the creation of new jobs stemming from the immi-

grants' own work. The immigrants' new spending creates demand for housing, groceries and other necessities, and their employers invest their expanding profits in new machinery and jobs. "It is called competitive capitalism," says Tony Carnevale of the American Society for Training and Development, "and it works. It's how America got rich."

Two forces, however, have recently helped to undercut the benefits of immigration: the welfare state and the steep decline in the skill levels of immigrants since 1970. In the last great decade of immigration, 1900 to 1910, public education and a little public health were the only services provided to those migrating to New York and other Northeastern cities. One third of the new immigrants simply failed and moved back home. Today dozens of welfare programs—from food stamps to unemployment compensation—cushion failure and attract immigrants who might otherwise stay home. In California, children born to illegal parents now account for one in eight beneficiaries of one program alone, Aid to Families with Dependent Children (AFDC). The state-run Medicaid program provided $489 million in health care to more than 400,000 illegal aliens last year. Legal aliens got hundreds of millions more.

Donald Huddle, an immigration expert at Rice University, recently calculated that the 19.3 million legal, illegal and amnestied aliens accepted into the United States since 1970 utilized $50.8 billion worth of government services last year. They paid $20.2 billion in taxes. So the net burden on native-born taxpayers was $30.6 billion—a social-welfare cost per immigrant of $1,585. Huddle projects these immigrants will cost taxpayers another $50 billion a year on average over the next 10 years.

A decline in the skills of new immigrants helps to explain these numbers. Ninety percent of current immigrants arrive from Third World countries with income and social-service levels one tenth or even one twentieth those of the United States'. Their education levels relative to those of native-born Americans are steadily declining. So are their earnings. George Borjas of the University of California, San Diego, says that in 1970 the average immigrant actually earned 3 percent more than a native-born American but by 1990 was earning 16 percent less. "Each year the percentage is heading downward," says Borjas. What's more, welfare dependency has steadily climbed and is now above that of native-borns. In 1990, 7.7 percent of native Californians received

public assistance vs. 10.4 percent of new immigrants.

The welfare costs of immigration should dramatically decrease as the California and U.S. economies recover. The long-term benefits of immigrant labor and business enterprise will then be more apparent. But the age of innocence in the American immigration experience is over. The rise of the U.S. welfare state has placed a cushion under the immigrant experience—and diminished the benefits of immigration to the country at large.

RICH THOMAS *with* ANDREW MURR
in Los Angeles

NEWSWEEK POLL

Was immigration a good thing or a bad thing for this country in the past?

59% Good thing
31% Bad thing

Is immigration a good thing or a bad thing for this country today?

29% Good thing
60% Bad thing

Is the U.S. still a melting pot, or do immigrants today maintain their national identity more strongly?

20% Still a melting pot
66% Maintain identity

THE NEWSWEEK POLL, JULY 29-30, 1993

Golden Venture or the young Latinos who scale the fence at Tijuana every night.

Bill Clinton's goal, like that of most defenders of continued large-scale immigration, is to drive home the distinction between legal immigration (good) and illegal immigration (very, very bad). Illegal immigration is undeniably out of control. Congress tried to stop it in 1986 with a law called IRCA, the Immigration Reform and Control Act, which was based on a two-pronged strategy. IRCA

offered amnesty and eventual citizenship to an estimated 3.7 million illegal aliens and, at the same time, aimed at shutting down the U.S. job market by making it illegal for employers to hire undocumented aliens. The act has failed. Despite the amnesty, the estimated number of illegals has once again risen to between 2 million and 4 million people. "For the first two years there was a significant drop . . . because folks thought there was a real law here," says Lawrence H. Fuchs, acting chair of the

U.S. Commission on Immigration Reform. "But the word got out" that IRCA had no teeth, Fuchs says, and the influx resumed. Fuchs concedes that as many as 500,000 illegals now enter this country each year, though he admits it is impossible to know for sure.

The concern over illegal immigration is fueled, in part, by two conflicting fears. Illegals are vulnerable to exploitation by employers and are often victimized—extorted, kidnapped, raped, tortured and sometimes killed—by crimi-

1820–1870
The potato famine of the mid-1840s sent the Irish scurrying to the promised land, while economic depression in Germany triggered an exodus

start a family and invest in the next generation. Immigration is for the young: it takes courage, stamina and determination to pull up your roots, say goodbye to all that is dear and familiar, and hit the long and difficult trail to El Norte. Illegal immigration, with all its hazards, is for the truly daring: the Latino men who wait on Los Angeles street corners, hoping for daywork, have faced more risk than most Americans will ever know.

You can argue, then, that the distinction between legal and illegal immigration is nearly meaningless. Immigrants are immigrants: how they got here is a detail. And, in fact, the arcane system of regulation created by the 1965 law, together with its amendments and adjustments since, implicitly accepts this argument. The law recognizes three reasons to award immigrant visas—job skills, especially those that somehow match the needs of the U.S. economy; a demonstrable reason to seek refuge from war or political persecution, and kinship to an American citizen or a legal alien. This triad of goals replaced the national-origin quota system of 1924, which heavily favored immigrants from North-

nals and smugglers. At the other extreme, in cities like Los Angeles, they flood the labor market and set off bitter competition with American workers and legal immigrants for jobs.

But the real problem is the subversion of U.S. law and policy, and that creates two dilemmas for the federal government. The first is what to do about the undocumented aliens who have made their way into this country since IRCA: another amnesty, obviously, would only encourage more illegal immigration. The second dilemma is worse. There is no particular reason to believe that the current influx of illegals cannot rise from 500,000 a year to 600,000 a year or even beyond. This is conjectural but not necessarily alarmist: as Fuchs says, the word is out. Looking around the world, "one can't find the natural forces that will bring down the flow," says Harvard University sociologist Nathan Glazer. "The first impact of prosperity will be to increase it. Look at China. These people don't come from the backward areas, they come from the progressive parts. As they learn how to run a business, they say to themselves, 'Why not go to the United States and do even better?' "

The same applies to Bangladesh, the Dominican Republic, Mexico or the Philippines. The dynamic, as Fuchs says, is rooted in powerful macroeconomic forces now at work all around the globe—rising birthrates and the conquest of disease, prosperity or the hope of prosperity, even modern telecommunications. (The glittery materialism of American TV shows is now being broadcast everywhere.) Much as Americans tend to regard the new immigrants as poor, uneducated and less skilled, the vast majority are surely enterprising. What they seek is opportunity—the opportunity to hold two jobs that no Americans want, to buy a television set and a beat-up car, to

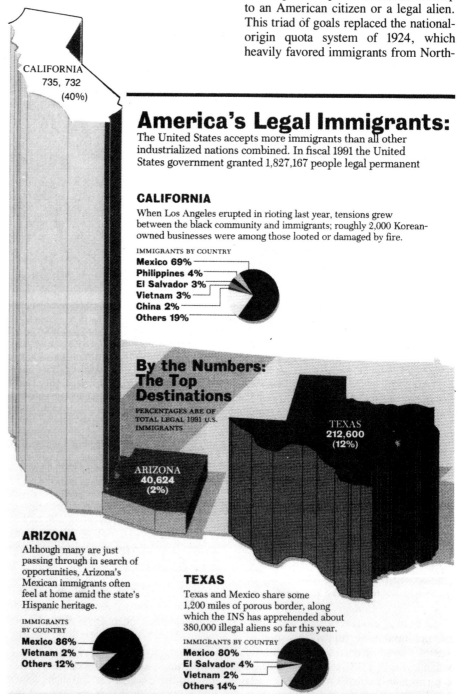

America's Legal Immigrants:
The United States accepts more immigrants than all other industrialized nations combined. In fiscal 1991 the United States government granted 1,827,167 people legal permanent

CALIFORNIA
When Los Angeles erupted in rioting last year, tensions grew between the black community and immigrants; roughly 2,000 Korean-owned businesses were among those looted or damaged by fire.

IMMIGRANTS BY COUNTRY
Mexico 69%
Philippines 4%
El Salvador 3%
Vietnam 3%
China 2%
Others 19%

CALIFORNIA
735, 732
(40%)

By the Numbers: The Top Destinations
PERCENTAGES ARE OF TOTAL LEGAL 1991 U.S. IMMIGRANTS

TEXAS
212,600
(12%)

ARIZONA
40,624
(2%)

ARIZONA
Although many are just passing through in search of opportunities, Arizona's Mexican immigrants often feel at home amid the state's Hispanic heritage.

IMMIGRANTS BY COUNTRY
Mexico 86%
Vietnam 2%
Others 12%

TEXAS
Texas and Mexico share some 1,200 miles of porous border, along which the INS has apprehended about 380,000 illegal aliens so far this year.

IMMIGRANTS BY COUNTRY
Mexico 80%
El Salvador 4%
Vietnam 2%
Others 14%

ern and Western Europe and severely restricted immigration from everywhere else. It is a matter of lasting national shame that Congress, throughout the 1930s and even after World War II, refused to adjust the law to admit the victims of the Holocaust. That shabby record outraged Jews and had much to do with the passage of [the] act of 1965. So did the old law's bias against Slavs, Poles, Italians, the Chinese and the Japanese.

But all three of these goals have been steadily distorted—chipped at, twisted out of shape—by the realities of immigration since 1965. Kinship to U.S. citizens, known as the "family-reunification policy," has become the overwhelming

1880–1920
Persecution and poverty throughout Europe unleashed the greatest flock of immigrants ever; no fewer than 12 million sought refuge here

favorite of visa seekers and the primary reason the pattern of immigration has shifted so hugely to the Third World. It was never intended to be: given the fact

that most immigration to the United States had always been from Europe, those who voted for the act of 1965 generally assumed that family-reunification visas would be used by Europeans. They also assumed that there would be no large increase in immigration to the United States. "Our cities will not be flooded with a million immigrants annually," Sen. Edward Kennedy told a subcommittee hearing. "Under the proposed bill, the present level of immigration [about 300,000 a year] remains substantially the same. . . ."

That is not what happened. Immigration from Latin America, the Caribbean and Asia, a trickle in 1965, has steadily widened so that it now comprises about 90 percent of the total. Legal immigration from 1971 to 1990 was 10.5 million people—but if 3 million illegals are (conservatively) added in, the total is pretty much the same as 1900–1920, the peak years in American history. Owing partly to a further liberalization of the law in 1990 and partly to the IRCA amnesty, the United States now accepts more immigrants than all other industrialized nations *combined*. (Upwards of 80 percent are persons of color: so much for the myth that U.S. policy is racist.) Proponents of further immigration argue that the current influx is actually lower than the 1900–1920 peak when considered as a percentage of the U.S. population. They are right: it was 1 percent of the population then and about one third of 1 percent now. But it is still a lot of people.

Who They Are and Where They Go

residence. Seventy-nine percent of these legal immigrants, looking for everything from freedom to financial opportunity, chose the seven states below as their new homes.

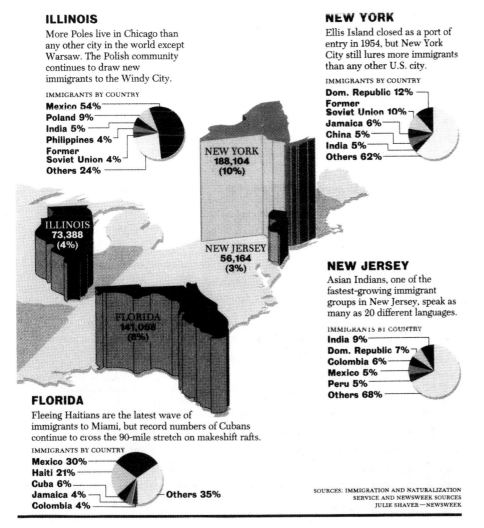

ILLINOIS
More Poles live in Chicago than any other city in the world except Warsaw. The Polish community continues to draw new immigrants to the Windy City.

IMMIGRANTS BY COUNTRY
Mexico 54%
Poland 9%
India 5%
Philippines 4%
Former Soviet Union 4%
Others 24%

NEW YORK
Ellis Island closed as a port of entry in 1954, but New York City still lures more immigrants than any other U.S. city.

IMMIGRANTS BY COUNTRY
Dom. Republic 12%
Former Soviet Union 10%
Jamaica 6%
China 5%
India 5%
Others 62%

NEW JERSEY
Asian Indians, one of the fastest-growing immigrant groups in New Jersey, speak as many as 20 different languages.

IMMIGRANTS BY COUNTRY
India 9%
Dom. Republic 7%
Colombia 6%
Mexico 5%
Peru 5%
Others 68%

FLORIDA
Fleeing Haitians are the latest wave of immigrants to Miami, but record numbers of Cubans continue to cross the 90-mile stretch on makeshift rafts.

IMMIGRANTS BY COUNTRY
Mexico 30%
Haiti 21%
Cuba 6%
Jamaica 4%
Colombia 4%
Others 35%

NEW YORK 188,104 (10%)
ILLINOIS 73,388 (4%)
NEW JERSEY 56,164 (3%)
FLORIDA 141,088 (8%)

SOURCES: IMMIGRATION AND NATURALIZATION SERVICE AND NEWSWEEK SOURCES
JULIE SHAVER—NEWSWEEK

And the law is full of holes. A majority of those who get family-reunification visas (235,484 in 1992) come in with no numerical restriction at all: for them, at least, immigration is a form of entitlement program. Others game the system by forging documents, faking job histories and hiring smart American lawyers to get them eligible for resident visas and green cards. This is known in federal jargon as "adjusting status," and in most years it works for more than 200,000 immigrants. The asylum hustle is the newest wrinkle. By claiming political asylum, would-be immigrants circumvent the normal rules and, because the jails are full, are usually freed to stay and work. Many simply vanish into the underground economy. "We didn't [expect] the asylum problem," says Lawrence Fuchs. "We thought of it as the ballerina in the tutu saying, 'I defect, I defect'."

Immigration policy is simultaneously a statement of America's relationship with the rest of the world and a design for the national future: it is, and probably should be, a mixture of altruism and self-interest. Current U.S. policy contains elements of both—but it is a blurry, heavily brokered policy that has been cobbled together over the decades to reflect the changing fads and competing interests of domestic politics. A purely selfish policy would accept only immigrants who could contribute to economic or social progress. But this idea—awarding visas on the basis of talent or skill—

has always been opposed by organized labor and other groups, and it is a minor feature of today's law, totaling about 140,000 out of 810,000 visas annually. Conversely, providing a haven for refugees is in the best tradition of the American conscience, and the United States has taken a lot of refugees since 1970—1.5 million Vietnamese, Laotians, Cambodians, Cubans, Russians and other oppressed nationalities.

But the vast majority of those who get here are ordinary folks pursuing a better life—and although this, too, is part of the American tradition, the question can and should be asked: What's in it for *us*?

What does all this immigration do for America and Americans? Julian Simon, a University of Maryland economist, says he knows the answer: more immigration means more economic growth—more wealth and more progress for all Americans, period. Pat Buchanan, the talk-show host and erstwhile presidential candidate, has a different answer: more immigrants mean more social friction and the slow erosion of the English-speaking, hybrid European culture we call "American."

There is a third issue as well: how many people, really, can the territorial United States support? Immigration now

Immigrant Schools: The Wrong Lessons

UNION AVENUE ELEmentary school, a dusty sprawl of concrete, asphalt and chain-link fence just west of downtown Los Angeles, bears all the scars of the inner city. Yellow caution signs mark the perimeter: NARCOTICS ENFORCEMENT AREA. RESIDENTS ONLY. In the distance a police helicopter circles over a crime scene. After school, parents anxiously hook their fingers through the fence and wait for their kids to emerge. But because Union Avenue draws from a heavily immigrant neighborhood, its 2,000 students have even more to surmount than the grim realities of crime and poverty. They also face the enormous obstacles, educational and societal, that stand in the way of foreign-born newcomers.

The student body is more than 93 percent Latino. The second largest group is Filipino, at 2.9 percent. A third of the students were born outside the United States, and well over half are not proficient in English. As many as half may be children of illegal aliens. There are as few Anglos as there are Native Americans: six. In the school library there are books in Tagalog, Korean, Vietnamese, Spanish and English. But

not even a third of the faculty can speak Spanish. The others rely on bilingual teacher assistants to translate the lessons. This is an explosive subject here. Many claim that bilingual education has done more to divide teachers than to help Spanish speakers. Defenders see it as a multicultural keystone. The faculty has been Balkanized by bilingualism: at lunchtime the two sides segregate themselves by table.

Most of the newest immigrants come from Central America, and many bring with them the trauma of war. Asked whether he had witnessed much fighting in his hometown of San Rafael, El Salvador, which he left three years ago, fifth grader Angel Alfaro nods but doesn't want to talk about it. Asked about his school and what he would do to fix it, he perks up and says in unaccented English, "Nothing. It's perfect."

The Union Avenue kids' eagerness to please, and to learn, is irrepressible. Yet it is hard to be optimistic about their future. For all of its inadequacies, the school is a relatively calm way station. Most of the kids will go on to Virgil Middle School, where education competes with gangs, graffiti tag-

gers and drugs. Fifth grader Reggie Perez, whose parents are Guatemalan, says he is going to go to a school in North Hollywood "because at Virgil there are just too many gangs." Out of 15 students interviewed last week (the school is in session year round), all but one said their parents were trying to get them into a parochial school or bused to a school in a better neighborhood. Still, most of the fifth graders will end up at Virgil.

Schools like Union Avenue are making a valiant effort. But as a recent report from the Rand Corp. says, "School systems that are beset by debt, declining and unstable revenues, dilapidated buildings and inadequate instructional resources cannot improve simply by trying harder." The federal government has all but ignored the needs of states with large immigrant populations like California, New York, Texas, Florida and Illinois. The single federal program that targets immigrant students is funded at $30 million a year—or $42 per child. In California, where budget tightening has hit specialized programs especially hard, state officials estimate that they are short 8,000 bilingual teachers.

NEWSWEEK POLL

Do you agree or disagree: (percent saying agree)

62% Immigrants take the jobs of U.S. workers

78% Many immigrants work hard—often taking jobs that Americans don't want

59% Many immigrants wind up on welfare and raise taxes for Americans

THE NEWSWEEK POLL, JULY 29-30, 1993

Historically, a solid education has been the quickest road to assimilation. But today, during the greatest surge in immigration since the turn of the century, the schools are failing the 2 million children who have been part of the influx. Their education is isolating them from the mainstream, rather than helping them to join it, and exposing them to all of the pathologies of ghetto life. Meanwhile, as the NEWSWEEK Poll indicates, anti-immigrant sentiment is on the rise. Such a charged atmosphere "doesn't make the job any easier," said Lorraine M. McDonnell, coauthor of the Rand report. The kids, instead of getting the best that their new home has to offer, often get the worst.

STRYKER McGUIRE *in Los Angeles*

produces about a third of U.S. population growth, and projections for the future range from a population of about 383 million in 2050 to 436 million by the year 2090. All of these projections are shaky—based on complex assumptions about birth and death rates as well as immigration policy. Some environmentalists (and many Californians) think the United States should immediately halt immigration to protect the ecosystem and the quality of life. Fuchs says his commission has consulted environmentalists and population experts. "They persuaded us that the population growth is terribly serious on a planetary scale, but not in the United States," he says. "So migration to the United States perhaps has a beneficial effect on the global environmental problem." Still, Congress took no notice of this question when it voted to increase immigration in 1990—and given the wide disparity of current views, picking the "right" number of future Americans is ultimately a combination of taste and guesswork.

1965–1993
The face of immigration has changed over the last few decades, adding non-European cultures, languages and religions to the melting pot

The further question is one that troubles Pat Buchanan and many others: can America absorb so many people with different languages, different cultures, different backgrounds? The answer, broadly, is yes—which does not mean there will be no ethnic friction and does not mean that assimilation is easy for anyone. Assimilation is a generational thing. The first generation—the immigrants themselves—are always strangers in the land. The second generation is halfway between or (kids will be kids) rejects the immigrant culture. The third generation is hyphenated-American, like everybody else, and begins the search for Roots. The tricky part, which worries Fuchs considerably, is that America's "civic culture" is unique in all the world. It is the belief, as embodied in the Constitution and our political tradition, "that it is individual rights, not group rights, that hold this country together." So here is the question for all of us, native-born and immigrant alike. At what point do policies like affirmative action and minority-voting rights stop being temporary remedies for past injustices and start being permanent features of the system? The whole concept of group rights, as Fuchs says, is tribalism—the road to Bosnia, not East L.A. And that, surely, is not what Israel Zangwill had in mind when he described America as the crucible of a new civilization.

With ADAM WOLFBERG and BOB COHN in Washington, ANDREW MURR in Los Angeles and bureau reports

JAPAN'S INFLUENCE ON AMERICAN LIFE

There's more to it than team building and sushi. The Japanese are changing Americans' self-image—and inspiring an urge to learn.

Stratford P. Sherman

REMEMBER when America was the greatest country in the whole wide world? After World War II a euphoric sense of supremacy—*No. 1, by God, and proud of it!*—seemed the birthright of U.S. citizens. But the feeling has faded, and even the whipping America gave Saddam Hussein couldn't quite bring it back. The changed mood accompanies a new respect for the Japanese, who rose to mastery and power while Americans were horsing around with LBOs, credit cards, and cocaine.

Suddenly, all around the U.S., Japanese are settling in as neighbors, classmates, and employers—over 200,000 at last count, with more coming all the time. Many are executives whose decisions affect thousands of workers. Unlike earlier arrivals on these shores, these people have no intention of becoming Americans. They

REPORTER ASSOCIATES *Mark D. Fefer and Jung Ah Pak*

come not as immigrants, but as expatriates—and conquerors.

Japan has much more to offer than the business ideas, such as just-in-time manufacturing, that already have altered the habits of many U.S. corporations. What most Americans don't yet see is Japan's deeper effect on their society. The barriers of language and race are formidable, and Japanese expatriates often seem more eager to fit in than impose their culture on the U.S.

But buy a round of drinks for the patrons at Rumors, a dimly lit bar on the outskirts of Lexington, Kentucky, and they'll talk your ear off about Japan's growing influence. The bar is a few miles down the road from Toyota's Georgetown plant—where 68 Japanese, 3,650 Americans, and a whole lot of robots build the Camry sedans that J.D. Power & Associates rates as the nation's top-quality auto. Rumors is a

blue-collar hangout where customers keep their caps on while they drink—beer, mostly, and Seven-and-Seven. Country-western music videos play on the cable TV; tacked to a rafter over the bar is a bumper sticker with an American flag that reads TRUCKERS FOR THE TROOPS.

These country boys aren't about to start wearing kimonos, but they are remarkably cosmopolitan and aware. Bartender Sam Thurman, 31, who wears one earring, a black T-shirt, and shorts emblazoned with the words "Rude Dogs," is a house framer by trade who works at Rumors to evade unemployment. "The Japanese come in here sometimes," he says. "They're down-to-earth people, and they've proved that they have a lot of good ideas." Counters Buck Arnett, 31, a union pipefitter who was working 60-hour weeks at a Dow Corning plant before being laid off in April: "I don't

From *Fortune,* June 17, 1991, pp. 115-116, 118, 120, 122, 124. © 1991 by The Time Inc. Magazine Company. All rights reserved. Reprinted by permission.

like the Japs." But when asked why Japan so often bests America in business, Arnett doesn't flinch: "It's our own damn fault." The others all nod and raise their brewskies in agreement. "Hell, yes!" they say.

THAT RECOGNITION represents a turning point for grass-roots America. Says David Halberstam, whose book *The Reckoning* explored U.S.-Japanese competition in autos: "It's the end of an illusion we've had since the Battle of Midway, that if America does it, it's the best." Now Americans are asking themselves why they can't do as well as the Japanese.

When folks in Kentucky and elsewhere first saw Japanese companies clobber their U.S. counterparts years ago, many reacted as if the Japanese had landed from Mars, equipped with some kind of extra-smart mutant genes. But as greater numbers of ordinary Americans meet Japanese face to face, many respond just like Barbara Tinnell, 26, a team leader at the Toyota plant, who has spent six weeks in Japan on training tours. Says she: "From how good they're doing you almost expect the Japanese to be superior people—but they're not different, really." Perceptions like hers are priceless because they imply a responsibility to measure up.

But how? Americans like Tinnell are finding one answer in the Japanese management practice of *kaizen*, or continuous improvement—and in the enthusiasm for learning that is the real force behind it. Japan's towering achievement in manufacturing is the sum of countless small advances by individual workers and companies. For Americans raised to regard learning as something that happens in school, that is a profoundly new way of looking at things.

The 1987 film *Tampopo* illustrates the Japanese attitude. The picture (available on videocassette) tells the story of a widow who runs an unsuccessful noodle shop. Inspired by a customer's fierce criticism, she painstakingly masters the art of making *ramen* soup. That's all there is to the plot, but it plays like an adventure. How different from, say, *Rocky*, in which the hero spends most of the time bulking his biceps.

JAPANESE-STYLE learning typically involves lots of personal contact. For Americans, there is now more opportunity to meet people from Japan than ever before. Japanese companies currently employ over 400,000 people in the U.S. Some 35,000 Americans are taking college-level courses in Japanese, and enrollment continues to rise. Over a million Americans visited Japan in 1990, 40% more than five years ago, while three million Japanese sojourned in the U.S., mostly as tourists or students.

Japan's expatriates are spread all over the U.S. More than a third live on the West Coast, particularly in California, where 20% of all Japanese-owned U.S. factories are located. Roughly a quarter have gathered in New York City and nearby suburbs. The rest are scattered in smaller groups from Wyoming to Georgia, where Yamaha makes golf carts. The Japanese Chamber of Commerce of Georgia has almost 300 members.

In California, where the influx of Asian peoples began more than a century ago, the influence of Japanese expatriates is diluted and blurred. They compete for attention with newcomers from countries as diverse as Cambodia and Peru, and with a large and well-assimilated population of Americans of Japanese descent. To see signs—often contradictory—of what lies ahead, one must go to towns like Fort Lee, New Jersey, and Georgetown, Kentucky, where, in an atmosphere of awkward affability, Japanese and Americans are learning to live together.

A disproportionate number of the Japanese expatriates around New York City have gathered in a couple of suburbs. In Fort Lee, across the Hudson River from Manhattan, Mayor Nicholas Corbiscello remembers the day when the only Asians he saw there were the people who pressed his shirts. Now 15% of the students in the public schools are citizens of Japan. That figure understates the Japanese presence, since many of the children transfer to Japanese schools in New York City after fifth grade.

"I don't think there's any question that the Japanese will change America. I've seen a change right before my eyes," says Alan Sugarman, Fort Lee's superintendent of schools. He is a fervent believer in multiculturalism, the idea that ethnic groups can no longer be expected to abandon their distinctiveness in the traditional melting pot: "We can't stampede newcomers into being Americans anymore." But that's okay, he says. The Asian kids' diligent study habits set the standard for everyone else, leading American students to work harder. Achievement scores in Fort Lee are rising, and 90% of high school graduates go to college, vs. 75% in the mid-Seventies.

Japanese and American cultures often clash. That is the case in Scarsdale, New York, where a fifth of public-school students are from Japan. Unlike Fort Lee, which includes diverse ethnic and immigrant groups, Scarsdale is wealthy, homogeneous, and somewhat stunned from the sudden influx from Japan. American and Japanese adults there lead mostly separate lives, in part because the expatriate group is large enough to sustain itself. Like U.S. expatriates of an earlier era, who earned the epithet "Ugly Americans" by herding together in ignorance of local ways, the Japanese are most comfortable with one another.

THE CHILDREN have no choice but to meet and compete at school. A college sophomore, who says he didn't often speak to the Japanese while at Scarsdale High, draws this broad lesson from his experience: "Racial tension between Asians and Americans is just inevitable." Principal Judy Fox is trying hard to promote harmony: Scarsdale High is preparing a course in Japanese language and culture, has put Japanese-English dictionaries in every classroom, and hired "bias-reduction consultants," who encourage students to talk out their differences.

The efforts, though well intended, have yet to bear fruit. "I don't think students here know much about Japanese culture, considering how many Japanese are here," remarked senior Jimmy Zednik, 18, who said he had spent a year in Yokohama. Indeed, a recent visit to the school— during an "International Day" festival, as it happened—suggests that only a few American students mingle with the Japanese.

The kids gathered in the gym at lunchtime to sample foods of their ancestral lands, from Africa to Korea. The U.S. table, offering pretzels, potato chips, and brownies, attracted almost nobody, while the Japan table, serving noodles and sushi, was mobbed. But when Americans and Japanese sat on the floor to eat, they stayed apart. Asked about the apparent conflict, an American girl gestured to a nearby Asian, saying, "*She's* my friend." Replied the Asian: "Yeah—but I'm not Japanese."

Across the room, a group of young Americans eagerly confessed their racist feelings to a visitor, all the while chowing down on Japanese food. Their bluntest remarks don't deserve to be printed, but the sources of their anger are plain. "They're smarter than us," said one, pointing with his chin to some nearby Japanese. Added another: "You hear your parents talking about how they're taking over."

A few feet away, Futa Sakamoto, a ninth-grader, sat with a group of Japanese. He said he does mix with Americans but wishes his schoolmates were more friendly: "*We'll* change, but the Americans don't want to." Part of the trouble, his companions acknowledge, is the language barrier that encourages the Japanese to stick together. Yoshi Ito, 15, gratefully remembered his experience as one of the few Japanese in an American summer camp: "It was very nice to be alone. If there were more Japanese people there, I wouldn't learn."

JAPANESE companies in the area are catching on to the problem. Hitachi, for one, now advises expatriate employees to spread out instead of congregating in the U.S. equivalent of the foreigners' ghettos that Japanese disdainfully call *gaijin mura*. The company also suggests that they take part in community activities, and the Japanese know how to take a hint: Yasushi Sayama, who was general manager of corporate administration before returning to Japan a few months ago, joined a local Lutheran church, even though he's not Christian.

Compared with the tensions of Scarsdale, multiculturalism comes easy in the beautiful state of Kentucky. For one thing, there aren't that many Japanese living around Georgetown or nearby Harrodsburg,

WHY MADONNA ISN'T JAPANESE

Ardent consumers of American popular culture, the Japanese have been largely unable thus far to enrich it. Sure, U.S. children play Nintendo and read Japanese-influenced comics like *Usagi Yojimbo*, which chronicles the adventures of a samurai rabbit. Rare is the American who doesn't own a Japanese VCR, Walkman, or car. And yes, Japanese cuisine is winning converts: According to Kenji Kishimoto of Suntory, which sells its beer in the U.S. mostly in Japanese restaurants, the States boasts roughly 3,500 such eateries. That's 40% more than in 1980, but so what? Even *Wendy's* has that many outlets.

In U.S. pop culture, Japanese ideas seem to succeed only when watered down. Ninjas are big, but you'd have to go into some kind of trance to find much Confucian thought in *Teenage Mutant Ninja Turtles II*. The last Japanese tune to reach *Billboard*'s hit parade was "Sukiyaki" in 1963. (Idiotically named for the U.S. market, it was actually about love, not lunch.) Hollywood has lavishly honored director Akira Kurosawa, whose film *Ran* was Japan's biggest U.S. box-office hit. Total ticket sales? Only $7 million, about what it costs to lure Jack Nicholson out of bed.

Nor has Japanese culture made major inroads into ordinary consumer marketing. Smith & Hawken, a specialized mail-order house, does well with Japanese garden tools. But despite a recent plug on *thirtysomething*, the highbrow Signals catalogue has sold only a few hundred of the desktop Zen rock gardens it offers for $45 each. Kellogg has introduced what it calls an "Oriental cereal" named Kenmei with a bold ideogram on the box meaning grain plant. The stuff is like Rice Krispies minus the snap-crackle-pop, and it isn't making much noise in the marketplace, either. Perhaps wisely, ads for Anheuser-Busch's successful Bud Dry beer don't mention that the lengthy dry brewing process, which causes extra fermentation, comes from Japan.

In time, all this may change. The trendy young tastemakers in New York and L.A. went Japanese years ago. They're drawn to artists like Masami Teraoka and fashion designers like Rei Kawakubo, who sells $100 million of clothing annually under her Comme des Garçons label. They admire the thoughtful spareness of Japanese design—and the way things work in America, that means someday you probably will too.

where Hitachi makes auto parts. Of that factory's 490 employees, only 14 are Japanese. The expatriates—managers and engineers—seemed to fit right in while eating lunch at the local Pizza Hut.

The other great difference here is that the Japanese provide a powerful boost to the Kentucky economy, and the Americans likeliest to meet Japanese are those who work for them. In this unprosperous corner of the world, people are thankful just to hold a job.

The Japanese are shrewd employers. In Kentucky, which lost many sons in World War II—Harrodsburg has a memorial to victims of the Bataan death march—the Japanese hire mostly young people with no memory of that war and little chance of finding a better job anywhere else. The Japanese can be more de-

manding than boot-camp drill instructors, but they pay well and reward outstanding performance. And the plants make products that sell, which translates into pride and job security for workers.

Some become enthusiasts. Dean Lee has been promoted twice in his three years at Hitachi; only 27, he manages the plant's production planning. An intelligent man who holds a degree in industrial technology from Morehead State University, Lee sounds like a Moonie when he says, with conviction, "We're an American company"—as if Japanese ownership and management counted for nothing.

Working for Hitachi, he says, "has just changed me totally." Among the lessons learned from his employers: patient deliberation in making decisions. Instead of just buying a car this year, Lee pondered his choices for four months before settling on a Mercury, which, he notes, uses Hitachi parts. He recently sold his house but plans to rent an apartment and carefully consider his options before buying again.

John Beets, 35, a Toyota team leader, learned a lot by observing the Japanese at play. "They know how to relax," he says, "but a party or a golf game with them lasts two or three hours at the maximum—then the schedule kicks in and they go off somewhere else. Now I tend to set schedules for myself more. I make sure I have flexibility but also try to get something done at certain points along the day."

FOR Karen Satterly, 24, a born-again Baptist who assembles circuitboards at Hitachi, the lesson is more personal. In her high school she says many Americans felt inferior to their few Japanese schoolmates, the offspring of expatriate managers. When she joined Hitachi, she felt uncertain of her ability to meet the company's standards. "The Japanese are such particular people," she explains. In time Satterly learned how to make the parts the precise way her employers want them. She's proud of her work now, and of herself. "I think a lot of people feel inferior, and that tends to make them a little mean," she says. "That's just something they have to overcome."

Experiences like these are the essence of Japan's influence in America: an accumulation of personal discoveries, small in themselves, that could add up to something big.

Is White Racism the Problem?

Arch Puddington

ARCH PUDDINGTON, a former aide to the late civil-rights leader, Bayard Rustin, writes frequently on race relations. He works for Radio Free Europe-Radio Liberty in New York.

A CONSPICUOUS feature of the commentary on the recent Los Angeles riot was the many comparisons between racial conflict in America and the most murderous ethnic strife abroad. More than once, Los Angeles was likened to Yugoslavia, and frequent parallels were drawn between conditions here and in South Africa, with neighborhoods like South-Central Los Angeles identified as the American version of Soweto. Ethnic and religious hatred in the Middle East was also invoked. The British *Guardian* headlined one article, "Beirut in L.A."; inevitably, black neighborhoods were portrayed as similar to the West Bank, with blacks cast as America's Palestinians, and the riots characterized as a black *intifada*.

Some black political figures, particularly Jesse Jackson and Maxine Waters (who represents South-Central L.A. in Congress), referred to the riot as a rebellion, with the implication that the rioters should be regarded as the heroes of a struggle against despotism. Yet the black mobs who beat into senselessness white motorists who had strayed into the wrong neighborhoods were not participating in a rebellion; and most of the victims of the killing, burning, and looting were members of their own race. As for those engaged in the looting, it was difficult to believe that they were telling us anything other than that human beings will often yield to temptation if there appear to be no sanctions involved.

Of course, the commentators who drew comparisons between the Los Angeles disorders and conditions in other distressed corners of the globe had in mind the political similarities as well as the physical ones. But the view of an America plagued by a racial conflict as lethal as the struggle pitting Serbs against Croats or the Hezbollah against Maronite Christians cannot long be sustained.

To begin with, whites here are not killing blacks; less than 3 percent of wrongful deaths in 1990 involved white assailants and black victims, half the percentage of cases where blacks were the assailants and whites the victims.

Nor are American whites unmoved by cases of racial injustice. By overwhelming majorities whites expressed bewilderment and outrage over the not-guilty verdict rendered in the case of the four white Los Angeles police officers accused of beating a black man (Rodney King), the incident which triggered the riots in L.A. and several other cities. Whites might not have been ready to label the residents of Ventura County, where the trial was held, as reactionary white suburbanites (in the words of a black California politician, Willie Brown). But there was certainly a willingness to accept the proposition that blacks are treated less fairly than whites by the criminal-justice system, even though whites are aware of the high rates of black crime.

Nor is it accurate to accuse white Americans of complacency about the plight of the black poor. Many may believe that affirmative action has elevated blacks to the status of a preferred class, but most recognize that blacks are more likely than other groups to be afflicted by poverty, inadequate medical care, and a multitude of other such problems.

A more accurate statement is that Americans have suffered from a lack of leadership on racial matters, from both the Right and the Left. The Left's shortcomings were on display in black political leaders like Representative Ron Dellums and Jesse Jackson, who responded to the riots by demanding massive transfers from the military budget to the inner city, attacking foreign aid and free-trade policies, and issuing silly declarations about the bailout of the savings-and-loan industry. There was also the spectacle of Representative Waters assuring America that she did not condone violence and looting, and then, again and again, coming perilously close to doing just that.

Conservatives, on the other hand, were left with no credible response to the repeated references by liberals to "twelve years of neglect" under Presidents Reagan and Bush. For there was no denying that both of these administrations gave every sign of obliviousness to the racial problem and in the process reinforced the impression that conservatives simply do not care much whether blacks succeed or not.

Reprinted from *Commentary*, July 1992, pp. 31-36, by permission. All rights reserved.

FOR some commentators, finally, responsibility lay not with American leadership but with America itself. They were convinced, in other words, that America is a thoroughly racist society—that racism, and not the failure of this or that program, or the policies of this or that administration, is the source of the seemingly intractable problems of the inner-city black poor.

Charges of racism have, of course, been hurled about quite promiscuously in recent years, with the result that many Americans see it as one of those political terms which have been stripped of meaning through misuse by demagogues. Recognizing this, those who attributed the Los Angeles events to white racism usually refrained from the kind of generalized indictment of American society that was routinely voiced during the 1960's. Instead, they focused on specific institutions, such as the Los Angeles Police Department, the criminal-justice system, or the banks (for their reluctance to provide loans to inner-city businesses).

There was, however, at least one voice prepared to blame the riots on the bigotry of individual whites and the racism of American institutions: Andrew Hacker, the white political scientist whose controversial book, *Two Nations: Black and White, Separate, Hostile, and Unequal*, was published just a few weeks before the riots.* *Two Nations* was already on the best-seller lists when the Los Angeles riot broke out, and it climbed steadily in sales thanks to the consequent revival of concern over the country's racial troubles.

The thesis of *Two Nations* is set forth in the very first paragraph. Race, Hacker tells us, "has been an American obsession since the first Europeans sighted 'savages' on these shores." While the American Indians would eventually be "subdued" or "slaughtered," the importation of African slaves would ensure a permanent racial crisis for the new society. Today, the fact that America was once a slave-owning society "remains alive in the memory of both races and continues to separate them." "Black Americans," Hacker adds, "are Americans, yet they still subsist as aliens in the only land they know." Thus America is in reality "two separate nations," where blacks "must endure a segregation that is far from freely chosen."

These phrases resonate with the apocalyptic language used in 1968 by the National Advisory Commission on Civil Disorder in what became popularly known as the Kerner Report. In its most frequently quoted passage, the Kerner Report declared that America was becoming "two societies, one white, one black—separate and unequal," and placed the burden of responsibility for this development on "white racism."

The Kerner Report's long-term effect on social policy is debatable. Without doubt, however, the report had the unintended consequence of alienating many whites from the civil-rights agenda. These whites interpreted the more pointed Kerner formulations as blaming them for the rash of riots which had engulfed the nation's major cities, and they reacted with predictable indignation. Some black leaders also found the report unfortunate insofar as it focused attention on the psychology of individual whites rather than on the source of black economic inequality.

Yet Hacker is even more insistent than the Kerner Report was about the racism both of individual Americans and American institutions. He damns everything from the police to the schools to corporate executives to popular culture as complicit in a regime of racial subordination—a condition, he asserts, which exists because that is the way whites want it.

In addition, then, to echoing the Kerner Report, Hacker's analysis—for all the concise, matter-of-fact, dry prose in which it is couched—pulsates with the spirit of the radical 60's, when New Left and Black Power ideologues discovered systemic bias throughout American life. Hacker even betrays an attraction for the kind of theorizing which gained currency during the sourest period of racial radicalism and urban chaos. He is, for example, attracted to the young Eldridge Cleaver's ruminations about rape as an instrument of political revenge against white society, along with the late James Baldwin's proposition that whites "need the nigger"—that is, that whites have a stake in seeing blacks as inferior, in order to bolster their own illusion of racial superiority.

In general, Hacker uses racism the way Marxists use class oppression, as a ready-made explanation for all social phenomena, a sterile approach preordained to reach the gloomy, if sensationalistic, conclusion that racial progress will invariably be thwarted by a white majority living in constant dread of challenges to its supremacy.

TAKE Hacker's discussion of income inequality. He begins by noting that while whites have always earned considerably more than blacks on average, the income gap did narrow by a substantial amount in the three decades before 1970. The most pronounced improvement occurred in the years 1940-59—a period when Jim Crow prevailed in the South, where most blacks then lived, and when thousands of blacks were finding employment in the industrial centers of the North and Midwest. But since 1970, Hacker notes, the racial gap has narrowed hardly at all.

The trends emphasized by Hacker would seem to substantiate the conclusions of the sociologist, William Julius Wilson, that the failure of blacks to continue their march toward income parity stems primarily from their having been disproportionately hurt by the decline in industrial employ-

_____
* Scribners, 258 pp., $24.95.

ment. But this theory clashes with Hacker's basic argument which traces inequality to racism and racism alone, and so he does not dwell on it. Likewise, he conveniently ignores the fact that working-class Americans of all races have suffered income stagnation during the past twenty years, another trend which challenges his book's main premise.

Nor is Hacker drawn to the idea that blacks should emulate the model of recent immigrant groups by seeking economic advancement through small businesses sustained by dawn-to-dusk hours and the mobilization of entire families. Hacker recognizes that during the period of legal segregation black-owned businesses often served black neighborhoods, but he seems to sympathize with the position now taken by many blacks that, having lived in America for generations, they should not have to make the sacrifices which newcomers are compelled to make. Hacker adds that whites themselves are less likely to engage in small business than such groups as Koreans, Japanese, and Cubans, and for this reason should refrain from passing judgment on blacks for their lack of entrepreneurial enthusiasm.

From just about every perspective, this is a thoroughly insidious argument, guaranteed to feed the flames of ghetto defeatism. Yes, there are whites who preach unappetizing sermons which counterpose the achievements of Asian immigrants to the failures of the black poor. Yet whites are still twice as likely as blacks to own their own businesses, and in any case whites are not confronted by the kind of economic crisis which now afflicts generation after generation of inner-city black poor.

Blacks, of course, do face certain hurdles to successful business ownership, and where government can assist in lowering these barriers, action should be aggressively taken. But part of the problem clearly involves the negative attitudes of young blacks not merely to business ownership but to the entire world of work.

To be sure, these attitudes are not shared by all or even most black males; we are, after all, familiar with the pictures of thousands of workers, mainly black, lining up to apply for a handful of positions at the post office or the assembly-line plant. There is, however, another image, one highlighted in an illuminating post-riot *MacNeil-Lehrer* segment, in which a group of young male Harlemites had no hesitation in telling an interviewer of their unwillingness to accept jobs advertised at a local placement office because the pay was too low.

Here, we were informed, was a graphic example of the dilemma confronting young black men whose employment opportunities were limited to "dead-end jobs." Yet it was not pointed out—it seldom is—that historically people without much education have very often started out at precisely such dead-end jobs, acquired a respect-

able work record, and then moved on to better-paying positions in other fields.

Even today, according to a recent study, 90 percent of those applying for new taxi-driver licenses in New York are foreign-born; and only a portion of the 10 percent who are native-born is black. Now, driving a taxi may not be the most lucrative job in the world, but it is not the kind of minimum-wage position which black men often deride; in many ways, it is an ideal transitional job for young men without a clear sense of what they want to do with their lives. Racial discrimination is not a problem, and hiring standards are far from stringent. Here, one would think, is an occupation ready-made for heavy black participation. That this is not the case inevitably raises questions about black male attitudes toward the world of work that Hacker, for one, does not even begin to deal with.

Yet this issue must be placed on the table, along with institutional racism, prejudice, and the changing nature of the economy, if the full and frank discussion about race advocated by Hacker and others is to be conducted.

One likely outcome of such a discussion might be the discovery that black attitudes are strongly conditioned by the repeated stress on the black community as the helpless victim of white society. Blacks like the writer Shelby Steele and the community activist Robert Woodson have argued persuasively that blacks cannot move forward as long as they see themselves in this way, since it leads to passivity, resentment, and demoralization. Hacker, by contrast, regards victimhood as the defining feature of American blacks, and in a self-defeating vicious circle dismisses any emphasis on personal responsibility and self-discipline as merely the latest weapon in white America's ongoing project of racial humiliation.

HACKER'S approach to the critical question of out-of-wedlock births is even more shocking than his treatment of employment. Thus, he makes much of the fact that over the past several decades there has been a proportionately higher increase in unmarried parents among whites than among blacks, the point being that whites have no standing to sermonize about the structure of the black family. Hacker may consider this an effective debater's point, but it is irrelevant, or worse, to any serious examination of the dynamics of black poverty, and is a piece of blatant evasion from a writer who takes pride in candor and plain speaking.

For one thing, there remains a huge difference in the proportion of single parents among blacks and whites. More to the point, a phenomenon which for whites represents a serious but containable problem is for blacks something truly catastrophic, as can be seen by reading the biographies of the teenagers who kill other teenagers over something so trivial as who was first in line at a fast-food restaurant. Almost always, the assailant is a black boy who knew his father fleetingly, if at all.

Hacker is just as bad on the question of education as a vehicle for racial progress. He suggests, correctly, that there is a genuine clash between the goal of employing more black teachers and the challenge of strengthening national educational standards. In states which have devised tests to measure teacher competence as part of a reform package, white teachers have consistently and by wide margins outperformed blacks. In a typical situation, 75 percent of a state's white teachers will pass competency tests, as compared with 45-50 percent of black teachers. In one state, Louisiana, the rate for whites was 78 percent; for blacks, it was a dismayingly low 15 percent—meaning that white teachers were five times as likely to achieve a passing mark.

Hacker's analysis of scores on the Scholastic Aptitude Test (SAT) also makes for disturbing reading. On this examination, so critical for college admission, blacks lag not only behind whites, but behind the sons and daughters of recent immigrants from Asia and Latin America. This is true even when the comparison is limited to low income immigrants whose mastery of English is weak. In 1990, whites and Asians scored some 200 points higher than blacks on average, a huge difference. Hispanic students scored almost 70 points higher, even though their income levels were about equal to those of blacks, even though a similarly low percentage of their parents had attended college, and even though two-thirds of them described English as their second language.

It has, to be sure, been argued—and Hacker appears to agree—that the SAT is culturally biased against blacks. But he adds the intriguing observation that it is not so much "white" values which are reflected in standardized examinations as values which demonstrate a familiarity with the skills necessary to cope with the modern world generally. These modern skills and ideas may have had their origin in the United States and Europe, but through the globalization of the economy and the spread of mass communications they have by now filtered through to what was once known as the third world. It is this transnational flow of values, Hacker contends, which accounts for the impressive performance of recent immigrant children on American standardized tests.

The unsettling implication of this analysis is that within black America there is a generation of young people totally unprepared for modern economic competition. Is this, as Hacker insists, due to white racism? Or are there other causes—sensitive factors relating to the culture of inner-city life—which must eventually be addressed? How does Hacker's one-track explanation square with the fact that the earnings of black women have reached over 90 percent of average white female earnings? Or with the fact that college-educated black women earn *more* than comparably educated white women?

In times past, even during the pre-civil-rights period, urban blacks moved rather easily into the job market—the private job market, it should be stressed, since it has only been in recent times that blacks have been heavily represented in government employment. Clearly, the white racism invoked by Hacker—the de-facto segregation purposely set up by whites because they consider blacks a "degraded species of humanity"—cannot explain what is happening today. And it certainly cannot point us toward a way out.

IN THE aftermath of the riots of 1992, no institution of American life has been subjected to a scrutiny more intense, or angrier, than law enforcement. And indeed, the most frequent complaint of blacks is that they are systematically mistreated by the police. This complaint has been voiced by black corporate executives, physicians, actors, and university professors, as well as by the inner-city poor, with many black professionals recounting stories of abject humiliation at police hands.

On the surface, the King verdict would seem to reinforce Hacker's thesis of an inherently racist America, where whites automatically identify with state power even when the rights of blacks have clearly been violated. Yet the jury in the King case did not come across in press accounts as comprised of arrant bigots. Interviews with individual jurors reveal men weeping and women praying for divine guidance as a decision was reached, and of twelve average Americans agonizing over every detail of evidence. In other words, the jury was behaving much like juries in other lengthy, highly publicized trials of recent memory. Members of the jury took their mission with dead seriousness, and if, as seems likely, an error was made, it was committed by twelve people who were engaged in an earnest attempt to see that justice was done.

It is also possible that the jurors were motivated by an unconscious bias against blacks. Or, what is more likely, by a combination of attitudes, in which the police were seen as the last defense against society's predatory elements and Rodney King, a large man with a checkered, criminal past, as precisely the kind of person against whom society needs to be protected. If so, the reason can be found in the statistics assembled by Hacker himself, which point to the near-impossibility today of separating the issue of race from the issue of crime.

Drawing on arrest figures collected from local law-enforcement agencies by the Federal Bureau of Investigation, Hacker shows that in practically every category of violent crime, blacks are overrepresented by huge margins. Blacks comprise 61 percent of those arrested for robbery—

five times their proportion of the population (12 percent). The figure for murder is 55 percent; for rape, 43 percent; for weapons possession, nearly 40 percent; for aggravated assault, 38 percent.

To make matters worse, these statistics are nationwide in scope. They include the states (nearly half) in which blacks make up less than 5 percent of the population, and the many areas of industrialized states where the black presence is minuscule. Obviously, this means that in urban areas the proportion of blacks among the suspects in violent crimes is much, much higher even than the high numbers cited by Hacker.

Even if allowance is made for racial bias among police or for the ability of white criminals to elude arrest, these figures demonstrate, in stark terms, that to regard casually dressed young black men warily is a matter of prudence, not prejudice. The figures do show that in the murder and rape categories, black assailants choose black victims by overwhelming margins. On the other hand, the victims of robbery by blacks tend to be white.

A RELATED issue, from the perspective of the police, is the belief that black criminals are more likely to use violence in resisting arrest. Certainly blacks are better armed than in the past. By some measurements, the Los Angeles riot was less severe and less costly in terms of property loss than previous disorders, some of which raged for days and saw entire blocks destroyed. Yet more deaths occurred in Los Angeles in 1992 than in Newark, Detroit, or Watts in the 60's, and the reason almost certainly was the large number of sophisticated weapons among the rioters and the increased tendency of black criminals to shoot with deadly intent.

As one Los Angeles gang member told Ted Koppel of *Nightline*, the difference between Watts some 25 years ago and the most recent turbulence was the prevalence of Uzis and assault weapons among those participating in the two riots.

Given this lethal combination of skyrocketing violent crime, well-armed criminals, and a long history of hostility between blacks and police, one would expect fatal shootings of blacks by the police to be on the rise. Indeed, within the black community a whole mythology has emerged in which the victims of the police are regarded as heroes of racial struggle. Spike Lee dedicated his movie, *Do the Right Thing*, to blacks who died in controversial incidents at the hands of New York City police, and Hacker seems to feel that blacks are justified in looking upon the victims of police shooting as martyrs.

In reality, however, fatal shootings of blacks by the police have undergone a steady *decline* in recent years, amounting to 40 percent less than two decades ago. The same period has also seen a major increase in the number of blacks in big-city police departments. Nationwide, blacks comprise 40 percent of new police hires over the past two

decades, and blacks are well represented on all major police forces, including the one in Los Angeles.

True, blacks are still three times more likely than whites to be killed by a policeman's bullet. But one simply cannot ascribe this to racism, since blacks are also three-to-five times more likely than whites to be arrested for crimes of violence. An interesting sidelight is that those blacks who die at the hands of the police are disproportionately the victims of black policemen. Hacker's comment, typically, is that "now there is a tendency to use blacks to control blacks" in the major cities.

F OR the past two decades, the strategy of America's black leadership has rested on two main pillars: securing jobs in the professions, skilled trades, and government service through affirmative-action programs, and gaining more and more political power, particularly local power in big cities. After Los Angeles, that strategy lies in ruins.

Affirmative action will continue: that was ensured by the passage of the most recent civil-rights act. But court decisions, the general political mood, and the wording of the new civil-rights law itself have combined to make it unlikely that racial-preference programs will expand beyond their current level. And as civil-rights leaders themselves acknowledge, policies of racial preference cannot deal with the problems of the urban underclass, the chief source of racial tension today.

Nor have the black poor derived much benefit from the impressive increase in black political power. Three of the cities hardest hit by the recent wave of disorders—Los Angeles, Atlanta, and Seattle—are led by black mayors, and Atlanta's political establishment is today predominantly black. Black political officials are not responsible for the persistence of poverty and the explosion of inner-city drugs and crime. Nevertheless, whether under white or black leadership, the problems of the black underclass persist. Meanwhile, immigrant groups which have eschewed serious political involvement while focusing single-mindedly on economic achievement continue their march toward integration and prosperity.

Despite the obvious failure of race-specific policies in meeting the needs of the underclass, we can be sure that the riots of 1992 will ignite new and ever more ambitious demands for racially balanced juries, police forces, and legislative bodies, along with renewed calls for multicultural education and an Afrocentric curriculum in urban schools. It would be highly unfortunate if such demands were acceded to: they represent an attempt to buy racial peace, similar to the Johnson administration's handing out of anti-poverty grants to youth gangs and posturing militants during the 60's, and they serve to reinforce the dangerous myth that the road to black economic integration will be significantly different from the road taken by all other groups.

On the positive side, the response to the riots has summoned forth a number of voices grounded in common sense and optimism. Of particular note have been the neighborhood activists, those involved in bringing business to black neighborhoods, working with the police to provide better street safety, trying to stimulate a more livable inner-city environment. Where national black leaders harp on the theme of white racism and call for urban Marshall Plans, many local leaders insist that measures be taken to ensure a level playing field for black businessmen and drive home the point that the solutions to the problems of black America will ultimately be found in the inner resources of black people themselves.

After Los Angeles, America has a clear choice in its approach to racial division. It could, on the one hand, follow Andrew Hacker and those, both white and black, who think as he does, into a soul-searching debate over white racism, much like the debate which followed the riots of the 60's. The result, this time, would be similar: bitterness, frustration, and little concrete action. Or we could begin paying heed to people, also both white and black, who have new thoughts about race, and especially new thoughts about reaching the underclass—thoughts based on the centrality of moral and spiritual factors like personal responsibility and initiative. It is this latter course, and only this latter course, that offers the possibility of new hope for blacks, and for all the rest of us as well.

Drug and Sexual Issues

One basic question facing society is "How far should we go in attempting to regulate the private lives of our members?" We expect that when the actions of one person impact negatively on others, those others can demand and expect that the guilty party change or eliminate these behaviors. In such cases there is an identifiable victim who can seek redress. However, in many cases involving behaviors, the victim and the criminal/perpetrator are one and the same, so the legislating of morality becomes an issue. No one is "hurt" by these actions, but the potential for serious offense exists. These are known in the sociological literature as "victimless" crimes, because the so-called victim and the criminal are the same. In other words, there is no complaining party. The complainant is often a third party who is offended by the actions of the individual. One could always argue that there are no true victimless crimes because what a person does to him- or herself does impact on significant others, i.e., family, close friends, and children.

"Born or Bred?" addresses the issue of what causes homosexuality. Is it learned or conditioned by the individual's social environment, or is it genetic? The article presents research data that would appear to support the genetic argument. It also raises questions as to the social consequences for homosexuals and prospective parents if homosexuality is proven to be genetic.

"Shape Up or Ship Out" addresses the explosive issue of homosexuals serving in the military. President Clinton's attempt to fulfill campaign promises to lift the ban on gays in the military has been met with strong resistance both within and outside the military. Will gays in the military undermine military effectiveness and morale? The answer to this question is unknown. But as sociologists have discovered, it is not reality that affects the behaviors of individuals or groups, it is the perception of reality that governs behaviors.

"Truth and Consequences: Teen Sex" explores the implications of earlier and earlier experiences of teen sexual activities. The sexual revolution is into its thirtieth year, and the results are far from positive. The authors look at the social, medical, psychological, and economic costs and what, if anything, can be done to reduce them.

In "The CIA Connection," the author discusses how the U.S. government, in attempting to ensure that its international interests were realized, made deals that not only winked at drug-related activities but actually encouraged them. Thus our current drug problem is partly a legacy of international policies whereby the end justified the means.

"A Society of Suspects: The War on Drugs and Civil Liberties" is being waged simultaneously. While trying to win the war on drugs, law enforcement personnel insist their hands are being tied. But those constraints were established by our Founding Fathers to protect the rights of every American citizen to be free from unwarranted searches, entry into homes, and arrest. This author argues that constitutional rights are being systematically limited and redefined because of this "war."

Looking Ahead: Challenge Questions

Which of the two sides of the "born" or "bred" controversy concerning homosexuality appears to be the most convincing?

What difference does it really make if homosexuality is born or bred?

Just why are we so concerned, as a society, about drugs?

Distinguish between the harmful effects of societally approved drugs, (alcohol, tobacco, and caffeine), and those that are not (heroin, cocaine, marijuana).

In what major ways can raising the fears of the members of a society impact on their rights as citizens?

Do the ends always justify the means used in a society to combat drug use/abuse?

What responsibility must the U.S. government assume for the state of the drug problem in the nation today?

Is supporting corrupt dictatorships to further U.S. objectives ever justified?

Which of the three sociological theoretical positions do you think most clearly helps to understand the issues/problems covered in this unit?

What are the values, rights, obligations, and harms associated with the each of the activities included in this unit?

BORN OR BRED?

Science and psychiatry are struggling to make sense of new research that suggests that homosexuality may be a matter of genetics, not parenting

Until the age of 28, Doug Barnett* was a practicing heterosexual. He was vaguely attracted to men, but with nurturing parents, a lively interest in sports and appropriate relations with women, he had little reason to question his proclivities. Then an astonishing thing happened: his identical twin brother "came out" to him, revealing he was gay. Barnett, who believed sexual orientation is genetic, was bewildered. He recalls thinking, "If this is inherited and we're identical twins—what's going on here?" To find out, he thought he should try sex with men. When he did, he says, "The bells went off, for the first time. Those homosexual encounters were more fulfilling." A year later both twins told their parents they were gay.

Simon LeVay knew he was homosexual by the time he was 12. Growing up bookish, in England, he fit the "sissy boy" profile limned by psychologists: an aversion to rough sports, a strong attachment to his mother, a hostile relationship with his father. It was, LeVay acknowledges, the perfect Freudian recipe for homosexuality—only he was convinced Freud had cause and effect backward: hostile fathers didn't make sons gay; fathers turned hostile because the sons were "unmasculine" to begin with.

Last year, LeVay, now a neuroscientist at the Salk Institute in La Jolla, Calif., got a chance to examine his hunch up close.

*Not his real name.

What he found is still reverberating among scientists and may have a profound impact on how the rest of us think about homosexuality. Scanning the brains of 41 cadavers, including 19 homosexual males, LeVay determined that a tiny area believed to control sexual activity was less than half the size in the gay men than in the heterosexuals. It was perhaps the first direct evidence of what some gays have long contended—that whether or not they choose to be different, they are born different.

Doug Barnett, meanwhile, got an opportunity to make his own contribution to the case. Two years ago he was recruited for an ambitious study of homosexuality in twins, undertaken by psychologist Michael Bailey, of Northwestern University, and psychiatrist Richard Pillard, of the Boston University School of Medicine. Published last December, only months after LeVay's

> **Many people have welcomed the indication that gayness begins in the chromosomes**

work, the results showed that if one identical twin is gay, the other is almost three times more likely to be gay than if twins are fraternal—sugesting that something in the identical twins' shared genetic makeup affected their sexual orientation.

In both studies, the implications are potentially huge. For decades, scientists and the public at large have debated whether homosexuals are born or made—whether their sexual orientation is the result of a genetic roll of the dice or a combination of formative factors in their upbringing. If it turns out, indeed, that homosexuals are born that way, it could undercut the animosity gays have had to contend with for centuries. "It would reduce being gay to something like being left-handed, which is in fact all that it is," says gay San Francisco journalist and author Randy Shilts.

But instead of resolving the debate, the studies may well have intensified it. Some scientists profess not to be surprised at all by LeVay's finding of brain differences. "Of course it [sexual orientation] is in the brain," says Johns Hopkins University psychologist John Money, sometimes called the dean of American sexologists. "The real question is, when did it get there? Was it prenatal, neonatal, during childhood, puberty? That we do not know."

Others are sharply critical of the Bailey-Pillard study. Instead of proving the genetics argument, they think it only confirms the obvious: that twins are apt to have the same sort of shaping influences. "In order for such a study to be at all meaningful, you'd have to look at twins raised apart," says Anne Fausto Stirling, a developmen-

From *Newsweek*, February 24, 1992, pp. 46-50, 52-53. © 1992 by Newsweek, Inc. All rights reserved. Reprinted by permission.

tal biologist at Brown University, in Providence, R.I. "It's such badly interpreted genetics."

In the gay community itself, many welcome the indication that gayness begins in the chromosomes. Theoretically, it could gain them the civil-rights protections accorded any "natural" minority, in which the legal linchpin is the question of an "immutable" characteristic. Moreover, it could lift the burden of self-blame from their parents. "A genetic component in sexual orientation says, 'This is not a fault, and it's not your fault'," says Pillard.

Yet the intimation that an actual gene for gayness might be found causes some foreboding. If there is a single, identifiable cause, how long before some nerdy genius finds a "cure"? Many scientists say it's naive to think a single gene could account for so complex a behavior as homosexuality. Yet at least three research projects, one of them at the National Institutes of Health, are believed to be searching for a "gay gene" or group of genes. LeVay, for one, thinks a small number of sex genes may be isolated, perhaps within five years: "And that's going to blow society's mind."

For some people, it is not too great a leap from there to Nazi-style eugenics. In the nightmare scenario, once a gay fetus is detected in utero, it is aborted, or a genetic switch is "flipped" to ensure its heterosexuality. The gay population simply fades away. Would mothers permit such tampering? Even parents who've come to terms with their child's homosexuality might. "No parent would choose to have a child born with any factor that would make life difficult for him or her," says Laurie Coburn, program director of the Federation of Parents and Friends of Lesbians and Gays (ParentsFLAG).

On this subject, feelings are seldom restrained. But cooler voices can be heard, mainly those of lesbians. Many of them say their choice of lesbianism was as much a feminist statement as a sexual one, so the fuss over origins doesn't interest them. "It's mostly fascinating to heteros," says one gay activist. On the whole, lesbians are warier of the research, and their conspicuous absence from most studies angers them. "It's part of the society's intrinsic sexism," says Penny Perkins, public-education coordinator for Lambda Legal Defense and Education Fund, which works to promote lesbian and gay men's rights. Frances Stevens, editor in chief of Deneuve, a lesbian news magazine, admits her personal history supports biological causes; although she came from a wholesome "Brady Bunch" family, she knew she was gay "from day one." But she is skeptical of the studies, she says. "My response was: if the gay guy's [hypothalamus] is smaller, what's it like for dykes? Is it the same size as a straight male's?" That's something researchers still have to find out.

Gay men have their own reasons to be irate: as they see it, looking for a "cause" of homosexuality implies it is deviant and heterosexuality is the norm. When John De Cecco, professor of psychology at San Francisco State University and editor of the Journal of Homosexuality, began one of his classes recently by suggesting students discuss the causes of homosexuality, someone called out, "Who cares?" and the class burst into applause.

All the same, homosexuals must care deeply about how the straight world perceives them. History has taught them that the consequences of those perceptions can be deadly. Over the centuries they have been tolerated or reviled, enfranchised or oppressed. According to John Boswell's 1980 book, "Christianity, Social Tolerance and Homosexuality," things didn't turn truly nasty until the 13th century, when the church, on the heels of a diatribe from Saint Thomas Aquinas, began to view gays as not only unnatural but dangerous.

In our own century of *sex et lux*, beginning with Sigmund Freud, psychiatrists ascribed male homosexuality to unconscious conflicts and fixations that have their roots in early childhood. (Freud was always foggier on female sexuality.) But that view was officially dropped in 1973, when more stringent diagnostic standards—and the lobbying of gay activists—persuaded the American Psychiatric Association to expunge homosexuality from the list of emotional disorders. The decision was bitterly disputed; 37 percent of APA members voted against it in a 1974 referendum. But younger psychiatrists now are taught that rather

---

SIMON LEVAY

A grieving scientist's labor of love convinces him that biology is destiny

In the long-running debate over whether homosexuality begins in the genes or the nursery, Simon LeVay was an unlikely champion for the genetic side. As a homosexual himself (with a homosexual brother), he seemed a textbook-perfect product of nurture. "When I look back," he says, "I definitely see things that went along with being gay: not liking rough sports, preferring reading, being very close with my mother." And the classic clincher—"I hated my father as long as I can remember." By Freudian lights, that should have made an open-and-shut case for nurture. But LeVay believed even then that nature comes first. "My point would be that gays are extremely different when they're young and as a *result* they can develop hostile relationships with their fathers. It's just a big mistake to think it's the other way around and the relationships are causative."

An Englishman with a Ph.D. in neuroanatomy, LeVay spent 12 years at Harvard before moving on to the Salk Institute to pursue his field of research—which, ironically, included the influence of environment on development. But when his lover of 21 years, Richard Hersey, died of AIDS, LeVay went into a deep depression. Hospitalized for two weeks, he began reevaluating his goals. "It makes you think what your life is about," he says. Around that time, a UCLA lab announced its finding that a portion of the male hypothalamus that regulates sex was more than twice as large as women's. Suddenly, it seemed to LeVay there was a thesis to pursue: was it also larger than that of gays? "I felt if I didn't find anything, I would give up a scientific career altogether."

After nine months' work, LeVay did find that in at least one group of gays, the sex-regulating area was smaller than in straight men. The work brought him instant fame and a round of talk shows, where he's often obliged to contend with the unconvinced. But he thinks it's worth it, if it promotes the idea that homosexuality is a matter of destiny, not choice. "It's important to educate society," he says. "I think this issue does affect religious and legal attitudes." From here on he'll be spreading the word as codirector of the West Hollywood Institute for Gay and Lesbian Education, on leave from Salk. The new institute opens in September as one of the first free-standing schools for homosexual studies. LeVay may have to abandon research. But he's still on the compassionate course he set out on after the death of his lover.

than trying to "cure" homosexuals, they should help them feel more comfortable about themselves.

LeVay resolved to look for sex differences in the brain after the slow, wrenching death from AIDS of his companion of 21 years (box). He'd been impressed by a study done by a UCLA graduate student, Laura Allen, working with biologist Robert Gorski, showing that a portion of the hypothalamus in the brains of males was more than twice as large as that of women. LeVay's report, published in the journal Science on Aug. 30, 1991, was based on his own yearlong study of the hypothalamus in 41 cadavers, including 19 self-avowed homosexual men, 16 heterosexual men and 6 heterosexual women. All the homosexuals had died of AIDS, as had seven of the heterosexuals—including one of the women. What emerged with almost startling clarity was that, with some exceptions, the cluster of neurons known as INAH 3 (the third interstitial nucleus of the anterior hypothalamus, which LeVay calls "the business end as far as sex goes") was more than twice as large in the heterosexual males as in the homosexuals, whose INAH 3 was around the same size as in the women. In the sensation that greeted the report, its cautious wording was all but ignored. "What I reported was a difference in the brain structure of the hypothalamus," says LeVay. "We can't say on the basis of that what makes people gay or straight. But it opens the door to find the answer to that question."

One of the major criticisms of the study was that AIDS could have affected the brain structure of the homosexual subjects. LeVay has been able to field that one by pointing out that he found no pathology suggesting such damage either in gay or straight men who died of the disease. Later, in fact, he examined the brain of a homosexual who died of lung cancer, and again found INAH 3 much smaller.

The trickier question is whether things might work the other way around: could sexual orientation affect brain structure? Kenneth Klivington, an assistant to the president of the Salk Institute, points to a body of evidence showing that the brain's neural networks reconfigure themselves in response to certain experiences. One fascinating NIH study found that in people reading Braille after becoming blind, the area of the brain controlling the reading finger grew larger. There are also intriguing conundrums in animal brains. In male songbirds, for example, the brain area associated with mating is not only larger than in the female but varies according to the season.

Says Klivington: "From the study of animals, we know that circulating sex hormones in the mother can have a profound effect on the organization of the brain of the fetus. Once the individual is born, the story gets more complex because of the interplay between the brain and experience. It's a feedback loop: the brain influences behavior, behavior shapes experience, experi-

ence affects the organization of the brain, and so forth."

LeVay knows he is somewhat vulnerable on that score. Because his subjects were all dead, he knew "regrettably little" about their sexual histories, besides their declared or presumed orientation. "That's a distinct shortcoming of my study," he concedes. Did the gay men play the passive or aggressive roles in sex? Were some bisexual, another variable, and could that have affected their neuron clusters? To find answers, LeVay plans next to study living subjects with the new MRI (magnetic resonance imaging) technology. But he remains convinced that biology is destiny. "If there are environmental influences," he says, "they operate very early in life, at the fetal or early-infancy stage, when the brain is still putting itself together. I'm very much skeptical of the idea that sexual orientation is a cultural thing."

The Bailey-Pillard twin study had its own shortcomings. The numbers alone were impressive. The researchers found that of 56 identical twins, 52 percent were both gay, as against 22 percent of fraternal twins, who have somewhat weaker genetic bonds. (Of the adoptive, nongenetically related brothers in the study, only 11 percent were both gay.) The suggestion of a shared genetic destiny is strong, but many critics have wondered: what about the discordant twins—those where only one was homosexual? Many in the study were not only discordant, but dramatically different.

Most sexuality studies use the Kinsey

ANNETTE BRENNER

For parents, a child's 'coming out' can lead to painful episodes of soul-searching

Annette E. Brenner remembers joking when her oldest son was 4 that she'd approve his marrying outside the family's faith as long as he married a woman. When he "came out" to her and her husband at 17, one of her first reactions was to try to "negotiate" him out of his gayness. She offered him a car, a house, if only he would wait and try marriage. He was at boarding school in Connecticut at the time, and she was convinced it was "just a stage." She remembers thinking, "Sure, this week you're a homosexual. Enjoy the experiment, have fun. Next week you'll be a Hare Krishna." Then she became enraged. "What is this kid doing to me?" she'd ask herself. What was he doing to his grandparents, his brother and sister?

Years of gay activism haven't made coming out much easier on parents. At the Chicago-area office of ParentsFLAG (Parents and Friends of Lesbians and Gays), the national support organization Brenner joined, parents often call in tears. Some, she says, have had nervous breakdowns over the news of their child's homosexuality. Brenner had a terrible time accepting her son's revelation. For a while she wondered about the Freudian explanation. "We replayed his whole life" looking for some environmental reason, she says. She wondered whether she had been too domineering. They sent him to a therapist, only to be told he was comfortable with his gayness. Finally, they came to terms with it, too—her husband more easily than she did. She understands now why her son had such a poor self-image at school, why he endured falling grades and bouts of depression.

Her son is 28 now, and he brings his lover home for visits. "He's happy because his family accepts him," says Brenner. Still, she frets about AIDS, and she knows he hasn't been tested. He's been "bashed" a couple of times—and she worries about his physical safety. Even seeing how content her son is, Brenner says, "Had I known that I was to have a gay child, I would probably not want to have a gay child."

At FLAG, parents are firmly behind any research that implicates biology as the source of gayness. It assuages the raging guilt some of them feel that they might be responsible. "Especially if my child gets AIDS," says Brenner, "can you imagine what that would be like?" Probably, it would be shattering. Gays may come out and get on with their lives, often happily. But for parents, the doubts and the dread never seem to stop.

scale, which rates orientation on a seven-point spectrum from strictly heterosexual to exclusively homosexual. The study found that most of the discordant identical twins were at opposite ends of the Kinsey spectrum. How could two individuals with identical genetic traits and upbringing wind up with totally different sexual orientation? Richard Green, a noted UCLA researcher of homosexuality, says he believes research should focus on that finding, which he deems "astounding." Although Pillard and Bailey are certain that biology plays the dominant role, Bailey acknowledges: "There must be something in the environment to yield the discordant twins."

What that might be is uncertain. None of the usual domineering-mother, distant-father theories has been conclusively shown to determine sexuality. Meanwhile the case for biology has grown stronger. "If you look at all societies," says Frederick Whitam, who has researched homosexuality in cultures as diverse as the United States, Central America and the Philippines, "homosexuality occurs at the same rates with the same kinds of behavior. That suggests something biological going on. The biological evidence has been growing for 20 or more years."

"Something in the environment," "something biological"—the truth is, the nature-nurture argument is no longer as polarized as it once was. Scientists are beginning to realize there is a complex interplay between the two, still to be explored. June Reinisch, director of the Kinsey Institute, prefers to think we are only "flavored, not programmed." Genetics, she says, only give us "a range of outcomes."

> ## 'There are talk shows where people still say, homosexuality is an abomination, it's vile.'
>
> *Novelist Jacquelyn Holt Park*

Should it really matter to gays what makes them gay? Whitam says it does matter. In a 1989 study of attitudes toward gays in four different societies, those who believed homosexuals "were born that way" represented a minority but were also the least homophobic. Observes Whitam: "There is a tendency for people, when told that homosexuality is biological, to heave a sigh of relief. It relieves the families and homosexuals of guilt. It also means that society doesn't have to worry about things like gay teachers."

For the most part, gays remain doubtful that even the strongest evidence of biological origins will cut much ice with confirmed homophobes. Many find the assumption naive. "Our organization considers the studies useless," says Dr. Howard Grossman, a gay doctor who heads New York Physicians for Human Rights. "It's just like the military—

you can show them a thousand studies that show gay soldiers aren't a security risk and they still don't care."

The doctor's pessimism is not unwarranted. Jacquelyn Holt Park, author of a moving novel about the sorrows of growing up lesbian in the sexually benighted 1940s and '50s, is just back from a 9,000-mile book tour where she was astonished to find how little has changed. "There are talk shows," says Park, "where fundamentalists and the like still say [homosexuality] is an abomination, it's vile. They said, 'You're not black, blacks can't change their color, but you can change.' I guess these new studies might address some of those feelings."

Even within the enlightened ranks of the American Psychoanalytic Association there is still some reluctance to let homosexual analysts practice. As arrested cases themselves, the argument goes, they are ill equipped to deal with developmental problems. The belief that homosexuality can and should be "cured" persists in some quarters of the profession.

Others are exasperated by that view. Richard Isay, chairperson of the APA's Committee on Gay, Lesbian and Bisexual Issues, is convinced analysis can be more damaging than beneficial to gays. "I still see many gay men who come to me after they've been in analysis where the therapist has been trying to change their orientation," he says. "That's extremely harmful to the self-esteem of a gay man." Isay thinks the approach, instead, should be to try to clear away "roadblocks" that may interfere with a gay's ability to function.

Perhaps the most voluble spokesman for

MIKE

Through therapy, a gay widower seeks an end to a lifestyle of cruising

"Mike" is a 49-year-old widower who was married for 18 years and has a teenage son. Although he says he loved his wife, he was secretly cruising gay bars during his marriage and engaging in short-term homosexual encounters. After his wife died, he found his way to Dr. Joseph Nicolosi, whom he consulted for eight months.

"I went on binges, just like an alcoholic would do. [After my wife died] Saturday nights were terrible. I'd go to a heterosexual bar and end up jumping in my car and going to some bath or gay bar. I was at a point in my life whether either I was a homosexual and I was going to be open and public about it, or I was not going to be a homosexual and be otherwise. I was in the pits. Whatever I was doing was not making me happy. I was not going to continue living the lie that I was living.

"I kept searching for somebody to help me, but you always heard that nothing could be done about this and anybody who came to your attention was usually a gay therapist. I was more than in a closet, I was in a coffin. I had never revealed this to anybody before. I never trusted anybody. In the very first session [with Dr. Nicolosi], I realized we were on the same wavelength.

"I never had a man in my life who taught me how to be a man. I never had a role model. I realize how my dad's failure to be present for me screwed me up. I was very angry toward my dad. And I never knew why. I [also] felt I'd been castrated by women. When I got into therapy, the resentment toward my mother was far greater than toward my dad. There was a lot of anger, a lot of deep feeling at not having your mother accept your maleness. When I started loving myself, when I started to know who I was, my maleness came with it." (*Six months after completing therapy, Mike says he has not had any homosexual encounters. Does he feel "cured"?*)

"I would have to answer, yes, I still do sometimes have homosexual feelings. But I don't get upset if I get them because I understand them now. Now Saturday night comes and goes and I don't even think about it."

the "fix it" school is Charles Socarides, a New York City analyst who claims a flourishing practice in turning troubled homosexuals into "happy, fulfilled heterosexuals." To Socarides, the only biological evidence is "that we're anatomically made to go in male-female pairs." Thus he "reconstructs" patients' lives to learn why they can't mate with opposite-sex partners. There can be many reasons, he says: "abdicating fathers, difficult wives, marital disruptions." From there, he "opens up the path" to hetero happiness, for which, he says, one gratified customer cabled him recently: "The eagle has landed."

Some psychiatrists still see the removal of homosexuality from the official list of emotional disorders as a mistake. (Instead, it was innocuously identified as "sexual orientation disturbance.") "Psychology and psychiatry have essentially abandoned a whole population of people who feel dissatisfied with their feelings of homosexuality," says psychologist Joseph Nicolosi, author of "Reparative Therapy of Male Homosexuality" *(Jason Aronson. 1991).* In graduate school, says Nicolosi, he found the stance was that if a client came in complaining about his gayness, the therapist's job was to teach him to accept it. "It was like the old joke of the patient who tells the doctor his arm hurts when he bends it and the doctor advises him not to bend it."

Nicolosi tries to do more than that for his patients, most of them men in their 20s and 30s who are unhappy with their homosexuality. As director of the Thomas

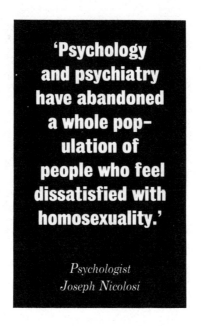

'Psychology and psychiatry have abandoned a whole population of people who feel dissatisfied with homosexuality.'

Psychologist Joseph Nicolosi

Aquinas Psychology Clinic in Encino, Calif., he tries to bolster his patients' sense of male identity, which he sees as crucial to their orientation. The biological evidence is inconclusive, Nicolosi says; there is much more proof for familial causes of homosexuality. "Research has shown repeatedly that a poor relationship with a distant, aloof father and an overpossessive, domineering mother could cause homosexuality in males," he says.

In fact, some of that research, dating back to the 1950s, has been discredited because of faulty techniques, among other

problems. Nicolosi is at any rate modest in his own claims. No cures as such, but "a diminishment of homosexual feelings" to the point where some patients can marry and have families. How long is treatment? "Probably a lifetime process," he says.

With the debate over origins still going strong, comes one more exhibit in evidence. Recently, Bailey and Pillard divulged just a tidbit from their not-yet-published study of lesbian twins. Finding enough females for the study took twice as long as their earlier project, says Bailey, but apparently it was worth the effort. "If there are genes for homosexuality, they're not gender blind," he says. Lesbians in the study had more lesbian sisters than they did gay brothers.

Nature? Nurture? Perhaps the most appropriate answer comes from Evelyn Hooker, who showed in an important 1950s study that it is impossible to distinguish heterosexuals from homosexuals on psychological tests. Hooker takes the long view of the search for origins. "Why do we want to know the cause?" she asks. "It's a mistake to hope that we will be able to modify or change homosexuality . . . If we understand its nature and accept it as a given, then we come much closer to the kind of attitudes which will make it possible for homosexuals to lead a decent life in society." The psychiatric profession heeded Hooker when it stopped calling homosexuality an illness. At 84, her voice has grown fainter, but the rest of us could do worse than listen to her now.

DAVID GELMAN *with* DONNA FOOTE *in Los Angeles,* TODD BARRETT *in Chicago,* MARY TALBOT *in New York and bureau reports*

Shape up or ship out

The military is willing to let homosexuals serve — but only if they remain in the closet

Every Thursday morning at Fort Hood, Texas, is "sergeant's time," when the noncommissioned officers of the Army's 1st Cavalry Division train their young soldiers. Sgt. Mark McLaughlin, one of the division's top noncommissioned officers, knows how to teach men to be soldiers and how to hammer a group of strangers into a team.

But as the Clinton administration lifts the ban on homosexuals in the military, Sergeant McLaughlin will be asked to lead a revolution in the nation's close-knit, tradition-minded military society. "I've been in eight years, and I'm confident that you can throw anything at me," he says. "But this is the first time where you can give me a mission and I don't know what to do."

Congress and the military brass are not eager to tackle the issue, either. "The discomfort level of the majority of members is incredibly high," says Republican Sen. John McCain of Arizona, a former Vietnam POW who opposes lifting the ban. "This has been mishandled from the beginning. Now everyone understands the volatility of the issue—and the need to find some compromise."

In the closet. That will be difficult. Congressional hearings begin this week, and when Pentagon officials testify later in April, they are likely to propose that homosexuals be permitted to serve in the military so long as they remain in the closet. "We won't ask the question," says a senior officer who has been studying the issue closely. "But as soon as a person is identified as homosexual by their behavior, that person will be discharged."

That idea may not fly. When President Clinton said he will consider barring ho-mosexual troops from some jobs, his comments outraged gay activists, who fear the president is folding under pressure. David Mixner, a gay adviser to the Clinton campaign, called the suggestion "morally repugnant."

Senate Armed Services Committee Chairman Sam Nunn of Georgia, who balked at Clinton's decision to lift the ban, wants to defuse the emotion and keep the first set of congressional hearings on the subject as "neutral, bland and boring as possible," says one committee source. So historical and legal presentations, discussions of unit cohesion and a look into the experiences of foreign military forces will be the start of a two-month process that also will include field trips to military installations.

By this summer, Congress will be ready to hear from the Pentagon brass, which has until July 15 to present the White House with a proposal for lifting the gay ban but has been slow to launch its study of the issue. Sources say the study group's members have been chosen but they have not been officially commissioned to begin work. The group will be headed by Air Force Lt. Gen. Robert Alexander and will include flag officers from each of the services. In addition, the sources say, the White House has picked two lawyers for the nine-member panel.

Senior officers say they understand the military's obligation to "respond to the democratically elected civilian leadership," as one puts it, and they say they understand the military's role in American society. But many have made no secret of their opposition to lifting the ban on homosexuals, and they resent what they think is an attempt to use the military as a social laboratory to legitimize gay and lesbian lifestyles.

At the heart of the military's presentation to the Armed Services Committee will be the claim that it will be difficult to open the ranks without compromising the military's ability to fight. "A soldier has to think of homosexuals in the context of war-fighting," says a senior officer assigned to help formulate the Pentagon's position on the issue, who agreed to speak with *U.S. News* on condition of anonymity. "Our business is to fight and to win wars. I don't make a profit; I don't make cars. We kill people in the name of national security. No one else in our society is asked to do that." The bottom line, in the officer's view: "Does it help me or hinder me in winning at war?"

Although thousands of gays and lesbians have served honorably and with distinction, and while many soldiers say they have had no problems serving alongside homosexual comrades, many officers fear that allowing declared homosexuals to serve will destroy the military's chemistry and cohesion. "The most important thing we do with soldiers is try to bind the force together," says the senior officer. "On the battlefield it's the commitment to the team that carries the day."

Blood brothers. Soldiers from the 2nd Armored Division at Fort Hood agree. "In combat you have to rely on every single guy at any moment, at any time," says Cpl. John Owens. "And if you're in combat and you mistrust somebody, it's over. You want to have that cohesion. And if you lose that cohesion, that's your life."

"The military is not an ordinary job," says Spc. Daniel Malecha. "We work to-

From *U.S. News & World Report*, April 5, 1993, pp. 24-26, 31, 33. © 1993 by U.S. News & World Report. Reprinted by permission.

gether but we actually live together. And sometime in the future we might have to go to war together. You've got to think of your job. You can't have any distraction or anything. If you think of something else, you might get yourself killed, you might get someone else killed."

The military contends that in a host of ways, from infringing upon a soldier's privacy to increasing the risk of AIDS, accepting avowed homosexuals into the ranks could undermine morale and effectiveness. Among the areas of concern to the Pentagon:

■ **Violation of privacy.** "An army at war is a peculiar thing," says a senior officer. "If my staff here at the Pentagon were all homosexual it wouldn't make a bit of difference." In the field, though, soldiers sleep together, shower together and live together. "You don't have choices," the officer says. "You abandoned your right to choose who you live with."

"We spend a lot of time in the field, sometimes 30, 45 days at a time, and we're elbow to elbow with people in the dirt," says Staff Sgt. Randall Benton of the 2nd Armored Division. "And it's uncomfortable working around people who you feel have a sexual preference that is not what you believe is right."

■ **AIDS.** The military requested data from the Centers for Disease Control and Prevention in Atlanta. Based on its study of that information, which says that two thirds of all AIDS cases are attributable to homosexual behavior, the Pentagon has concluded that HIV-positive military personnel hurt military readiness. A memo prepared by the joint staff adds: "A lot of blood is spilled in battle . . . each member of the team must be ready to provide immediate, battlefield first aid. Fear of AIDS, whether founded or not, can preclude the performance of first aid to a service member who is known or even suspected to be a homosexual."

The memo continues: "The military services rely on their own people for whole blood, even to the extent of arm-to-arm transfusions. We must ensure that this vital source remains untainted and has the complete confidence of our medical personnel and its potential users. If we don't, AIDS-infected blood will cause some of our young American warriors to die." There are about 9,000 cases of HIV in the armed services; the military calculates their cost at $985 million.

■ **Losing good people.** The Pentagon says parents are asking recruiters whether gays will be admitted into the military. Many good soldiers are already worried about their future in a smaller military; they may use the homosexual issue as an excuse to get out.

In the end, the military wants to insist that homosexuals who choose to serve must restrict their behavior. "We will

equalize the opportunity to come into the service," says one officer. "But people will have to subordinate their lifestyle to the good of the military service."

Pentagon officials argue that the military regulates the behavior of its heterosexual members. It enforces stringent rules governing the length of men's hair, and until fairly recently, it expected officers to obey a guide to social etiquette. An officer never held hands with his wife on post, in order to signal that he treated her as a lady, not as an intimate.

Pandora's box. The joint staff's "Statement on Homosexuals," approved by Gen. Colin Powell, chairman of the Joint Chiefs of Staff, goes even further, however, suggesting a need to virtually require homosexuals to stay in the closet or be discharged. Otherwise, military leaders fear, the Pentagon will have to decide whether to recognize homosexual couples, what benefits homosexual partners are entitled to, whether gay couples and lesbian couples are entitled to live together in base housing and how to ensure fairness in promotions and assignments.

Nor is the military an equal opportunity employer. "By the nature of the military mission and environment, we deny civil rights all the time," Powell's memo says. The military does not accept people who fail to meet its height, weight or age restrictions, people with certain medical conditions or people who fail to meet education standards. "We regard service as a privilege, not a right," says a senior officer.

The most difficult question will be how to deal with a soldier who declares his homosexuality but does his job and is not disruptive. "If I tell you I'm homosexual, that's going to have the same effect as if you catch me in the act," argues a senior officer. "Behavior and announced orientation must be treated as one." The U.S. Circuit Court, in the 1989 case of *Ben-Shalom v. Marsh*, allowed the Army to discharge an acknowledged lesbian solely on the basis of her statement. The court reasoned that her statement suggested "a desire and propensity to engage in homosexual conduct."

Who is to blame? But if the military loses the political fight and does not retain the right to discharge avowed homosexuals, soldiers will face tough choices. For an M-1A1 tank or a Bradley fighting vehicle commander, typically a 30-year-old sergeant responsible for a four- or five-man crew, an avowed homosexual who performs his job impeccably poses a dilemma. If the crew's morale suffers, who is to blame? The homosexual or the other members of the team who resent the homosexual?

No matter how the policy debates in Washington are resolved, in the field it

will be the sergeants and petty officers who will determine whether the military really accepts homosexuals or simply finds more subtle ways to discriminate against them. And even with President Clinton's help, gays and lesbians will have to fight an uphill battle against deeply entrenched attitudes.

The military's midlevel managers are getting mixed signals from superiors who say they will follow orders but who openly oppose Clinton's policy. And many noncommissioned officers are resolutely opposed to accepting homosexuals on moral or military grounds — or both. "They're going to have to take us off to the side and educate us on whatever reason it might be right [to lift the ban on homosexuals]," says Sergeant Benton of the 2nd Armored Division, "but I don't think they're ever going to show me the reason that it's right." "How do you break down what for 27 years my parents told me?" asks 1st Cavalry Sergeant McLaughlin. "A slide show in a theater won't change that."

Some noncommissioned officers also find it difficult to understand why one soldier's right to be openly gay is more important than the morale and cohesion of his unit. "I couldn't honestly go up and take the [gay] man and say 'you're out of here' and make up situations to get rid of him," says Sergeant Benton. "But I'm going to guarantee you, it's easier to eliminate one problem instead of four. You've got to be honest with these [four] guys. They're right, in my opinion, and this guy over here is morally wrong."

Without violating their orders to accept gays in the ranks, noncommissioned officers can find a variety of ways to discourage homosexuals from pursuing careers in the all-volunteer military. "Guess who's going to go work on garbage detail or in the grease pit?" says Staff Sgt. Xavier Hernandez of the 2nd Armored Division.

Following orders. But soldiers also are trained to obey orders. "The bottom line is: We will fight when we're told to fight," says III Corps Command Sgt. Maj. Richard Cayton, the senior noncommissioned officer at Fort Hood. "And if our executives tell us this is the order, then we're going to follow the order to the best of our ability. If we have to do it, it'll be a rough transition, but we'll do it to the best of our ability. That's professionalism." Adds 1st Sgt. Tommy Carter of the 2nd Armored: "As long as we're discussing it, it's a discussion. Once a decision has been made, it's insubordination."

Clear guidelines about how homosexuals are to behave and how they must be treated will be as important as direct orders. "If you've got your guidelines in place," says Staff Sgt. David Durham, a

COMING OUT TOO SOON

Hit by friendly fire

Sgt. Justin Elzie is a 10-year marine with an outstanding record. In 1989, he was named marine of the year at his eight-battalion support group on Okinawa. He stood embassy duty in Egypt during the gulf war and in Helsinki during the 1990 Bush-Gorbachev summit.

But Elzie felt he had one final mission before he left the corps. So on January 29, buoyed by President Clinton's announced intention to end the ban on gays in the military, Elzie announced on national television that he was a homosexual. "I came out to show people that there *are* gay marines down here," he said from Camp Lejeune. "What I wanted to do was stand up and join the fray and try to make a positive difference."

Elzie, however, may have stood up too soon. He had planned to leave the Marines under a voluntary-separation program in April. He hoped that his fine record and Clinton's vague promise that investigations of gay soldiers would be put on hold would allow him to receive an honorable discharge and a promised $25,000 separation bonus. But on February 10, he got a letter from his commanding officer telling him the corps had begun proceedings to administratively discharge him because of his homosexuality. The early separation and bonus would not be forthcoming. If the corps has its way at a hearing this week, Elzie will be put into unpaid standby reserve status, where he will wait until the Clinton administration and the Pentagon sort out the military's policy on gays.

Marine Corps Capt. Todd Yeatts, a public affairs officer at Camp Lejeune, says the corps has no choice but to proceed against homosexuals. "We're doing it the way we've always done it," says Captain Yeatts. "The Marine Corps' policy is set until we get specific guidance to change it."

Not safe yet. Gay-rights leaders say that, despite the administration's promises, they are telling service members not to come out. "It's not a safe time. People are going to be prosecuted," says Torie Osborn, executive director of the National Gay and Lesbian Task Force in Washington.

Still, Elzie thinks it has been worth it. He has shown his fellow marines, with whom he has trained, worked and showered for years, that gays can be good marines. He says other marines have been mostly supportive, and that he knows of other cases where peers and commanders have not turned in openly gay marines and sailors. "What I've noticed is, on a one-to-one basis, they don't give a damn," he said.

BY PETER CARY

tank commander in the 2nd Armored, "then basically he's got a choice of following them and doing his job or seeking employment elsewhere. It's pretty cut and dried. I guess if the homosexual guy is operating within the guidelines that are in place, there's not a whole lot you're going to be able to do to him."

Sensitivity training holds some promise, if only because many soldiers' views are grounded in stereotypes. Although many gays and lesbians have served, most soldiers don't think they know anyone who is homosexual, and many assume that homosexuals choose to be so, despite physiological evidence suggesting that there may be biological causes. "Homosexuality is viewed as abnormal," says a senior officer.

In the end, many military leaders are hoping that most homosexuals who want to serve will continue to keep their sexual preference to themselves. "The military can continue to operate if we never again ask about an individual's sexual preference," says a senior officer. "Gays have been in the military since the dawn of time," says Spc. Eduardo Castilleja of the 2nd Armored Division. "We understand that. But they never stood out. They never made it clear to anybody. And I prefer it to stay like that." Gay and lesbian soldiers, however, want to know why they must hide their true identities in order to serve their country.

BRUCE B. AUSTER AT FORT HOOD
WITH GLORIA BORGER

Truth and Consequences
TEEN SEX

Douglas J. Besharov with Karen N. Gardiner

Douglas J. Besharov is a resident scholar at the American Enterprise Institute. Karen Gardiner is a research assistant at the American Enterprise Institute.

Ten million teenagers will engage in about 126 million acts of sexual intercourse this year. As a result, there will be about one million pregnancies, resulting in 406,000 abortions, 134,000 miscarriages, and 490,000 live births. Of the births, about 313,000, or 64 percent, will be out of wedlock. And about three million teenagers will suffer from a sexually transmitted disease such as chlamydia, syphilis, gonorrhea, pelvic inflammatory disease, and even AIDS.

This epidemic of teen pregnancy and infection has set off firestorms of debate in school systems from Boston to San Francisco. Last May, Washington, D.C. Mayor Sharon Pratt Kelly announced that health officials would distribute condoms to high school and junior high school students. Parents immediately protested, taking to the streets with placards and angry shouts. And the New York City Board of Education was virtually paralyzed for weeks by the controversy surrounding its plans for condom distribution.

Both sides have rallied around the issue of condom distribution as if it were a referendum on teen sexuality. Proponents argue that teenagers will have sex whether contraceptives are available or not, so public policy should aim to reduce the risk of pregnancy and the spread of sexually transmitted diseases by making condoms easily available. Opponents claim that such policies implicitly endorse teen sex and will only worsen the problem.

The causes of teen pregnancy and sexually transmitted diseases, however, run much deeper than the public rhetoric that either side suggests. Achieving real change in the sexual behavior of teenagers will require action on a broader front.

Thirty Years into the Sexual Revolution

Some things are not debatable: every year, more teenagers are having more sex, they are having it with increasing frequency, and they are starting at younger ages.

There are four principal sources of information about the sexual practices of teenagers: the National Survey of Family Growth (NSFG), a national in-person survey of women ages 15–44 conducted in 1982 and again in 1988; the National Survey of Adolescent Males (NSAM), a longitudinal survey of males ages 15–19 conducted in 1988 and 1991; the National

Survey of Young Men (NSYM), a 1979 survey of 17- to 19-year-olds; and the Youth Risk Behavior Survey (YRBS), a 1990 questionnaire-based survey of 11,631 males and females in grades 9–12 conducted by the Centers for Disease Control (CDC). In addition, the Abortion Provider Survey, performed by the Alan Guttmacher Institute (AGI), collects information about abortions and those who provide them.

With minor variations caused by differences in methodology, each survey documents a sharp increase in the sexual activity of American teenagers. All these surveys, however, are based on the self-reports of young people and must be interpreted with care. For example, one should always take young males' reports about their sexual exploits with a grain of salt. In addition, the social acceptability of being a virgin may have decreased so much that this, more than any change in behavior, has led to the higher reported rates of sexual experience. The following statistics should therefore be viewed as indicative of trends rather than as precise and accurate measures of current behavior.

A cursory glance at Figure 1 shows that there was indeed a sexual revolution. The 1982 NSFG asked women ages 15–44 to recall their first premarital sexual experience. As the figure shows, teenagers in the early 1970s (that is, those born between 1953 and 1955) were twice as likely to have had sex as were teenagers in the early 1960s (that is those born 1944 to 1946).

From *The American Enterprise*, January/February 1993, pp. 52-59. © 1993 by The American Enterprise Institute for Public Policy Research. Distributed by The New York Times Special Features.

The trend of increased sexual activity that started in the 1960s continued well into the late 1980s. According to the 1988 NSFG, rates of sexual experience increased about 45 percent between 1970 and 1980 and increased another 20 percent in just three years, from 1985–1988, but rates have now apparently plateaued. Today, over half of all unmarried teenage girls report that they have engaged in sexual intercourse at least once.

These aggregate statistics for all teenagers obscure the second remarkable aspect of this 30-year trend: sexual activity is starting at ever-younger ages. The 1988 NSFG found that the percentage of 18-year-olds who reported being sexually active increased about 75 percent between 1970 and 1988, from about 40 percent to about 70 percent. Even more startling is that the percentage of sexually experienced 15-year-old females multiplied more than fivefold in the same period, from less than 5 percent to almost 27 percent.

Moreover, the increase in sexual activity among young teens continued beyond 1988. In 1990, 32 percent of ninth-grade females (girls ages 14 and 15) reported ever having had sex, as did 49 percent of the males in the same grade. At the same time, the proportion of twelfth-grade females (ages 17 and 18) who reported ever engaging in sex remained at 1988 levels.

Teenagers are not only having sex earlier, they are also having sex with more partners. According to the NSAM, the average number of partners reported by males in the 12 months preceding the survey increased from 2.0 in 1988 to 2.6 in 1991. Almost 7 percent of ninth-grade females told the YRBS that they had had intercourse with four or more different partners, while 19 percent of males the same age reported having done so. By the twelfth grade, 17 percent of girls and 38 percent of boys reported having four or more sexual partners.

A major component of these increases has been the rise in sexual activity among middle-class teenagers. Between 1982 and 1988, the proportion of sexually active females in families with incomes equal to or greater than 200 percent of the poverty line increased from 39 percent to 50 percent. At the same time, the proportion of females from poorer families who had ever had sex remained stable at 56 percent.

Until recently, black teenagers had substantially higher rates of sexual activity than whites. Now, the differences between older teens of both races have narrowed. But once more, these aggregate figures obscure underlying age differentials. According to the 1988 NSAM, while 26 percent of white 15-year-old males reported engaging in sex compared to 67 percent of blacks, by age 18 the gap narrowed to 71 percent of whites and 83 percent of blacks. A similar trend appears among females. Twenty-four percent of white 15-year-old females have engaged in sex, compared to 33 percent

of their black counterparts, reports the 1988 NSFG. By age 16, the proportions increase to 39 percent and 54 percent, respectively. Even by age 17, fewer white females have started having sex (56 percent) than have blacks (67 percent). On the other hand, white teen males reported having had almost twice as many acts of intercourse in the 12 months preceding the 1988 NSAM than did black teen males (27 versus 15). The white males, however, had fewer partners in the same period (2 versus 2.5).

The Social Costs

Among the consequences of this steady rise in teen sexuality are mounting rates of abortion, out-of-wedlock births, welfare, and sexually transmitted diseases.

Abortion. About 40 percent of all teenage pregnancies now end in abortion. (Unmarried teens account for about 97 percent.) This means that of the 1.6 million abortions in 1988, over 400,000—or a

The trend of increased sexual activity that started in the 1960s continued well into the late 1980s. . . . Today, over half of all unmarried teen-age girls report that they have engaged in sexual intercourse at least once.

FIGURE ONE: TRENDS IN PREMARITAL SEXUAL ACTIVITY FOR ALL FEMALE TEENAGERS

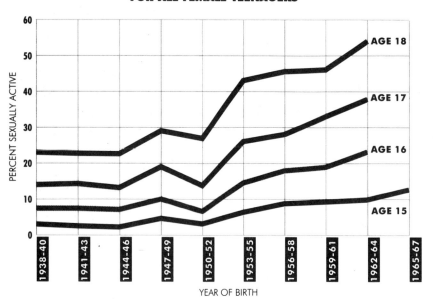

SOURCE: S. Hofferth, J. Kahn, and W. Baldwin, "Premarital Sexual Activity Among U.S. Women Over the Past Three Decades," *Family Planning Perspectives*, Vol. 19, No. 2, March/April 1987.

quarter of the total—were performed on teenagers. In the 11 years between 1973 and 1984, the teenage abortion rate almost doubled, from about 24 to about 44 per 1,000 females ages 15–19. (Between 1984 and 1988, the rate stabilized.)

A study by AGI's Stanley Henshaw found that between 1973 and 1988, the abortion rate for girls ages 14 and under increased 56 percent (from 5.6 to 8.6 per 1,000), 62 percent for those ages 15–17 (from 18.7 to 30.3), and among older teens, almost 120 percent (from 29 to 63.5). In absolute numbers, the youngest group had about 13,000 abortions, the

middle group had 158,000, and the oldest group had 234,000.

Out-of-Wedlock Births. Over 300,000 babies were born to unwed teenagers in 1988. That's three-fifths of all births to teenagers. Although the total number of births to teenagers declined between 1970 and 1988, the percentage born out of wedlock more than doubled (from 29 percent to 65 percent), and the teenage out-of-wedlock birth rate increased from about 22 per 1,000 to 37 per 1,000. Over 11,000 babies were born to children under 15 years old in 1988.

Welfare. Few teen mothers place

their children up for adoption as was often done in the past. And yet most are not able to support themselves, let alone their children. Consequently, about 50 percent of all teen mothers are on welfare within one year of the birth of their first child; 77 percent are on within five years, according to the Congressional Budget Office. Nick Zill of Child Trends, Inc., calculates that 43 percent of long-term welfare recipients (on the rolls for ten years or more) started their families as unwed teens.

As Table 1 shows, welfare dependency is more a function of a mother's age and marital status than of her race. White and black unmarried adolescent mothers have about the same welfare rate one year after the birth of their first child. After five years, black unmarried mothers have a somewhat higher rate of welfare dependency than whites (84 percent versus 72 percent), but various demographic factors such as family income, educational attainment, and family structure account for this relatively small difference.

Disease. Over three million teenagers, or one out of six sexually experienced teens, become infected with sexually transmitted diseases each year, reports the Centers for Disease Control (CDC). One Philadelphia clinic administrator laments that she used to spend $3 on contraceptives for every $1 on disease screening and related health issues. Today, the ratio is reversed. Susan Davis, a contraception counselor at a Washington, D.C. area Planned Parenthood clinic, explains, "The risk of infection is greater than the risk of pregnancy for teens." These diseases can cause serious

TABLE ONE: PERCENT OF ADOLESCENT MOTHERS ON AFDC

	BY FIRST BIRTH	WITHIN ONE YEAR OF BIRTH	WITHIN FIVE YEARS OF BIRTH
All	7%	28%	49%
Married	2	7	24
Unmarried	13	50	77
White	7	22	39
Black	9	44	76
White, Unmarried	17	53	72
Black, Unmarried	10	49	84

SOURCE: Congressional Budget Office, Sources of Support for Adolescent Mothers, Government Printing Office: Washington, D.C., 1990

problems if left untreated. The CDC estimates that between 100,000 and 150,000 women become infertile every year because of sexually transmitted disease-related pelvic infections.

The recent explosion of these diseases is in large measure caused by the sexual activity of teenagers; sexually transmitted disease rates decline sharply with age. Take gonorrhea, for example. According to AGI, there were 24 cases per 1,000 sexually experienced females ages 15–19 in 1988. Among women ages 20–24, the rate declined to 15 and fell rapidly with age. For women ages 25–29, 30–34, and 35–39, the rates are 5, 2, and 1 per 1,000, respectively. Except for AIDS, most sexually transmitted diseases follow a similar pattern.

AIDS has not reached epidemic proportions in the teen population—yet. According to the Centers for Disease Control, fewer than 1,000 cases of AIDS are among teenagers. However, there are 9,200 cases among 20–24 year-olds and 37,200 cases among 25–29 year-olds. Given the long incubation period for the AIDS virus (8–12 years), many of these infections were probably contracted during adolescence.

According to Lawrence D'Angelo and his colleagues at the Children's National Medical Center in Washington, D.C., the rate of HIV (the virus that causes AIDS) infection among teenagers using the hospital increased rapidly between 1987 and 1991. For males, the rate increased almost sevenfold, from 2.47 per 1,000 in 1987 to 18.35 per 1,000 in 1991. The female rate more than doubled in the same period, from 4.9 to 11.05. These statistics only reflect the experience of one hospital serving a largely inner-city population, but they illuminate what is happening in many communities.

Use, Not Availability

Many people believe that there would be less teen pregnancy and sexually transmitted diseases if contraceptives were simply more available to teenagers, hence the call for sex education at younger ages, condoms in the schools, and expanded family planning programs in general. But an objective look at the data reveals that availability is not the prime factor determining contraceptive use.

Almost all young people have access to at least one form of contraception. In a national survey conducted in 1979 by Melvin Zelnik and Young Kim of the Johns Hopkins School of Hygiene and Public Health, over three-quarters of 15- to 19-year-olds reported having had a sex education course, and 75 percent of those who did remembered being told how to obtain contraception.

Condoms are freely distributed by family planning clinics and other public health services. They are often sitting in a basket in the waiting room. Edwin Delattre, acting dean of Boston University's School of Education and an opponent of condom distribution in public schools, found that free condoms were available at eight different locations within a 14-block radius of one urban high school.

And, of course, any boy or girl can walk into a drug store and purchase a condom, sponge, or spermicide. Price is not an inhibiting factor: condoms cost as little as 50¢. Although it might be a little embarrassing to purchase a condom—mumbling one's request to a pharmacist who invariably asks you to speak up used to be a rite of passage to adulthood—young people do not suffer the same stigma, scrutiny, or self-consciousness teenagers did 30 years ago.

Teenagers can also obtain contraceptives such as pills and diaphragms from family planning clinics free of charge or on a sliding fee scale. In 1992, over 4,000 federally funded clinics served 4.2 million women, some as young as 13. According to AGI, 60 percent of sexually active female teens use clinics to obtain

SLEEP AROUND AND YOU COULD WIND UP HAVING MORE THAN A GOOD TIME.

Gonorrhea   Syphilis   AIDS   Herpes

When you're a teenager, the consequences of sex can stay with you a lot longer than the memories. **THE CHILDREN'S DEFENSE FUND**

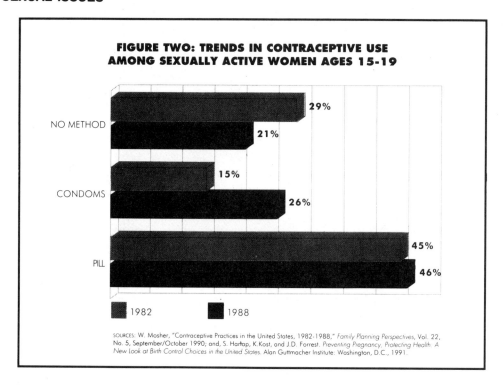

FIGURE TWO: TRENDS IN CONTRACEPTIVE USE AMONG SEXUALLY ACTIVE WOMEN AGES 15-19

NO METHOD — 29% (1982), 21% (1988)

CONDOMS — 15% (1982), 26% (1988)

PILL — 45% (1982), 46% (1988)

■ 1982   ■ 1988

SOURCES: W. Mosher, "Contraceptive Practices in the United States, 1982-1988," *Family Planning Perspectives*, Vol. 22, No. 5, September/October 1990; and, S. Harlap, K.Kost, and J.D. Forrest. *Preventing Pregnancy, Protecting Health: A New Look at Birth Control Choices in the United States.* Alan Guttmacher Institute: Washington, D.C., 1991.

contraceptive services, while only 20 percent of women over 30 do. In all states except Utah, teenagers can use clinic services without parental consent. To receive free services under the Medicaid program, however, a teenager must present the family's Medicaid card to prove eligibility.

In 1990, total public expenditures for family planning clinics amounted to $504 million. Adjusted for inflation, however, combined federal and state funding for clinics has declined by about one-third since 1980. But the impact of these cuts is unclear. On the one hand, the U.S. Department of Health and Human Services reports that the number of women using publicly funded clinics actually rose between 1980 and 1990, from 4.0 million to 4.2 million. When William Mosher of the National Center for Health Statistics analyzed the NSFG data, however, he found a slight decline between 1982 and 1988 in the proportion of respondents who had visited a clinic in the 12 months preceding the survey (37 percent versus 35 percent).

Whatever the effect of these cuts, the evidence suggests that as with condoms, teens know how to find a clinic when they want to. When they are younger, they do not feel the need to go to a clinic since condoms tend to be their initial form of contraception.

Susan Davis of Planned Parenthood explains, "The most common reason teenagers come is because they think they are pregnant. They get worried. Or they get vaginal infections. I had a whole slew of girls coming for their first pelvic exam and they all had chlamydia." The median time between a female teenager's first sexual experience and her first visit to a clinic is one year, according to a 1981 survey of 1,200 teenagers using 31 clinics in eight cities conducted by Laurie Zabin of the School of Hygiene and Public Health at the Johns Hopkins University in Baltimore.

The Conception Index

Two pieces of evidence further dispel the notion that lack of availability of contraception is the prime problem. First, reported contraceptive use has increased even more than rates of sexual activity. By 1988, the majority of sexually experienced female teens who were at risk to have an unintended pregnancy were using contraception: 79 percent. (This represents an increase from 71 percent in 1982.) When asked what method they use, 46 percent reported using the pill, 26 percent reported using condoms, and 2 percent reported using foam (see figure 2). In addition, the proportion of teen females who reported using a method of contraception at first intercourse increased from 48 percent in 1982 to 65 percent in 1988.

The second piece of evidence is that as they grow older, teenagers shift the forms of contraception they use. Younger teens tend to rely on condoms, whereas older teens use female-oriented methods, such as a sponge, spermicide, diaphragm, or the pill, reflecting the greater likelihood that an older female will be sexually active.

A major reason for this increase in contraceptive use is the growing number of middle-class youths who are sexually active. But it's more than this. Levels of unprotected first sex have decreased among all socioeconomic groups. Among teens from wealthier families, the proportion who reported using no method at first sex decreased between 1982 and 1988 from 43 percent to 27 percent. During the same period, non-use among teens from poorer families also declined, from 60 percent to 42 percent.

Unprotected first sex also decreased among racial groups. Between 1982 and 1988, the proportion of white females who reported using a method of contraception at first intercourse increased from 55 percent to 69 percent. Among blacks, the increase was from 36 percent to 54 percent.

It's not just that teens are telling interviewers what they want to hear about contraception. Despite large increases in sexual activity, there has not been a corresponding increase in the number of conceptions. Between 1975 and 1988,

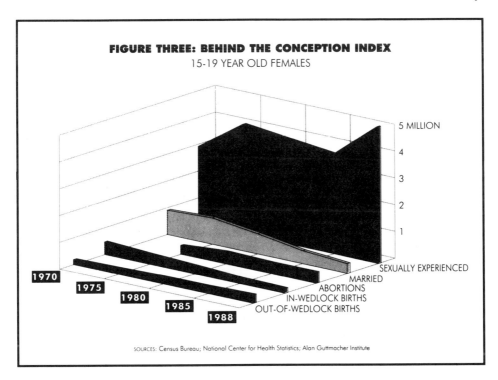

FIGURE THREE: BEHIND THE CONCEPTION INDEX
15-19 YEAR OLD FEMALES

SOURCES: Census Bureau; National Center for Health Statistics; Alan Guttmacher Institute

when about 1.3 million more teen females reported engaging in sex (a 39 percent increase), the absolute number of pregnancies increased by less than 21 percent (see figure 3).

In fact, one could create a crude "teen conception index" to measure the changing rate of conception (composed of abortions, miscarriages, and births) among sexually active but unmarried teenagers. If we did so, the 1988 index would stand at .87, representing a decline of 13 percent from 1975 (down from 210 to 182 per 1,000 sexually active, unmarried teens). Most of this decline occurred between 1985 and 1988 as more middle-class teenagers had sex.

The Challenge

Although the conception index among teens is declining, the enormous increase in sexual activity has created a much larger base against which the rate is multiplied. Thus, as we have seen, there have been sharp increases in the rates of abortion, out-of-wedlock births, welfare dependency, and sexually transmitted diseases as measured within the whole teen population.

Teenage sexuality does not have to translate into pregnancy, abortion, out-of-wedlock births, or sexually transmitted diseases. Western Europe, with roughly equivalent rates of teen sexuality, has dramatically lower rates of un-

wanted pregnancy. According to a 1987 AGI study, the pregnancy rate among American teens (96 per 1,000 women) was twice as high as that in Canada (44), England and Wales (45), and France (43). It was almost three times higher than Sweden's (35) and more than six times higher than in the Netherlands (14). The answer, of course, is effective contraception.

The magnitude of the problem is illustrated by data about reported condom use. Between 1979 and 1988, the reported use of a condom at last intercourse for males ages 17–19 almost tripled, from 21 percent to 58 percent. A decade of heightened concern about AIDS and other sexually transmitted diseases probably explains this tripling. According to Freya Sonenstein and her colleagues at the Urban Institute, over 90 percent of males in their sample knew how AIDS could be transmitted. Eighty-two percent disagreed "a lot" with the statement, "Even though AIDS is a fatal disease, it is so uncommon that it's not a big worry."

As impressive as this progress was, 40 percent did not use a condom at last intercourse. In fact, the 1991 NASM found that there has been no increase in condom use since 1988—even as the threat of AIDS has escalated.

The roots of too-early and too-often unprotected teen sex reach deeply into our society. Robin Williams reportedly

asked a girlfriend, "You don't have anything I can take home to my wife, do you?" She said no, so he didn't use a condom. Now both Williams and the girlfriend have herpes, and she's suing him for infecting her. (She claims that he contracted herpes in high school.) When fabulously successful personalities behave this way, should we be surprised to hear about an inner-city youth who refuses his social worker's entreaties to wear a condom when having sex with his AIDS-infected girlfriend?

According to the 1988 NSAM, while 26 percent of white 15-year-old males reported engaging in sex compared to 67 percent of blacks, by age 18 the gap narrowed to 71 percent of whites and 83 percent of blacks.

This is the challenge before us: How to change the behavior of these young men as well as the one in five sexually active female teens who report using no method of contraception. First, all the programs in the world cannot deal with one vital aspect of the problem: many teenagers are simply not ready for sexual relationships. They do not have the requisite emotional and cognitive maturity. Adolescents who cannot remember to hang up their bath towels may be just as unlikely to remember to use contraceptives. Current policies and programs do not sufficiently recognize this fundamental truth.

At the same time, the clock cannot be turned all the way back to the inno-cent 1950s. Sexual mores have probably been permanently changed, especially for older teens—those who are out of high school, living on their own or off at college. For them, and ultimately all of us, the question is: How to limit the harm being done?

The challenge for public policy is to pursue two simultaneous goals: to lower the rate of sexual activity, especially among young teens, and to raise the level of contraceptive use. Other than abstinence, the best way to prevent pregnancy is to use a contraceptive, and the best way to prevent sexually trans-mitted diseases is to use a barrier form of contraception. Meeting this challenge will take moral clarity, social honesty, and political courage—three commodi-ties in short supply these days.

The CIA Connection

O nce it is packaged in plastic envelopes, heroin from Pakistan, Burma, or Mexico is ready for its trip to the United States via an infinite variety of couriers—airline attendants, diplomats, merchants, gangsters—and almost invariably financed and organized by one of the major American distribution syndicates. To the average American who witnesses the dismal spectacle of the narcotics traffic at the street level, it must seem inconceivable that the Government is implicated. But America's heroin plague is of its own making.

Unfortunately, during the long years of the Cold War, American diplomats and CIA agents have been involved in the narcotics traffic at three levels:

¶ coincidental complicity through covert alliances with groups actively engaged in the drug traffic;

¶ support of the traffic by covering up for drug-lord allies and thus condoning their involvement;

¶ active engagement in the transport of opium and heroin.

ALFRED W. McCOY

Alfred W. McCoy is professor of history at the University of Wisconsin, Madison. This article, copyright © 1991, Alfred W. McCoy, is adapted from "The Politics of Heroin: CIA Complicity in the Global Drug Trade" (a completely revised and expanded edition of "The Politics of Heroin in Southeast Asia"), published by Lawrence Hill Books (June 1991).

Such U.S. complicity played a catalytic role in the buildup of Burma's opium trade in the 1950s and the growth of the Golden Triangle heroin traffic in Southeast Asia during the 1960s and 1970s. Official U.S. tolerance for drug dealing by our clandestine allies also occurred in the borderlands of Afghanistan and Pakistan in the early 1980s, rapidly transforming this remote region into one of the world's leading producers of heroin.

Despite the global prohibition of opium and coca sales, a vast illicit industry continues to link the highlands of the Third World with the cities of the First.

Over the past century, peasants of the Andes and the southern rim of Asia have relied on these drugs as their major source of cash. In such remote, rugged regions with costly transport and poor roads, narcotics—with their light weight and sure market—remain the only viable cash crops.

These mountain regions, moreover, provide refuge to rebels who find narcotics, with both production and marketing outside government control, an ideal economic base for revolution. The Asian and Latin American highland zones lie at the intersection of trade routes, terrain, national boundaries, and ethnic frontiers that make them natural outlaw zones beyond the reach of most modern states. The merchants who control the opium or coca crop are often legitimate tribal leaders who can mobilize arms and armies to defend their trade. Whether at peace or in rebellion, many highland regions of Asia and Latin America are dominated by narcotics, which create potent political support for the survival of this lucrative trade.

As the raw drugs come down from the highlands, they usually move to centers of secondary services essential to the global traffic—processing, finance, and smuggling. Since the farmers need credit and markets for each new crop, a major expansion of drug production has three requirements—finance, logistics, and politics.

What happened in Southern Asia beginning in the late 1970s is a case in point.

B y May 1980, Dr. David Musto, a Yale University psychiatrist and White House adviser on drugs, was an angry man. In late 1977, he had accepted President Jimmy Carter's appointment to the White House Strategy Council on Drug Abuse with the understanding that this statutory, policymaking body would "determine Federal strategy for prevention of drug abuse and drug trafficking."

Over the next two years, Musto found that the CIA and other intelligence agencies denied the council—whose members included the Secretary of State and the Attorney General—access to all classified information on drugs, even when it was necessary for framing new policy.

At one memorable briefing by CIA specialists on Colombia, Musto came armed with current World Bank data on the role

From *The Progressive*, July 1992, pp. 20-26. Excerpted from *The Politics of Heroin: CIA Complicity in the Global Drug Trade* by Alfred W. McCoy. © 1991 by Alred W. McCoy. Reprinted by permission on the publisher, Lawrence Hill Books, Brooklyn, NY.

of the U.S. dollar in the cocaine trade. The agency experts responded to his loaded questions with a direct lie about the dollar. When Musto confronted them with his World Bank data, the CIA men retracted their false statements without a blush. Musto's complaints to the White House about CIA lying produced no response.

When President Carter reacted to the Soviet invasion of Afghanistan in December 1979 by shipping arms to the mujahideen guerrillas, Musto's disquiet grew. "I told the council," he recalls, "that we were going into Afghanistan to support the opium growers in their rebellion against the Soviets. Shouldn't we try to avoid what we had done in Laos? Shouldn't we try to pay the growers if they will eradicate their opium production? There was silence." As heroin from Afghanistan and Pakistan poured into the United States, Musto noted that the number of drug-related deaths in New York City rose by 77 per cent.

Concerned by the mounting "heroin crisis," Musto joined Dr. Joyce Lowinson, another White House Drug Council member, in writing an op-ed-page article for *The New York Times* to protest the Carter Administration's failings. The two expressed their "worry about the growing of opium poppies in Afghanistan and Pakistan by rebel tribesmen" and asked: "Are we erring in befriending these tribes as we did in Laos when Air America (chartered by the Central Intelligence Agency) helped transport crude opium from certain tribal areas?"

While the two drug experts could only guess at the reasons for the expanded opium production, they had no doubts about the consequence—a flood of heroin. "On the streets, this drug is more potent, cheaper and more available than at any time in the last twenty years," they wrote. Although denied official intelligence, these two medical doctors warned, quite accurately as it turned out, that "this crisis is bound to worsen."

At the same time that Musto was voicing his concerns about a possible flood of Afghan heroin in late 1979, field agents for the Drug Enforcement Administration (DEA) were already finding that his possibility was fast becoming their reality. Following a decade of major victories in the global drug war, the sudden surge of heroin from Southern Asia—Afghanistan and Pakistan—disheartened the drug agents. As the first shipments of the new heroin began to arrive, the DEA called a special "Middle East Heroin Conference" at New York's Kennedy Airport in December 1979.

The DEA's intelligence chief opened the gathering of his agents by introducing the "new Middle Eastern heroin threat," the agency's terminology for the Pakistan-Afghanistan heroin surge which seemed to be rising without restraint.

Flying in from the Middle East for the conference, agent Ernie Staples added to the gloom. Since the "political situations" in the region were unfavorable, he reported, the DEA's "first line of defense"—interception near the growing areas—had collapsed. In a frank admission of failure, Staples stated flatly that there were "no longer any DEA personnel working effectively in these source countries." Grown and processed without restraint, Southern Asian heroin was capturing the European market.

"Europe at present is being flooded with Middle Eastern heroin," said Staples. As supply surged, wholesale heroin prices in Europe were falling and purity had risen to a new high—a statistic confirmed by 500 recent deaths from drug overdose in West Germany.

With ample supplies of Southern Asian opium and morphine, Marseille's Corsican syndicates were cooperating with the Sicilian Mafia. Judging from a recent seizure of New York-bound heroin in Italy, Sicilian Mafia groups based in Palermo were starting to smuggle the new heroin into the United States. "All indications," concluded Staples, "point to an increase of trafficking between Europe and the United States."

As DEA agents from Boston to Chicago stood in succession, they added details that revealed a developing crisis. Responsible for the nation's premier heroin market, the New York agents had been the first to see the impact of the new Southern Asian heroin. There was every sign that the New York heroin market of some 150,000 addicts was coming out of a long drought—police exhibits showed a "dramatic increase in purity," hepatitis cases were up, and city police had recorded a sharp rise in heroin arrests.

Changes in the New York market were soon felt in the rest of the country. The DEA's Washington, D.C., office, for example, reported an "increase in overdose death statistics." Within a year, these trends, seen so clearly by both Musto and the DEA in late 1979, began to transform the nature of the U.S. drug problem.

During the 1980s, America experienced an unprecedented drug crisis. Rising from insignificant levels, cocaine use doubled between 1982 and 1985. Eclipsed by the media glare on cocaine and crack, global heroin production and U.S. consumption rose steadily as well. Between 1983 and 1986, the number of heroin-related deaths doubled. And, while casual use of drugs declined toward the end of the decade, the hard core of regular users grew steadily.

Although the drug pandemic of the 1980s had complex causes, the growth in global heroin supply could be traced, in large part, to two key aspects of U.S. policy: the failure of the DEA's interdiction efforts and the CIA's covert operations.

By attacking heroin trafficking in separate sectors of Asia's extended opium zone in isolation, the DEA simply diverted heroin exports from America to Europe and shifted opium production from Southern to Southeast Asia and back again—raising both global production and consumption with each move.

Ironically, the increasing opium harvests in Burma and Afghanistan, America's major suppliers, were in large part the product of both the DEA's ill-fated attempts at interdiction and certain of the CIA's covert operations. Just as CIA support for Nationalist Chinese troops in the Shan states had increased Burma's opium crop in the 1950s, so the agency's aid to the mujahideen guerrillas in the 1980s expanded opium production in Afghanistan and linked Pakistan's nearby heroin laboratories to the world market. After a decade as the sites of major CIA covert operations, Burma and Afghanistan ranked, respectively, as the world's largest and second-largest suppliers of illicit heroin in 1989.

In the ten years that followed his prediction, Musto's dismal vision of America's coming drug crisis has been fulfilled.

Covert CIA operations in Afghanistan transformed Southern Asia from a self contained opium zone into a major supplier of heroin for the world market. Since the Sixteenth Century, when recreational opium-eating first developed, Southern Asia had constituted a self-sufficient drug market. In the highlands spanning Iran, Afghanistan, and northwest India (now Pakistan), tribal farmers grew limited quantities of opium and sold it to merchant caravans bound for the cities of Iran and India.

During the decade of Cold War confrontation with the Soviet Union in Afghanistan, however, CIA intervention provided the political protection and the logistics that opened that nation's poppy fields to heroin markets in Europe and America. Although Soviet forces have withdrawn and CIA aid has now slackened, there is every indication that Afghanistan, like Burma before it, will remain a major heroin supplier.

Long something of a backwater in U.S. foreign policy, Southern Asia emerged in the late 1970s as a flashpoint in the Cold War. As the United States and its allies sent in covert operatives, secret arms shipments, and military aid to meet the escalating political crises, opium production soared and heroin poured out of the region into European and American markets.

The Iranian revolution of February 1979 was the first in a series of major events that changed the character of both the region's politics and its narcotics traffic. Waves of strikes and mass demonstrations in Teheran toppled the Shah and his apparatus of repression, breaking his once-tight controls over the country's opium trade. His successor, the Ayatollah Khomeini, denounced drug dealers as "first-class traitors and a danger to society," but the new Islamic regime, reflecting Iran's traditional tolerance for the drug, did not place opium in the same forbidden category as alcohol, thereby creating an ambiguity that allowed the traffic to flourish. Six months after the revolt, the CIA reported that drugs were being sold openly on Teheran's streets and that the Revolutionary Guards, with many addicts in their ranks, did "not interfere with the dealers."

By September, CIA analysts in the U.S. embassy estimated that Iran's next poppy harvest would raise opium production from the current 200 tons to an estimated 325 tons. They argued that Iran's opium boom had "created a new 'golden triangle' comprised of Iran, Pakistan, and Afghanistan." Once the new bumper crop was harvested, Iran's opium "will join that . . . flowing over the 'silk route' of Marco Polo to Turkey and from there to Western Europe." The CIA concluded its report with a warning: "The world must brace itself for a flood of opium and heroin from Iran."

As events turned out, the CIA was half right. Beginning in 1979, Southern Asia did increase its heroin exports, but the drugs came from the Pakistan-Afghan borderlands, not Iran. As it had for two centuries, Iran showed a remarkable appetite for drugs and absorbed all of its own opium harvests, now greatly expanded under the new regime. Although Iran did not produce a surplus for export, its increased harvests now met its own needs, freeing Afghanistan's opium for export to Europe.

Initially, a peculiar twist in the global drug trade brought Southern Asia's heroin to Europe in 1979. Although the Pakistan-Afghanistan opium harvest rose steadily from 400 tons in 1971 to 1,200 tons in 1978, almost all of the increased production was consumed locally. Small quantities first appeared in Europe in 1975. But in the months following the region's bumper crop of 1978, European police still seized only forty-nine kilograms of Southern Asian heroin, a tenth of the 451 kilograms intercepted from Southeast Asia. Then the monsoon rains failed for two years in Southeast Asia, reducing Burma's opium production to a record low.

Nature, combined with covert-action nurture, soon turned Southern Asia's local opium traders into suppliers to the world.

As a network of heroin laboratories opened in 1979-1980 along the Afghan-Pakistan border to service the global markets opened by Southeast Asia's drought, Pakistan's opium production soared to 800 tons, far above its 1971 harvest of some ninety tons. By 1982, the Afghan poppy fields, linked with laboratories across the border in Pakistan, supplied more than half the heroin demand in America and Europe. To cite statistics, European seizures of Pakistani heroin shot from 121 kilograms in 1978 to 880 kilograms in 1980. Only three years after the first CIA arms reached the mujahideen, Southern Asia, never before a source, supplied 60 per cent of the U.S. heroin market. Inside Pakistan itself, the number of heroin addicts soared from only 5,000 in 1980 to 1.3 million in 1985.

During the ten years of CIA covert support for the mujahideen resistance, U.S. Government and media sources were silent about the involvement of leading Afghan guerrillas and Pakistan military in the heroin traffic.

Southern Asia became the focus of a crisis in U.S. foreign policy so grave that three successive Administrations, from Carter to Bush, gave the CIA unlimited funds and unrestrained authority to do whatever had to be done. After Iranian mobs toppled the Shah in 1979, America lost its military surrogate in the Persian Gulf, gateway for the West's oil supplies. A year earlier, various communist factions of the Afghan army had overthrown the dictator Mohammad Daoud and established a pro-Soviet regime in that strategic nation, the historic threshhold for Russian expansion toward the Indian Ocean. After months of internecine fighting among Kabul's communists, Soviet troops invaded Afghanistan in December 1979, occupying Kabul, the capital, and installing a pliable Afghan communist as president.

President Carter reacted with ill-concealed rage, using his diplomatic and covert-action resources to mobilize military aid for the mujahideen guerrillas. Within weeks, massive arms shipments began—hand-held missiles and antitank weapons from China, Kalashnikov assault rifles from Egypt, munitions from Saudi Arabia, and a variety of U.S. weapons from the CIA.

But Carter's covert-aid effort was limited by the coolness of his relations with General Mohammad Zia ul-Haq, leader of Pakistan's harsh martial-law regime. Soon after President Ronald Reagan took office in 1981, however, the White House announced a $3 billion program of military aid to Pakistan, including the latest F-16 fighters.

With Pakistan now openly committed to the mujahideen, General Zia's military assumed a dominant role in supplying the Afghan resistance forces. The Saudis delivered their clandestine aid directly to client guerrilla units inside Afghanistan. But most allied agencies worked with Pakistan's Inter-Service Intelligence (ISI), Zia's chosen instrument, which he was then building into a powerful covert-operations unit with the advice and assistance of the CIA. The agency's relationship with ISI was a complex give-and-take that makes simple caricatures inappropriate—that ISI was the agency's errand runner on the Afghan border or, conversely, that ISI manipulated the CIA into writing a blank check for General Zia's own Afghan policies. Whatever the nuances of covert relations may have been, the partnership produced a transformation of Pakistan's heroin trade.

When the Soviet Union began infiltrating Afghanistan in early 1979, the CIA worked through ISI to organize the first mujahideen resistance groups. "Throughout most of the war," explains Afghanistan expert Barnett Rubin, "the United States subcontracted to General Zia and ISI the main political decision about which Afghans to support." The U.S. program to aid the Afghan guerrillas began in April 1979, eight months before the full-scale Soviet invasion.

The following month at Peshawar in Pakistan's North-West Frontier Province, a CIA special envoy from the Islamabad station first met Afghan resistance leaders, all carefully selected by Pakistan's ISI—which was in effect offering the agency an alliance with its own Afghan client, Gulbuddin Hekmatyar, leader of the small Hezbi-i-Islami guerrilla group. The CIA accepted and, over the next decade, gave more than half its covert aid to Hekmatyar's guerrillas.

It was a dismal decision. Unlike the later resistance leaders who commanded strong popular followings inside Afghanistan, Hekmatyar, by all accounts brutal and corrupt, led a guerrilla force that was a creature of the Pakistani military. After the CIA built his Hezbi-i-Islami into the largest Afghan guerrilla army, he would use his arms—with the full support of ISI and the tacit tolerance of the CIA—to become Afghanistan's leading drug lord.

Among the legion of American correspondents who covered the Afghan resistance during the 1980s, few bothered to probe the background of Hekmatyar, the CIA's chosen instrument. An Islamic militant and former engineering student, Hekmatyar had founded Afghanistan's Muslim Brotherhood and led student demonstrations in Kabul during the late 1960s to oppose the king's secular reforms. In the early 1970s, according to a 1990 report in *The New York Times*, "he had dispatched followers to throw vials of acid into the faces of women students who refused to wear veils." Accused of murdering a leftist student in 1972, Hekmatyar fled into Pakistan's North-West Frontier where, as a member of Pushtun tribes that straddle the border, he was able to continue his political work. Living in Peshawar, Hekmatyar allied himself with Pakistan's Jama'at-i Islami (Party of Islam), a fundamentalist and quasi-fascist group with many followers inside the Pakistani officer corps.

Through these contacts with the military, Hekmatyar would become commander of a Pakistani covert operation to destabilize a new government in Kabul in 1974—five years before the Soviet invasion. When Mohammad Daoud, a former prime minister, led a coup against the Afghan king and established a republic in 1973, Pakistan's Prime Minister Zulfikar Ali Bhutto ordered his military to begin training a secret force of 5,000 Afghan rebels at clandestine camps inside Pakistan.

Armed and supplied by Islamabad, Hekmatyar led these guerrillas into Afghanistan and launched a revolt in the Panjsher valley north of Kabul in July 1975. Hekmatyar's propaganda that Daoud's conservative republic was a "godless communist-dominated regime" was unconvincing, and his mercenary force found itself without popular support. The Afghan army encountered little resistance when it marched into the valley to mop up. While Kabul put ninety-three of his captured mercenaries on trial, Hekmatyar retreated into Pakistan with most of his forces intact.

A year later, a communist coup in Kabul ousted Daoud and revived the fortunes of Hekmatyar's exile army. When the CIA station chief in Islamabad met the ISI's selected Afghan leaders in May 1979 and agreed to provide arms to Hekmatyar's guerrillas, it was a momentous decision, although nobody knew it at the time. CIA covert aid would increase markedly over the next two years, but Hekmatyar remained the prime beneficiary. Similarly, in June 1981, when President Reagan and General Zia agreed to support a full-scale war inside Afghanistan, the flood of clandestine military aid still followed the same patterns set at Peshawar by the CIA, ISI, and Hekmatyar two years earlier.

With generous U.S. aid, Pakistan opened its borders to three million Afghan refugees and allowed the CIA to conduct its secret war without restraint. Along the border, American operatives ran training camps for the mujahideen; in Islamabad, the CIA maintained one of its largest foreign stations to direct the war. CIA Director William Casey gained direct access to General Zia and was warmly received on regular visits. And, unique in a region where the official attitude toward the United States ranges from the unfriendly to the hostile, Zia allowed the CIA to open an electronic intelligence station facing the Soviet Union in northern Pakistan and permitted U.S. spy flights over the Indian Ocean from his air bases near the Persian Gulf.

Aside from $3 billion in direct aid, the Pakistan military gained control over distribution of the $2 billion in covert aid the CIA shipped to the Afghan guerrillas during the ten-year war. For General Zia's loyalists within the military, these contracts were a source of vast wealth.

At an operational level, General Zia's men controlled the delivery of CIA arms shipments when they arrived in Pakistan. Once the arms landed at the port of Karachi, the Pakistan army's Logistics Cell trucked them north to the Afghan guerrillas in the North-West Frontier. The governor of this province was Lieutenant General Fazle Huq, President Zia's closest confidant and the de facto overlord of the mujahideen. Even as the ranks of the resistance swelled after 1981, the ISI still insisted that Hekmatyar receive the bulk of CIA arms shipments.

ISI also gave Hekmatyar a free hand to rule the Afghan refugee camps that sprawled around Peshawar, and he used it to run what one U.N. worker called a "reign of terror," gaining control of rival resistance groups through violence. During the decade of the Afghan resistance war, such organizations as Asia Watch and Amnesty International received numerous reports of human-rights violations by his Hezbi-i-Islami guerrillas. But the American press still published positive reports about *our* mujahideen, ignoring the abuses and drug-dealing.

A year after the Soviet withdrawal in 1989, *The New York Times* finally reported what it called "the sinister nature of Mr. Hekmatyar." By then, his atrocities had caused the president of Afghanistan's new interim government to denounce Hekmatyar—his own foreign minister—as a "criminal" and a "terrorist."

As the Cold War confrontation wound down, the international press finally broke its decade of silence to reveal the involvement of the Afghan resistance and Pakistani military in the region's heroin trade. In May 1990, for example, *The Washington Post* published a front-page article charging that the United States had failed to take action against Pakistan's heroin dealers "because of its desire not to offend a strategic ally, Pakistan's military establishment." The *Post* article said U.S. officials had ignored

Afghan complaints of heroin trafficking by Hekmatyar and the ISI, an allegation that at least one senior American official confirmed. And *The Post* reported that "Hekmatyar commanders close to ISI run laboratories in southwest Pakistan" and "ISI cooperates in heroin operations."

The independent Pakistani press, angered by the country's own heroin epidemic, had reported many of the details years before. But while Pakistani heroin flooded Europe and America in the early 1980s, the Western press maintained a public silence on the origins of this new narcotics supply.

As the ISI's mujahideen clients used their new CIA munitions to capture prime agricultural areas inside Afghanistan, the guerrillas urged their peasant supporters to grow poppies, thereby doubling the country's opium harvest to 575 tons between 1982 and 1983. Mullah Nasim Akhundzada, a mujahideen commander, for example, controlled the best opium lands—once the breadbasket of Afghanistan—during most of the war. He decreed that half of all peasant holdings would be planted in opium. A ruthless leader and bitter enemy of Hekmatyar, Mullah Nasim issued opium quotas to every landowner and maintained his control by killing or castrating those who defied him.

In early 1986, *New York Times* correspondent Arthur Bonner spent a month traveling in the region, where he found extensive poppy fields in every town. "We must grow and sell opium to fight our holy war against the Russian nonbelievers," explained Nasim's elder brother Mohammed Rasul.

This admission contradicted the assurances the U.S. embassy in Islamabad had been giving about the Afghan drug trade. Typical of its disinformation on the subject, just two months before, the embassy had issued a formal denial that Afghan guerrillas "have been involved in narcotics activities as a matter of policy to finance their operations."

While Mullah Nasim ruled the prime opium fields of the Helmand Valley, Hekmatyar held the complex of heroin laboratories just across the border in Pakistan, operating under the protection of Governor Fazle Huq.

By 1988, there were an estimated 100 to 200 heroin refineries in the province's Khyber district alone. Trucks from the Pakistani army's logistics cell arriving with CIA arms from Karachi often returned loaded with heroin—protected from police search by ISI papers.

Writing in *The Nation* three years later, Lawrence Lifschultz cited numerous police sources charging that Governor Fazle Huq, President Zia's intimate, was the primary protector of the heroin industry. Lifschultz said that Huq "had been impli-

cated in narcotics reports reaching Interpol" as early as 1982. Both European and Pakistani police claimed that all investigations of the province's major heroin syndicates had "been aborted at the highest level."

With seventeen agents assigned to the U.S. embassy in Islamabad, the Drug Enforcement Administration compiled detailed reports identifying "forty significant narcotics syndicates in Pakistan." Despite the high quality of DEA intelligence, not a single major syndicate was investigated by Pakistani police for nearly a decade.

In marked contrast to the seventeen DEA agents who shuffled papers without result in the U.S. embassy, a single Norwegian detective broke a heroin case that led directly to Zia's circle. Arrested at Oslo airport with 3.5 kilograms of heroin in December 1983, Pakistani trafficker Raza Qureshi traded details about his drug syndicate for a reduced sentence. After Norway's public prosecutor filed formal charges against three Pakistani heroin merchants in September 1985, Pakistan's Federal Investigation Agency ordered their arrest. When police picked up Hamid Hasnain, vice president of the government's Habib Bank, they searched his briefcase and found the personal banking records of President Zia.

There was evidence, moreover, of a major heroin syndicate inside the Pakistan military. In June 1986, police arrested an army major driving from Peshawar to Karachi with 220 kilograms of heroin. Two months later, police arrested an air force lieutenant carrying an identical amount, indications of a tidy military mind organizing uniform deliveries. Before the two could be interrogated, both officers escaped from custody under what Pakistan's *Defense Journal* called "mystifying circumstances." These were only two of sixteen military officers arrested in 1986 for heroin trafficking.

The blatant official corruption continued until August 1988, when General Zia's death in a plane crash brought an eventual restoration of civilian rule. Typical of the misinformation that had blocked any U.S. action against Pakistan's heroin trade, the State Department's semi-annual narcotics review in September called Zia—who counted the country's leading drug lords as his confidants and close allies—"a strong supporter of anti-narcotics activities in Pakistan."

Soon after assuming office through open elections, the new prime minister, Benazir Bhutto, declared war on drugs by dismissing two of ISI's top military administrators and creating a new ministry to attack the drug trade. Despite her good intentions, however, Bhutto's commitment to the drug war was soon compromised and the outlook for an effective attack on the country's highly developed heroin industry seemed bleak. After ten years of unchecked growth under General Zia, drugs were now too well entrenched in the country's politics and economy for simple police action.

Conservative economists estimated that total annual earnings from Pakistan's heroin trade were $8 billion to $10 billion, far larger than Pakistan's government budget and equal to one-quarter of its gross domestic product. With so much heroin money flowing into the country, Pakistani commentators feared that the country's politics would take on a Colombian cast—that is, that the drug lords would start using money and arms to influence the nation's leaders.

Indeed, the first signs were not long in coming. Facing a no-confidence motion in the national assembly in late 1989, Prime Minister Bhutto charged that drug money was being used to destabilize her government. When she claimed that heroin dealers had paid 194 million rupees (the U.S. equivalent of about $9 million at the time) for votes against her, many observers found the allegation credible.

Moreover, the heavily armed tribal populations of the North-West Frontier Province were determined to defend their opium harvests. Police pistols would prove ineffective against tribal arsenals that now, thanks to the CIA, included automatic assault rifles, anti-aircraft guns, and rocket launchers. "The government cannot stop us from growing poppy," one angry tribal farmer told a foreign correspondent in 1989. "We are one force, and united, and if they come with their planes we will shoot them down."

By early 1990, the CIA's Afghan operation had proved doubly disastrous. Shortly after the Soviet withdrawal from Afghanistan in early 1989, the U.S. financed a mujahideen assault on Jalalabad, confidently predicting a victory as the first step toward a communist collapse. Instead, the attack failed and the communist regime still rules Kabul today, two years later.

After ten years of covert operations at a cost of $2 billion, America was left with mujahideen warlords whose skill as drug dealers exceeded their competence as military commanders. As the Cold War ended and the Bush Administration's war on drugs began, such Afghan leaders as the opium warlord Hekmatyar became a diplomatic embarrassment for the United States.

Following the policy of radical pragmatism it had employed before in Burma and Laos, the CIA had again allied itself with an opium warlord. Despite direct complaints from other Afghan guerrilla leaders about Hekmatyar's heroin dealing, the CIA evidently refused to do anything that might lessen his effectiveness as an instrument of its covert operations.

In mountain ranges along the southern rim of Asia—whether in Afghanistan, Burma, or Laos—opium is the main currency of external trade and thus a key source of political power. Since agency operations involve alliances with local power brokers who serve as the CIA's commanders, the agency has repeatedly found its covert operations enmeshed with Asia's heroin trade.

By investing a local asset such as Hekmatyar with the authority of its alliance, the CIA draws him under the mantle of its protection. So armed, a tribal leader, now less vulnerable to arrest and prosecution, can use his American protection to expand his share of the local opium trade. Once the CIA has invested its prestige in one of these opium warlords, it cannot afford to compromise a major covert-action asset with drug investigations.

Respecting the national-security imperatives of CIA operations, the DEA keeps its distance from agency assets, even when they are major drug lords. During the ten years of the Afghan war, some seventeen DEA agents sat in the U.S. embassy at Islamabad watching—without making a single major arrest or seizure—as the flood of Afghan-Pakistan heroin captured 60 per cent of the U.S. drug market. Operating along the Afghan border, CIA agents delivered several hundred million dollars' worth of arms to Hekmatyar's heroin convoys and cooperated closely with his corrupt protectors in Pakistan's ISI.

Over the past twenty years, the CIA has repeatedly denied any involvement in the Asian opium traffic. Although admitting that some of its allies might have dabbled in drugs, the agency insists that it has always avoided direct culpability. But critics who look for the CIA's officers to actually dirty their hands with drugs in the line of duty are missing the point. In most covert actions, the CIA avoids direct involvement in combat or espionage and instead works through local clients whose success often determines the outcome of an agency operation. Thus, the CIA's involvement in drugs usually revolves around indirect complicity in the drug dealing of its assets, not in any *direct* culpability in the actual traffic.

Still, the difference is moot on the streets of America. As David Musto demonstrated with his prescient questions in 1980, CIA complicity in opium traffic has a certain predictability to it, wherever and however it occurs.

A Society of Suspects:
THE WAR ON DRUGS AND CIVIL LIBERTIES

Property seized in drug raids, including large amounts of money, may be forfeited to the government without proof of the owner's guilt.

A decade after Pres. Reagan launched the War on Drugs, all we have to show for it are city streets ruled by gangs, a doubled prison population, and a substantial erosion of constitutional protections.

Steven Wisotsky

Mr. Wisotsky, professor of law, Nova University, Ft. Lauderdale, Fla., is a member of the advisory board of the Drug Policy Foundation, Washington, D.C., and author of Beyond the War on Drugs. *This article is based on a Cato Institute Policy Analysis.*

O N DEC. 15, 1991, America celebrated the 200th anniversary of the Bill of Rights. On Oct. 2, 1992, it marked the 10th anniversary of an antithetical undertaking—the War on Drugs, declared by Pres. Ronald Reagan in 1982 and aggressively escalated by Pres. George Bush in 1989. The nation's Founders would be disappointed with what has been done to their legacy of liberty. The War on Drugs, by its very nature, is a war on the Bill of Rights.

In their shortsighted zeal to create a drug-free America, political leaders—state and Federal, elected and appointed—have acted as though the end justifies the means. They have repudiated the heritage of limited government and individual freedoms while endowing the bureaucratic state with unprecedented powers.

That the danger to freedom is real and not just a case of crying wolf is confirmed by the warnings of a few judges, liberals and conservatives alike, who, insulated from elective politics, have the independence to be critical. Supreme Court Justice Antonin Scalia, for example, denounced compulsory urinalysis of Customs Service employees "in the front line" of the War on Drugs as an "invasion of their privacy and an affront to their dignity." In another case, Justice John Paul Stevens lamented that "this Court has become a loyal foot soldier" in the War on Drugs. The late Justice Thur-

good Marshall was moved to remind the Court that there is "no drug exception" to the Constitution.

In 1991, the Court of Appeals for the Ninth Circuit declared that "The drug crisis does not license the aggrandizement of governmental power in lieu of civil liberties. Despite the devastation wrought by drug trafficking in communities nationwide, we cannot suspend the precious rights guaranteed by the Constitution in an effort to fight the 'War on Drugs.'" In that observation, the court echoed a 1990 ringing dissent by the chief justice of the Florida Supreme Court: "If the zeal to eliminate drugs leads this state and nation to forsake its ancient heritage of constitutional liberty, then we will have suffered a far greater injury than drugs ever inflict upon us. Drugs injure some of us. The loss of liberty injures us all."

Those warnings are cries in the wilderness, however, unable to stop the relentless buildup of law enforcement authority at every level of government. In fact, the trend toward greater police powers has accelerated. One summary of the Supreme Court's 1990-91 term observed that its criminal law decisions "mark the beginning of significant change in the relationship between the citizens of this country and its police."

Despite such warnings, most Americans have yet to appreciate that the War on Drugs is a war on the rights of all of us. It could not be otherwise, for it is directed not against inanimate drugs, but against people—those who are suspected of using, dealing in, or otherwise being involved with illegal substances. Because the drug industry arises from the voluntary transactions of tens of millions of individuals—

all of whom try to keep their actions secret—the aggressive law enforcement schemes that constitute the war must aim at penetrating their private lives. Because nearly anyone may be a drug user or seller of drugs or an aider and abettor of the drug industry, virtually everyone has become a suspect. All must be observed, checked, screened, tested, and admonished—the guilty and innocent alike.

The tragic irony is that, while the War on Drugs has failed completely to halt the influx of cocaine and heroin—which are cheaper, purer, and more abundant than ever—the one success it can claim is in curtailing the liberty and privacy of the American people. In little over a decade, Americans have suffered a marked reduction in their freedoms in ways both obvious and subtle.

Among the grossest of indicators is that the war leads to the arrest of an estimated 1,200,000 suspected drug offenders each year, most for simple possession or petty sale. Because arrest and incarceration rates rose for drug offenders throughout the 1980s, the war has succeeded dramatically in increasing the full-time prison population. That has doubled since 1982 to more than 800,000, giving the U.S. the highest rate of incarceration in the industrialized world.

It has been established that law enforcement officials—joined by U.S. military forces—have the power, with few limits, to snoop, sniff, survey, and detain, without warrant or probable cause, in the war against drug trafficking. Property may be seized on slight evidence and forfeited to the state or Federal government without proof of the personal guilt of the owner.

From *USA Today Magazine*, July 1993, pp. 17-21. © 1993 by The Society for the Advancement of Education. Reprinted by permission.

Finally, to leverage its power, an increasingly imperial Federal government has applied intimidating pressures to shop owners and others in the private sector to help implement its drug policy.

Ironically, just as the winds of freedom are blowing throughout central and eastern Europe, most Americans and the nation's politicians maintain that the solution to the drug problem is more repression—and the Bill of Rights be damned. As Peter Rodino, former chairman of the House Judiciary Committee, said in expressing his anger at the excesses of the Anti-Drug Abuse Act of 1986, "We have been fighting the war on drugs, but now it seems to me the attack is on the Constitution of the United States."

In the beginning, the War on Drugs focused primarily on supplies and suppliers. Control at the source was the first thrust of anti-drug policy—destruction of coca and marijuana plants in South America, crop substitution programs, and aid to law enforcement agencies in Colombia, Peru, Bolivia, and Mexico.

Because this had no discernible, lasting success, a second initiative aimed to improve the efficiency of border interdiction of drug shipments that had escaped control at the source. There, too, success was elusive. Record numbers of drug seizures—up to 22 tons of cocaine in a single raid on a Los Angeles warehouse, for instance—seemed only to mirror a record volume of shipments to the U.S. By 1991, the amount of cocaine seized by Federal authorities had risen to 134 metric tons, with an additional amount estimated at between 263 and 443 tons escaping into the American market per year.

A reasonable search and seizure in the War on Drugs is interpreted very broadly and favors local police and Federal drug agents.

As source control and border interdiction proved futile, a third prong of the attack was undertaken: long-term, proactive conspiracy investigations targeted at suspected high-level drug traffickers and their adjuncts in the professional and financial worlds—lawyers, accountants, bankers, and currency exchange operators. This has involved repeated and systematic attacks by the Federal government on the criminal defense bar, raising dark implications for

the integrity of the adversarial system of justice. Defense lawyers have been subjected to grand jury subpoenas, under threat of criminal contempt, to compel disclosures about their clients. Informants have been placed in the defense camp to obtain confidential information. In each instance, the effect has been to undermine the protections traditionally afforded by the attorney / client relationship. This demonstrates the anything-goes-in-the-War-on-Drugs attitude of the Department of Justice, which publicly defended using lawyers as informants as "a perfectly valid" law enforcement tool.

As these expanding efforts yielded only marginal results, the war was widened to the general populace. In effect, the government opened up a domestic front in the War on Drugs, invading the privacy of people through the use of investigative techniques such as urine testing, roadblocks, bus boardings, and helicopter overflights. Those are dragnet methods; to catch the guilty, everyone has to be watched and screened.

Invading privacy

Drug testing in the workplace. Perhaps the most widespread intrusion on privacy arises from pre- or post-employment drug screening, practiced by 80% of Fortune 500 companies and 43% of firms employing 1,000 people or more. Strictly speaking, drug testing by a private employer does not violate the Fourth Amendment, which protects only against government action. Nevertheless, much of the private drug testing has come about through government example and pressure. The 1988 Anti-Drug Abuse Act, for instance, prohibits the award of a Federal grant or contract to an employer who does not take specified steps to provide a drug-free workplace. As a result of these and other pressures, tens of millions of job applicants and employees are subjected to the indignities of urinating into a bottle, sometimes under the eyes of a monitor watching to ensure that clean urine is not smuggled surreptitiously into the toilet.

In the arena of public employment, where Fourth Amendment protections apply, the courts largely have rejected constitutional challenges to drug testing programs. In two cases to reach the U.S. Supreme Court, the testing programs substantially were upheld despite, as Justice Scalia wrote in dissent in one of them, a complete absence of "real evidence of a real problem that will be solved by urine testing of customs service employees." In that case, the Customs Service had implemented a drug testing program to screen all job applicants and employees engaged in drug interdiction activities, carrying firearms, or handling classified material. The Court held that the testing of such applicants and employees is "reasonable" even without

probable cause or individualized suspicion against any particular person, the Fourth Amendment standard.

For Scalia, the testing of Customs Service employees was quite different from that of railroad employees involved in train accidents, which had been found constitutional. In that case, there was substantial evidence over the course of many years that the use of alcohol had been implicated in causing railroad accidents, including a 1979 study finding that 23% of the operating personnel were problem drinkers. Commenting on the Customs case, Scalia maintained that "What is absent in the government's justifications—notably absent, revealingly absent, and as far as I am concerned dispositively absent—is the recitation of even a single instance in which any of the speculated horribles actually occurred: an instance, that is, in which the cause of bribe-taking, or of poor aim, or of unsympathetic law enforcement, or of compromise of classified information, was drug use."

Searches and seizures. Other dragnet techniques that invade the privacy of the innocent as well as the guilty have been upheld by the Supreme Court. In the tug-of-war between the government's search and seizure powers and the privacy rights of individuals, the Court throughout the 1980s almost always upheld the government's assertion of the right of drug agents to use the airport drug courier profile to stop, detain, and question people without warrant or probable cause; subject a traveler's luggage to a sniffing examination by a drug-detecting dog without warrant or probable cause; search without warrant or probable cause the purse of a public school student; and search at will ships in inland waterways.

The right of privacy in the home seriously was curtailed in decisions permitting police to obtain a search warrant of a home based on an anonymous informant's tip; use illegally seized evidence under a "good faith exception" to the exclusionary rule (for searches of a home made pursuant to a defective warrant issued without probable cause); make a trespassory search, without a warrant, in "open fields" surrounded by fences and no trespassing signs and of a barn adjacent to a residence; and conduct a warrantless search of a motor home occupied as a residence, a home on the consent of an occasional visitor lacking legal authority over the premises, and the foreign residence of a person held for trial in the U.S. The Court also validated warrantless aerial surveillance over private property—by fixed-wing aircraft at an altitude of 1,000 feet and by helicopter at 400 feet.

Similarly, it significantly enlarged the powers of police to stop, question, and detain drivers of vehicles on the highways on suspicion with less than probable cause or with no suspicion at all at fixed checkpoints or roadblocks; make warrantless searches of automobiles and of closed containers therein; and conduct surveillance of suspects by placing transmitters or beepers on vehicles or in containers therein.

The foregoing list is by no means comprehensive, but it does indicate the sweeping expansions the Court has permitted in the investigative powers of government. Indeed, from 1982 through the end of the 1991 term, the Supreme Court upheld government search and seizure authority in approximately 90% of the cases. The message is unmistakable—the Fourth Amendment prohibits only ''unreasonable'' searches and seizures, and what is reasonable in the milieu of a War on Drugs is construed very broadly in favor of local police and Federal drug agents.

Surveillance of U.S. mail. Another casualty of the War on Drugs is the privacy of the mail. With the Anti-Drug Abuse Act of 1988, the Postal Service was given broad law enforcement authority. Using a profile, investigators identify what they deem to be suspicious packages and place them before drug-sniffing dogs. A dog alert is deemed probable cause to apply for a Federal search warrant. If an opened package does not contain drugs, it is resealed and sent to its destination with a copy of the search warrant. Since January, 1990, using this technique, the Postal Service has arrested more than 2,500 persons for sending drugs through the mail. The number of innocent packages opened has not been reported.

Wiretapping. As a result of the War on Drugs, Americans increasingly are being overheard. Although human monitors are supposed to minimize the interception of calls unrelated to the purpose of their investigation by listening only long enough to determine the relevance of the conversation, wiretaps open all conversations on the wiretapped line to scrutiny.

Court-authorized wiretaps doubtless are necessary in some criminal cases. In drug cases, though, they are made necessary because the ''crimes'' arise from voluntary transactions, in which there are no complainants to assist detection. The potential is great, therefore, for abuse and illegal overuse.

Stopping cars on public highways. It is commonplace for police patrols to stop ''suspicious'' vehicles on the highway in the hope that interrogation of the driver or passengers will turn up enough to escalate the initial detention into a full-blown search. Because the required ''articulable suspicion'' rarely can be achieved by observation on the road, police often rely on a minor traffic violation—a burned-out taillight, a tire touching the white line—to supply a pretext for the initial stop. In the Alice-in-Wonderland world of roving drug patrols, however, even lawful behavior can be used to justify a stop. The Florida Highway Patrol Drug Courier Profile, for example, cautioned troopers to be suspi-

cious of ''scrupulous obedience to traffic laws.''

Another tactic sometimes used is the roadblock. Police set up a barrier, stop every vehicle at a given location, and check each driver's license and registration. While one checks the paperwork, another walks around the car with a trained drug-detector dog. The law does not regard the dog's sniffing as the equivalent of a search on the theory that there is no legitimate expectation of privacy in the odor of contraband, an exterior olfactory clue in the public domain. As a result, no right of privacy is invaded by the sniff, so the police do not need a search warrant or even probable cause to use the dog on a citizen. Moreover, if the dog ''alerts,'' that supplies the cause requirement for further investigation of the driver or vehicle for drugs.

Monitoring and stigmatizing. In the world of anti-drug investigations, a large role is played by rumors, tips, and suspicions. The Drug Enforcement Administration (DEA) keeps computer files on U.S. Congressmen, entertainers, clergymen, industry leaders, and foreign dignitaries. Many persons named in the computerized Narcotics and Dangerous Drug Information System (NADDIS) are the subject of ''unsubstantiated allegations of illegal activity.'' Of the 1,500,000 persons whose names have been added to NADDIS since 1974, less than five percent, or 7,500, are under investigation by DEA as suspected narcotic traffickers. Nevertheless, NADDIS maintains data from all such informants, surveillance, and intelligence reports compiled by DEA and other agencies.

The information on NADDIS is available to Federal drug enforcement officials in other agencies, such as the Federal Bureau of Investigation, the Customs Service, and the Internal Revenue Service. State law enforcement officials probably also can gain access on request. Obviously, this method of oversight has troubling implications for privacy and good reputation, especially for the 95% named who are not under active investigation.

Another creative enforcement tactic sought to bring about public embarrassment by publishing a list of people caught bringing small amounts of drugs into the U.S. The punish-by-publishing list, supplied to news organizations, included only small-scale smugglers who neither were arrested nor prosecuted for their alleged crimes.

Military surveillance. Further surveillance of the citizenry comes from the increasing militarization of drug law enforcement. The process began in 1981, when Congress relaxed the Civil War-era restrictions of the Posse Comitatus Act on the use of the armed forces as a police agency. The military ''support'' role for the Coast Guard, Customs Service, and other anti-drug agencies created by the 1981 amendments expanded throughout the 1980s to the point that the

U.S. Navy was using large military vessels—including, in one case, a nuclear-powered aircraft carrier—to interdict suspected drug smuggling ships on the high seas.

By 1989, Congress designated the Department of Defense (DOD) as the single lead agency of the Federal government for the detection and monitoring of aerial and maritime smuggling into the U.S. DOD employs its vast radar network in an attempt to identify drug smugglers among the 300,000,000 people who enter the country each year in 94,000,000 vehicles and 600,000 aircraft. Joint task forces of military and civilian personnel were established and equipped with high-tech computer systems that provide instantaneous communication among all Federal agencies tracking or apprehending drug traffickers.

The enlarged anti-drug mission of the military sets a dangerous precedent. The point of the Posse Comitatus Act was to make clear that the military and police are very different institutions with distinct roles to play. The purpose of the military is to prevent or defend against attack by a foreign power and to wage war where necessary. The Constitution makes the president commander-in-chief, thus centralizing control of all the armed forces in one person. Police, by contrast, are supposed to enforce the law, primarily against domestic threats at the city, county, and state levels. They thus are subject to local control by the tens of thousands of communities throughout the nation.

Since the 1987 enactment of the Uniform Sentencing Guidelines, the penalties for drug crimes have become extreme and mandatory.

To the extent that the drug enforcement role of the armed forces is expanded, there is a direct increase in the concentration of political power in the president who commands them and the Congress that authorizes and funds their police activities. This arrangement is a severe injury to the Federal structure of our democratic institutions. Indeed, the deployment of national military forces as domestic police embarrasses the U.S. in the international arena by likening it to a Third World country, whose soldiers stand guard in city streets, rifles at the ready, for ordinary security purposes.

The dual military/policing role also is a danger to the liberties of all citizens. A likely military approach to the drug problem would be to set up roadblocks, checkpoints, and roving patrols on the highways, railroads, and coastal waters, and to carry out search-and-destroy missions of domestic drug agriculture or laboratory production. What could be more destructive to the people's sense of personal privacy and mobility than to see such deployments by Big Brother?

Excessive punishment

These are some of the many ways the War on Drugs has cut deeply—and threatens to cut deeper still—into Americans' privacy, eroding what Justice Louis D. Brandeis described as "the right to be let alone—the most comprehensive of rights and the right most valued by civilized men." Working hand-in-hand with the political branches, the courts have diminished constitutional restraints on the exercise of law enforcement power. In addition to expanded powers of surveillance, investigation, and prosecution, punishment has been loosed with a vengeance, against enemy and bystander alike.

Punishments have become draconian in part because of permission conferred by Justice William Rehnquist's 1981 circular dictum: "the question of what punishments are constitutionally permissible is not different from the question of what punishments the Legislative Branch intended to be imposed." The penalties have become so extreme, especially since the 1987 enactment of the Uniform Sentencing Guidelines, that many Federal judges have begun to recoil. U.S. district court Judge J. Lawrence Irving of San Diego, a Reagan appointee, announced his resignation in protest over the excessive mandatory penalties he was required to mete out to low-level offenders, most of them poor young minorities. Complaining of "unconscionable" sentences, the judge said that "Congress has dehumanized the sentencing process. I can't in good conscience sit on the bench and mete out sentences that are unfair."

Judge Harold Greene of the District of Columbia went so far as to refuse to impose the minimum guideline sentence of 17.5 years on a defendant convicted of the street sale of a single Dilaudid tablet, pointing to the "enormous disparity" between the crime and the penalty. In the judge's view, the minimum was "cruel and unusual" and "barbaric." Fourth circuit Judge William W. Wilkins objected to mandatory penalties because "they do not permit consideration of an offender's possibly limited peripheral role in the offense." Agreeing with that thinking, the judicial conferences of the District of Columbia, Second, Third, Seventh, Eighth, Ninth, and Tenth circuits have adopted resolutions opposing mandatory minimums.

As drug control policymakers came to realize that the drug dealers were, in an economic sense, merely entrepreneurs responding to market opportunities, they learned that attacks on dealers and their supplies never could succeed as long as there was demand for the products. Thus, they would have to focus on consumers as well as on suppliers. Pres. Reagan's 1986 Executive Order encouraging or requiring widespread urine testing marked a step in that direction. By 1988, Administration policy was being conducted under the rubric of "zero tolerance." In that spirit, Attorney General Edwin Meese sent a memorandum to all U.S. Attorneys on March 30, 1988, encouraging the selective prosecution of "middle and upper class users" in order to "send the message that there is no such thing as 'recreational' drug use. . . . "

Because of the volume of more serious trafficking cases, however, it was not remotely realistic, as the Attorney General must have known, to implement such a policy. Indeed, in the offices of many U.S. Attorneys, there were minimum weight or money volume standards for prosecution, and the possession and small-scale drug cases routinely were shunted off to state authorities. In fact, in many districts, the crush of drug cases was so great that the adjudication of ordinary civil cases virtually had ceased. The courthouse doors were all but closed to civil litigants.

In the name of zero tolerance, Congress purposely began enacting legislation that did not have to meet the constitutional standard of proof beyond a reasonable doubt in criminal proceedings. In 1988, it authorized a system of fines of up to $10,000, imposed administratively under the authority of the Attorney General, without the necessity of a trial, although the individual may request an administrative hearing. To soften the blow to due process, judicial review of an adverse administrative finding is permitted, but the individual bears the burden of retaining counsel and paying court filing fees. For those unable to finance a court challenge, this system will amount to punishment without trial. Moreover, it has been augmented by a provision in the Anti-Drug Abuse Act of 1988 that may suspend for one year an offender's Federal benefits, contracts, grants, student loans, mortgage guarantees, and licenses upon conviction for a first offense.

Both sanctions are a form of legal piling on. The legislative intent is to punish the minor offender more severely than is authorized by the criminal law alone. Thus, the maximum penalty under Federal criminal law for a first offense of simple possession of a controlled substance is one year in prison and a $5,000 fine, with a minimum fine of $1,000. Fines up to $10,000 plus loss of Federal benefits obviously exceed those guidelines.

The most recent innovation of this kind is a form of greenmail, a law that cuts off highway funds to states that do not suspend the driver's licenses of those convicted of possession of illegal drugs. The potential loss of work for those so punished and the adverse consequences on their families are not considered. The suspension is mandatory.

Seizure and forfeiture

The War on Drugs not only punishes drug users, it also penalizes those who are innocent and others who are on the periphery of wrongdoing. The most notable example is the widespread and accelerating practice, Federal and state, of seizing and forfeiting cars, planes, boats, houses, money, or property of any other kind carrying even minute amounts of illegal drugs, used to facilitate a transaction in narcotics, or representing the proceeds of drugs. Forfeiture is authorized, and enforced, without regard to the personal guilt of the owner. It matters not whether a person is tried and acquitted; the owner need not even be arrested. The property nonetheless is forfeitable because of a centuries-old legal fiction that says the property itself is "guilty." Relying on it, in March, 1988, the Federal government initiated highly publicized zero tolerance seizures of property that included the following:

● On April 30, 1988, the Coast Guard boarded and seized the motor yacht *Ark Royal*, valued at $2,500,000, because 10 marijuana seeds and two stems were found on board. Public criticism prompted a return of the boat, but not before payment of $1,600 in fines and fees by the owner.

● The 52-foot *Mindy* was impounded for a week because cocaine dust in a rolled up dollar bill was found on board.

● The $80,000,000 oceanographic research ship *Atlantis II* was seized in San Diego when the Coast Guard found 0.01 ounce of marijuana in a crewman's shaving kit. The vessel eventually was returned.

● A Michigan couple returning from a Canadian vacation lost a 1987 Mercury Cougar when customs agents found two marijuana cigarettes in one of their pockets. No criminal charges were filed, but the car was kept by the government.

● In Key West, Fla., a shrimp fisherman lost his boat to the Coast Guard, which found three grams of cannabis seeds and stems on board. Under the law, the craft was forfeitable whether or not he had any responsibility for the drugs.

Not surprisingly, cases like the foregoing generated a public backlash—perhaps the only significant one since the War on Drugs was declared in 1982. It pressured Congress into creating what is known as the "innocent owner defense" to such *in rem* forfeitures, but even that gesture of reasonableness is largely illusory.

First, the defense does not redress the gross imbalance between the value of property forfeited and the personal culpability of the owner. For example, a Vermont man was found guilty of growing six marijuana plants. He received a suspended sentence, but he and his family lost their 49-acre farm. Similarly, a New York man forfeited his $145,000 condominium because he sold cocaine to an informant for $250. The law provides no limit to the value of property subject to forfeiture, even for very minor drug offenses.

Second, the innocent owner defense places the burden on the property claimant to demonstrate that he or she acted or failed to act without "knowledge, consent or willful blindness" of the drug activities of the offender. Thus, the Federal government instituted forfeiture proceedings in the Delray Beach, Fla., area against numerous properties containing convenience stores or other businesses where drug transactions took place, claiming that the owners "made insufficient efforts to prevent drug dealings."

Placing the burden on the claimant imposes expense and inconvenience because the claimant must hire a lawyer to mount a challenge to the seizure. Moreover, many cases involve the family house or car, and it often is difficult to prove that one family member had no knowledge of or did not consent to the illegal activities of another. For instance, a Florida court held that a claimant did not use reasonable care to prevent her husband from using her automobile in criminal activity; thus, she was not entitled to the innocent owner defense.

A particularly cruel application of this kind of vicarious responsibility for the wrongs of another is seen in the government's policy of evicting impoverished families from public housing because of the drug activities of one unruly child. The Anti-Drug Abuse Act of 1988 specifically states that a tenant's lease is a forfeitable property interest and that public housing agencies have the authority to hire investigators to determine whether drug laws are being broken. The act authorizes eviction if a tenant, member of his or her household, guest, or other person under his or her control is engaged in drug-related activity on or near public housing premises.

To carry out these provisions, the act funded a pilot enforcement program. In 1990, the Departments of Justice and Housing and Urban Development announced a Public Housing Asset Forfeiture Demonstration Project in 23 states. The project pursued lease forfeitures and generated considerable publicity.

In passing this law, it must have been obvious to Congress that many innocent family members would suffer along with the guilty. Perhaps it was thought vital, nonetheless, as a way of protecting other families from drugs in public housing projects. As experience proves, however, even evicted dealers continue to deal in and around the projects. It is hard to take public housing lease forfeitures very seriously, therefore, other than as a symbolic statement of the government's tough stand against illegal drugs.

Destructive consequences

A policy that destroys families, takes property from the innocent, and tramples the basic criminal law principles of personal responsibility, proportionality, and fairness has spillover effects into other public policy domains. One area in which the fanaticism of the drug warriors perhaps is most evident is public health. Drugs such as marijuana and heroin have well-known medical applications. Yet, so zealous are the anti-drug forces that even these therapeutic uses effectively have been banned.

Marijuana, for instance, has many applications as a safe and effective therapeutic agent. Among them are relief of the intraocular pressure caused by glaucoma and alleviating the nausea caused by chemotherapy. Some AIDS patients also have obtained relief from using cannabis.

Yet, marijuana is classified by the Attorney General of the U.S., not the Surgeon General, as a Schedule I drug—one having a high potential for abuse, no currently accepted medicinal use, and lack of accepted safety for utilization. It thereby is deemed beyond the scope of legitimate medical practice and thus is not generally available to medical practitioners.

The only exception was an extremely limited program of compassionate treatment of the terminally or seriously ill, but even that has been eliminated for political

---

The intensive pursuit of drug offenders has generated an enormous population of convicts held in prison for very long mandatory periods of time; so much so that violent criminals (murders, robbers, and rapists) often serve less time than the drug offenders.

---

reasons. Assistant Secretary James O. Mason of the Department of Health and Human Services announced in 1991 that the Public Health Service's provision of marijuana to patients seriously ill with AIDS would be discontinued because it would create a public perception that "this stuff can't be so bad." After a review caused by protests from AIDS activists, the Public Health Service decided in March, 1992, to stop supplying marijuana to any patients save the 13 then receiving it.

There also are beneficial uses for heroin. Terminal cancer patients suffering from intractable pain generally obtain quicker analgesic relief from heroin than from morphine. Many doctors believe that heroin should be an option in the pharmacopeia. Accordingly, in 1981, the American Medical Association House of Delegates adopted a resolution stating that "the management of pain relief in terminal cancer patients should be a medical decision and should take priority over concerns about drug dependence." Various bills to accomplish that goal were introduced in the 96th, 97th, and 98th Congresses. The Compassionate Pain Relief Act was brought to the House floor for a vote on Sept. 19, 1984, but was defeated by 355 to 55. Although there were some concerns voiced about thefts from hospital pharmacies, the overwhelming concern was political and symbolic—a heroin legalization bill could not be passed in an election year and, in any event, would send the public the "wrong message."

The final and perhaps most outrageous example in this catalog of wrongs against public health care is the nearly universal American refusal to permit established addicts to exchange used needles for sterile ones in order to prevent AIDS transmission among intravenous drug users. In 1991, the National Commission on AIDS recommended the removal of legal barriers to the purchase and possession of intravenous drug injection equipment. It found that 32% of all adult and adolescent AIDS cases were related to intravenous drug use and that 70% of mother-to-child AIDS infections resulted from intravenous drug use by the mother or her sexual partner. Moreover, the commission found no evidence that denial of access to sterile needles reduced drug abuse, but concluded that it did encourage the sharing of contaminated needles and the spread of the AIDS virus. Notwithstanding the commission's criticism of the government's "myopic criminal justice approach" to the drug situation, the prevailing view is that needle exchange programs encourage drug abuse by sending the wrong message.

Public safety is sacrificed when, nationwide, more than 18,000 local, sheriff's, and state police officers, in addition to thousands of Federal agents, are devoted full time to special drug units. As a result, countless hours and dollars are diverted from detecting and preventing more serious violent crimes. Thirty percent of an estimated 1,100,000 drug-related arrests made during 1990 were marijuana offenses, nearly four out of five for mere possession. Tax dollars would be spent better if the resources it took to make approximately 264,000 arrests for possession of marijuana were dedicated to protecting the general public from violent crime.

The intensive pursuit of drug offenders has generated an enormous population of convicts held in prison for very long periods of time as a result of excessive and/or mandatory jail terms. It is estimated that the operating cost of maintaining a prisoner ranges from $20,000 to $40,000 per year, depending upon the location and level of security at a particular prison. With more than 800,000 men and women in American correctional facilities today, the nationwide cost approaches $30,000,000,000 per year. This is a major diversion of scarce resources.

These financial burdens are only part of the price incurred as a result of the relentless drive to achieve higher and higher arrest records. More frightening and damaging are the injuries and losses caused by the early release of violent criminals owing to prison overcrowding. Commonly, court orders impose population caps, so prison authorities accelerate release of violent felons serving non-mandatory sentences in order to free up beds for non-violent drug offenders serving mandatory, non-parolable terms.

For example, to stay abreast of its rapidly growing inmate population, Florida launched one of the nation's most ambitious early release programs. However, prisoners serving mandatory terms—most of them drug offenders, who now comprise 36% of the total prison population—are ineligible. As a result, the average length of sentence declined dramatically for violent criminals, while it rose for drug offenders. Murderers, robbers, and rapists often serve less time than a "cocaine mule" carrying a kilo on a bus, who gets a mandatory 15-year term.

A Department of Justice survey showed that 43% of state felons on probation were rearrested for a crime within three years of sentencing. In short, violent criminals are released early to commit more crimes so that their beds can be occupied by non-violent drug offenders. Civil libertarians are not heard often defending a societal right to be secure from violent criminals, much less a right of victims to see just punishment meted out to offenders. In this they are as shortsighted as their law-and-order counterparts. The War on Drugs is a public safety disaster, making victims of us all.

However uncomfortable it may be to admit, the undeniable reality is that drugs always have been and always will be a presence in society. Americans have been paying too high a price for the government's War on Drugs. As Federal judge William Schwarzer has said, "It behooves us to think that it may profit us very little to win the war on drugs if in the process we lose our soul."

Global Issues

- **Environmental (Articles 37–39)**

- **Cultural and Economic (Articles 40–42)**

Many of the social problems facing Americans today are shared by people world wide, such as the environment, pollution, and inflation. Some problems facing the whole world are fueled by the consumerism of Americans, and some problems facing the United States are the product of other nations' improvements in production and their desire to improve their economic conditions. The world is no longer the exclusive marketplace for U.S. goods. What we do impacts on the world, and what happens around the world impacts on the United States.

"Enough Is Enough: Assessing Global Consumption" is one example of how America's lifestyle has impacted on many other nations. We have moved from a nation of producers to a nation of consumers. This voracious appetite for consumption is emulated in other nations, and it is making a horrendous impact on the world's environment.

"The Rape of the Oceans" focuses on the impact that technology, fishing policies, and international competition are having on marine life. The very attributes that made fishermen rugged, individualistic heroes are the attributes that may destroy their occupations.

The benefits of global warming are never discussed in the mass media. Global warming is seen as the beginning of the end for mankind. But this may not be true, and in fact, the exact opposite may be true. In the article "Benefits of Global Warming," the author examines the statistics on global warming and finds little if any support that it is occurring or that it is having negative consequences.

"Islam's Violent Improvisers" are small, isolated, unorganized groups of angry young men. Attempts to control Islamic terrorists by placing pressure on specific nations such as Iran, Liberia, and Iraq cannot succeed. These new radicals hold no allegiance to any political state. Their allegiance is to a specific charismatic individual and that person's particular interpretation of what constitutes true Islamic law. Most Islamic states are a loose and uneasy mix of modern politics and religious traditions and are not seen as Islamically pure. As more and more Islamic radicals question the legitimacy of any state, their actions will be very difficult to control.

"Outer Limits to America's Turn Inward" focuses on Americans' tendency to believe that the world exists to make sure America survives. But, with increasing inflation, the deterioration of our cities, crime, and so on, other countries have began to invest elsewhere. They no longer see us as a place of unlimited opportunities, and we can no longer expect that their money will bail us out of our current economic mess.

In "A Decade of Discontinuity," the author points out that humankind can no longer expect a future of ever-increasing productivity. World population growth is increasingly outstripping its food production and fossil fuel capacity. Scientists are concerned that the technological innovation that kept pace in the past may not be capable of doing so in the future.

Looking Ahead: Challenge Questions

What are the negative implications of consumerism (a) for those nations that are consuming and (b) for those nations meeting the demands of the consumers?

In what major ways will the abuse to which we have subjected our oceans eventually impact on us?

Why is international cooperation so vital if we are to save our oceans?

Is there any valid empirical evidence that global warming is occurring? If it is, will it be necessarily bad?

To what degree are "terrorist nations" responsible for Islamic terrorist acts such as the 1993 bombing of the World Trade Center in New York City?

Why are the activities of members of Islamic charismatic terrorist groups difficult to control?

Can we, as a nation, continue to be the police force or savior of the world?

Can technological innovation continue to meet the worldwide ever-increasing demand for food, fuel, and security?

What are the implications for world peace of increasing populations and shrinking resources?

In what significantly different ways would the three major sociological theoretical perspectives argue that we should study global issues?

What are the major values, rights, obligations, and harms associated with each of the issues covered in this unit?

Enough is Enough

Assessing global consumption

Alan Durning

ALAN DURNING is a senior researcher at the Worldwatch Institute. This article is adapted from "Asking How Much Is Enough," Chapter Nine, in *State of the World 1991*.

"Our enormously productive economy ... demands that we make consumption our way of life, that we convert the buying and use of goods into rituals, that we seek our spiritual satisfaction, our ego satisfaction, in consumption. ... We need things consumed, burned up, worn out, replaced, and discarded at an ever increasing rate."

Victor Lebow, U.S. retailing analyst, 1955

Across the country, Americans have responded to Victor Lebow's call, and around the globe, those who could afford it have followed. And many can: Worldwide, on average, a person today is four-and-a-half times richer than were his or her great-grandparents at the turn of the century.

Needless to say, that new global wealth is not evenly spread among the earth's people. One billion live in unprece-dented luxury; one billion live in destitu-tion.Overconsumption by the world's fortunate is an environmental problem unmatched in severity by anything except perhaps population growth. Surging ex-ploitation of resources threatens to ex-haust or unalterably disfigure forests, soils, water, air, and climate. High con-sumption may be a mixed blessing in human terms, too. Many in the industrial lands have a sense that, hoodwinked by a consumerist culture, they have been fruit-lessly attempting to satisfy social, psychological, and spiritual needs with material things.

Of course, the opposite of overcon-sumption—poverty—is no solution to either environmental or human problems. It is infinitely worse for people and bad for the natural world. Dispos-sessed peasants slash and burn their way into Latin American rain forests, and hungry nomads turn their herds out onto fragile African range land, reducing it to desert. If environmental destruction results when people have either too little or too much, we are left to wonder how much is enough. What level of consump-tion can the earth support? When does

From *Dollars & Sense,* June 1991, pp. 15-18. *Dollars & Sense* is a monthly progressive economics magazine published in Somerville, Massachusetts. First-year subscriptions cost 16.95 and may be ordered by writing *Dollars & Sense,* One Summer St., Somerville, MA 02143 having more cease to add appreciably to human satisfaction?

THE CONSUMING SOCIETY

Consumption is the hallmark of our era.

The headlong advance of technology, rising earnings, and cheaper material goods have lifted consumption to levels never dreamed of a century ago. In the United States, the world's premier consuming society, people today on average own twice as many cars, drive two-and-a-half times as far, and travel 25 times further by air than did their parents in 1950. Air conditioning spread from 15% of households in 1960 to 64% in 1987, and color televisions from 1% to 93%. Microwave ovens and video cassette recorders reached almost two-thirds of American homes during the 1980s alone.

Japan and Western Europe have displayed parallel trends. Per person, the Japanese today consume more than four times as much aluminum, almost five times as much energy, and 25 times as much steel as they did in 1950. They also own four times as many cars and eat nearly twice as much meat. Like the Japanese, Western Europeans' consumption levels are only one notch below Americans'.

The late 1980s saw some poor societies begin the transition to consuming ways. In China, the sudden surge in spending on consumer durables shows up clearly in data from the State Statistical Bureau: Between 1982 and 1987, color televisions spread from 1% to 35% of urban Chinese homes, washing machines quadrupled from 16% to 67%, and refrigerators expanded their reach from 1% to 20%.

Meanwhile, in India, the emergence of a middle class, along with liberalization of the consumer market and the introduction of buying on credit, has led to explosive growth in sales of everything from automobiles and motorbikes to televisions and frozen dinners.

Few would begrudge anyone the simple advantages of cold food storage or mechanized clothes washing. The point, rather, is that even the oldest non-Western nations are emulating the high-consumption lifestyle. Long before all the world's people could achieve the American dream, however, we would lay waste the planet.

The industrial world's one billion meat eaters, car drivers, and throwaway consumers are responsible for the lion's share of the damage humans have caused common global resources. Over the past century, the economies of the wealthiest fifth of humanity have pumped out two-thirds of the greenhouse gases threatening the earth's climate, and each year their energy use releases three-fourths of the sulfur and nitrogen oxides causing acid rain. Their industries generate most of the world's hazardous chemical wastes, and their air conditioners, aerosol sprays, and factories release almost 90% of the chlorofluorocarbons destroying the earth's protective ozone layer. Clearly, even one billion profligate consumers is too much for the earth.

Beyond the environmental costs of acquisitiveness, some perplexing findings of social scientists throw doubt on the wisdom of high consumption as a personal and national goal: Rich societies have had little success in turning consumption into fulfillment. Regular surveys by the National Opinion Research Center of the University of Chicago reveal, for example, that no more Americans report they are "very happy" now than in 1957.

Likewise, a landmark study by sociologist Richard Easterlin in 1974 revealed that Nigerians, Filipinos, Panamanians, Yugoslavians, Japanese, Israelis, and West Germans all ranked themselves near the middle of a happiness scale. Confounding any attempt to correlate affluence and happiness, poor Cubans and rich Americans were both found to be considerably happier than the norm.

If the effectiveness of consumption in providing personal fulfillment is questionable, perhaps environmental concerns can help us redefine our goals.

IN SEARCH OF SUFFICIENCY

By examining current consumption patterns, we receive some guidance on what the earth can sustain. For three of the most ecologically important types of consumption—transportation, diet, and use of raw materials—the world's people are distributed unevenly over a vast range. Those at the bottom clearly fall below the "too little" line, while those at the top, in the cars-meat-and-disposables class, clearly consume too much.

Approximately one billion people do their traveling, aside from the occasional donkey or bus ride, on foot. Unable to get to jobs easily, attend school, or bring their complaints before government offices, they are severely hindered by the lack of transportation options.

Another three billion people travel by bus and bicycle. Kilometer for kilometer, bikes are cheaper than any other vehicle, costing less than $100 new in most of the Third World and requiring no fuel.

The world's automobile class is relatively small: Only 8% of humans, about 400 million people, own cars. The automobile makes itself indispensable: Cities sprawl, public transit atrophies, shopping centers multiply, workplaces scatter.

The global food consumption ladder has three rungs. According to the latest World Bank estimates, the world's 630 million poorest people are unable to provide themselves with a healthy diet. On the next rung, the 3.4 billion grain eaters of the world's middle class get enough calories and plenty of plant-based protein, giving them the world's healthiest basic diet.

The top of the ladder is populated by the meat eaters, those who obtain close to 40% of their calories from fat. These 1.25 billion people eat three times as much fat per person as the remaining four billion, mostly because they eat so much red meat. The meat class pays the price of its diet in high death rates from the so-called diseases of affluence—heart disease, stroke, and certain types of cancer.

The earth also pays for the high-fat diet. Indirectly, the meat-eating quarter of humanity consumes nearly 40% of the world's grain—grain that fattens the livestock they eat. Meat production is behind a substantial share of the environmental strains induced by agriculture, from soil erosion to overpumping of underground water.

In consumption of raw materials, such as steel, cotton, or wood, the same pattern emerges. A large group lacks many of the benefits provided by modest use of nonrenewable resources—particularly durables like radios, refrigerators, water pipes, tools, and carts with lightweight wheels and ball bearings. More than two billion people live in countries where per capita consumption of steel, the most basic modern material, falls below 50 kilograms a year.

Roughly 1.5 billion live in the middle class of materials use. Providing each of them with durable goods every year uses between 50 and 150 kilograms of steel. At the top of the heap is the industrial world or the throwaway class. A typical resident of the industrialized fourth of the world uses 15 times as much paper, 10 times as much steel, and 12 times as much fuel as a Third World resident.

In the throwaway economy, packaging becomes an end in itself, disposables proliferate, and durability suffers. Americans toss away 180 million razors annually, enough paper and plastic plates and cups to feed the world a picnic six times a year, and enough aluminum cans to make 6,000 DC-10 airplanes. Similarly, the Japanese use 30 million "disposable" single-roll cameras each year, and the British dump 2.5 billion diapers.

THE CULTIVATION OF NEEDS

What prompts us to consume so much? "The avarice of mankind is insatiable," wrote Aristotle 23 centuries ago. As each of our desires is satisfied, a new one appears in its place. All of economic theory is based on that observation.

What distinguishes modern consuming habits, some would say, is simply that we are much richer than our ancestors, and consequently have more ruinous effects on nature. While a great deal of truth lies in that view, five distinctly modern factors play a role in cultivating particularly voracious appetites: the influence of social pressures in mass societies, advertising, the shopping culture, various government policies, and the expansion of the mass market into households and local communities.

In advanced industrial nations, daily interactions with the economy lack the face-to-face character prevailing in surviving local communities. Traditional virtues such as integrity, honesty, and skill are too hard to measure to serve as yardsticks of social worth. By default, they are gradually supplanted by a simple, single indicator—money. As one Wall Street banker put it bluntly to the *New York Times*, "Net worth equals self-worth."

Beyond social pressures, the affluent live completely enveloped in pro-consumption advertising messages. The sales pitch is everywhere. One analyst estimates that the typical American is exposed to 50-100 advertisements each morning before nine o'clock. Along with their weekly 22-hour diet of television, American teenagers are typically exposed to three to four hours of TV advertisements a week, adding up to at least 100,000 ads between birth and high school graduation.

Marketers have found ever more ways to push their products. Ads are piped into classrooms and doctors' offices, woven into the plots of feature films, placed on board games, mounted in bathroom stalls, and played back between rings on public phones in the Kansas City airport. Even the food supply may go mass media: The Viskase company of Chicago now offers to print edible ad slogans on hot dogs, and Eggverts International is using a similar technique to advertise on thousands of eggs in Israel.

Advertising has been one of the fastest growing industries during the past half-century. In the United States, ad expenditures rose from $198 per capita in 1950 to $498 in 1989. Worldwide, over the same period, per person advertising expenditures grew from $15 to $46. In developing countries, the increases have been astonishing. Advertising billings in India jumped fivefold in the 1980s; newly industrialized South Korea's advertising industry grew 35-40% annually in the late 1980s.

Shopping, particularly in the United States, seems to have become a primary cultural activity. Americans spend six hours a week shopping. Some 93% of American teenage girls surveyed in 1987 deemed shopping their favorite pastime.

Government policies also play a role in promoting consumption and in worsening its ecological impact. The British tax code, for example, encourages businesses to buy thousands of large company cars for employee use. Most governments in North and South America subsidize beef production on a massive scale.

Finally, the sweeping advance of the commercial mass market into realms once dominated by family members and local enterprise has made consumption far more wasteful than in the past. More and more, flush with cash but pressed for time, households opt for the questionable "conveniences" of prepared, packaged foods, miracle cleaning products, and disposable everything—from napkins to shower curtains. All these things cost the earth dearly, and change households from productive units of the economy to passive, consuming entities.

Like the household, the community economy has atrophied—or been dismembered—under the blind force of the money economy. Shopping malls, super-highways, and strips have replaced corner stores, local restaurants, and neighborhood theaters—the very places that help create a sense of common identity and community. Traditional Japanese vegetable stands and fish shops are giving way to supermarkets and convenience stores, and styrofoam and plastic film have replaced yesterday's newspaper as fish wrap.

All these things nurture the acquisitive desires that everyone has. Can we, as individuals and as citizens, act to confront these forces?

THE CULTURE OF PERMANENCE

The basic value of a sustainable society, the ecological equivalent of the Golden Rule, is simple: Each generation should meet its own needs without jeopardizing the prospects of future generations to meet theirs.

For individuals, the decision to live a life of sufficiency—to find their own answer to the question "how much is enough?"—is to begin a highly personal process. Social researcher Duane Elgin estimated in 1981—perhaps optimistically—that 10 million adult Americans were experimenting "wholeheartedly" with voluntary simplicity. India, the Netherlands, Norway, Western Germany, and the United Kingdom all have small segments of their populations who adhere to a non-consuming philosophy. Motivated by the desire to live justly in an unjust world, to walk gently on the earth, and to avoid distraction, clutter, and pretense, their goal is not ascetic self-denial but personal fulfillment. They do not think consuming more is likely to provide it.

Realistically, voluntary simplicity is unlikely to gain ground rapidly against the onslaught of consumerist values. And, ultimately, personal restraint will do little if not wedded to bold political and social steps against the forces promoting consumption. Commercial television, for example, will need fundamental reorientation in a culture of permanence. As religious historian Robert Bellah put it, "That happiness is to be attained through limitless material acquisition is denied by every religion and philosophy known to humankind, but is preached incessantly by every American television set."

Direct incentives for overconsumption are also essential targets for reform. If goods' prices reflected something closer to the environmental cost of their production, through revised subsidies and tax systems, the market itself would guide consumers toward less damaging forms of consumption. Disposables and packaging would rise in price relative to durable, less-packaged goods; local un-processed food would fall in price relative to prepared products trucked from far away.

The net effect might be lower overall consumption as people's effective purchasing power declined. As currently constituted, unfortunately, economies penalize the poor when aggregate consumption contracts: Unemployment skyrockets and inequalities grow. Thus arises one of the greatest challenges for sustainable economics in rich societies—finding ways to ensure basic employment opportunities for all without constantly stoking the fires of economic growth.

In the final analysis, accepting and living by sufficiency rather than excess offers a return to what is, culturally speaking, the human home: to the ancient order of family, community, good work, and good life; to a reverence for excellence of skilled handiwork; to a true materialism that does not just care about things but cares for them; to communities worth spending a lifetime in. The very things that make life worth living, that give depth and bounty to human existence, are infinitely sustainable.

THE RAPE OF THE OCEANS

America's last frontier is seriously overfished, badly polluted, poorly managed and in deepening trouble

With Capt. Joe Testaverde at the helm, the trawler Nina T slips into its Gloucester, Mass., mooring at sunset. Joe's father, Salvatore Testaverde, and his Sicilian father before him were Gloucester fishermen, and the family has trawled Northeastern waters for close to 80 years. This night seems a comforting continuum as the fish are unloaded and the crew members josh with dockside onlookers, exaggerating the size of the catch. The scene in this snug New England harbor is as timeless and reassuring as the tides—and as deceptive as a roseate dawn.

In bygone years, Joe Testaverde's father and grandfather would return to port with their boats packed from bilge to gunwale with haddock and flounder, and with jumbo codfish weighing 50 pounds or better. Sal Testaverde recalls pulling up 5,000 pounds of cod in a one-hour tow. Today, if he can find them, son Joe might haul in 2,000 pounds of middling-sized cod in eight hours of hard trawling. And he won't even waste time searching for flounder and haddock. The Nina T, more than likely, will return with hake, whiting, spiny dogfish or skate—species despised in Sal Testaverde's day as "trash" fish. Shipped abroad or retailed in ethnic markets for about $1 a pound, they are the dominant and devalued currency of the Georges Bank, once the nation's richest fishing ground.

The precipitous, perhaps irreversible decline of New England's groundfish is one of the major casualties of an unrelenting assault on the nation's coastal oceans. The principal problems are overfishing, burgeoning seaside development, loss of coastal wetlands and pollution of bay and estuary fish breeding grounds. Compounding these pressures is the profligate waste of hundreds of millions of pounds of edible "bycatch" fish. And a political

---

About 1.5 million dolphins and other small whales are killed each year by tuna fishermen, by pollution or in targeted hunts.

---

consensus between fishing and federal bureaucrats to better manage the vast and valuable marine resources has yet to be reached. This looming disaster extends from the coastlines out to the 200-mile limit in the Atlantic and Pacific oceans, the Gulf of Mexico, the Gulf of Alaska and the Bering Sea. Together, they represent the country's last open frontier.

These 2.2 million square miles contain about one fifth of the world's harvestable seafood; enormous populations of marine birds and mammals, and spectacular undersea reefs, banks and gardens teeming with life forms that have barely been studied. "We have two choices—conserve and de-

velop a sustainable resource, or squander and destroy it," says Roger McManus, head of the Center for Marine Conservation, the only national environmental group devoted solely to the oceans' welfare. "Our record so far is abysmal."

Earth Summit. There is a growing belief among environmentalists that the world's overexploited and ailing oceans will replace tropical rain forests as the next global ecology concern. At the United Nations Earth Summit in Rio de Janeiro that wrapped up last week, participants pledged to try and control overfishing, pollution and coastal development. But the agreement contained no bold new initiatives and few specific goals or enforcement mechanisms. Not surprisingly, amid the rancorous parley that saw the United States excoriated for its independent stance on global warming, forest protection and biodiversity, marine issues drew scant attention from the media or from official delegates.

But elsewhere, the alarms are sounding—especially in America. Front-line U.S. environmental groups like Greenpeace, the National Audubon Society and the World Wildlife Fund are following the lead of the Center for Marine Conservation and turning their attention to ocean biodiversity. Until recently, they paid little attention to such unglamorous issues as fish. They favored instead emotional, hot-button topics like the killing of dolphins, harp seals and whales; birds and mammals

From *U.S. News & World Report*, June 22, 1992, pp. 64-68, 70-71, 75. © 1992 by U.S. News & World Report. Reprinted by permission.

dying in drift nets, or saving endangered species like manatees and sea turtles. "Marine fisheries are the nation's single most threatened resource," says Amos Eno of the nonprofit National Fish and Wildlife Foundation. "There has been weak involvement by major environmental groups and poor federal management."

Close to half of U.S. coastal finfish stocks are now overexploited—meaning that more are being caught than are replenished by natural reproduction. Scientists say 14 of the most valuable species—New England groundfish, red snapper, swordfish, striped bass and Atlantic bluefin tuna among them—are threatened with commercial extinction, meaning that too few would remain to justify the cost of catching them.

Only drastic conservation measures will restore these threatened stocks. However, a five-to-10-year fishing ban to allow rebuilding could spell economic disaster for segments of the fishing industry. Virtually all the remaining commercial finfish stocks—except in Alaskan waters—are now being harvested to their limits.

In 1990, Japanese drift netters dumped 39 million unwanted fish, 700,000 sharks, 270,000 sea birds and 26,000 mammals. Most were dead.

Further fishing pressure could put more species in jeopardy. Between 1986 and 1991, the finfish and shellfish catch off the lower 48 states declined by 500 million pounds, from 4.8 billion pounds to 4.3 billion. The harvest of menhaden—used to make poultry feed, fish oil and other products—dropped last year by 300 million pounds. "When Nature is at her best, you can fish with impunity and get away with it," says Lee Weddig, executive director of the National Fisheries Institute, a trade organization. "We can do that no longer."

Pollution's toll. The assault on the oceans begins at the shoreline. About half the U.S. population lives within 50 miles of the coastline, and the booming development is hard to control. The result: massive changes in coastal ecology that are destroying or damaging habitat for finfish and shellfish. Coastal wetlands are gobbled up: Louisiana, for example, loses about 50 square miles of piscatorial breeding ground annually. In California, only 9 percent of the state's original 3.5 million acres of coastal wetlands remain. These bays and estuaries are the breeding grounds and nurseries for fully 75 percent of commercial-seafood species. But they are being increasingly befouled by sewage, industrial waste water and runoff from cities and farms.

Half the fish in areas polluted by toxic chemicals fail to spawn and suffer from weakened immune systems. Chemical nutrients from smokestacks and sewers and from pesticides and fertilizers used on farms and front lawns stimulate explosive algae growth that blocks sunlight and eventually depletes the waters of oxygen, creating undersea dead zones. One acre of Narragansett Bay, R.I., or Delaware Bay, for example, now gets more nitrogen and phosphorus annually from urban and farm runoff than an average acre of cotton, soybeans or wheat grown in the United States.

At any given time, fully one third of the nation's oyster, clam and other shellfish beds are closed because of contamination. Some 27 marine mammals and birds in American coastal waters are now listed as threatened or endangered, and the rising phenomenon of mass die-offs of dolphins and seals is blamed on toxins like PCBs that are rapidly accumulating in the marine environment. And as every beachgoer knows, trash is piling up in ever increasing amounts. Some shorelines along the Gulf of Mexico are strewn with 2 tons of marine debris per mile.

This assault on the marine environment is being felt most keenly by the nation's commercial fisheries. Both the fiercely independent industry and the

National Marine Fisheries Service, which tries hard to regulate it, are struggling over ways to control overfishing, reduce the number of boats, curb the waste of bycatch fish and find more efficient ways to manage and harvest the stocks. At present, fisheries are the least regulated of public resources. Enforcement of even the lax regulations is spotty, compliance is weak and there is simply no real incentive for individual fishermen to conserve.

Atlantic bluefin tuna—a sushi delicacy—have declined 90 percent since 1970. In Japan, a single fish can wholesale for $30,000.

The severely depleted finfish stocks in the lower 48 states, and the government's failure to manage effectively the coastal oceans for the commonweal, raise several questions. Should the seas up to the 200-mile limit be treated as a public resource—like federal lands—and administered like other natural assets? Industries pay the government to drill for offshore oil, cut national-forest timber and mine coal on public lands. Should fishermen pay to harvest seafood in federal waters? Before the Taylor Grazing Act of 1934, Western rangelands were nearly destroyed by cattle because ranchers had free access. Could this tragedy-of-the-commons be repeated in America's oceans?

Questions of control. The root cause of today's overfishing goes back to 1977, when the Magnuson Act extended U.S. coastal jurisdiction from 12 miles to 200 miles and the dominant foreign factory vessels were kicked out of American waters. Ironically, the nation managed to gain control of its coastal oceans but in so doing, simply traded overfishing by foreigners for unrestrained plunder by domestic fishermen.

Meanwhile, the rust-bucket American fleet was gradually replaced—

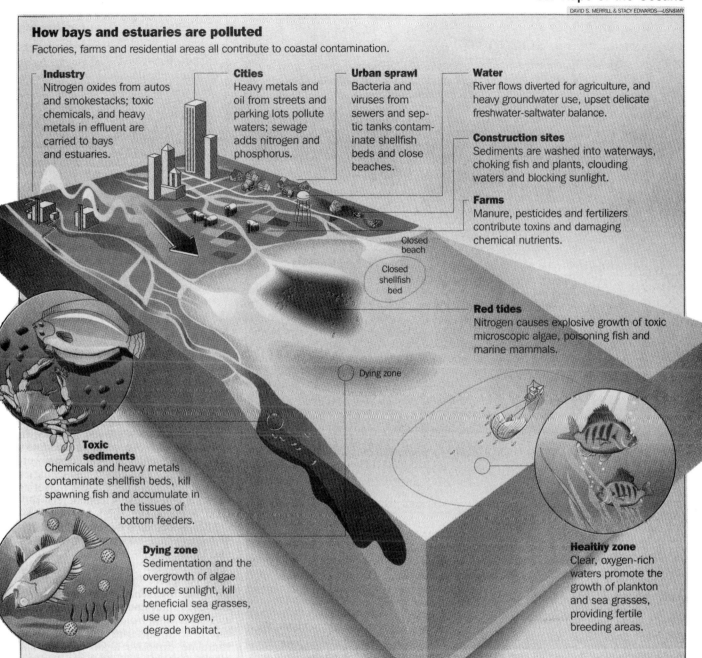

How bays and estuaries are polluted
Factories, farms and residential areas all contribute to coastal contamination.

Industry
Nitrogen oxides from autos and smokestacks; toxic chemicals, and heavy metals in effluent are carried to bays and estuaries.

Cities
Heavy metals and oil from streets and parking lots pollute waters; sewage adds nitrogen and phosphorus.

Urban sprawl
Bacteria and viruses from sewers and septic tanks contaminate shellfish beds and close beaches.

Water
River flows diverted for agriculture, and heavy groundwater use, upset delicate freshwater-saltwater balance.

Construction sites
Sediments are washed into waterways, choking fish and plants, clouding waters and blocking sunlight.

Farms
Manure, pesticides and fertilizers contribute toxins and damaging chemical nutrients.

Closed beach

Closed shellfish bed

Red tides
Nitrogen causes explosive growth of toxic microscopic algae, poisoning fish and marine mammals.

Dying zone

Toxic sediments
Chemicals and heavy metals contaminate shellfish beds, kill spawning fish and accumulate in the tissues of bottom feeders.

Dying zone
Sedimentation and the overgrowth of algae reduce sunlight, kill beneficial sea grasses, use up oxygen, degrade habitat.

Healthy zone
Clear, oxygen-rich waters promote the growth of plankton and sea grasses, providing fertile breeding areas.

thanks to more than $500 million in federal loan guarantees—with efficient, high-tech boats. And a $1.3 billion fleet of some 70 factory vessels, American-registered but mostly owned by Japanese, Scandinavian and Korean interests, now plies the Gulf of Alaska and the Bering Sea. From Gloucester, Mass., to Cordova, Alaska, the industry has too many fishing boats—but there is no consensus on how to control this armada or limit access to the fisheries.

The fishing capacity of the new boats is staggering and, more than

The world eats 90 million metric tons of seafood annually. Replacing it with red meat would require 200 million steers or 750 million hogs.

anything else, has exacerbated the destructive pressure on the fish stocks. Just a decade ago, many fishermen still

used binoculars, shoreside landmarks and oilcan buoys to mark and relocate productive areas. Today, the smallest vessels employ sophisticated electronics that can pinpoint a single codfish at 100 fathoms or guide a captain to within 100 feet of a favorite hot spot. East Coast fishermen seeking increasingly scarce swordfish in the warm Gulf Stream waters, for example, once lowered thermometers over the side or scanned the surface for blue warm-water eddies. Now they can get ocean temperatures faxed to their boats via satellite.

GOODBYE 'JAWS'

Can sharks survive?

After 400 million years of evolution, the shark is the top predator in the ocean. At the apex of the food chain, cruising its domain in perpetual, primordial motion, it is the undisputed king of the undersea jungle.

But it has taken man—an even more ruthlessly efficient killer—just a single decade to threaten the shark's survival. Hunted for their meat and their fins, many species are in a dizzying ecological plunge. "In America, and around the world, sharks are being fished to oblivion," says University of Miami shark expert Samuel Gruber. "Without drastic conservation measures, some species will be lost."

Making soup. Sharks became gourmet fare in the late 1970s, after the National Marine Fisheries Service encouraged the harvesting of what had been widely regarded as an underutilized "trash" fish—good only for crab bait or sport angling. But the heaviest pressure to harvest sharks now comes from the rising demand in Asia for shark fins to make soup. Depending on the species, fins can be worth $5 to $30 a pound to U.S. fishermen. In parts of Asia, choice fins sell for as much as $150 a pound. The boom has boosted the number of commercial boats targeting sharks or taking them as a bonus bycatch. It has also led to the gruesome and wasteful practice of "finning": Fishermen cut off the two valuable fins and toss the helpless animal back to starve.

The prospects for saving endangered shark species are complicated by the fact that the animals are slow to mature and reproduce. But for marine biologist Gruber, the idea of seas lacking sharks is deeply disturbing. Without the primary predator, fish populations would rapidly expand, possibly setting off a chain reaction that could upset the delicately balanced marine ecosystem all the way down to plankton. "We don't know enough about the true mechanics of the biosphere to predict with certainty what would happen," he says. "But we do know a diverse, balanced ecosystem is good. And for that, we need sharks."

Medical value. Some 350 species—from 8-inch cigar sharks to 35-foot whale sharks—inhabit the oceans. Beyond their food value, they show promising medical potential for humans. Their cartilage is used as artificial skin for burn victims, their corneas have been used for human replacement and shark liver oil is a principal ingredient in many hemorrhoid ointments. Scientists are interested in studying their high resistance to cancers and their regenerative powers that allow wounds to heal rapidly. "It's amazing, the damage they suffer and how quickly they recover," Gruber says. "I've seen them with badly lacerated corneas and massive wounds from mating that heal very quickly. I've seen them with stingray spines stuck through their mouths or piercing the brain or heart cavity. They do fine."

A federal shark-recovery plan announced in January calls for an end to finning and for strict commercial- and sport-fishing limits designed to protect 39 coastal and high-seas species whose survival is threatened. Gruber says the plan is a good beginning, although for him, it comes about four years too late. In 1988, he was forced to abandon 30 years of behavioral studies of lemon sharks in the Florida Keys after the population was wiped out for crab bait. "When I was a student, I thought the oceans were so wide and so vast that it was impossible to degrade the system," he says. "I thought it was a great sink for chemicals and pollution, and there was no way to put a dent in the marine populations. Boy, was I wrong."

1981, for example, New England fishermen pressured their regional council to remove all catch quotas on cod, haddock and flounder. That led to the disastrous depletion of the most valuable commercial species. Short of a politically difficult multiyear fishing freeze, the NMFS wants to limit gradually the fishermen's days at sea, increase net-mesh sizes to reduce mortality of small, unwanted fish and ban new boats from entering the fishery. The alternative Darwinian solution is to let the fishermen fight for the dwindling supply.

David versus Goliath. Rooted in the colonial era and steeped in tradition, New England fisheries have long resisted regulation. Alaska's modern fisheries, developed in recent decades, more readily accept tight controls. But common problems are magnified in the Northern Pacific and they threaten the resource. Alaska's high-tech, industrial-strength fleet has too many boats, and there is enormous waste.

Some 70 factory ships are locked in fierce competition with thousands of small vessels in the Bering Sea and Gulf of Alaska. Together, the David and Goliath fleets have enough capacity to scoop up the entire annual Alaskan quota of about 4.8 billion pounds of groundfish in less than six months. With factory ships worth $75 million tied up in port and shoreside plants served by the small vessels periodically idled, with no fish to process, there is relentless lobbying by the rival fleets for a bigger share of the catch.

The very fecundity of the Alaskan waters, like that of other regions, encourages waste. Fishing everywhere produces bycatch that is thrown back—invariably dead or dying—because the fish are too small, too big, have lower market value than the target species, or because it is illegal to keep them. For every pound of shrimp hauled from the Atlantic Ocean and the Gulf of Mexico, for example, an estimated 9 pounds of red snapper, croaker, mackerel, sea trout, spot, drum and other species are brought up in the nets and tossed overboard. This annual shrimp-fishery bycatch alone is estimated by the NMFS at more than 1 billion

To marine biologists, the decline of New England's prized cod, flounder and haddock stocks is a warning for all American fisheries. Many blame the mess on weak leadership by the National Marine Fisheries Service and on the New England Fishery Management Council, one of eight regional groups set up nationwide by the NMFS to govern the industry. Critics contend that the councils are dominated by commercial-fishing interests that are less concerned with conservation than with maximizing profits. In pounds—a waste that equals 10 percent of the entire U.S. harvest.

"National scandal." In 1990, Alaskan trawlers fishing for pollock and cod jettisoned some 25 million pounds of halibut—worth about $30 million—plus vast quantities of salmon and king crab, because they were an incidental, prohibited bycatch. They also reported throwing away 550 million pounds of groundfish because they were the wrong size or to save space for more valuable species.

NMFS officials think the waste is actually higher than 550 million pounds because that total is largely reported by vessel captains and thus is unverifiable. Larry Cotter, a Juneau, Alaska, fisheries consultant and former bycatch chairman for the NMFS regional management council, calls the waste "a national scandal and an unconscionable disgrace."

PCBs in the milk of Canadian Beluga whales— "The world's most polluted animals"—are 3,400 times the safe levels for drinking water.

Another pressing problem in Alaskan waters emanates from the traditional free-for-all culture that allows anyone with a boat to try his luck. So many fishermen compete for the valuable Pacific halibut that the entire year's quota—once harvested over a leisurely six-month season—is now taken in two frantic 24-hour periods.

Last year's derby for the giant flatfish was typical. At noon on September 3, some 6,000 vessels raced out of Alaskan ports in a maritime version of the Oklahoma land rush and began hauling in halibut like sharks in a feeding frenzy. At noon the next day, when the season ended, many vessels limped back to port dangerously overloaded. The Coast Guard handled 29 Mayday calls from sinking boats. There was no loss of life, but during the earlier one-day spring season, two crewmen had drowned. The September boats landed 23.7 million pounds but about 4 million pounds rotted because it couldn't be frozen quickly enough. And the massive glut hitting the market in one day meant no fresh halibut for most consumers.

To fix many of the problems on all three coasts, the National Marine Fisheries Service is eager to manage the nation's seafood stocks through a system of individual transferable quotas, called ITQs. Based on their previous fishing history, boat owners would be given a permit allowing them to harvest a fixed amount of finfish or shellfish each year. The permits could be leased, sold or passed on in a family. "We need to get fishermen to act more like farmers—give them an ownership privilege and a vested interest in the stocks," says NMFS conservation chief Richard Schaefer. "Fishermen don't own a fish until it's flopping around on the deck. If they own it before it is caught, they will manage it rationally."

The ITQ system is already being tested in two East Coast clam fisheries, and Alaskan halibut is one of several other species under consideration for

ITQs. But while many fishermen favor temporary limits on the number of boats entering the industry, there is little enthusiasm for permits, quotas or other regulations. Their reluctance exemplifies the freewheeling, entrepreneurial independence that fishermen cling to—the right to get rich or go broke, unfettered or unprotected by Uncle Sam. "ITQs will destroy us," says Edward Lima, executive director of the Cape Ann Vessel Association in Gloucester. "Corporations will buy up permits and swallow us like corporate farms gobbling up family farmers." His friend Joe Testaverde agrees. And he objects on less tangible grounds, as well. "Quotas remove the lure and romance of fishing," he says. "Part of the thrill is to go out one day and catch nothing, then come home the next and beat out the other guy."

But dwindling stocks and the urgent need for conservation mean that fishermen will have to adapt and change—or risk destroying the very resource that sustains them. Like any good fisherman, Joe Testaverde is cheerfully optimistic. If the cod, haddock and flounder don't come back, he will fish for something else. "Yesterday, on the sonar screens, I saw tons and tons of small fish—whiting, mackerel, butterfish, squid and herring," he says. "If I didn't see that, I'd be scared of the future. We're the last surviving hunters and gatherers. I know I'm *always* gonna catch fish." Testaverde's attitude reflects much of what is right—and what is wrong—with the fishing industry. It is also the reason why America's oceans are in deepening trouble.

Michael Satchell

Benefits of Global Warming

S. Fred Singer

S. Fred Singer is professor of environmental sciences at the University of Virginia. He is director of the Science and Environmental Policy Project at the Washington Institute for Values in Public Policy. He has written widely on environmental and related issues. Among his books are Global Effects of Environmental Pollution; Free Market Energy: The Way to Benefit Consumers; *and* The Changing Global Environment.

Global catastrophes have always held a special fascination for the human mind. Since ancient times, philosophers and theologians have contemplated worldwide cataclysms. In recent years, it has been the global environment that has taken center stage and has engaged scientists, politicians, environmental activists, and the media.

The new wave of global environmental concern has focused on global climate warming. It extends beyond apocalyptic visions and intense hype from environmental groups and the media—with passive cooperation from bureaucracies and scientists—to a political drive to establish international controls over industrial processes and business operations. The scientific base for such drastic action is uncertain and contentious. However, this type of policy is sure to stifle economic growth and, hence, reduce human welfare.

Climate warming, as a possible consequence of greenhouse effects, has emerged as the major environmental issue of the 1990s. The easing of international tension with the Soviet Union could make the greenhouse effect, along with other global environmental concerns, a leading foreign policy issue. The wide acceptance of the Montreal Protocol, which limits and rolls back manufacture on chlorofluorocarbons (CFCs) to avert future changes in stratospheric ozone, has encouraged environmental activists to call for similar controls of carbon dioxide (CO2) from the burning of fossil fuel. At conferences in Toronto (1988), at The Hague (1989), and in Geneva (1990), they have expressed disappointment with the American government for not supporting immediate action. But should the United States assume leadership in a campaign that could cripple our economy? Would it not be more prudent first to assure, through scientific research, that the problem is both real and urgent?

The scientific base for greenhouse warming includes some facts, lots of uncertainty, and just plain ignorance requiring more observations, better theories, and more extensive calculations. Specifically, there is consensus about the increase in so-called greenhouse gases in the earth's atmosphere as a result of human activities. The strength of "sources and sinks" for these gases, that is, their rate of generation and the rates of removal is somewhat uncertain. Major uncertainty and disagreements exist on the question of whether this increase has caused a change in the climate during the last one hundred years. The scientific community also disagrees on predicted changes from further increases in greenhouse gases. The computer models used to calculate future climate are not yet good enough.

As a consequence of this "shaky" science, we cannot be sure whether the next century will bring a warming that is negligible or one that is significant. Even if there were to be global warming and associated climate changes, it is debatable whether the consequences will be good or bad. Likely, we would get some of each. The scientific base for an enhanced greenhouse warming due to human activity is too uncertain to justify drastic action at this time.

There is little risk in delaying policy responses to this century-old problem, since scientific understanding can be expected to improve substantially within the next few years. Instead of panicky, premature, and

From *Society*, Vol. 29, No. 3, March/April 1992, pp. 33-40. © 1992 by Transaction Publishers. Reprinted by permission.

likely ineffective actions that would only slow down, but not stop, the further growth of CO2, we should use the same resources—several trillion dollars, by some estimates—to increase our economic resilience so that we can then apply specific remedies, when necessary. This is not to say that prudent steps cannot be taken now. Many kinds of energy conservation and efficiency increases make economic sense even without the threat of greenhouse warming.

Greenhouse Gases

It has been common knowledge for about a century that burning of fossil fuels—coal, oil, and gas—increases the atmospheric content of carbon dioxide (CO2). Conventional wisdom predicts an enhancement of the natural greenhouse effect and a warming of the global climate as a result. Advances in spectroscopy have produced evidence that CO2 (and other molecules made up of more than two atoms) absorb infrared radiation. Consequently, a build-up in CO2 would impede the escape of heat radiation from the earth's surface. In fact, it is the greenhouse effect from naturally occurring carbon dioxide and water vapor that has warmed the earth's surface for billions of years. Without the natural greenhouse effect, ours would be a frozen planet without life.

The policy issue now is whether the nearly 30 percent increase in CO2, mainly since the Second World War, calls for immediate and drastic action. According to the prevailing theory, and taking into account increases in the other trace gases that produce greenhouse effects, we have already gone halfway to an effective doubling of greenhouse gases—this cannot be reversed in a century or more. Thus, the theory says we are locked into a temperature increase of 1.5° to 4.5° Celsius (2.7° to 8.1° Fahrenheit). The average global temperature should now be increasing at the rate of 0.3° C per decade!

Precise measurements of the increase in the atmospheric CO2 date to the International Geophysical Year of 1957 to 1958. More recently it has been discovered that other greenhouse gases—gases that absorb strongly in the infrared portion of the spectrum—have also been increasing. This is due, at least in part, to human activities. These gases currently produce a greenhouse effect nearly equal to that of CO2, but could soon outdistance carbon dioxide's greenhouse effect. A list of these non-CO2 greenhouse gases follows:

• Methane is produced in large part by sources that relate to population growth. Among these sources are rice paddies, cattle, and oil-field operations. Methane, now 20 percent of the greenhouse gas effect but growing twice as fast as CO2, has more than doubled since pre-industrial times. It would become the most important greenhouse gas if CO2 emissions were to stop.

• Nitrous oxide has increased by about 10 percent, most likely because of soil bacterial action promoted by the increased use of nitrogen fertilizers.

• Ozone from urban air pollution adds about 10 percent to the global greenhouse effect. It may decrease in the United States as a result of clean air legislation but increase in other parts of the world.

• Chlorofluorocarbons (CFC's or "freons"), manufactured for use in refrigeration, air conditioning, and industrial processes, could make a significant contribution but will soon be replaced by less-polluting substitutes.

• The most effective greenhouse gas by far is water vapor.

The last item on the list, water vapor, is not a man-made gas, but is assumed to amplify the warming effects of the man-made gases. It is not really known whether water vapor has increased in the atmosphere or whether it will increase in the future although all model calculations assume this to be so. Predictions of future warming should depend not only on the amount but also on the horizontal and especially the vertical distribution of water vapor, and on whether it will be in the atmosphere in the form of a gas, as liquid cloud droplets, or as ice particles. The current computer models are not refined enough to test these crucial points.

Climate Record

Has there been a climate effect caused by the sharp increase in greenhouse gases during the last few decades? The data are ambiguous. Advocates for immediate action profess to see a global warming of about 0.5° C since 1880. They point to record temperatures experienced in the 1980s and confidently predict a warming of as much as 5° C in the next century.

An Intergovernmental Panel on Climate Change (IPCC), sponsored by the United Nations, has been laying the groundwork for an international convention aimed at averting such a climate catastrophe. Its scientific base is a "Policymakers Summary" on greenhouse warming, released in June 1990, said to represent a "scientific consensus." Far from it. The summary ignores valid scientific objections to the theoretical calculations that predict a global warming. It is silent about other human activities, notably the emission of sulfur dioxide in industrial processes, that are thought to promote a climate cooling. It plays fast and loose with the historical climate data that clearly disagree with the standard greenhouse warming theory. It also puts a "spin" on its major conclusions that can only serve to mislead the nonscientist decision makers who are earnestly seeking answers to global problems.

For example, to claim "certainty"—as the IPCC summary does—that "there is a natural greenhouse effect which already keeps the earth warmer than it would otherwise be" is on par with revealing that we know for sure that the earth is round. The greenhouse effect has been known for over a century and has been studied for several decades. To claim certainty that emissions of gases from human activities (carbon dioxide, methane, chlorofluorocarbons, nitrous oxide) "will enhance the greenhouse effect," is not particularly startling either, unless one can show that the additional warming is really significant.

The greenhouse effect has been known for over a century and has been studied for several decades.

Yet these two conclusions, issued without further qualifications, must suggest to the unwary a future in which the United States heartland is turned into a parched desert by near continuous droughts, its coasts lashed by frequent hurricanes or, worse still, flooded by oceans as sea levels rise to unprecedented heights. These images are assiduously promoted by many politicians and environmental groups and reported uncritically by the media, anxious to exaggerate cataclysmic disasters. They are not, however, based on scientific fact, and are not even supported by the details in the bulk of the IPCC report itself.

The IPCC report is based on faith in existing mathematical models that have not been able to "hindcast" the temperature changes experienced in the past century and, furthermore, have been in a state of flux. To match more closely what is happening in nature, the predictions of the global-warming models have generally been scaled downward within the last two years and include a more sophisticated accounting of cloud and ocean current effects.

The report's claim to scientific consensus does nothing to enhance its credibility. Nevertheless, former British Prime Minister Margaret Thatcher, while still in office, latched on to it as a means of demonstrating her environmental credentials. She announced that she was joining ranks with other European leaders and had broken ranks with the Bush administration by pledging that Britain would eliminate growth in carbon dioxide emissions over the next fifteen years—provided other industrialized countries would do the same. Leaving

herself this large loophole, she further stated that she was prepared to recommend a 30 percent reduction "in the currently projected levels of future carbon dioxide emissions." But since her projection included a healthy economic growth rate, the reduction amounts to nothing more than a leveling of emissions at about the present level.

White House officials have been more cautious, with Michael R. Deland, chairman of the president's Council on Environmental Quality, stating that the IPCC report was not the final word. Congressional science advisor D. Allan Bromley did not think that the report would have a major effect on the administration's actions. However, there are now several bills introduced in Congress which would have the United States restrict the use of energy—unilaterally, if necessary—to reduce the emission of carbon dioxide from the burning of fossil fuel.

The Other View

Many scientists do not accept the IPCC conclusions and call attention to the fact that the strongest temperature increase occurred before the major rise in greenhouse gas concentration. This increase in both Northern Hemisphere land (NHT-Land) and marine air temperatures (NMAT) was followed by a thirty-five-year temperature decrease, between the years 1940 and 1975, when concern arose about an approaching ice age. Following a sharp increase in average temperatures between 1975 and 1980, there has been no increase during the 1980s in spite of record increases in greenhouse gases. Similarly, global atmospheric (rather than surface) temperatures, as measured by weather satellites, show no trend in the last decade.

Climatologists at the National Oceanographic and Atmospheric Administration (NOAA) find no overall warming in the U.S. temperature record. Using a technique that eliminates urban "heat islands" and other local distorting effects, they confirm the temperature rise before 1940, but then show a general decline. Reginald Newell and colleagues at Massachusetts Institute of Technology report no substantial change in the global sea surface temperature in the past century. This is important because the ocean, with its much greater heat inertia, should control any atmospheric climate change.

Perhaps most significant are the studies that document a relative rise in nocturnal temperatures in the United States in the last sixty years, while daytime values stayed the same or declined. This is just what one would expect from the increase in atmospheric greenhouse gas concentration. But its consequences, as Patrick Michaels of the University of Virginia has pointed out, are benign: a longer growing season, fewer frosts, and no increase in soil evaporation.

The most precise measurement, free of local influences on temperature gauges and covering the whole globe including the oceans, comes from a microwave experiment in satellites. Microwave data measure the temperature of the lower atmosphere—globally, continuously, day and night, and with high precision. They show essentially no net temperature change during the past ten years. The time span, however, is still too short to draw definite conclusions.

Data collected over the next decade should allow us to test the IPCC projection that global temperatures will rise by about 0.3°C per decade on average, resulting in a global increase of 2° C by the year 2025 and 6°C by the end of the twenty-first century. It is, therefore, fair to say that we have not seen the huge greenhouse warming of about 1.5°C expected by now from some theories and played up by the media.

Mathematical Models

Modelers generally agree that some global warming is desirable, but actual estimates vary widely. Models predict that if effective greenhouse gases double, the average global temperature should increase between 1.5° and 4.5° C. (These projections of global warming were unchanged for many years, then crept up, and have recently dropped back.) In 1989, some modelers cut their predictions in half as they tried to model clouds and ocean currents more accurately. Modelers also disagree on the regional distribution of this warming and on where the increased precipitation will go. One British computer model forecast equal levels of rainfall for the Sahara Desert and Scotland.

Models are "tuned" to give the right mean temperature and seasonal temperature variation, but they fall short of modeling other important atmospheric processes, such as the poleward transport of energy. Nor do they routinely encompass longer-scale processes that involve the oceans or the ice and snow in the earth's cryosphere. Fine-scale processes that involve convection, cloud formation, boundary layers, or the earth's detailed topography are inadequately incorporated into the models.

Serious discrepancies also exist between model results and the actual experience from the detailed climate record of the past century. The "fingerprints" characteristic of greenhouse warming are not found in the record. Here are some of the expected results of greenhouse warming and the actual findings:

• Existing models predict a strong warming of the polar regions and of the tropical upper atmosphere—all contrary to observations.

• Contrary to model predictions, observations suggest that warming has been more rapid over the oceans than over the land, and over the southern than over the northern hemisphere.

• The bulk of the warming occurred before 1940, before more than a quarter of the fossil fuel CO_2 had been released into the atmosphere and before half of the biospheric release of CO_2 had occurred. Yet during the period of 1940 to 1975, cooling occurred in spite of the rapid release of CO_2 from fossil fuel burning.

• The bulk of the warming occurred in two short bursts, around 1920 and again between 1975 to 1980. The models, however, do not yield ready explanations of these occurrences.

Impact of Climate Change

Based on extrapolation of the climate record, the most likely outcome of the buildup in greenhouse gases is a modest warming of less than 1° C (average) in the next century, with the increase concentrated at high latitudes and in the winter. Is this necessarily a bad result? One should perhaps recall that only a decade ago, when climate cooling was a looming issue, a United States government study calculated a huge national cost associated with such cooling. More to the point perhaps, actual climate cooling, experienced during the Little Ice Age or in the famous 1816 New England "year without a summer," which caused large agricultural losses and even famines.

If cooling is bad, then warming should be good. This statement is predicated on warming being slow enough so that adjustment is easy and relatively cost-free. Even though some crop varieties can benefit from higher temperatures with either more or less moisture, the soils may not be able to adjust as quickly. Agriculturalists expect that with increased atmospheric CO_2—which is, after all, plant food—plants will grow faster and need less water. The warmer night temperatures suggested by NOAA climatologist Tom Kafi's research translate to longer growing seasons and fewer frosts. Increased global precipitation should also be beneficial to plant growth.

It is important to keep in mind that year-to-year changes at any location are far greater and more rapid than might be expected from greenhouse warming. Nature, crops and people have already adapted to such large short-term swings. Extreme climate events—crippling winters, persistent droughts, killer hurricanes—that cause the great ecological and economic problems. But there is no indication from modeling or from actual experience that such extreme events would become more frequent if greenhouse warming ever becomes appreciable. The exception might be tropical cyclones, which, according to Robert Balling and Randall Cerveney of Arizona State University, would be more frequent but weaker, cooling vast areas of the ocean surface and increasing annual rainfall by 10 to 15 percent. Climate models predict that polar temperatures should warm the most, thus reducing the driving force for severe winter weather.

Finally, there is the fear of sea-level rise and catastrophic flooding as glaciers melt. The cryosphere contains enough ice to raise sea level by 100 meters. Conversely, during recent ice ages enough ice accumulated to drop sea level 100 meters below the present level. These are extreme possibilities. For example, tidal gauge records of the past century suggest that sea level has risen modestly, by about 0.1 to 0.2 meters. But the gauges measure only relative sea level, and many of their locations have dropped because of land subsidence. Besides, the locations are too highly concentrated geographically (mostly on the East Coast of the United States) to permit global conclusions. The situation will improve greatly in the next few years as precise global data become available from a variety of satellite systems.

Satellite radar-altimeters have already given a surprising result. As reported by NASA scientists, Greenland's ice sheets are gaining in thickness. A net increase in the ice stored in the cryosphere and an inferred drop in sea level leads to somewhat different predictions of future sea levels. It is clearly important to verify these results by other techniques and also to get more direct data on current sea-level changes.

Summarizing the available evidence, we conclude that even if significant warming were to occur in the next century, the net impact may well be beneficial. This conclusion would be even more compelling if the long-anticipated ice age were on its way.

In view of the uncertainties about the degree of warming, and the even greater uncertainty about its possible impact, what should we do? In the time it takes for an expanded research program to reduce or eliminate these uncertainties, we can implement policies and pursue approaches that make sense even if the enhanced greenhouse effect does not exist. A variety of sensible actions suggest themselves.

Energy Conservation and Efficiency

Global energy conservation can best be achieved by pricing rather than by command-and-control methods. Prices should include the external costs that are avoided by the user and transferred to someone else. The idea is to have the polluter or the beneficiary pay the cost. An example is peak pricing for electric power. Yet another example, appropriate to the greenhouse dis-

cussion, is to increase the tax on gasoline to make it a true highway user fee instead of the current method of having most capital and maintenance costs paid by various state taxes. Congress has so far lacked the courage for such a direct approach, preferring instead regulation (such as the Corporate Average Fuel Econ-

---

Over-conservation can waste as much energy as under-conservation.

---

omy standards) that is mostly ineffective and produces large indirect costs for the consumer. Energy efficiency should be attainable without much intervention, provided it pays for itself. A good rule of thumb is: if it is not economical, then it probably wastes energy and we should not do it. Over-conservation can waste as much energy as under-conservation. But provided that energy is properly priced. the job for government is to remove institutional and other road blocks.

Helpful government actions include, but are not limited to, these steps:

• Providing information to consumers, especially on life-cycle costs for home heating, lighting, refrigerators, and other appliances.

• Encouraging turnover and replacement of older, less efficient (and often more polluting) capital equipment, such as cars, machinery, and power plants. Existing policies that make new equipment too costly run counter to this goal.

• Stimulating development of more efficient systems by the private sector, such as combined-cycle power plants or a more efficient internal combustion engine.

Non-Fossil Fuels

Nuclear power is, in many countries, cheaper than fossil-fuel power, yet it is often opposed on environmental grounds. The problems cited against nuclear energy, such as disposal of spent nuclear fuel, are mostly political and ideological rather than technical. Nuclear energy from fusion rather than uranium fission may be a longer-term possibility, but the time horizon for this development is uncertain. Solar energy and other forms of renewable energy should also become more competitive as their costs drop and as fossil-fuel prices rise. However, solar energy is both highly variable and very dilute. In fact, it takes a football field of solar cells in a sunny climate to supply the total energy needs of the average American household. Wind energy and biomass are other forms of energy that are competitive in certain applications. Schemes to extract energy from temperature differences in the ocean have been suggested as inexhaustible sources of non-polluting hydrogen fuel, if we can solve the daunting technical problems.

Solution of the Future

If greenhouse warming ever becomes a real problem, numerous proposals have been made for removing CO_2 from the atmosphere—that is, increasing CO_2 "sinks." Reforestation is widely talked about, but probably not cost-effective. Natural expansion of boreal forests in a warming climate would sequester atmospheric CO_2. A novel idea, proposed by California oceanographer John Martin, is to fertilize the Antarctic Ocean and let plankton growth do the job of converting CO_2 into bio-material. The limiting trace nutrient may be iron, which could be supplied and dispersed more economically.

And, if all else fails, "venetian blinds" satellites can be put into earth orbit to modulate the amount of sunshine reaching the earth. These satellites could also generate electric power and beam it to earth, as originally suggested by Peter Glaser of the A. D. Little organization. Such a scheme may sound farfetched, and possibly it is, but many other futuristic projects (like covering the Sahara with solar cells or Australia with trees) have been discussed seriously.

False Solutions

Environmental groups and congressmen have renewed demands for immediate action on greenhouse warming. A key point of the various bills already introduced is for the United States to cap and reduce—unilaterally, if necessary—the emission of the major greenhouse gas, carbon dioxide resulting from fossil-fuel burning. The president would be well advised to resist such pressure to place scientifically arbitrary and economically ruinous limits on energy generation. Many people are hyping the greenhouse "threat" to push their pet agendas. They seem undeterred by the growing scientific evidence that there are no climate effects from the increase in atmospheric greenhouse gases. For example, global temperatures did not increase during the past decade—contrary to cataclysmic predictions. Yet the *Today* show, PBS television specials like "Crisis in the Atmosphere," and most of the print media still preach impending doom in the form of the collapse of global agriculture or a catastrophic rise in sea levels. An editor of *Time* magazine even assures journalists that it is all right to become environmental advocates, never mind scientific facts.

Why do so many different groups focus on greenhouse warming? Because this issue provides a wonderful excuse for doing what they already want to do, under the guise of saving the planet. In one corner proponents of nuclear energy (which emits no CO_2) see a chance to refurbish their public image. Natural gas producers are keen on beating out competition from cheaper, but more polluting coal. Even scientists are becoming cheerleaders. Budgets for climate research have jumped to over one billion dollars.

Ineffective and Costly Policies

In another corner are the proponents of energy conservation and renewable energy. These are commendable goals except for those uneconomical measures that waste more energy than they save. The extremists oppose all energy growth and economic growth. Most dangerous are those with hidden political agendas, most often oriented against business, the free market, and the capitalistic system. After the collapse of socialism in Eastern Europe it is no longer fashionable to argue for state ownership of industrial concerns. The alternative is to control private firms by regulating every step of every manufacturing process.

And then there are those for whom global warming is a vehicle for international action, preferably with lots of treaties and protocols to control CO_2 or perhaps even methane. Some view the greenhouse effect as a launch platform for an ambitious foreign aid program, others as the justification for global multi-billion dollar afforestation projects, while still others would use it to encourage (or even enforce) global population control.

The notion of capping CO_2 emissions, or even rolling back emissions by 20 to 50 percent is based on the idea that energy conservation can be achieved by decree. It is often combined with the idea of a carbon tax to make it sound like a free-market proposal. If enacted unilaterally, this would hamper U.S. economic growth. The impact would fall mainly on the poorer segment of the population, as so many pollution control proposals do.

If applied to the rest of the world, capping CO_2 emissions would certainly be denounced as "eco-imperialism," a scheme to stop economic development in the less-developed countries (LDCs). The billions of people in the LDCs want cars, refrigerators, television sets, and air conditioning. It might take a large bribe to make them go along with any scheme that would deny them the quality of life that comes with the use of energy and electricity.

A carbon tax, imposed primarily on coal, has many strikes against it:

• Coal is used mainly to produce electric power. Since public utilities would pass the increased fuel cost along to ratepayers, a carbon tax amounts to little more than a regressive value-added tax.

• A carbon tax is not only unfair but also counter-productive to the national goal of reducing oil imports. Cutting the use of domestically produced coal would also give a windfall to oil and gas producers (read: OPEC), at the expense of consumers. Of course, all this exclusive emphasis on limiting energy generation and coal use is misplaced and irrational.

• CO_2 is added to the atmosphere by activities other than energy generation. Deforestation and soil erosion, primarily in the LDCs, are believed to provide 25 percent or more of the CO_2 in the atmosphere. By contrast, U.S. forest inventories have been growing since 1920, sequestering carbon dioxide from the atmosphere. A further uncertainty is the fraction of CO_2 that is absorbed into the ocean. Estimates run as high as 50 percent. Until these numbers are made more precise, it is difficult to predict the result of any remedial policy.

• The United States is only a modest contributor to atmospheric carbon dioxide from fossil-fuel burning, currently less than 25 percent. More importantly, this percentage is shrinking rapidly as LDCs increase both their populations and their standards of living. According to Worldwatch Institute, a widely cited environmental think tank, CO_2 contributions from LDCs have grown rapidly in the last decades and can be expected to explode in the coming century. Between 1960 and 1987, carbon dioxide emissions from fossil fuels increased by 54 percent for the United States, 26 percent for France, 22 percent for West Germany, 161 percent for the area of the former Soviet Union, 292 percent for Japan, 176 percent for China, 307 percent for Brazil, and 357 percent for India—while the United Kingdom's emissions actually decreased by 3 percent.

• Most important, carbon dioxide will be losing its pre-eminent position as a greenhouse gas to other gases, like methane, for which no control strategy has been developed. How does one control emissions from rice paddies and cows, which are among the primary sources of methane? Currently, CO_2 contributes over 50 percent of the greenhouse effect, but carbon dioxide is becoming "saturated"—an increase in its atmospheric concentration no longer produces a proportional increase in the effect.

The upshot of all these considerations is that even our most drastic measures to limit fossil-fuel burning can do little to stave off an inevitable rise in atmospheric greenhouse gases. Doubling of these gases could be delayed from perhaps the year 2040 to 2045 but would cost our economy a trillion dollars by some estimates.

Evidence indicates that the net impact of significant warming in the next century may well be beneficial. Yale economist William Nordhaus, one of the few who has been trying to deal quantitatively with the economics of the greenhouse effect, has pointed out that "those who argue for strong measures to slow greenhouse warming have reached their conclusion without any discernible analysis of the costs and benefits."

Those charged with policy decisions that can affect economic growth and the welfare of billions of people would do well to move cautiously and insist on a thorough understanding of the physics of the atmospheric greenhouse before taking hasty, far-reaching actions that would drive energy prices sky-high. Stringent controls enacted now would be economically devastating without affecting greatly the growth of greenhouse gases in the atmosphere. Energy conservation, efficiency increases, and use of non-fossil fuels are all prudent policies, as long as they are cost-effective. But more drastic, precipitous—and especially, unilateral—steps to delay the putative greenhouse impacts can cost jobs and economic prosperity without being effective.

Global temperatures have been declining since the dinosaurs roamed the earth some 70 million years ago. About two million years ago a new "ice age" began most probably as a result of the drift of the continents and the build-up of mountains. Since then the earth has seen at least seventeen cycles of glaciation, interrupted by short (10,000 to 12,000 years) interglacial (warm) periods. We are now in such an interglacial interval, the Holocene, that started 10,800 years ago; the onset of the next glacial cycle cannot be very far away.

The length of a cycle, about 100,000 to 120,000 years, is believed to be controlled by small changes in the seasonal and latitudinal distribution of solar energy received as a result of changes in the earth's orbit and spin axis. While this theory can explain the timing, the detailed mechanism is not well understood—especially the sudden transition from full glacial to interglacial warming. Very likely, an ocean/atmosphere interaction is triggered and becomes the direct cause of the transition in climate. The climate record also reveals evidence for major climatic changes on time scales shorter than those for astronomical cycles. During the past millennium the earth experienced a "climate optimum" around 1100 A.D., when the Vikings found Greenland to be green and Vinland (Labrador?) able to support grape growing. The "Little Ice Age" found European glaciers advancing well before 1600, and suddenly retreating starting in 1860. The warming of 0.5° C, reported in the global temperature record since 1880, may be the end of this little ice age rather than the beginning of the human greenhouse.

Islam's Violent Improvisers

Without a formal structure, new religious radicals are hard to combat

Steve Coll and David Hoffman

Washington Post *Foreign Service*

On a dreary December dawn, four young Palestinians in an old sedan entered the streets of Lod, a mixed Arab-Jewish town in central Israel. They spotted Israeli border guard Nissim Toledano walking to work, ran him down, drove him back to their village just north of Jerusalem and dumped him in a cave. Two days later, frustrated that Israel had rebuffed their demands for a prisoner exchange, the men decided to kill Toledano. But since they did not know how to use a gun, they stabbed and strangled him.

Another morning, another city: In Cairo's timeworn Zeinhoum district last month, an Egyptian army officer was driving to work when automatic-weapons fire pierced the clamorous, crowded streets. The officer escaped, but a policeman and a bystander were killed, as were two attackers—members of Egypt's revolutionary Islamic Group. Estimated cost of the Islamic Group's poorly aimed but deadly ambush, including assault rifles, hand grenades and forged identity papers: about $7,700.

These incidents and dozens like them reflect the new face of violent Islamic radicalism in Israel and Egypt and across the Middle East—a swelling wave of grass-roots movements that are improvised in their military operations, modest in budgetary requirements, diffuse in organization and committed to radical pan-Islamic ideology.

From Tel Aviv to Cairo to New York, a frustrated alliance of pro-Western governments is struggling to unravel the insurgents' intricate structures and their sources of financial and material support—all in the hope of containing the radicals' political and military power. But because the radicals are so loosely organized, the effort has proven immensely difficult.

"Radical Islam today is wheels within wheels within wheels," says Israeli scholar Ifrah Zilberman. "That's what makes it so frustrating for outside analysts and counter-terrorist efforts."

The movements arise from broadly based opposition politics in generally undemocratic countries. They seek to impose strict Islamic law on societies now mainly governed by an uneasy mix of modern politics and religious tradition. Frequently under intense pressure from their governments, these radical Islamic movements have given birth to extremist factions or groups that seek to achieve their goals through direct revolutionary violence.

The ascendant movements mark a basic change in the structure and character of Middle Eastern political violence. The tightly organized revolutionary organizations sponsored during the 1970s and 1980s by such governments as Syria, Iraq and Libya—including the Palestine Liberation Organization and the group headed by the Palestinian Sabri Banna, or Abu Nidal—are in decline. On the rise in the 1990s is a much more fluid trend—unorganized groups of angry young men involved in self-proclaimed religious war and broadly based protest politics.

The recent terrorism cases in New York can be seen as part of this broader picture, according to the evidence so far. More evidence may yet be mustered in court about links between the New York defendants and outside governments or other sponsors, but it seems clear that the sums of money required for their terrorist operations were small and that their support networks were organized largely around family, informal contacts and local institutions, such as neighborhood mosques.

Yet at the same time, some defendants have ties to international, charismatic personalities, such as radical Egyptian preacher Sheik Omar Abdel Rahman, as well as to transnational institutions like Brooklyn's Alkifah Refugee Center, which helped send Muslim volunteer fighters to Afghanistan and runs branch offices in Pakistan and Croatia.

Seeking to mollify their publics and to find sympathy in the United States, Egyptian and Israeli politicians sometimes blame Iran's revolutionary Islamic government in Tehran for funding and stoking these radical movements. After the killing of Toledano in December—an incident that triggered the expulsion from Israel of more than 400 suspected Islamic activists—Prime Minister Yitzhak Rabin pointed the finger at "radical-fanatic Muslim insanity," which he described as "a megalomaniac system headed by Iran."

"The Arab world—the world in general—will pay, if the cancer of the radical-fundamentalist Islam is not halted at

From *The Washington Post National Weekly Edition*, August 9-15, 1993, pp. 6-7. © 1993 by The Washington Post. Reprinted by permission.

the house of study of [ayatollah Ruhollah] Khomeini and his followers in Iran," Rabin declared. Egyptian President Hosni Mubarak has made similar accusations about Iran's role during the last six months.

But the Israeli and Egyptian charges are misleading in many ways, according to results of those countries' police investigations, as well as interviews with dozens of participants in the Islamic movements, officials and specialists. Iran provides funding to Islamic radicals abroad, including in Israel, they say. But these Islamic movements are in many ways home-grown. The outside support they receive comes more often from wealthy individuals in Saudi Arabia, other Persian Gulf countries and elsewhere than it does from Iran, say movement participants, Israeli and Egyptian officials and Western specialists.

Iran's strengths as it competes for influence with Islamic movements are the inspirational power of its original revolution and its willingness to defy the West and Israel. But Iran is hampered in its efforts to export revolution. Iran's Shiite Islamic faith is in the minority throughout the Arab world, and its strong ethnic Persian identity raises hackles with many Arabs, regardless of Islamic ideology.

The Islamic movements now so dynamic in Israel, Egypt and other countries arise from complex factors, including the failures of secular institutions, economic troubles, an absence of democracy, perceptions of injustice, the deep cultural roots of Islamic faith, the legacy of the war in Afghanistan and rapid social change in the Muslim world.

That outside support for these movements comes, to a large extent, from wealthy individuals in Saudi Arabia and other Persian Gulf countries reflects the diffuse, often informal character of the present Islamic revival.

Funding from abroad to Egypt's Islamic Group "either comes through individuals or bank transfers to individuals not known to security," says Egyptian Interior Minister Hassan Mohammed Alfi. "We do not know the exact amount" of money coming from gulf sources. "These operations took place secretly," he says. "It has to be large sums of money."

According to Palestinian and Israeli sources familiar with Hamas, the largest Islamic organization among the 1.8 million Palestinians in the Israeli-occupied West Bank and Gaza Strip, most outside support to the movement comes not from Iran but from private groups and individuals in Saudi Arabia and the Persian Gulf emirates and is often passed through Jordan.

Although the transfers are well hidden, it is known that some comes as charitable contributions for such institutions as schools, clinics and mosques, and some is cash for military operations smuggled by individuals across the Allenby Bridge into the West Bank.

All told, this outside support may amount to $20 million a year—just a fraction of the estimated $500 million a year that the secular Palestine Liberation Organization reaped until recently from the gulf states.

Neither are the movements' relatively small budgets coherently organized. The institutional and financial heart of the Muslim world's vibrant Islamic revival lies in the *"jamaa,"* an Arabic word that means "group" or "society" and is chosen by modern Islamic radicals to connote loose structure but firm commitment to religious principles.

In dissecting the transnational finances of these organizations, it is difficult to draw a line between private, cross-border Islamic charitable contributions to legitimate institutions and patronage of violent Islamic revolutionaries. Some groups attract militant young radicals prone to violence. But most such organizations publicly forswear violence, promoting radical Islam through charity, education or unions.

Governments seeking to quell Islamic movements often have trouble distinguishing one sort of jamaa from another—indeed, the peaceful and violence-prone ones are sometimes interconnected, say participants, specialists and officials. In other cases, mosques or Islamic education societies originally funded from abroad for peaceful, evangelical purposes have more recently been taken over in such places as Upper Egypt and the Israeli-occupied West Bank by younger Islamic radicals committed to violent revolution, they say.

"Islamic movements must be understood on two levels—organizations and structures, and then secondly as fluid, multidimensional, interactive," says Khurshid Ahmed, a leading Pakistani Islamic activist and charity manager with wide contacts in the radical Arab world.

Typically, formal outside sponsorship is not central to an Islamic jamaa. Rather, the group depends on *zakaat*, the 2.5 percent annual contribution set down by Islamic law and demanded of wealthy Muslims who expect to reach heaven.

Zakaat "has nothing to do with the borders of countries," says Rachid Ghannouchi, exiled leader of Tunisia's radical Nahda, or Renaissance, movement. "The Islamic movement relies on this individual sharing, financial participation."

Pious Muslims with the most to give tend to live in Saudi Arabia and other oil-rich gulf states. Their contributions often involve cash or diversions through legitimate businesses or charities; the use of prolific modern technology—such as fax machines, computers and electronic banking—and informal, person-to-person cross-border contacts.

In Egypt's case, "there is a group of Islamic Group members working in Saudi Arabia," explains one of the radical movement's lawyers in Upper Egypt. "They are both Egyptians and Saudis, and they try to help people here financially."

The Egyptians involved are not from the Islamic Group's military or proselytizing wings, but are among the "affiliated but undeclared members" who clandestinely cooperate with the radical movement, the lawyer says.

"Likewise, there are Saudis who belong to the Islamic Group who are undeclared," he adds. "So they meet in various places far from the eyes of authority. For example, someone from here goes to Saudi as a doctor or engineer or lawyer, and he interacts with Saudis. . . . Both groups are looking for someone to convey the real *sharia*" or Islamic law, he says.

To understand what these splintered and voluntary Islamic movements look like on the ground and why they so vex the secular, pro-Western governments seeking to contain them, consider the developments underway today in Jenin, a dusty, violence-wracked city of 220,000 on the northern side of the Israeli-occupied West Bank. Jenin used to be a stronghold of the secular PLO, which stateless Palestinians looked on for decades as a surrogate state. Besides fighters, the PLO financed an array of institutions from schools to hospitals to newspapers, as well as payments to families whose sons and fathers were imprisoned or had been killed. But the PLO is running out of money, and its network is falling apart. The Islamic movement is filling the vacuum.

Like the PLO, the Islamic movement has many faces. In addition to its military wing, Hamas is a broadly based religious movement with a foundation in mosques and a political and social service movement that has drawn the Palestinian merchant and intellectual classes, as well as the poor.

One of the movement's landmarks in Jenin is a gleaming new Islamic medical center, topped by a mosque, on a ridge above the city center. The hospital has room for up to 100 patients—nearly double the capacity of Jenin's only other medical center, an aging facility run by the Israeli military administration. The hospital has modern technology; orthopedic, pediatric and emergency services; a pharmacy and a laboratory. Funding for the hospital, mosque and a kindergarten—about $3 million since the mid-1980s—came from individual benefactors in the Persian Gulf, says Sheik Zaid Mahmoud Zakarneh, head of the zakaat fund that raised the money. Fund leaders wrote letters and traveled from the West Bank to Saudi Arabia and other gulf countries to solicit money from individual donors. Eventually, they found an exiled palestinian businessman in Riyadh, a Saudi Arabian businessman in Jeddah, a government charity in Kuwait and a Palestinian charity in Canada that were willing to send significant sums, Zakarneh says.

"It depends on Islam . . . on the understanding that every Muslim should by faith give part of his income," Zakarneh says. Among wealthy Saudis, adds Zakarneh's colleague Fuaz Hamad, "it is also a matter of prestige. He [the donor] says, 'I donated for Palestine,' and they ask for a certificate and put it on the wall."

The beneficiaries are Jenin's impoverished Palestinians. Families pay less than 60 cents to visit the medical center, and those who can afford more pay just a few dollars. In the dental clinic, a patient says he came because "they are a humane and charitable society" and because "they're cheaper than anyone else. Because of good services, they have a good reputation."

The picture is equally striking in the Gaza Strip. The Islamic Society in Gaza, which began as a small sports club in a mosque at the Beach Refugee Camp, today provides hundreds of youths with activities, including a computer camp, kindergartens and lectures. "The people are in need of any services, from any institution," says Saleh Berheet, a society manager.

The group's budget is supported by individual and charity donations from the gulf, society officials say. So is the budget of Gaza's Islamic University, long the center of Islamic radicalism in the territory. "They [Saudis] don't know what they are donating to, but they want to salvage their souls," says Mordechai Abir, a former policy planning chief in the Israeli Defense Ministry and the country's leading specialist on Saudi Arabia. "And let's be honest with ourselves—what is peanuts to them is real money in the West Bank or Gaza."

Does the efficient, proselytizing Islamic religiosity of these charities, hospitals and schools really make them, per se, a part of the infrastructure of the violent factions of the Islamic movement? Officials at the facilities say that is preposterous—they describe themselves as undertaking social work, not sowing violent revolution. But the Israeli government sees these institutions as the superstructure of a broad Islamic movement whose most militant wing is openly dedicated to violent religious struggle. Thus, Israel has lately sought to contain the activities of the movement's support institutions, despite their benign appearance.

In Jenin, records and computer disks at the Islamic hospital were confiscated by Israeli authorities. Several doctors and board members, charged with being members of Hamas, were deported to Lebanon in December. Israel has denied permission for the Jenin clinic to import new equipment and an ambulance, say hospital and Israeli officials.

Elsewhere in the occupied territories, Israel recently closed a dozen or so mosques thought to be centers of radicalism. Board members from other Islamic charities and institutions were deported in December. The Israelis have tried to stanch the flow of money from abroad, but they confess they cannot keep track of it.

Dissecting its own radical Islamic opposition, Egypt's government faces a similar quandary. U.S. academic researcher Dennis Sullivan estimates that 2,000 Islamic charitable societies are registered in Egypt. Many are associated with the Muslim Brotherhood, once a violent Islamic movement publicly dedicated for the last 20 years to a peaceful, evolutionary transition to an Islamic state in Egypt.

Brotherhood members forced into exile in Saudi Arabia and Europe during the 1960s have built up over the years a rich network of Islamic banks, companies and other institutions, in and out of Egypt. Some Egyptian government officials contend these elderly Brotherhood members are using their resources to fund the younger generation of Egyptian Islamic radicals committed to street violence. But the government has never produced evidence of such funding, and the local Brotherhood chapter denies any link to the younger radicals.

Attempts by Egypt and Israel to trace the support networks of young Islamic activists who pull the triggers in acts of religious or insurgent violence have yielded similar portraits of complexity and diffusion. One example is the recent finding of Israeli police investigators in the Toledano killing, a turning point for Israel in that it prompted the largest deportation in the country's peacetime history. The four Palestinians accused of the killing, arrested after months on the run, turned out to be in some respects an amateurish gang with no connections to Hamas's military wing when they undertook their campaign of violence. They decided to kidnap Toledano with "bare hands," as an Israeli security official puts it, and they had no experience with weapons.

The network they constructed was informal, built on a single acquaintance. After killing Toledano, one gang member contacted Ibrahim Nawadeh, an alleged Hamas activist and preacher he had known at an Islamic college and who had become the Jordanian-salaried imam in a small Jenin mosque, investigators say. From Nawadeh the gang sought money and guns. He gave them an Israeli-made Uzi submachine gun, a pistol and 4,000 Jordanian dinars (about $6,000), investigators say. When the Uzi proved defective, the preacher replaced it with another and helped the gang buy a new car similar to the kind driven by Israeli police and army officers, so the activists could not be easily detected.

Nawadeh was a go-between, but the gang picked their own targets, the investigators say. The preacher obtained money from yet another Hamas figure. When dealing with the gang, he "didn't give them orders," and he "didn't give them instructions," one investigator says.

Nawadeh's father, a retired merchant, denies that his son was involved with Hamas and says the charges against him are "exaggerated." He describes Nawadeh as a product of religious schools and says he had long been the most fervently religious member of his family.

The gang Nawadeh allegedly funded was not typical of all Hamas military cells—they were at the same time more ambitious and less well-prepared than many. Yet their efforts underscore the often fractured structure of contemporary violent Islamic radicals. "It is organic—there's no need for a department of this or a department of that," says Israeli scholar Zilberman. "It's organized around charisma or religious scholarship. . . . The best way to destroy charisma is to become bureaucratic."

Outer Limits to America's Turn Inward

Depending on the Kindness of Strangers

Walter Russell Mead

Author of Mortal Splendor: The American Empire in Transition, *Walter Russell Mead is a member of NPQ's Board of Advisors.*

Is a return to prewar isolationism, or even a more narrow internationalism, really an alternative for the self-doubting superpower? Won't economic protection lead to depression? Won't America's environmental isolationism worsen global warming? Is it wise to bite the Japanese hand that finances our deficits? With the free trade agreement pending, can Mexico and the U.S. separate foreign and domestic issues?

In this section, we examine the outer limits to America's turn inward.

"I have always depended on the kindness of strangers," said Blanche DuBois as they hauled her off to the asylum at the end of Tennessee Williams' play *A Streetcar Named Desire.*

Blanche's motto was America's, too, during the last 12 years of idiotic misgovernance. Was the deficit out of control? Had the government thrown away trillions of taxpayer dollars on the bungled deregulation of the savings and loans and the banking system? Had our financial markets degenerated into rigged casinos as CEOs looted the companies they were supposed to build? Had our infrastructure rotted away while social cancers ate at our inner cities?

No matter, said America in the last 12 years. The kindness of strangers would bail us out. Yes, we had stopped saving for the future. Yes, we had saddled ourselves with incompetent managerial and government elites. Yes, we had allowed our educational and health care systems to decay into vastly expensive and unproductive ruin.

But so what? America could always depend on the kindness of strangers. Foreign investors would buy up the bonds of our debauched Treasury. Foreign investors would snap up our overbuilt office parks. Foreign investors would buy the shares of our mismanaged companies

and invest in the technology that, someday, might begin to allow us to repair the damage of our 12-year binge.

And they did, for a while. All during the 1980s foreigners bought our companies, our T-bills and our office buildings—usually for prices no Americans could match. As the Japanese bought up everything from Rockefeller Center to Hollywood, a few Americans grumbled about losing control of our destiny. Protectionists warned that we were being colonized by Japanese and European investors—that our kids would flip burgers for foreign-owned chains.

That never happened, but something else has—something worse.

The strangers wised up. They took a long, hard look at the U.S. and decided to be a little less kind.

Foreign investment, which topped $70 billion in 1989, dried up after that—down to $22 billion last year, a drop of two-thirds. The British alone invested almost that much in 1989; Japanese investment in this country dropped by three-quarters—from an average of $17.3 billion in 1987–89 to $4.3 billion in 1991.

It turns out that the American economy wasn't a good buy. A recent Commerce Department report estimates that the total average annual return on foreign investment in the United States during the 1980s was 2.6 percent. The *total* return on foreign investment in the U.S. last year was a pathetic $361 million. Superpatriots can relax: There will be no throngs of rich foreigners snapping up our golf courses and office parks for some time to come. The strangers are taking their money home.

Capital can choose from dozens of countries and hundreds of cities eager for new investments. The recent riots in Los Angeles, and the signs of racial unrest in other great American cities, make the U.S. a less attractive place to do business even as they make Americans more aware of our need for increased urban investments. If American banks and insurance companies have red-lined our inner cities, what makes us think foreigners will invest there? If American politicians have largely written off our inner

Reprinted with permission from *New Perspectives Quarterly*, Vol. 9, No. 3, Summer 1992, pp. 28-30.

cities and their inhabitants, why will foreign governments and investors be more optimistic? Peter Ueberroth, charged with drumming up investment to rebuild L.A. in the aftermath of the riots, will face a tough sell when he goes abroad to raise money.

Investments weren't the only kindness we looked for from strangers. We expected them to buy our products and so pull us out of the recession. Until recently, this too, was working. In 1991, even as the U.S. economy shrank by some $35 billion, our exports surged almost $40 billion. Translation: The recession would have been twice as bad without the kindly strangers who bought our goods.

If American politicians have largely written off our inner cities and their inhabitants, why will foreign governments and investors be more optimistic?

But now recession is spreading in the rest of the world, and foreign countries are no longer eager to snap up our wares. U.S. exports fell by $1 billion in the first quarter of 1992, and there could be more bad news to come.

The global recession may be severe. Japan, Germany, Britain, Canada and France are all in or near recession—and all of them will be cutting back on their imports, and trying harder to get out of their recessions by stepping up their exports to us.

Economists are guardedly optimistic about the American outlook. The statistics are still mixed, but signs of recovery have multiplied through the first half of the year. One black cloud remains: the U.S. still depends on capital from abroad, and the global recession is reducing the amount of available capital. The worst case is Japan, where the Nikkei stock market index has lost almost half its value in the last three years. The Tokyo property market has also crashed, and most observers see further declines in the future. Japanese banks, hard-hit by falling stock prices and bad real estate loans, have less money to lend; businesses around the world will have a harder time finding money to borrow.

Real estate is a global problem now. Olympia & York, the world's largest and one of its best-respected real estate companies, now teeters on the brink of collapse. Olympia & York's lenders face potential losses of hundreds of millions, possibly more; the commercial real estate market looks more troubled than ever.

The U.S. budget deficit is setting new records; our banks are still reeling from their real estate losses; foreign capital is staying home. Potentially, this could mean a credit crunch and capital shortage in the U.S. that would strangle any economic recovery in its cradle.

The world economy has been here before. The U.S. was the Japan of the 1920s—rich, pacifistic and looking to

invest overseas. In those days it was Europe that depended on the kindness of strangers. Germany needed to borrow money to repay war debts to Britain and France; Britain and France needed the German payments to pay *their* debts to the U.S.

It all worked, for a while. But something happened to the strangers: the 1929 stock market crash in the U.S. Suddenly, Americans were no longer flush with cash, no longer ready to pay inflated prices for German assets. The dollars headed home; American brokers, banks and individual investors needed their money to pay off their market losses.

Without American money, the European economy came crashing down. The German banking system fell apart; the British and French governments defaulted on their debts; the European collapse then worsened the American problems, and the Depression's vicious cycle got under way.

A mild case of this has helped prolong the American recession. As Japanese money pulled out of the U.S., the American economy sagged. The weakness in America, Japan's largest market, made Japan's corporations look vulnerable, undermining their stock prices. As stock prices fell, the Japanese sold more American assets, weakening our economy once again.

Nobody really know how bad the global recession will get. Until now, the U.S. has always been the locomotive that pulled the global economy out of a slump. When the world economy slowed, the U.S. would spend more money, pumping up the budget and trade deficits to give the world economy a quick start. The last and most dramatic ride of the American locomotive came when Ronald Reagan spent his way out of the recession of 1981–82. Once again the stimulus worked, but the resulting fiscal chaos in the U.S. left most observers convinced that the old locomotive had come to the end of the line.

If decent blue-collar jobs continue to disappear, and white and black workers continue to scuffle over the few that remain, what will the U.S. look like by 2002?

This time, the U.S. *can't* rescue the rest of the world. Our deficit exceeds $250 billion; nobody wants to see it go higher. Germany is too busy with reunification and inflation to take responsibility for the global economy, and Japan is too worried about its own problems to help anybody else.

There is, or there should be, nothing surprising about the fix we are in. Everyone has known since the '70s that the U.S. could no longer, single-handedly, manage the global economy. But, like Blanche DuBois, America's leaders preferred to ignore the unpleasant reality, and made no provisions to meet the coming challenge.

There is something breathtakingly casual in the way the American elite responds to its failures. The savings and loan debacle, the disintregation of our inner cities, the budget deficit: Our public and private elites don't care about them. Perhaps because they grew up in the years when the U.S. faced no real economic challenges and knew no real limits, they don't understand that failure has a price.

If so, this new failure—the failure to develop an international system to hedge against the possibility of world-wide depression—will open their eyes to their folly. Hundreds of million—billions—of people around the world have pinned their hopes on the international market economy. They and their leaders have embraced market principles—and drawn closer to the West—because they believe that our system can work for them.

But what if it can't? What if the global economy stagnates—or even shrinks? In that case, we will face a new period of international conflict: South against North, rich against poor. Russia, China, India—these countries with their billions of people and their nuclear weapons will pose a much greater danger to world order than Germany and Japan did in the '30s.

Closer to home, as the suppressed rage of America's inner cities boils forth anew, one must ask about the domestic consequences of a slow-growth economy. The rising tide of the '80s failed to lift the boats of most inner city residents; how will they fare when the tide has stopped rising? And how will their responses, and the reactions of the white majority, shape American politics in the '90s?

Beyond the inner cities, the American lower-middle class has watched helplessly as its real earnings have stagnated over the last generation. The secular slowdown in growth has reduced opportunities and incomes for non-college-educated white males below the levels reached when Richard Nixon was in the White House. If decent blue-collar jobs continue to disappear, and white and black workers continue to scuffle over the few that remain, what will the U.S. look like by 2002?

The winds are picking up and the dark clouds thicken on the horizon, but it is business as usual in Washington. Politicians squabble with each other and do favors for their friends, oblivious to the dangers of the gathering storm.

"I don't want realism" said Blanche, "I want magic!" We may all need some magic to get through the stagnant global economy that currently looks set to last well into the '90s.

A DECADE OF DISCONTINUITY

The 1980s may have been the last decade in which humankind could anticipate a future of ever-increasing productivity on all fronts. By one measure after another, the boom we have experienced since mid-century is coming to an end.

LESTER R. BROWN

When the history of the late 20th century is written, the 1990s will be seen as a decade of discontinuity—a time when familiar trends that had seemed likely to go on forever, like smooth straight roads climbing toward an ever-receding horizon, came to abrupt bends or junctures and began descending abruptly. The world's production of steel, for example, had risen almost as reliably each year as the sun rises in the morning. The amount of coal extracted had risen almost uninterruptedly ever since the Industrial Revolution began. Since the middle of this century, the harvest of grain had grown even faster than population, steadily increasing the amount available both for direct consumption and for conversion into livestock products. The oceanic fish catch, likewise, had more than quadrupled during this period, doubling the consumption of seafood per person.

These rising curves were seen as basic measures of human progress; we *expected* them to rise. But now, within just a few years, these trends have reversed—and with consequences we have yet to grasp. Meanwhile, other trends that were going nowhere, or at most rising slowly, are suddenly soaring.

That such basic agricultural and industrial outputs should begin to decline, while population continues to grow, has engendered disquieting doubts about the future. These reversals, and others likely to follow, are dwarfing the discontinuities that occurred during the 1970s in the wake of the 1973 rise in oil prices. At that time, an overnight tripling of oil prices boosted energy prices across the board, slowed the growth in automobile production, and spurred investment in energy-efficient technologies, creating a whole new industry.

The discontinuities of the 1990s are far more profound, originating not with a handful of national political leaders as with the OPEC ministers of the 1970s, but in the collision between expanding human numbers and needs on the one hand and the constraints of the earth's natural systems on the other. Among these constraints are the capacity of the oceans to yield seafood, of grasslands to produce beef and mutton, of the hydrological cycle to produce fresh water, of crops to use fertilizer, of the atmosphere to absorb CFCs, carbon dioxide, and other greenhouse gases, of people to breathe polluted air, and of forests to withstand acid rain.

Though we may not have noticed them,

From *World Watch*, July/August 1993, pp. 19-26. © 1993 by Worldwatch Institute, Washington, DC. Reprinted by permission.

these constraints drew dramatically closer between 1950 and 1990, as the global economy expanded nearly fivefold. Expansion on this scale inevitably put excessive pressure on the earth's natural systems, upsetting the natural balances that had lent some stability to historical economic trends. The trends were driven, in part by unprecedented population growth. Those of us born before 1950 have seen world population double. In 1950, 37 million people were added to the world's population. Last year, it was 91 million.

Against the Grain

The production of grain, perhaps the most basic economic measure of human well-being, increased 2.6 fold from 1950 to 1984. Expanding at nearly 3 percent per year, it outstripped population growth, raising per capita grain consumption by 40 percent over the 34-year period, improving nutrition and boosting consumption of livestock products—meat, milk, eggs, and cheese—throughout the world.

That period came to an end, ironically, around the time the United States withdrew its funding from the United Nations Population Fund. During the eight years since 1984, world grain output has expanded perhaps one percent per year. In per capita terms, this means grain production has shifted from its steady rise over the previous 34 years to a *decline* of one percent per year since then—a particularly troubling change both because grain is a basic source of human sustenance and because of the likely difficulty in reversing it (see Figure 1).

This faltering of basic foodstuffs was triggered by other, earlier discontinuities of growth—in the supply of cropland, irrigation water, and agricultural technologies. Cropland, measured in terms of grain harvested area, expanded more or less continuously from the beginning of agriculture until 1981. The spread of agriculture, initially from valley to valley and eventually from continent to continent, had come to a halt. Since 1981, it has not increased. Gains of cropland in some countries have been offset by losses in others, as land is converted to nonfarm uses and abandoned because of erosion.

Irrigation, which set the stage for the emergence of early civilization, expanded gradually over a span of at least 5,000 years. After the middle of this century, the growth in irrigated area accelerated, averaging

nearly 3 percent per year until 1978. Around that time, however, as the number of prime dam construction sites diminished and underground aquifers were depleted by overpumping, the growth of irrigated area fell behind that of population. Faced with a steady shrinkage of cropland area per person from mid-century onward, the world's farmers since 1978 have faced a shrinking irrigated area per person as well.

Although there was little new land to plow from mid-century onward, the world's farmers were able to achieve the largest expansion of food output in history by dramatically raising land productivity. The engine of growth was fertilizer use, which increased ninefold in three decades—from 14 million tons in 1950 to 126 million tons in 1984—before starting to slow (see Figure 2).

In 1990, the rise in fertilizer use—what had been one of the most predictable trends in the world economy—was abruptly reversed. It has fallen some 10 percent during the three years since the 1989 peak of 146 million tons. Economic reforms in the former Soviet Union, which removed heavy fertilizer subsidies, account for most of the decline. Letting fertilizer prices move up to world market levels, combined with weakened demand for farm products, dropped fertilizer use in the former Soviet Union by exactly half between 1988 and 1992. This was an anomalous decline, from which there should eventually be at least a partial recovery.

More broadly, however, growth in world fertilizer use has slowed simply because existing grain varieties in the United States, Western Europe, and Japan cannot economically use much more fertilizer. U.S. farmers, matching applications more precisely to crop needs, actually used nearly one-tenth less fertilizer from 1990 to 1992 than they did a decade earlier. Using more fertilizer in agriculturally advanced countries does not have much effect on production with available varieties.

The backlog of unused agricultural technology that began to expand rapidly in the mid-19th century now appears to be diminishing. In 1847, German agricultural chemist Justus von Leibig discovered that all the nutrients removed by plants could be returned to the soil in their pure form. A decade later, Gregor Mendel discovered the basic principles of genetics, setting the stage for the eventual development of high-yielding, fertilizer-responsive crop varieties.

Falling Capacities: *With human population growing by the equivalent of 12 New York Cities or 11 Somalias a year, the world's food-producing capacity has been seriously strained—and the amount per person now shows signs of reversing its historic growth.*

Figure 1. Grain, the basic staple of both direct human consumption and livestock feed, is now falling in per-person production after decades of growth.

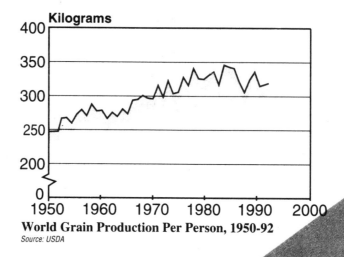

World Grain Production Per Person, 1950-92

Source: USDA

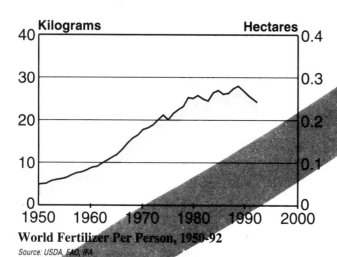

World Fertilizer Per Person, 1950-92

Source: USDA, FAO, IFA

Figure 2. Fertilizer use, the engine that drove up farm productivity worldwide, is sputtering—and in per-capita terms, is falling.

Figure 3: Fish from the oceans, once thought virtually limitless in supply, may already have reached its global limit—launching a decline in the catch per person that will continue to worsen as long as human population grows.

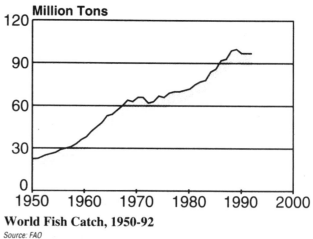

World Fish Catch, 1950-92

Source: FAO

As the geographic frontiers of agricultural expansion disappeared in the mid-20th century, the adoption of high-yielding varieties and rapid growth in fertilizer use boosted land productivity dramatically. In the 1960s, an array of advanced technologies for both wheat and rice producers was introduced into the Third World—giving rise to a growth in grain output that was more rapid than anything that had occurred earlier, even in the industrial countries.

Although it cannot be precisely charted, the backlog of unused agricultural technology must have peaked at least a decade ago. Most of the known means of raising food output are in wide use. The highest-yielding rice variety available to farmers in Asia in 1993 was released in 1966—more than a quarter-century ago. Today, the more progressive farmers are peering over the shoulders of agricultural scientists looking for new help in boosting production, only to find that not much is forthcoming. Agricultural scientists are worried that the rapid advance in technology characterizing the middle decades of this century may not be sustainable.

Less Meat *and* Less Fish

The growth in meat production, like that of grain, is slowing. Between 1950 and 1987, world meat production increased from 46 million tons to 161 million tons—boosting the amount per person from 18 kilograms in 1980 to 32 kilograms (about 70 pounds) in 1987. Since then, however, it has not increased at all. The one percent decline in per capita production in 1992 may be the beginning of a gradual world decline in per capita meat production, another major discontinuity.

Underlying this slowdown in overall meat production is a rather dramatic slowdown in the production of beef and mutton, resulting from the inability of grasslands to support more cattle and sheep. From 1950 to 1990, world beef output increased 2.5-fold. Now, with grasslands almost fully used—or overused—on every continent, this growth may be nearing an end. From 1990 to 1992, per capita beef production for the world fell 6 percent.

The supply of fish, like that of meat, no longer keeps pace with increases in human numbers. Here, too, there has been a reversal of the historic trend. Between 1950 and 1989, the global catch expanded from 22 million tons to 100 million tons. The per

capita seafood supply increased from 9 to 19 kilograms during this period. Since 1989, the catch has actually declined slightly, totalling an estimated 97 million tons in 1992 (see Figure 3). United Nations marine biologists believe that the oceans have reached their limit and may not be able to sustain a yield of more than 100 million tons per year.

Throughout this century, it has been possible to increase the fish take by sending out more ships, using more sophisticated fishing technologies, and going, literally, to the farthest reaches of the ocean. That expansion has now come to an end. The world's ocean catch per capita declined 7 percent from 1989 until 1992, and is likely to continue declining as long as population continues to grow. As a result, seafood prices are rising steadily.

Getting more animal protein, whether it be in the form of beef or farm-raised fish, now depends on feeding grain and soybean meal. Those desiring to maintain animal protein intake now compete with those trying to consume more grain directly.

Table 1. Growth and Decline in Production of Fossil Fuels, 1950-92

Fossil Fuel	Growth Period		Decline Period	
	Years	Annual Rate (percent)	Years	Annual Rate (percent)
Oil	1950-79	+ 6.4	1979-92	- 0.5
Coal	1950-89	+ 2.2	1989-92	- 0.6
Natural Gas	1950-92	+ 6.2		

Fossil Fuels: The Beginning of the End

While biological constraints are forcing discontinuities in agriculture and oceanic fisheries, it is atmospheric constraints—the mounting risks associated with pollution and global warming—that are altering energy trends. Throughout the world energy economy, there are signs that a major restructuring is imminent. On the broadest level, this will entail a shifting of investment from fossil fuels and nuclear power toward renewables—and toward greater energy efficiency in every human activity.

We cannot yet see the end of the fossil fuel age, but we can see the beginning of its decline. World oil production peaked in 1979 (see Table 1). Output in 1992 was four percent below that historical high. World coal production dropped in 1990, in 1991, and again in 1992 (partly because of the recession), interrupting a growth trend that had spanned two centuries. If strong global warming policies are implemented, this could be the beginning of a long-term decline in coal dependence.

Of the three fossil fuels, only natural gas is expanding output rapidly and is assured of substantial future growth. Gas burns cleanly and produces less carbon dioxide than the others, and is therefore less likely to be constrained by stricter environmental policies. While oil production has fallen since 1979, gas production has risen by one-third.

With oil, it was the higher price that initially arrested growth. More recently, it has been the pall of automotive air pollution in cities like Los Angeles, Mexico City, and Rome that has slowed the once-unrestrained growth in motor vehicle use and, therefore, in oil use. With coal, it was neither supply nor price (the world has at least a few centuries of coal reserves left), but the effects of air pollution on human health, of acid rain on forests and crops, and of rising CO_2 concentrations on the earth's climate that have sent the industry into decline. Several industrial countries have committed themselves to reducing carbon emissions. Germany, for example, plans to cut carbon emissions 25 percent by 2005. Switzerland is shooting for a 10 percent cut by 2000, and Australia for 20 percent by 2005. Others, including the United States, may soon join them.

With the beginning of the end of the fossil fuel age in sight, what then will be used to power the world economy? Fifteen years ago, many would have said, with little hesitation, that nuclear power will. Once widely thought to be the energy source of the future, it has failed to live up to its promise (the problems of waste disposal and safety have proved expensive and intractable) and is being challenged on economic grounds in most of the countries where it is produced.

Nuclear generating capacity reached its historical peak in 1990. Though it has declined only slightly since then, it now seems unlikely that there will be much, if any, additional growth in nuclear generating capacity during this decade—and perhaps ever.

The Winds of Change

Even as the nuclear and fossil fuel industries have faltered, three new technologies that harness energy directly or indirectly from the sun to produce electricity—solar thermal power plants, photovoltaic cells, and wind generators—are surging. In wind power, particularly, breakthroughs in turbine technol-

ogy are setting the stage for rapid expansion in the years ahead. Wind electricity generated in California already produces enough electricity to satisfy the residential needs of San Francisco and Washington, D.C. Indeed, it now seems likely that during the 1990s, the growth in wind generating capacity will exceed that in nuclear generating capacity. Three countries—Denmark, the Netherlands, and Germany—have plans to develop a minimum of a thousand megawatts of wind

Table 2. World Economic Growth by Decade, 1950-93

Decade	Annual Growth of World Economy	Annual Growth Per Person
1950-60	4.9	3.1
1960-70	5.2	3.2
1970-80	3.4	1.6
1980-90	2.9	1.1
1990-93 (prel.)	0.9	−0.8

generating capacity by 2005. China aims to reach the same goal by 2000. Given the rapid advances in the efficiency of wind generating machines and the falling costs of wind generated electricity, the growth in wind power over the remainder of this decade could dwarf even current expectations.

The potential for wind power far exceeds that of hydropower, which currently supplies the world with one-fifth of its electricity. England and Scotland alone have enough wind generating potential to satisfy half of Europe's electricity needs. Two U.S. states—Montana and Texas—each have enough wind to satisfy the whole country's electricity needs. The upper Midwest (the Dakotas east through Ohio) could supply the country's electricity without siting any wind turbines in either densely populated or environmentally sensitive areas. And wind resource assessments by the government of China have documented 472,000 megawatts of wind generating potential, enough to raise China's electricity supply threefold.

For Third World villages not yet connected to a grid, a more practical source is photovoltaic arrays, which may already have a competitive advantage. With the World Bank beginning to support this technology, costs will fall fast, making photovoltaic cells even more competitive. Wind, photovoltaic cells, and solar thermal power plants all promise inexpensive electricity as the technologies continue to advance and as the economies of scale expand. Over the longer term, cheap solar electricity in various forms will permit the conversion of electricity into hydrogen, which will offer an efficient means of energy transportation and storage.

Technological advances that increase the *efficiency* of energy use are in some ways even more dramatic than the advances in harnessing solar and wind resources. Striking gains have been made in the energy efficiency of electric lighting, electric motors, the thermal efficiency of windows, and cogenerating technologies that produce both electricity and heat. One of the most dramatic, as recently noted in *World Watch* (May/June 1993), is the new compact fluorescent light bulb—which can supply the same amount of light as an incandescent bulb while using only one-fourth as much electricity. The 134 million compact fluorescent bulbs sold worldwide in 1992 saved enough electricity to close 10 large coal-fired power plants.

The discontinuities that have wreaked havoc with once-reliable trends are not random, but reflect an escalating awareness of the need to transform the global economy into one that is sustainable. They reflect the unavoidable reality that we have entered an era in which satisfying the needs of the 91 million people being added each year depends on reducing consumption among those already here. At this rate, by the year 2010, this growth will amount to a net addition equal to nearly 200 cities the size of New York, or 100 countries the size of Iraq—dramatically reducing the per capita availability of cropland and irrigation water. At some point, as people begin to grasp the implications of this new reality, population policy will become a central concern of national governments.

Economic Entropy
Whether in basic foodstuffs and fresh water, or in overall economic output, the decade of discontinuity has begun. Growth in the world economy reached its historical high at 5.2 percent per year during the 1960s (see Table 2). It then slowed to 3.4 percent per year in the 1970s, and 2.9 percent in the 1980s. Despite this slowdown, the per capita output of goods and services rose as overall economic growth stayed ahead of population growth. Now that, too, may be reversing.

From 1990 to 1992, the world economy expanded at 0.6 percent per year. If the International Monetary Fund's recent projection of 2.2 percent in world economic growth for 1993 materializes, we will find ourselves three years into this decade with an income per person nearly 2 percent lower than it was when the decade began. Even using an economic accounting system that overstates progress because it omits environmental degradation and the depletion of natural capital, living standards are falling.

Evidence is accumulating that the world economy is not growing as easily in the 1990s as it once did. The conventional economic wisdom concerning the recession of the early 1990s attributes it to economic mismanagement in the advanced industrial countries (particularly the United States, Germany, and Japan) and to the disruption associated with economic reform in the centrally planned economies. These are obviously the dominant forces slowing world economic growth, but they are not the only ones. As noted above, growth in the fishing industry, which supplies much of the world's animal protein, may have stopped. Growth in the production of beef, mutton, and other livestock products from the world's rangelands may also be close to an end. The world grain harvest shows little prospect of being able to keep pace with population, much less to eliminate hunger. And scarcities of fresh water are limiting economic expansion in many countries. With constraints emerging in these primary economic sectors—sectors on which much of the Third World depends—we may be moving into an era of slower economic growth overall.

The popular question of "growth or no growth" now seems largely irrelevant. A more fundamental question is how to satisfy the basic needs of the world's people without further disrupting or destroying the economy's support systems. The real challenge for the 1990s is that of deciding how the basic needs of all people can be satisfied without jeopardizing the prospects of future generations.

Of all the discontinuities that have become apparent in the past few years, however, it is an upward shift in the population growth trend itself that may be most disturbing. The progress in slowing human population growth so evident in the 1970s has stalled—with alarming implications for the long-term population trajectory. Throughout the 1960s and 1970s, declining fertility held out hope for getting the brakes on population growth before it began to undermine living standards. The 1980s, however, turned out to be a lost decade, one in which the United States not only abdicated its leadership role, but also withdrew all financial support from the U.N. Population Fund and the International Planned Parenthood Federation. This deprived millions of couples in the Third World of access to the family planning services needed to control the number or timing of their children.

The concern that population growth could undermine living standards has become a reality in this decade of discontinuity. There is now a distinct possibility that the grain supply per person will be lower at the end of this decade than at the beginning, that the amount of seafood per person will be substantially less, and that the amount of meat per person will also be far less than it is today.

The absence of any technology to reestablish the rapid growth in food production that existed from 1950 to 1984 is a matter of deepening concern. In early 1992, the U.S. National Academy of Sciences and the Royal Society of London together issued a report that warned: "If current predictions of population growth prove accurate and patterns of human activity on the planet remain unchanged, science and technology may not be able to prevent either irreversible degradation of the environment or continued poverty for much of the world."

Later in the year, the Union of Concerned Scientists issued a statement signed by nearly 1,600 of the world's leading scientists, including 96 Nobel Prize recipients, noting that the continuation of destructive human activities "may so alter the living world that it will be unable to sustain life in the manner that we know." The statement warned: "A great change in our stewardship of the earth and the life on it is required, if vast human misery is to be avoided and our global home on this planet is not to be irretrievably mutilated."

The discontinuities reshaping the global economy define the challenge facing humanity in the next few years. It is a challenge not to the survival of our species, but to civilization as we know it. The question we can no longer avoid asking is whether our social institutions are capable of quickly slowing and stabilizing population growth without infringing on human rights. Even as that effort gets underway, the same institutions face the complex issue of how to distribute those resources that are no longer expanding, among a population that is continuing to grow by record numbers each year.

This article is adapted from the overview chapter of Vital Signs 1993: The Trends That Are Shaping Our Future, *by Lester R. Brown, Hal Kane, and Ed Ayres, published by W.W. Norton and the Worldwatch Institute in July.*

Credits/Acknowledgments

Cover design by Charles Vitelli

Introduction
Facing overview—United Nations photo by Paulo Fridman.

1. Parenting and Family Issues
Facing overview—Children Today photo by Jacquine Roland.

2. Crime, Delinquency, and Violence
Facing overview—United Nations photo.

3. Aging
Facing overview—United Nations photo by Sebastiao Barbosa.

4. Health and Health Care Issues
Facing overview—City of New York Department of Health.
110-112—Illustrations by Wayne Vincent.

5. Poverty and Inequality
Facing overview—Department of Housing and Urban Development.

6. Cultural Pluralism
Facing overview—New York Convention and Visitors Bureau.

7. Drugs and Sexual Issues
Facing overview—United Nations photo by John Robaton.

8. Global Issues
Facing overview—United Nations photo by J. Frank.

PHOTOCOPY THIS PAGE!!!*

ANNUAL EDITIONS ARTICLE REVIEW FORM

■ NAME: _____ DATE: _____

■ TITLE AND NUMBER OF ARTICLE: _____

■ BRIEFLY STATE THE MAIN IDEA OF THIS ARTICLE: _____

_____

_____

_____

_____

■ LIST THREE IMPORTANT FACTS THAT THE AUTHOR USES TO SUPPORT THE MAIN IDEA:

_____

_____

_____

_____

_____

_____

■ WHAT INFORMATION OR IDEAS DISCUSSED IN THIS ARTICLE ARE ALSO DISCUSSED IN YOUR TEXTBOOK OR OTHER READING YOU HAVE DONE? LIST THE TEXTBOOK CHAPTERS AND PAGE NUMBERS:

_____

_____

_____

_____

_____

_____

■ LIST ANY EXAMPLES OF BIAS OR FAULTY REASONING THAT YOU FOUND IN THE ARTICLE:

_____

_____

_____

_____

_____

■ LIST ANY NEW TERMS/CONCEPTS THAT WERE DISCUSSED IN THE ARTICLE AND WRITE A SHORT DEFINITION:

_____

_____

_____

_____

_____

*Your instructor may require you to use this Annual Editions Article Review Form in any number of ways: for articles that are assigned, for extra credit, as a tool to assist in developing assigned papers, or simply for your own reference. Even if it is not required, we encourage you to photocopy and use this page; you'll find that reflecting on the articles will greatly enhance the information from your text.

ANNUAL EDITIONS: SOCIAL PROBLEMS 94/95
Article Rating Form

Here is an opportunity for you to have direct input into the next revision of this volume. We would like you to rate each of the 42 articles listed below, using the following scale:

1. Excellent: should definitely be retained
2. Above average: should probably be retained
3. Below average: should probably be deleted
4. Poor: should definitely be deleted

Your ratings will play a vital part in the next revision. So please mail this prepaid form to us just as soon as you complete it.
Thanks for your help!

Annual Editions revisions depend on two major opinion sources: one is our Advisory Board, listed in the front of this volume, which works with us in scanning the thousands of articles published in the public press each year; the other is you—the person actually using the book. Please help us and the users of the next edition by completing the prepaid article rating form on this page and returning it to us. Thank you.

Rating	Article	Rating	Article
	1. Social Problems: Definitions, Theories, and Analysis		22. The Front Lines of Welfare Reform
	2. America's Family Time Famine		23. Going Private
	3. The American Family, 1992		24. Manufacturing Poverty
	4. Endangered Family		25. No Exit
	5. Bringing Up Father		26. The New Faces of Poverty
	6. Everyday Life in Two High-Risk Neighborhoods		27. When Problems Outrun Policy
	7. American Nightmare: Homelessness		28. An American Melting Plot
	8. The Whole Child Approach to Crime		29. America: Still a Melting Pot?
	9. Danger in the Safety Zone		30. Japan's Influence on American Life
	10. Ganging Up Against Violence		31. Is White Racism the Problem?
	11. Honey, I Warped the Kids		32. Born or Bred?
	12. When Cities Run Riot		33. Shape Up or Ship Out
	13. The Los Angeles Riots: Causes and Cures		34. Truth and Consequences: Teen Sex
	14. Old Money		35. The CIA Connection
	15. The New Face of Aging		36. A Society of Suspects: The War on Drugs and Civil Liberties
	16. Unplanned Parenthood		37. Enough Is Enough: Assessing Global Consumption
	17. The Story of a Nursing Home Refugee		38. The Rape of the Oceans
	18. Wasted Health Care Dollars		39. Benefits of Global Warming
	19. Risky Business		40. Islam's Violent Improvisers
	20. Deadly Migration		41. Outer Limits to America's Turn Inward
	21. Confronting the AIDS Pandemic		42. A Decade of Discontinuity

(Continued on next page)

ABOUT YOU

Name_____ Date_____

Are you a teacher? ☐ Or student? ☐

Your School Name _____

Department _____

Address _____

City_____ State _____ Zip _____

School Telephone #_____

YOUR COMMENTS ARE IMPORTANT TO US!

Please fill in the following information:

For which course did you use this book? _____

Did you use a text with this Annual Edition? ☐ yes ☐ no

The title of the text? _____

What are your general reactions to the Annual Editions concept?

Have you read any particular articles recently that you think should be included in the next edition?

Are there any articles you feel should be replaced in the next edition? Why?

Are there other areas that you feel would utilize an Annual Edition?

May we contact you for editorial input?

May we quote you from above?

ANNUAL EDITIONS: SOCIAL PROBLEMS 94/95

BUSINESS REPLY MAIL

First Class   Permit No. 84   Guilford, CT

Postage will be paid by addressee

The Dushkin Publishing Group, Inc.
Sluice Dock
DPG **Guilford, Connecticut 06437**

No Postage
Necessary
if Mailed
in the
United States